For Isadore Small

See pages
152, 278, 318, 320, 324

a passionate member

To his great-grandson
Albert Small

Stanley Rabinowitz
Rabbi

# THE ASSEMBLY

A Century in the Life of

The Adas Israel Hebrew Congregation

of Washington, D.C.

# THE ASSEMBLY

A Century in the Life of

The Adas Israel Hebrew Congregation

of Washington, D.C.

*Speak unto the entire assembly of Israel . . .*
—Exodus 12:3

by

STANLEY RABINOWITZ

Ktav Publishing House Inc.
Hoboken, New Jersey

ISBN 0-88125-443-6

Manufatured in the United States of America
KTAV Publishing House, Inc., 900 Jefferson St., Hoboken, NJ 07030

To

Anita,

Beloved

Friend, Companion, Critic, Wife

## TABLE OF CONTENTS

# PREFACE

In the preparation of this volume I had to consider several perplexing questions.

Should its scope be limited to the activities of the congregation or should it include a larger framework?

My research, which resolved that question, led me to see the congregation, not in isolation, but in the context of the origins of the Washington Jewish community, the founding of the Jewish Theological Seminary, and the beginnings of the Conservative Movement. Accordingly, in order to link the congregation to its background, I used a wide angle lens that encompassed the beginnings of Jewish life in Washington, the seminary and the Conservative movement to frame a sharper focus on the congregation.

Another question pertained to the selection of names. Who was to be included and who was to be omitted? Though well over a thousand men and women contributed to the making of Adas Israel in its first century, I was compelled, due to limitations of space, to mention only the officers and designated leaders. It must be kept in mind that others also served.

My third concern was how to avoid the egocentric predicament. As the text reached the decade of the sixties, it was inevitable that the third-person pronoun would give way to the first, since the author was also the rabbi of the congregation. I tried to detach myself as much as possible so as not to confuse the recording of events with self-glorification; others will decide whether I have succeeded. In any case, my role occupied only nine years of the congregation's first century.

The preparation of this history was facilitated by the writings of others whose research I gratefully acknowledge. First and foremost:

The late Samuel Holland, executive vice-president of the Jewish Historical Society of Greater Washington, whose marvelous curiosity led him to delve into the archives of the past and to lay the foundation for the history of Adas Israel and of the Washington Jewish community.

Evelyn Greenberg, art historian, now of Jerusalem, a pioneer in researching and recording the history of Washington Jewry and the origins of Adas Israel, who took the initiative in preserving the old Adas Israel Synagogue structure.

Rabbis Louis Stern and Abraham Simon, former rabbis of the Washington Hebrew Congregation, and Mr. Bernard Nordlinger, who have each written a history of the Washington Hebrew Congregation.

I have benefitted from reading the informative volume on the history of the Jewish Theological Seminary, entitled *A Different Spirit*, written by Rabbi Robert E. Fierstien, and from the research of Sarah Schmidt, now resident in Israel, undertaken at the instigation of Mr. Donald Wolpe, past president of Adas Israel and of the Jewish Historical Society.

I acknowledge with gratitude the cooperation of:

The Washington Hebrew Congregation, especially Lois England and its rabbis, Joshua Haberman and Joseph Weinberg.

The libraries and staff of:

The Historical Society of Washington D. C.

The Jewish Theological Seminary.

The Jewish Historical Society of Greater Washington and its director, Julian Feldman.

The American Jewish Historical Society.

The Jewish War Veterans, its archivist, Sandor B. Cohen, and its docent, Albert I. Lerner.

My correspondents:

Mr. Edgar L. Stromberg, archivist for the Behrend family.

Pamela S. Nadell, associate professor of Jewish Studies at the American University, author of *Conservative Judaism in America*, a sourcebook.

Two sons of former rabbis of Adas Israel: Rabbi Herman Grossman, son of Rabbi Benjamin Grossman, and Professor Hillel Shuval of the Hebrew University, son of Rabbi Louis Schwefel.

My colleagues:

Rabbis Abraham Karp, Wolfe Kelman, of blessed memory, Saul Teplitz, and Max Vorspan.

Within Adas Israel, I interviewed Flora Atkin, Isabelle Gichner, Louis Grossberg, Toba Hertzenberg, Estelle Jacobs, Samuel Lebowitz, Joseph Mendelson, Rabbi Samuel Weiss, Morton Wilner, and Herbert Wolf. All helped by offering their recollections of the past.

I am indebted to Rabbi Jeffrey Wohlberg and Cantor Arnold Saltzman for their cooperation and to Thelma Becker and Glenn Easton, executive directors, for their many kindnesses.

For their loyal service over many years and for their retrieval of important archival material, I am indebted to members of the maintenance staff, Carnalee Cauley, Calvin Casey, George Ford, James Young, and the late Preston Covington.

Throughout my tenure, I have been assisted by Mrs. Irwin Title, my secretary, whose amazing memory enabled her to recall significant details of the past that lesser mortals would have long forgotten and who was able to make the incomprehensible legible.

Achron, achron haviv, not the least, I am grateful to my wife, Anita, for her preliminary reading of the manuscript, for her valuable suggestions, and for her encouragement.

To recall the past is an act of resurrection. I therefore have drawn upon the recollections of others to record the memories of those who brought us to the present.

The first century of Adas Israel ended in 1969. It is for others to record the achievements of the second.

Stanley Rabinowitz

June 1992

# INTRODUCTION

It was on December 31, 1869, that approximately thirty-eight members officially withdrew from the Washington Hebrew Congregation to form the Adas Israel Hebrew Congregation. The resignations were but one step in a sequence that began in 1852 with the establishment of Washington's first congregation and led eventually to the legal recordation of the articles of incorporation of Washington's second congregation on September 9, 1870. The seventeen years between 1852 and 1869 remain a significant part of the early histories of what is today two separate congregations with differing ideologies.

The schism that led to the separation was a reflection of the social and religious stirrings in the American Jewish world of the mid-nineteenth century. Added to these forces were the differing personal temperaments and patterns of religous observance of the members of the original congregation. Thus, factors both external and internal were responsible for the division, just as they were for the increased diversity that would come to characterize American Jewish life.

The founders of Adas Israel, a handful of dedicated families, were determined to resist the threat of what to them seemed alien intrusions. They sought to preserve a form of Judaism that was familiar to them as a bridge between the Old World they had left behind and the New World they were cautiously eager to embrace.

To understand the motivations of the members who resigned from the original congregation, it is necessary to reach as far back as the early 1800s to recall the frightful conditions that prevailed in Europe during the period which brought the founders of the two congregations to Washington.

While this study focuses on the history of one congregation, it mirrors a segment of the mosaic of the American Jewish experience.

## THE FOUNDERS

The thirty-eight names and addresses listed below are taken from early congregational records and the Washington city directory for 1869–1870.

Levi Abraham
Abraham Brothers, Isaac and Levi, pawnbrokers, 412 11th Street N.W.

Isaac Alexander
Jeweler, 1229 Pennsylvania Avenue N.W.

Julius Baumgarten
Herman Baumgartgarten
Engravers, 319 Pennsylvania Avenue N.W.; boards: 3rd and Pennsylvania.

Bendiza J. Behrend
Gotthelf & Behrend, dry goods, 730 5th Street N. W.

John Boyer
Boyer & Poullans, pawnbrokers, 315 12th Street N.W.

Simon Coblenzer
Clerk, boards corner 8th and D Street N.W.

Levy Cohen
Shoemaker, 1302 7th Street N.W.
[Cohen was present at the Washington Hebrew Congregation's organizational meeting in 1852 and was one of the signers of its

articles of incorporation. The congregation conducted services in his home at the corner of H Street and Pennsylvania Avenue in 1854.]

Morris Cohen
Clerk, Post Office

Moses Coleman
Auctioneer, boards at 938 Pennsylvania Avenue N.W.

Charles Freirich
Salesman, 438 4th Street S.W.

Lewis Goldstein
Clerk, boards at 728 7th Street N.W.

Nathan Gotthelf
Gotthelf & Behrend Co., Dry Goods, 730 5th Street N.W.
[The city directory adds the words: "Business closed on Saturday."]

Herman Hammerschlag
Paper boxes, 1835 6th Street N.W.

Edward S. Hartogensis
Second-hand clothing, 1234 7th Street N.W.

Sam Hartong
Gents furnishings, 213 7th Street N.W.

Joseph Joseph
Liquors, near C Street S.W.

J. Jacobson
Clerk, boards at Pennsylvania Avenue, 5th Street N.W.

Isaac Levy
7th St, between N and O Streets N.W.

Jacob and Isaac Levi, paints, oil, and glass, 428 Massachusetts Avenue N.W.

Jacob Levy
1126 9th Street N.W.

Julius Lansburgh
Clerk, boards at 651 E Street N.W.

Sol Lewis
Jeweler, 1221 Pennsylvania Avenue N.W.; home: 930 E Street N.W.

Max Louis
Shoestore, 316 12th Street N.W.

M. Michaelis
Cigarmaker, 217 Pennsylvania Avenue N.W.; boards at 502 Pennsylvania Avenue N.W.

Simon Mundheim
Fancy Store, North Capitol, between G and H Streets N.E.

Leopold Oppenheimer
Clothier, 943 Pennsylvania Avenue N.W.

Manassas Oppenheimer
812 8th Street N.W.
[Oppeheimer was one of the signers of the petition to Congress seeking the right for the congregation to own property.]

Jacob Peyser
Clothier, 1127 7th Street N.W.; home: 1137 7th Street N.W.

Phillip Peyser
Clothier, 1146 7th Street N.W.

Elias J. Rasher
Hardware, 929 7th Street N.W.; home: 933 7th Street N.W.

Bernard Rich
1306 7th Street N.W.

Jacob Rich
Partner, Gotthelf & Behrend Co.
819 7th Street N.W.

Louis Roseman
Tailor, 412 Virginia Avenue S.W.

Louis Rosenberg
Clothier, 428 7th Street N.W.; home: 802 7th Street N.W.

Raphael Sanger
Clothier, 411 4 1/2 Street S.W.

Bernard Schlossberg
Peddler, boards at 279 7th Street N.W.

Moses Solomon
Furniture dealer, 311 7th Street S.W.

Abraham Walsky
Moses Walsky, clothing, 1203 7th Street N.W.

# 1

## THE FIRST JEWS

The first Jews to settle in the United States arrived in New Amsterdam in 1654 when the Dutch West India Company ruled what was to become New York with the heavy-handed agency of Peter Stuyvesant. They were Spanish-Portuguese in origin, Sephardim, as were the founders of many of America's other early Jewish communities. Later immigrants, who would come from Germany, Austria, and Central Europe, were Ashkenazim.

In 1789, the year of George Washington's first inauguration, the Jewish population of the United States was between 2,000 and 2,500 in a total population of 3.9 million and was concentrated in a handful of cities along the eastern seaboard. The first congregations in the United States were in New York, Newport, Savannah, Philadelphia, Richmond, and Charleston. All had been founded by immigrants of Spanish-Portuguese origin; all followed the Orthodox Sephardic ritual.

Between 1790 and 1820, the population of the United States reached 9.6 million, while the Jewish population increased to only 2,700. By mid-century, the Sephardic sources of migration were exhausted and the Ashkenazic surge began. The immigration of German, Austrian, and Central European Jews to the United States, which began as a trickle after the conclusion of the Napoleonic Wars in 1815, reached considerable proportions in later years, and before long the Ashkenazim outnumbered the Sephardim, whose dominance they challenged and then supplanted.

By 1840, when the Jewish population of the country as a whole was 15,000, there was less than a minyan in Washington, D.C. Unlike other cities along the East Coast, where both Sephardic and Ashkenazic Jews had settled, the Jews of Washington were virtually all German in origin and would remain so until the arrival of East European Jews in the 1880s; there was no Sephardic Jewish settlement in the city.

The earliest Jewish residents of Washington had settled briefly in nearby Baltimore, Maryland. From their beginnings, the Jewish communities of Washington and Baltimore were linked by common origins; both were founded by immigrants from Bavaria.

**Bavaria, Baltimore, and Washington**

Political upheaval and economic distress in Germany motivated emigration for Jew and Christian alike. German Jews had participated extensively in the country's liberal revolutionary movement in 1848–49, and when it failed, they emigrated in large numbers, as did many German Christians.[1] For Jews, however, there was the additional motivating factor of anti-Semitism; a wave of persecution had swept Germany following the collapse of the liberal revolution.

In Bavaria, conditions were especially harsh and appalling. In an attempt to reduce the size of its Jewish population, the Bavarian rulers restricted the right of marriage in each Jewish family. Munich, the capital of Bavaria, and a century later the birthplace of the Nazi Party, was even then a major center of anti-Semitism. The few Bavarian rulers who were willing to consider easing the restrictions on the Jews conditioned any concession on the demand that "the confessors of the Mosaic religion deny the authority of the Talmud and change their Sabbath from Saturday to Sunday."

In 1848, Leopold Kompert, a prominent Austrian Jewish novelist, echoing the mood of the biblical prophet Jeremiah, warned the Jews of the Austro-Hungarian Empire that they must find new homes: "The harvest is past, the summer is ended and we are not saved."[2] He was convinced that America offered the promise of mutually beneficial opportunities, since "the Jews do possess the qualities and virtues so indispensable for reconstruction in that country: foresight, sobriety, economy, discipline and loyalty."[3]

Driven by broken promises, discriminatory legislation, and a resurgence of crude xenophobic nationalism, even those who were not aware of Kompert's warning heeded his advice. For the most part, the migrating German Jews were attracted to the eastern seaboard and especially to New York, Philadelphia, and Baltimore. An unusually large number of Bavarian emigrants chose Baltimore as their port of entry into the new world because of an additional consideration—the price of steamship tickets.

Research by Moses Aberbach has revealed that many German Jews migrated to Baltimore rather than to other eastern cities because of the profitable relationship that existed between Baltimore and the German port of Bremen. Maryland exported wheat and tobacco through Baltimore to Europe. The tobacco was shipped to Bremen and the wheat to ever-famished Ireland. Reciprocal Irish and German exports, however, found no market in Maryland. Since it was unprofitable for the freighters to return to the United States with empty holds, shippers would entice passengers to fill their vessels for the return journey from Germany by offering passage to Baltimore at low rates.

Bavarian Jews seeking to embark for the United States were frequently approached by shipping agents and tobacco importers offering discounted tickets for passage to America via Bremen to

Baltimore. Benjamin Szold, who became a leading Baltimore rabbi and a founder of the Jewish Theological Seminary, was one of the many who came to the United States on a tobacco discount ticket. The linkage between the two port cities is the convincing explanation for the large Bavarian Jewish and Irish settlements in Baltimore.[4]

The Bavarian newcomers soon discovered that Baltimore was hardly the promised land they had expected. Economic opportunities were limited, and although the civic disabilities could not be compared to those in Bavaria, they found that, even in Maryland, because of a required "oath as a Christian," no Jew could be elected to state office. A so-called Jew Bill, passed in 1826, had granted Jews the right to appointive or elective office only on condition that they "subscribe to a belief in a future state of reward and punishments."

The newly arrived immigrants were often penniless and depended on those who had preceded them for assistance. Most were unskilled; neither were they suited for manual labor. Many became junk dealers, pawnbrokers, and itinerant peddlers, for these occupations required little capital or experience. Peddlers from Baltimore frequently passed through Washington, the capital city, and it was there that some ultimately settled. Other immigrants too, all seeking a livlihood, found their way to Washington.

For many years, Washington Jewry turned to Baltimore for its religious personnel and ritual requirements. Prior to the establishment of a congregation in Washington, Jews went to Baltimore for High Holiday services, and for lack of a Jewish burial ground, they turned to Baltimore's Jewish cemeteries.

As an example of the close relationship between Washington and Baltimore, the rabbi of the Eden Street Synagogue in East Baltimore, Henry Hocheimer, traveled to Washington every three months to test the students of the Washington Hebrew

Congregation's day school. He was also invited to deliver the farewell address, in German of course, when the congregation left its old quarters to occupy its new structure on 8th Street.

The Civil War marked the end of Washington's dependence on Baltimore. The cities differed in their political orientations. Maryland, a border state, with 87,000 slaves working its tobacco plantations, was divided in its loyalties. Being of the South, many of its citizens tended to favor the Democratic States Rights or Peace Party, while Washington, though south of Baltimore, was culturally northern and supported President Lincoln and the unity government. Following the Civil War, Washington was less dependent on Baltimore. For both cities, it was the end of the period of German immigration.

### Washington's First Jew

In the year that Washington became the nation's capital, 1791, the District of Columbia consisted of a ten-mile square of largely undeveloped rural wilderness carved out of a diamond-shaped section of Maryland and Virginia. Within its boundaries were two small tobacco-trading port settlements, Georgetown and Alexandria. It was nine years before the federal government would move from Philadelphia to Washington. At least one Jew took up residence five years earlier than either the Congress or the president.

Isaac Polock of Savannah, Georgia, a grandson of one of the founders of the synagogue in Newport, Rhode Island, was the first Jew to leave his mark on the capital city. He fled Savannah to escape the British occupation during the Revolutionary War, spending the war years in the North along with others who were in danger of being apprehended by the British as "revolutionists."[5]

Attracted by the building frenzy that swept Washington in the frantic attempt to convert marshland and forest into a city that could house the seat of government, Polock took up residence in Washington in 1795 and joined the effort to build a capital city befitting the new nation.[6]

Polock invested in several Washington developments. According to a deed dated September 17, 1795, "Morris and Nicholson conveyed to Isaac Polock for $34,000.00 all their property in the square."[7] Robert Morris and John Nicholson were the most active land speculators in Washington in the 1790s; both ended up in debtor's prison as overextended bankrupts.

Polock's most significant acquisition was a large parcel of land and its unfinished brick buildings located on Pennsylvania Avenue near the White House. James Greenleaf, another prominent speculator, had sold the lots to Polock with the stipulation that he complete the construction.[8]

Once completed, the buildings, from 2107 to 2117 Pennsylvania Avenue, were used as offices and residences of cabinet officials. Among the distinguished citizens who became Polock's tenants were James and Dolley Madison, when Madison was Secretary of State under President Thomas Jefferson. General Sam Houston, the first senator from Texas, lived in another. After the federal government moved to the District in 1800, another housed the first State Department. Still another was occupied by the first Secretary of the Navy. Polock himself lived in one of the houses from 1800 until his death in 1813.

According to a remarkable *Chronicle* covering the period from 1733 to 1803 and carefully recorded in Juedisch-Deutsch, first by Benjamin Sheftall, a pioneer Savannah settler, and continued by his son, Levi, Isaac Polock was a founding member of Savannah's first synagogue, the third to be established in the United States. In Savannah, Polock operated a "grocery and liquor store" and later built a brick building on the bay where importers and exporters stored their merchandise to await shipment.[9]

The Sheftall Chronicle noted that Isaac Polock was accorded the honor of *Hatan Torah* (i.e., being called to the Torah on the festival of Simchat Torah for the reading of the last section of Deuteronomy) in 1794, but was unavailable because he "would not be in town, for that he was going northward."[10] It was during his absence from Savannah that Polock made his way to Washington.[11]

Polock was buried in Washington in a burial ground on 23rd and E Streets N.W. known as Reservation 4, Observatory Hill, "near the north east corner of the Reservation."[12] Writing in 1901, a reporter named Wilber Birth recalled that a "priest" named Raphael Jones had officiated at Polock's funeral, and that Jones was German-born and a man of considerable learning who "wrote Hebrew and was acquainted with other languages."[13] Birth reported that Jones had married a seamstress who had resided in Birth's home.

After his marriage, Raphael Jones, the "Jew-Priest," had become a traveling salesman and later opened a grocery store in Georgetown, at the corner of Bridge and Potomac Streets. Birth reported that Jones "accumulated a fortune there and moved to Washington, where he established himself in the dry goods trade at what is now known as Kann's Sons and Co., corner 8th Street and Market Place."[14]

All but one of the buildings that Polock had built on Pennsylvania Avenue, and where he lived until his death, were demolished in the 1980s as part of the District's urban renewal program. The last one to stand, at 2109 Pennsylvania Avenue, became a restaurant and bar known as Billy's 3 and later as Tammany Hall, with an apartment on the second floor. It was demolished in 1987 to become a parking lot.

### Washington's First Jewish Family

A generation after Polock's death, Captain Alfred Mordecai and his family became occupants of one of the Polock buildings on

Pennsylvania Avenue. The city directory for 1834 lists Mordecai along with one other recognizably Jewish name, E. A. Cohen, the publisher of the directory.

Alfred Mordecai was the son of Jacob Mordecai and Judith Myers. His father was knowledgeable in Hebrew, according to his relative, the famed Rebecca Gratz, founder of the first Jewish Sunday school in the United States. Alfred Mordecai's grandfather, Moses Mordecai, had migrated to Philadelphia from his birthplace in Bonn, Germany, in 1750.

One of eleven children, Alfred Mordecai was born in Warrenton, North Carolina, on January 3, 1804. He married Sara Hays, whose maternal grandfather, Samuel Hays, was a descendant of a Dutch Jewish family that had migrated to the United States. The mother of Sara Hays was Rachel Gratz, a sister of the aforementioned Rebecca.

As a young officer, five years after his graduation from the West Point Military Academy in 1823, Alfred Mordecai came to Washington as assistant to the engineer of the Washington Arsenal. He rose in rank until he became superintendent of the Arsenal, which he commanded during the Mexican War. In 1855–56 he represented the United States Army as observer during the Crimean War.

The family papers and letters in the Library of Congress reveal that the Mordecai family, like the Hays and Gratz families, was religiously observant and involved in Jewish communal life, especially in Jewish education. The Hays and the Gratz families were prominent members of the Philadelphia Jewish community.

Alfred Mordecai's daughter, Rosa, born in 1839, was the first Jewish child to be born in Washington. When his second child, Frank, died in 1841, there were not enough Jews in Washington to make up a minyan for the funeral.[15]

At the outbreak of the Civil War, Alfred Mordecai, now a major, resigned his commission. Torn between loyalty to the Union and devotion to his native state, North Carolina, where most of his family still lived, he could not bring himself to take up arms against either side. He later moved to Philadelphia, where his two daughters, Rosa and Miriam, helped support the family by private teaching. Alfred Mordecai died in Philadelphia in 1887.

Rosa Mordecai returned to Washington in the 1890s, taking up residence in the Louise home on Massachusetts Avenue,* where she lived until her death in 1936. In Washington, she participated in civic and Jewish communal affairs after joining the local branch of the Council of Jewish Women, which had been organized in 1893, regularly reporting to the members as chairman of the committee on "Purity of the Press."

In one of her annual reports, she urged "mothers in Israel" to "implant purity in the hearts of your children" by practicing "the simple delights of the Friday evening services, the Seder with all its time honored associations."

In her handwritten will, dated May 10, 1920, Rosa Mordecai stated,

> All prayer books and Jewish books, except the old Daily Prayers belonging to Ellen Hays Etting, which I wish to put in my coffin, I leave my dear friends the Misses Solomons in memory of the many times we have used them together. I wish to be buried in Jewish Ground, preferably in Philadelphia.

The "Misses Solomons" were the daughters of Adolphus S. Solomons, one of the founders of Adas Israel. The obituary in the *Washington Post* on October 22, 1936, revealed Rosa Mordecai's link with Adas Israel through Rabbi Solomon Metz, its spiritual leader, who delivered the eulogy at her funeral.

One of Alfred Mordecai's grandsons, Major General William M. Miley, was the commander of the 17th Airborne Division, which

*The present address is 5425 Western Avenue N.W.

played an important role in the invasion of Germany during World War II.

~ *Gertrude (Mrs. Solomon) Metz* *Reflections*

Rabbi Metz used to visit elderly people and one of them was Rosa Mordecai, who was, during his visit to her counting the days of the *omer*.[17]

**The District of Columbia at Mid-Century**

In 1850, Washington had hardly begun to project the grandeur one would expect of the nation's capital city. The Capitol building, insignificantly domed, was yet to be completed. Unpaved streets and footpaths gave way to mud during the wet, sweltering summers. A rainstorm could transform Pennsylvania Avenue into a river of clay in the summer, and, in the winter, into a crenelated washboard of frozen ruts. During much of the year, when the President crossed the street from the White House to reach Blair House, a servant had to remove the clotted mud from his boots.

The Washington Monument, recently begun, was barely visible; the Potomac River flowed almost to its base. Public transportation was by horsedrawn omnibus with lines operating from Georgetown to the Navy Yard and from the wharves to 7th and 1st Streets. Congress had returned Alexandria and the trans-Potomac portion of the District of Columbia to Virginia in 1846, leaving Georgetown as the District's only commercial and social center.

The federal installation in Washington needed to expand to meet the demands of the growing country. Wagon trails awaited grading to be turned into streets; existing streets had to be paved. New buildings had to be constructed. Attracted by job opportunities, skilled craftsmen from around the world flocked into the District. Many of them were Germans, and some were Jews.[18]

Harriet Beecher Stowe's epic *Uncle Tom's Cabin*, published in March 1852, aroused the sensitivity and the passions of a people soon to be torn apart by a tragic and bloody conflict that would threaten to destroy the Union. Millard Fillmore was the President of the United States, completing the unfinished term of General Zachary Taylor, who had been inaugurated in 1849 only to die suddenly while attending a political rally in the summer of 1850. Daniel Webster was Secretary of State; Franklin Pierce would be the next President.

There were three Jews in Congress, or, more accurately, one Jew and two of dubious identity. David Levy Yulee, one of Florida's first U.S. senators, elected in 1845 after serving in the House of Representatives as his state's first territorial delegate to Congress, had changed his name from Levy to Yulee after his conversion to Christianity. The other two were Congressman Charles Lewis Levin, married to a Catholic, and a leader of the anti-alien American Party, who had been elected from a Philadelphia district to serve three terms, from 1845 to 1851, and Judah P. Benjamin, a Whig senator from Louisiana. Benjamin later became a leader of the Confederacy, second in importance only to its President, Jefferson Davis. Of the three, Benjamin was the only self-professed Jew, the first to be elected to the U.S. Senate.

Washington's German Jewish immigrants found kindred spirits in the Christian German community. They enjoyed speaking German to one another. Both regarded German as the language of *Kultur*, and English, at best, only as a means of earning a living in the new country. One of the Jewish immigrants, Max Cohenheim, launched Washington's first German-language newspaper, the *Columbia*. German Jews marched with German Lutherans, Evangelicals, and freethinkers in the city's parades. Together, they organized German societies and fraternal orders, of which the Odd Fellows was one.

Early German immigrants, Jews among them, settled in the section of the District now known as Foggy Bottom, an area bounded by Pennsylvania Avenue, between 19th and 24th Streets N.W. and 22nd and C Streets, originally called Hamburg because of its acquisition and development by a 1771 German immigrant named Jacob Funk.[19] From its beginning, the area attracted a large number of German immigrants.

German Jewish immigrants frequently turned to peddling in order to earn a livelihood, since it required little initial capital and offered a rapid means of accumulating more. It was a familiar pattern: peddle a few years and then strike roots by opening a store. At least four Washington Jewish merchants had begun their business careers as peddlers. One of them, Wolf Nordlinger, had peddled his wares along the East Coast until the Civil War compelled him to settle down in one city. He chose Washington and settled in Georgetown.

In 1850, Washington was little more than a village. Of the 52,000 inhabitants of the District of Columbia, at least twenty-one were Jews.[20] This was the number that gathered at the home of Herman Lissberger, who resided in the German neighborhood of Hamburg, on Pennsylvania Avenue near its intersection with 21st Street, a block previously developed by Washington's first Jew, Isaac Polock. It was in this home that a meeting had been called to consider the formation of a Jewish congregation. The year was 1852.

# 2

## THE FIRST CONGREGATION

The twenty-one Jews who gathered at the home of Herman Lissberger on April 25, 1852, affirmed their intention to form a "Hebrew Congregation," recording their discussion in minutes written in a flowing German script. They elected Solomon Pribram president; other officers elected included: Jacob Saqui (a Sephardi name) vice-president, Jonah Gluck, treasurer, and Albert Horwitz, secretary.*

The founding members were determined to retain their Jewish identity along with their German vernacular; they regarded German culture and language as only slightly less sacred than the Hebrew. They assessed themselves $1 per member to cover incidental costs. Among the founders were two, Leopold Oppenheimer and Levy Cohen, who, seventeen years later, would resign from the congregation to organize the Adas Israel Hebrew Congregation.

The country's only Jewish journal, the *Occident*, published in Philadelphia, noted that "the Israelites have bought a piece of land for a synagogue and that a congregation has been organized in the Capital of the United States. We knew that several families lived there, but not being acquainted with them, we never were informed of their proceedings."[1] Rabbi Isaac Leeser, the founding editor of the *Occident*, would later dedicate the congregation's first building.

*According to Rabbi Abram Simon of the Washington Hebrew Congregation, the organizational meeting took place at the home of W. Jacobi on 19th Street and Pennsylvania Avenue.

Historians have suggested that the first synagogues in the United States may have been organized not only as an expression of piety but as an attempt to cope with the loneliness of life in a strange new community as well as in response to what the immigrants believed to be an American expectation. This premise is supported by the address delivered on June 21, 1820, at the consecration of the newly built synagogue of Congregation Mikve Israel of Savannah, Georgia,* by its leader, Dr. Jacob de La Motta, who declared, "Were we not influenced by religious zeal, a decent respect to the custom of the community in which we live should actuate us to observe public worship."[2] Whatever the motives, the establishment of Washington's first congregation was clearly an affirmation of Jewish identity.

**Captain Jonas P. Levy**

The newly organized congregation gained considerable prestige from the affiliation of Jonas P. Levy, a captain in the U.S. Navy and a popular war hero. In 1857 he was elected president, succeeding Solomon Pribram, who became vice-president. Membership had by then grown to forty-four.

Jonas P. Levy (1807–1883), the son of Michael Levy and Rachel Phillips, was born into a prominent pioneer Philadelphia family whose members included Henry Phillips, a member of the 35th Congress of the United States, and Mordecai Manuel Noah, the noted author, dramatist, and politician. Jonas was the brother of Uriah P. Levy, also a naval hero, noted for having brought about the elimination of corporal punishment in the Navy and for his purchase of Monticello, the home of President Thomas Jefferson, whom he greatly admired.

*The congregation with which Isaac Polock was affiliated.

Jonas Levy's command of the U.S.S. *America* during the Mexican War and his association with prominent civic leaders gave him access to Washington's policy makers, a fact that proved useful in defending the rights of the small but growing Jewish community in the United States. He was instrumental in alleviating a distressing issue which aroused American Jewish opinion in 1851: the Swiss-American treaty.

Swiss Jews had long suffered from the discriminatory decrees of their government. Each Swiss canton had the right to decide whether or not to admit Jews; several cantons were closed to them. The Jews of America, quite naturally, objected to the Swiss policy, and in 1851, when the Senate was asked to ratify a treaty with Switzerland which included the provision that only American Christians would be allowed to live in that country, a furor erupted. Hundreds of protesting letters flooded senatorial offices in Washington. In the words of Isaac Leeser in the *Occident,*

> As American citizens we indignantly protest against the ratification by the Senate of the United States of a treaty containing a provision which strikes at the very root of the religious liberty of one hundred thousand American citizens.[3]

Mobilizing to oppose the treaty, Levy and Leeser organized a representative national Jewish committee to secure the support of sensitive Christians throughout the country to petition the Senate in opposition to ratification. They enlisted the aid of Secretary of State Daniel Webster and former Secretary of State Senator Henry Clay of Kentucky. Senator Judah P. Benjamin joined the petitioners.

The controversy, which persisted for almost fifteen years, remained unsettled until a new Swiss constitution finally endorsed religious liberty. The result was a victory not only for Swiss Jews but for the status of Jews throughout the world.

Writing in his journal, Leeser noted:

> Had the first step not been taken here, it is likely that neither American nor European governments would have troubled themselves about us. Those who wish to be free must themselves strike the blow. Let us be grateful that it has been done and one more land is open for the wandering sons of Israel.[4]

This would not be the last time that the capital's Jewish residents would play an important role in protecting the rights of Jews and other minorities.

### Places of Worship

The congregation conducted its first service in the home of Herman Lissberger on Pennsylvania Avenue. Later, as the membership outgrew his home's capacity, services were held on 10th Street, opposite the ill-fated Ford's Theatre, where President Lincoln was shot, and alongside Petersen's House, where he died.

Still later, as each of its rented quarters became inadequate, the congregation moved, in sequence, to 4th Street opposite City Hall, to 9th Street near D Street, and, later, to Harmony Hall on D Street between 12th and 13th Streets, a locale referred to as "Finkman's Hall near the Engine House."[5]

Wrote Rabbi Leeser in the *Occident*,

> We learn from the *Evening Star* that the Israelites are making strenuous exertions to provide themselves with a suitable place of worship. They are highly spoken of for their industry and general good conduct, and have won the good opinion of other denominations. They lately celebrated the receipt of a *Sepher Torah*, on which occasion they had a public dinner. We trust, however, to hear before many months have elapsed, that the contemplated Synagogue has

been completed, and is the resort of many and devout and pious Israelites.[6]

Leeser reported on a later visit to Washington in 1856:

> We visited the house lately fitted up [as] a place of worship.... They have a Hazan and Shochet in the person of the Rev. Mr. H. Melle. We learned... that... several Israelites in the District had not joined the Congregation; but we hope that the difficulties... may be speedily removed, so that the Israelites of the vicinity may contribute, to promote the welfare of their faith.[7]

An account in the local press gave details of the congregation's move to ninth and D streets in 1859.

> The ceremony of moving into a new synagogue, at the corner of Ninth and D Streets, took place on Friday afternoon, May 20 (Iyar 5619), with a full attendance of its members. The usual ceremony was performed by the Rev. Mr. Landsberg, minister of the Congregation, after which Capt. Jonas P. Levy made a... short address to the congregation.[8]

Soon after the dedication, the congregation sought to engage its first paid functionary. An ad in the *Occident* in June 1859 reveals its need.

> Wanted: By the first Hebrew Congregation of the City of Washington, A Hazzan, Shochet and Teacher in Hebrew, and, if possible, in the German language. The salary will be $400 a year, besides perquisites amounting to $150. Communications, with testimonials must be forwarded to
>
> Samuel Herman, Secretary

In 1860, the year Abraham Lincoln was elected president, Washington's Jewish population reached 400, according to a correspondent who visited Washington during the week of the election.

> Six years ago there was not a Minyan to be found in that city; now there are about four hundred Yehudim there.... Great credit should be accorded to Capt. Jonah P. Levy, through whose exertions and perseverance, not only a congregation has been formed, but a new building has just been purchased.
>
> We are informed that the Israelites of the national capital are now about closing the purchase of a beautiful large church on Tenth Street, between E and F Streets. The building cost originally $13,000, but the price to be paid for it is $10,000; first payment $2,000. . . . As the Washington Congregation is neither rich nor numerous, though steadily increasing, our friends would be greatly indebted to all Israelites to assist them to obtain a suitable house of worship.[9]

The correspondent confused the temporary rented quarters on 10th Street with the building on 8th Street, which would not be purchased until three years later on February 9, 1863. The 1861 tourist's guidebook to Washington, under the heading "*Synagogue of Israelites,*" stated, "Location of building not yet decided upon."[10]

The synagogue structure on 8th Street, still standing as later enlarged, was purchased in 1863 from the Methodist Episcopal Church, which had acquired it by default from the Central Presbyterian Church. Ground had been donated to the original owners, the Presbyterians, by John P. Van Ness in 1845. The Hebrew congregation purchased the building for $8,000, of which $2,000 was paid in cash and the balance deferred over a five-year period. Funds had been raised from the congregation's members and by soliciting the B'nai B'rith, the "Friends of Israel," and congregations in other communities.

In asking Jews in other parts of the United States for help, the congregation felt that its location in the nation's capital entitled it to their generosity. The following advertisement for support appeared in the *Occident*:

> **@TO THE BENEVOLENT OF EVERY SECT.@** The first (and only) Hebrew congregation of the city of Washington . . . ventures to the benevolent citizens of said city and other cities and places for aid. . . . They have long earnestly desired . . . a building in which they could . . . humbly and devoutly worship God; yet the smallness of their number (they are only sixty members) . . . puts it wholly out of their power to gratify this long cherished desire. But the time has come . . . to attempt its gratification. They have accordingly entered into a contract for the purchase of a church edifice. . . . From their slender means they have cheerfully contributed several thousand dollars. They earnestly and imploringly ask of the benevolent of the land to aid them in raising the additional amount, to enable them to pay the residue of the said purchase.
>
> Isaac Herzberg, President
>
> Adolph Adler, Recording Secretary. Trustees: J. H. Henlein, Emanuel Gutman, Moses Siegel.

The mayor of Washington, Richard Wallach, endorsed the appeal.

> Mayor's Office, Washington,
> Feb. 17, 1863
> This object is a laudable one, which commends itself to all. The parties engaged in the undertaking are residents of this city, personally well known to me, and are gentlemen of character.
>
> Richard Wallach, Mayor

Later, during the Civil War, Mayor Wallach would address an appeal to the Jews of New York for the support of Washington's indigent Jewish families. According to one history of the period, Wallach was a Jew, but it is likely that the author confused him with a member of the congregation who had the same name.*

**The Dedication**

The Civil War raged from 1861 to 1865. The impressive Union victory at Gettysburg in July 1863 was achieved at an extremely high cost to both sides: 23,000 Union casualties and 28,000 Confederate losses. The Gettysburg battle and the fall of Vicksburg the same month proved to be turning points in the war. It was during this tumultuous year that the congregation acquired the former church on 8th Street. The building had been redecorated and now needed to be consecrated.

The congregation dedicated its new home on July 31, 1863 with Rabbi Isaac Leeser, the recognized spokesman for traditional Judaism in America, delivering the dedicatory sermon. In his sermon, Leeser deplored the tragic loss of life exacted in the ongoing civil struggle.

The *Evening Star* described the service:

> Yesterday afternoon the new synagogue on Eighth Street between H and I Streets (formerly the M.E. Church South) was dedicated by the congregation with appropriate ceremonies in the presence of a large audience. Several of the clergy of the District were present. . . . also many prominent citizens, including the members of our City Council, members of the bar and the press.
>
> The ceremonies were begun at the old synagogue at Harmony Hall on D street between 12th and 13th streets, where the congregation assembled at 2:00 o'clock. Here the prayer Minchio [Mincha,

*Richard Wallach's father, who came from Romania, organized a Unitarian church in Washington. An Episcopalian minister officiated at Wallach's marriage, and another minister officiated at his funeral.

> the afternoon prayer] was said, and Dr. Archemier [Hochheimer] of Baltimore, delivered a short farewell address in German, after which the congregation repaired to the new synagogue. The five books of Moses, which are written on parchment enveloped in velvet, were taken in carriages in charge of the president of the congregation, Isaac Herzberg, assisted by the two oldest members, Jonah Gluck and Solomon Pribram, and the reader Samuel Weill.

Leeser, reporting on his Washington visit, wrote that "he had arrived in Washington on Wednesday, July 29, stayed at the home of Mr. Isaac Herzberg, the President, and had departed on Monday, August 3." He described the new synagogue as follows:

> The main hall is upstairs . . . 380 seats facing east. The gallery [for women] resting on iron pillars runs around three sides. The Ten Commandments surmount the whole, and in front [of the ark] is suspended a beautiful scarlet silk velvet curtain (Parocheth) [Leeser's parenthesis], the gift of the ladies.
>
> In the basement are apartments for the shamas, with meeting and school rooms, as also a Mikveh.
>
> In the evening we were invited to attend a ball given in honor of the opening of the Synagogue. . . . With our kind host and friends, we repaired to the Odd Fellow's Hall, where the festivities took place, and notwithstanding the great heat, there were assembled several hundred young Israelites, who filled the room to such an extent that all could not participate in the amusement at one time. We certainly had no idea that so many of our people could be brought together in Washington; but there they were, many the residents of the city, others of Alexandria and Baltimore, and some of New York even, all gathered together to do honor to the occasion.
>
> On Friday morning, the Rev. Rabbi Hyam Hochheimer of Baltimore, also arrived at Mr. Herzberg's to participate in the solemnities in the afternoon. At two o'clock a number of members repaired to the building which had been hitherto used for a Synagogue, and candor compels us to say, that it was so little in accordance with

> what it ought to be, that it was not abandoned a moment too soon, and we can well feel the pleasure of the people in quitting so inconvenient a place and so unsuitably situated, for a handsome structure, in an airy position, on an open street, with plenty of light all around it.
>
> The Rev. Mr. Weil, the Hazan, read the Minchah service, after which Rabbi Hochheimer delivered a brief parting address in German, taking for his text, "Blessed be thou at thy going out," showing how the act of quitting that spot may be made fruitful on entering the new building. . . .
>
> When the learned Rabbi had finished, the ministers and the president in one carriage, and the bearers of the four Sepharim in another, repaired to the new building, while the others present walked thither to receive the Law-books when they should arrive....
>
> Among the assembly were several Christian clergymen, lawyers, reporters, and many citizens; but none of the principal officers of the national or city government were present as far as we could learn. . . . and it bears a painful contrast with the late frequent attendance of the highest official persons in Europe at similar solemnities there.[11]

### Leeser's Sermon

Rabbi Leeser began the service of dedication on Friday afternoon by reciting the Shema Yisrael and the Shehechiyanu. Leeser later claimed that his sermon had been extemporaneous, which is difficult to believe, since by his own admission it "occupied somewhat less than an hour."

As his text, Leeser had selected the words King Solomon recited at the dedication of the First Temple in Jerusalem: "The heavens and the heaven of heavens cannot contain Thee; how much less then this house that I have built?"[12] The synagogue was built, declared Leeser, "not to attempt to enclose God, but to have a home for His law, where Jews may assemble to be instructed and to pray. The synagogue is a house of assembly and prayer." He continued:

> We Jews have been faithful guardians of Divine truth. We may not have excelled in inventiveness in the destructive engines of war; in this other nations have been our superiors; but our contributions to the common welfare have been the highest. The doctrines of all other faiths came from us.

As though mindful of the Christians present, he continued,

> The prejudice which has been excited against us in all ages is thus proven to be extremely unjust, for instead of being a burden to society we have been its greatest benefactors. And still, how long is it since every where we were spurned as enemies and outcasts? Who in the Middle Ages had pity on the Jew? Who commiserated his fallen condition?

He recalled the fanatical hatred of the Jews by prince and priest.

> Everyone thought himself at liberty to maltreat him for some fancied offence against the State and individuals, which was foreign to his heart and feeling. Nevertheless, he bore it all with patience. And he has lived to see the Scriptures diffused all over the earth, and to hear every where rising on High the Psalms and prayers of his own royal poet . . . Moses the man of God, and of the other sweet singers.

Now addressing the Jews, he charged,

> No, friends, it is not the size and elegance of the building which will please the Lord of all, but the spirit of the worshipers. . . . If then you, my brother Israelites, wish truly to hallow these walls, show yourselves worthy of your kindred, and let this house be the means to kindle in you a true devotion to the Eternal God . . . who released your ancestors from Egyptian bondage, to be to Him a perpetual inheritance.

With admirable dignity, Leeser made the most of the opportunity to defend and explain Judaism to the Christians present. He pointed out that Jews are in "an antagonistic position with the vast majority of mankind," for though the majority have derived their religion from the Bible, they believe in "a divided Godhead, as they term it, in a triune God."

> However Jews do not reject others because of this difference nor do they deny salvation to those who differ. Israelites have never been persecutors of their fellow-men . . . nor have we forced our faith on others. God is a universal God, and His sun shines equally for the Turk and Hindoo as the Hebrew.

By indirection, Leeser alluded to the widespread accusation that Jews were guilty of illegal trading with the South.

> Excluded so long from the sympathies of mankind, it is but natural that many [Jews] should have acquired habits not altogether commendable. But it is wrong to charge this fault upon all Israelites, as though all had sinned. The name of Jew has even become unjustly a term of reproach, although it has an honorable origin; since Leah when she had borne his fourth son to Jacob called him Judah (whence the name of Jew was by various changes derived). We may have lost much of our ancient high character through the course of so many terrible sufferings. But the heart of the Hebrew is still the seat of kindness . . . and few of us are ever guilty of violent robbery or of imbruing their hands in a fellow-man's blood.

In a scarcely veiled reference to the Confederacy, he observed,

> The banner which we received from Sinai has not been stained by treason; yet its white folds bear many a mark of blood; but it issued from the wounds in our own heart . . . which came from the wounds inflicted in our bosoms by the deadly weapon of our adversaries,

> who slew without mercy those who would not relinquish their belief to the demands of those who for the time bore rule over them, and whose favor could easily have been conciliated had they consented to forsake the God of their father, and united themselves with those around them.

Cued by the battle at Gettysburg earlier that month, Leeser declared,

> We as a class are faithful to the governments under which we live; and although until lately we were nearly every where excluded from the rights of citizenship and debarred from all offices, men belonging to our communion have fallen on the battle fields of contending nations, even where the combat was not for the rights of man, but the ambition of opposing potentates. And in the fearful struggle which now afflicts this land, our victims have not been wanting, who hastened to embark their life and fortune at the call of the authorities.
>
> We shall teach [our children] the holy precepts of the Scriptures ... "Thou shalt love thy neighbor as thyself," ... For it is charity alone which can accomplish our mission; the tree of life cannot flourish in the midst of violence; truth can be nursed only by the arts of peace.

Concluding in peroration,

> You, my Hebrew friends, I have to admonish solemnly to do honor to the name you bear; to prove by your conduct that you wish truly to consecrate this house, by an observance of the Sabbaths and festivals, by an honorable course of life as men and citizens, by training your children in the way they should go, and by showing in your whole conduct that you are sincere in your attachment to the law of Heaven.... united in bonds of love and kindness, may [we] give thanks and glory to the God of Israel and join in one universal Amen, Hallelujah.

Since it was not yet the Sabbath, "donations and subscriptions were received to a considerable amount." With the conclusion of the dedicatory service, the evening's Sabbath service was chanted by the hazzan assisted by the choir. Leeser reported that he was pleased with the rendition of Lecha Dodi and the Yigdal.

On Saturday morning the service began at 8:00 a.m. and concluded at 1:00 p.m. "owing to the calling up of some eighty persons to the Torah." Rabbi Hochheimer delivered the sermon, in German.

Evaluating his own address in the *Occident*, Leeser observed,

> The address was entirely extemporaneous, and made up after the speaker had taken a survey of his audience, which was largely composed of non-Israelites, wherefore he deemed it his duty to utter a defence of practical Judaism, the first time it was possible for him in the capital of the Union, and he trusts that it may not have been entirely without some good result.

Leeser's sermon, a remarkable expression of Jewish dignity, reflected the status of the Jew during the Civil War.

### Worship and Ritual

In defining their mode of worship, the founders of the congregation were determined to retain their familiar German Ashkenazic traditions and to replicate the sounds and procedures they recalled from their European synagogues. Preserving the familiar melodies would help them to overcome the culture shock that had followed their migration to a new, unfamiliar world.

The historian-sociologist Oscar Handlin noted the same tendency among Christian immigrants: "The immigrants thought it important to bring their churches to the United States, to reconstitute in their new homes the old forms of worship."[13]

The constitution of the congregation, adopted in 1856, specified that the services should follow the "Aschkeness minhag according to the Redolheimer prayer book, which shall not be altered unless by 3/4 votes of the congregation." The Roedelheim prayer book, published in Roedelheim, Germany, in 1806, was the standard prayer book for traditional congregations. Edited by Wolf Heidenheim, its formal name was *Siddur Safah Berurah* ("Prayers of Clear Speech").

Many years went by before the congregation permitted sermons or prayers to be rendered in English. Even when the practice of reciting the prayer for the government in English began, its repetition in Hebrew was required. The Haftarah, the portion from the Prophets, was allowed to be read in Hebrew or German. While English eventually became the language of public discourse, German long remained the preferred language of theology.

The constitution denied membership to the intermarried. Men and women sat separately; women were restricted to the gallery. Notices in German and English warned of a fine of $1 for anyone smoking in the building during hours of worship. There were detailed rules of procedure for "*Parseerchurs*" (i.e., *petichot*, opening the ark where the Torah scrolls were kept). Kohen and Levi were called to the Torah for the first and second honor, respectively, in accordance with traditional custom.

The constitution employed the term *Parnass* for president and *Gabai* for treasurer, terms found frequently in Sephardic congregations but not restricted to them. The president was to be installed during the fall festival of Simchat Torah. An 1861 revised constitution denied burial to the uncircumcised and prohibited marriages during the traditionally prohibited periods, three weeks prior to Tisha B'Av, the spring *sfirah* period, fast days, and the week-long festivals of Passover and Sukkot.

The congregation employed a shochet, a hazzan, and a *shamash*. Funds to pay wages and to sustain the budget were derived from diverse sources: dues, fees for the services of the shochet (referred to as *Schocath-Gelt*), fines for failure to attend daily services, sales of High Holiday seats to children of members, weddings, funerals, and the sale of burial lots. By 1869, the dues had been raised to $2 per month.

Simon Mundheim was engaged as *shochet* and Manassas Oppenheimer as *shamash* in 1867. Mundheim had been formally certified as a *shochet* in Germany; he was religiously observant in his personal life. By his own choice, he refused to serve members of the congregation accused of using or selling pork and "*traefer*" (nonkosher) meat. At the board's behest, he also declined to offer his services to members of the congregation who were in arrears in their payment of dues.

Mundheim was the great-grandfather of Louise Mundheim, who later was to marry Rabbi Norman Gerstenfeld, one of the distinguished spiritual leaders of the Washington Hebrew Congregation. Mundheim was also the father-in-law of Leopold Karpeles, a Civil War hero and the first Jew to receive the Congressional Medal of Honor.

Uncompromising in his observance of religious law, Mundheim would later be among those who withdrew from the Washington Hebrew Congregation to form the Adas Israel Hebrew Congregation, where he would continue to serve as shochet. Neither position sufficed for his livelihood. The city directory of 1869 lists Mundheim as operating a "fancy store" on North Capitol Street.

The duties of Manassas Oppenheimer, the *shamash*, included chanting the services on Yom Kippur and caring for the synagogue premises. Soon after his employment, he was asked to whitewash the walls of the synagogue and ordered not to permit ladies to nurse their infants in the "yard of the shule," but to usher them to an inside room. To discourage nursing mothers from congregating in the "yard of the shule" the board ordered the sale of the "benches laying about in the yard."[14]

Oppenheimer, too, would resign from the congregation, together with his son, Simon, to affiliate with the new group, which he would continue to serve as sexton.

### The Classroom

Concern for education was one of the most important reasons for joining a congregation. Public schools had not yet been established in the District of Columbia; its children were educated either in church schools or by private tutors. Apprenticeship was the usual method of vocational training.

For Jewish parents, schooling was important not simply to give their children a means of earning a livelihood but to impart sufficient Jewish knowledge to enable them to participate in religious services. Children were expected to learn three languages: English, for obvious reasons, Hebrew, for use in the synagogue, and German, which remained the language spoken at home.

The congregation was not able to establish a school until 1861, and, just as the Washington Hebrew Congregation was the first synagogue in the District, it was also the District's first Jewish religious school. As a parochial or all-day school, its curriculum included secular as well as religious studies, with instruction in English, German, and of course, Hebrew.

The school was named the Washington Hebrew Elementary School. Classes met daily from 9:00 a.m. to 4:00 p.m. The morning session was devoted to the study of Hebrew and German, the afternoon, to the teaching of "English and kindred subjects."[15] Members paid tuition of $1 a month per child; nonmembers paid

$1.50. An instructor was paid $83.33 per month. The school operated at a deficit.

Dr. Henry Hocheimer of Baltimore was engaged to administer examinations to the students every three months, reflecting the continuing dependance on Baltimore. The school committee's report in 1867 revealed that seventy-five children were enrolled, two teachers were employed, and nonmembers were expected to pay an extra fee. Confirmation, introduced in 1869, was restricted to children enrolled in the school. The school was supervised by a five-member school committee. Rules and Regulations drawn up in 1867 required teachers to teach six hours per day and to render quarterly reports on the progress of the school and the "general behavior of the scholars."

The school met on the premises of the synagogue, moving with it to each new rental until permanent quarters were acquired on 8th Street. The first instructor, charged with teaching Hebrew and German, was Rev. S. Weil, who served from 1860 through 1867. He was succeeded by Rev. Jacob S. Jacobson of Liverpool, England, who was driven to resign after only a few months, more for reasons of ideology than for the given reason of "health." English subjects were then assigned to Dr. Herman Baar, engaged in 1869, who was well qualified in English, having served previously as a teacher in England.

Public schools were established in Washington in 1862, the year slavery was abolished in the District. New school buildings were constructed, and "colored" children, were admitted into public education for the first time. One new school was named for the District's progressive mayor, Richard Wallach. Another, dedicated in 1869, the year of Adas Israel's founding, was called the Benjamin Franklin School.*

*The Benjamin Franklin School's building at 13th and K Street, N.W., was saved from the wrecker's ball by public outcry. Named a historic landmark, its exterior was restored with a grant from the Sigal/Zuckerman Company, and the structure was rededicated on May 5, 1992.

The congregation continued to operate its own school in the face of the competition of free education because it offered the advantage of instruction in German as well as Hebrew, subjects that remained important to the traditionally oriented recent German immigrants.

With each passing year, however, the lure of the American environment, the importance of learning English, and the obvious economic advantage of free education attracted more and more children to the public schools. Attesting to the inroads of the public school was the establishment of a supplementary Sunday religious school in 1868 under the initiative of Rev. Jacobson. The one-day-per-week school was intended to serve children who attended public school rather than the congregation's all-day school.

The *Occident* reported that the new Sunday school registered 140 children on its opening day and was expected to reach an enrollment of 200, compared to 75 in the all-day school. Jacob S. Jacobson was superintendent, with a staff of sixteen teachers, among them Sarah Kreslowski, Jacob Gotthelf, and Jacob Peyser.[16]

The immigrants soon realized that the public school system offered a more effective vehicle for becoming part of the American environment. By 1870, following the group secession from the congregation, the Washington Hebrew Elementary School closed its doors, to be replaced by a religious school meeting two afternoons per week, after public school hours, as well as on Sundays.

Adas Israel, soon after its formation, established its own religious school.[17]

### These Are The Names

For many years, the members of the Washington Hebrew Congregation referred to it merely as die Synagogue or die Shule, the German-Yiddish word for "synagogue." So long as it was the only congregation in the District, it required no further identification. Sensing the need for a formal designation to go with the dedication of their first building in 1863, the members selected "Shaarey Zedek Congregation." Although this name was never dropped, it was never commonly used. Newspaper articles, announcements, and the general public persisted in referring to the congregation as the "8th Street synagogue." Its name, "The Washington Hebrew Congregation" came about by inference and common acceptance before its official adoption which followed its decision to purchase a building.

In 1844 Congress, which had sole jurisdiction over the District of Columbia, passed the Religious Corporation Act, which enabled "congregations organized for religious worship" to acquire real estate. The congregation's leaders reasoned that the law applied to churches but not necessarily to synagogues. Given their German background and their Old World experience with government attitudes toward Jews, their conclusion was not unreasonable.

Seeking assurance that it would be legal for a synagogue to own property, they prepared a "Memorial" for submission to the 34th Congress on February 5, 1856, "praying" for an act of incorporation, since "the existing laws of this District contain no provisions as they were advised under which they can be constituted a congregation."*

In vain did the chairman of the Senate's District Committee, Senator Brown of Mississippi, point out that there was no need for the bill, since the Religious Corporation Act did not proscribe Jewish congregations from owning property even though synagogues were not specifically mentioned. Nonetheless, if "passage of the requested bill would make for the happiness of certain citizens of the District," he said, he would be pleased to recommend it.

*The petition names Leopold Oppenheimer as treasurer. Oppenheimer later became a leader of the group that founded Adas Israel and was a signatory of its articles of incorporation.

Ratified by the Senate on April 11, 1856, and by the House of Representatives on May 28, the bill was signed into law by President Franklin Pierce, who affixed his signature on June 2. It defined for all time not only the legal right of a synagogue to own property, but, by implication and perhaps inadvertently, the name of the congregation.

The new law carried the heading, "An Act for the benefit of the Hebrew Congregation in the City of Washington," and affirmed "that all the rights, privileges and immunities heretofore granted by law to the Christian churches in the City of Washington be, and the same hereby are extended to the Hebrew Congregation of said City."

"Hebrew Congregation" was a generic term for a Jewish congregation, just as in a previous instance the first Jewish congregation in Savannah, Georgia, was referred to by President George Washington as Savannah's Hebrew Congregation, though its official name was and remains Congregation Mickve Israel.

The generic heading of the bill, "An act for the Hebrew Congregation in Washington," soon overshadowed and displaced the congregation's original name, Shaarey Zedek. Nor did a later suggested name, Beth Elohim, ever achieve popular accceptance. The congregation would remain, for all time, The Washington Hebrew Congregation. When the group that seceded to form the District's second congregation they would adopt the name, Adas Israel Hebrew Congregation.

For much of the modern era, Jew and Christian alike favored the word "Hebrew" rather than "Jew" or "Jewish," which, more than likely, would be used today in corporate titles. Thus, George Washington, in addressing his letters to the Jewish congregations in Savannah and in Newport addressed the recipients as "Hebrews" whom the "wonder working Diety" had delivered from their Egyptian oppressors. Military "dog-tags" are still inscribed with an H rather than a J.*

Rabbi Isaac Meyer Wise, the leader of Reform Judaism, called the association of synagogues which he founded in 1873, "The Union of American Hebrew Congregations," and its college, "The Hebrew Union College." Still avoiding the term Jew, Wise called his journal, *The American Israelite* and its German edition, *Deborah*. For his journal, Leeser had chosen the *The Occident*.

The reason for avoiding the word Jew bears analysis. In Germany, the word Jude or Jew had become a word of approbrium. Influenced by the prevailing prejudice, German Reform Judaism asserted that Jews were either Israelites or Germans of the Mosaic persuasion. Jews in France during the period of the French Enlightenment expressed the same preference.

With the negative image of the term Jude still fresh in their minds, it is little wonder that the first generation of Jews in Washington, all of whom came from Germany, would select the names "The Washington Hebrew Congregation," and "The Adas Israel Hebrew Congregation."

Leeser's dedicatory address clearly recognized the low status of the word "Jew" when he stated, "The name of Jew has become unjustly a term of reproach."

Jews were determined to reclaim the dignity of their name. In Germany, as far back as 1832, Gabriel Riesser, an early champion of Jewish rights, deliberately chose the name *Der Jude* for his periodical, despite its negative connotation, as if to affirm proudly the name of Jew in the face of its detractors. For the same reason, for his widely distributed publication, Martin Buber, in 1916, adopted the same

*The Hebrew Union Veterans Organization, founded in 1896, changed its name to the Jewish War Veterans only in 1923.

name as that of Riessser's periodical. Buber, as other leading Jewish thinkers, was determined to reclaim the dignity of the Jewish name.

In the United States, an early effort to challenge the defamation of the Jewish name was mounted by Adolphus Solomons, an early supporter of Adas Israel, who wrote to the publishers of the popular Webster's Unabridged Dictionary and to the publishers of the less known Worcester's Dictionary, in 1872 ,objecting to the entry: "Jew, v.a. To cheat or defraud; to swindle, (Colloq.) [18]

G. and C. Merriam, publishers of Webster's, responded that "while they would be willing to undo any implied injustice, the objectional word was treated no worse than 'Jesuitical', to indicate artfulness and cunning, but that no offense was intended to the class, sect, race, or nation, from which the word was derived."

Brewer and Tileston, publishers of Worcester's, disclaimed responsibility, saying that their dictionary reflected usage and did not create it, and that the purpose of the dictionary was to give the "meaning of every word in the English language."

The publishers of Webster's argued, "as such a word has an existence, is it not better to stigmatize than to ignore it?" but ultimately agreed to delete the objectionable definition. Worcester's publishers persisted in its inclusion because, they wrote, they would find it "inconvenient to obliterate the line of type," and "it is necessary to keep the space occupied . . . they were not responsible that such a word exists and has a use." Ultimately, both dictionaries would make "amends" by labling the offensive definition "vulgar."

Later generations refused to accept the negative evaluation of the Jewish name. Sabato Morais, in 1886, selected the name Jewish Theological Seminary for the school which he established. The Nazi effort to degrade the name by inscribing the single word "Jude" on the yellow badge which every Jew under their control was forced to wear, turned the name into a badge of courage.

Today, the word "Jew" or "Jewish" has supplanted the use of both "Hebrew" or "Israelite."*

*William Safire, writing in the New York Times in 1991, noted that the University of Missouri Multi-cultural Management Program held that "some people find use of Jew alone offensive and prefer Jewish person.

# 3

## THE CIVIL WAR YEARS, 1861–1865

In the Dred Scott decision of 1857, a southern-dominated Supreme Court ruled that Negroes were not included in the "all men" whom the Declaration of Independence had proclaimed were "created equal," and, therefore, that a black person did not possess a citizen's right to sue in federal courts nor did a slave acquire freedom by being brought temporarily to a state that forbade slavery. It was a decision that the frail and sickly eighty-year-old Chief Justice Roger B. Taney had long wanted to write in defense of his southern culture.

It was also a decision that accentuated the bitter division between the southern slave-holding and the northern anti-slavery states. The twin issues of slavery and secession had been tearing the country apart long before the outbreak of the Civil War. The right of a state to secede from the Union was an issue as divisive as slavery in the presidential election of 1860. In view of his known position on the two issues, Lincoln's election in the November ballot as the sixteenth president of the United States fueled the determination of the secessionists to separate themselves from the federal government in Washington.

Not every southern leader favored withdrawing from the Union; some tried to stem the intense drive for secession which had been building up for years, hoping to achieve a workable compromise that would protect the interests of both North and South. Among the southerners favoring compromise was Judah P. Benjamin, the Jewish senator from Louisiana, who wrote to a friend, "The prudent and conservative men South [were not] able to stem the wild torrent of passion which is carrying everything before it. . . . It is a revolution . . . of the most intense character . . . and it can no more be checked by human effort, for the time, than a prairie fire by a gardener's watering pot."[1]

The Washington congregation faithfully observed the nationwide day of fasting and prayer which President James Buchanan had called for January 4, 1861 in an effort to mobilize national sentiment in the face of the threat of secession.[2] Neither prayer nor compromise, however, could undo the event that ultimately triggered secession: Abraham Lincoln's election by a solid bloc of northern states.

"No human power can save the Union, all the cotton states will go," said Jefferson Davis, U.S. senator from Mississippi and Franklin Pierce's Secretary of War. Judah P. Benjamin now agreed that "a settlement [is] totally out of our power to accomplish."[3] Less than a month before Lincoln's inauguration on March 4, 1860, seven southern states seceded to form the Confederate States of America; eventually there would be thirteen.

In the early morning of April 12, in an encounter having more symbolic than military significance, Confederate forces fired on Fort Sumter, situated on a manmade granite island at the bay entrance to Charleston, South Carolina. Two days later, on April 14, 1861, the American flag came down and the Confederate stars and bars rose over Sumter.

President Lincoln mobilized the Union Army on the following day. Thus began the tragedy of a divided nation struggling to define itself. The war would last far longer and be far bloodier than anyone on either side had expected at the outset. Its cost in American lives was as great as that of all of the nation's other wars combined, including the conflict in Vietnam.*

The Confederate states selected Montgomery, Alabama, as their temporary capital, moving to Richmond in July. The Confederacy named Jefferson Davis its President. Davis promptly invited Judah P. Benjamin to serve as his Attorney-General.

### Judah Philip Benjamin

Judah Benjamin attended services in Washington when the congregation worshipped at Harmony Hall in 1859. At a service celebrating the acquisition of a new Torah scroll he was given the honor of holding the scroll.[4]

Called by some "the brains of the Confederacy," Benjamin was born into a Sephardi family on the West Indian island of St. Croix in 1811. His family subsequently moved to Charleston, South Carolina, where his father, Philip, was one of the founders of Congregation Beth Elohim in 1824, the first Reform synagogue in the United States.

At fourteen, Benjamin entered Yale, but for still unknown reasons, he did not complete his degree. According to the *Universal Jewish Encyclopedia*, he had been assisted in entering Yale by Isaac Leeser and a Mr. Cardozo of Charleston.[5] After leaving Yale, he moved to New Orleans, where he was admitted to the bar and later married Nathalie St. Martin, of French parentage and a Catholic. It was not a tranquil marriage. Soon after the birth of their only child, Mrs. Benjamin moved permanently to Paris, where Benjamin visited her from time to time.

In 1852, when he was forty-one, Louisiana elected Benjamin to the United States Senate. Earlier the president had nominated him

*The Union dead numbered around 360,000, Confederate more than 260,000, for a grand total of more than 620,000 dead.

to the Supreme Court, but Benjamin had declined the appointment in favor of a political career.

Benjamin served the Confederacy as Attorney General until he was appointed Secretary of War to replace an ineffectual incumbent. Still later, President Davis named Benjamin to serve as his Secretary of State. The close relationship between the two Confederate leaders led to the unjustified identification of American Jews with secession and slavery.

Benjamin's Jewish identity made him a frequent target of anti-Semitic attacks; he presented a pretext for both sides to defame Jews as a group. His northern opponents referred to him as Davis's "Jewish puppeteer" and as "an Israelite with Egyptian principles." His southern opponents held him responsible for the problems of the Confederacy: shortage of supplies, military defeats, and diplomatic failures. To the credit of Jefferson Davis, he refused to sacrifice Benjamin's considerable talents to the taunting of southern critics.

After the war, fearing for his life, Benjamin fled to England, where he established a profitable law practice. He died in Paris on May 6, 1884, at the age of seventy-three, and was buried in a Catholic cemetery with last rites administered by a French priest. Since Benjamin left behind few private papers, having deliberately or accidentally burned his private files, he remains a mysterious and enigmatic figure in our history.

His biographer, Eli N. Evans, leaves no doubt about his assertion of Jewish identity,[6] nor did his obituary, which appeared in the *London Times*: "His main quality superior even to the superiority of his intellect and capacity for labour was an elastic resistance to evil fortune which to a lesser or greater extent exists in every Jew and which has enabled the Jewish people to resist exile and plundering, adversity and depression."[7]

**War and Slavery**

The 150,000 Jews in the United States were to be found on both sides of the tragic struggle. They divided with the nation, with approximately 7,000 serving in the Union army and 3,000 in the Confederate.

Most rabbis were sympathetic to the Union cause. David Einhorn of Baltimore and Sabato Morais of Philadelphia were among the most outspoken supporters of the Union. Einhorn, a leading Reform rabbi, was forced to flee Baltimore following threats on his life by Confederate sympathizers.

Sabato Morais, a descendant of Portuguese Marranos on his father's side and of German Ashkenazim on his mother's, who would later be the founding president of the Jewish Theological Seminary, was born in Livorno, Italy, on April 13, 1823. He moved to London in 1846 to become the Hebrew master of the orphanage of the Sephardic Bevis Marks Congregation, and five years later, in 1851, he migrated to the United States to succeed Isaac Leeser as the hazzan of Mikveh Israel, Philadelphia's Sephardic congregation.

In his sermons, Morais condemned slavery and secession. From his youth in Italy, Morais understood the evils of living under a despotic regime. He refused to be silenced even after several congregants asked him to limit his remarks to "religious subjects."

Throughout his career, Morais remained an outspoken critic of social evils. With the same vigour with which he had earlier opposed slavery, he championed the cause of striking garment workers against their employers, some of whom were members of his congregation. In the face of opposition, he demanded communal support for the newly arrived Russian Jewish immigrants and the Jewish farm communities in New Jersey. His social concerns were not limited to Jewish issues. He was an outspoken critic of laws restricting Chinese immigration.

In theology, Morais upheld an "enlightened Orthodoxy." During his forty-six-year tenure at Mikveh Israel, he influenced the thinking of many leaders of the emerging Conservative Movement, especially Cyrus Adler, who later became president of the Jewish Theological Seminary and who was for a brief time a member of Adas Israel.

After the war, in recognition of his vigorous support of the Union, he was invited to join the exclusive Union League Club of Philadelphia as an honorary member, probably the first Jew to be inducted.

Unlike Morais, Isaac Leeser, having served in Richmond, Virginia, where he retained many friendships, so sympathized with the people on both sides of the conflict that he could not bring himself to condemn either. He hoped that the war would be brief and urged Jews both South and North to "turn to the God of their fathers for support."[8]

Rabbi Isaac Mayer Wise, the leading spokesman for the emerging Reform movement, felt that the North had no right to compel the South to remain in the Union. To Wise, peace was more important than the preservation of the Union. A committed Democrat, he was not an admirer of Lincoln, whom he frequently criticized in print and sermon.

Rabbi George Jacobs of Richmond, who would succeed Leeser in Philadelphia in 1869 and would deliver the sermon at the dedication of the first Adas Israel synagogue, was himself a slaveowner. A female slave stayed with him even after her emancipation and continued to serve the family in Philadelphia throughout her life.*

*There were other outspoken rabbis on both sides of the conflict. We name only those who had a relationship with Washington's congregations.

### Impact on Washington

The 1860 census revealed fifty-six Jewish names in the roster of employed persons in the District of Columbia, most of them of German descent. With the outbreak of the Civil War, the Jewish population increased considerably along with the general population. Washington's prewar population of 75,000 mushroomed as military personnel, people seeking government employment, and thousands of escaped slaves eager to start new lives poured into the city. Contractors, merchants, purveyors of food, and other entrepreneurs rushed to the District to take advantage of the business opportunities created by the war. Journalists from other cities took up residence to report from Washington.

A correspondent writing in the *Jewish Messenger* in 1862 reported:

> The number of Israelites quartered in Washington and its vicinity (exclusive of those in the Army) cannot fall short of two thousand. As evidence of their presence, there are at least a half dozen kosher restaurants, all of which appear to flourish to the satisfaction of their proprietors. At one of them in particular, about dinner hour, there were forty guests seated at the same time, and, on their departure, an equal number ready to take their places. Many are the commercial establishments conducted under names familiar to a New Yorker. All departments of trade seem to be favored with a full representation from the metropolitan district.[9]

The war created new problems for the District's Jewish community. It often had to care for the impoverished families of Jewish volunteers who had come to Washington from other parts of the country, bringing their families with them.

A private in the Union Army received $13 per month in wages, when he was paid, usually several months in arrears. The Jews of Washington had neither the resources nor the facilities to cope with the needs of the local enlistees, much less with those of the many indigent Jewish newcomers. Neither did they possess the personnel or the funds to serve the large number of wounded Jewish soldiers convalescing in Washington's military hospitals.

A spokesman for the Jews of Washington wrote an open letter to the *Jewish Messenger* asking the New York community for assistance.

> .... The men, like true soldiers, say they willingly undergo every and any deprivation, but they feel it hard, indeed, as only our people can feel, to see those they love, and who have a right to look to them for their support, suffer for the necessaries of life.[10]

Richard Wallach, the mayor of Washington, also appealed to the Jews of New York for assistance.

> We have no fund to support the families of poor soldiers, and the unhappy consequence is, the wives and the children of these poor men are in abject want....

Few responses were received, but throughout the bitter years of the war, the congregation's women helped to care for the wounded and raised funds for the relief and assistance of Jewish soldiers and their families. As a means of fund-raising they sponsored bazaars called "Sanitary Fairs."* In 1864, the congregation raised $756.95 toward the communal goal. Only the fair sponsored by the Treasury Department exceeded this amount.

Captain Gunnel Levy appealed for aid for stricken Jewish soldiers. In a strongly worded statement he urged upon his readers

*Named for the U.S. Sanitary Commission, which administered wartime relief efforts. The term "sanitary" in this context was adopted from the name of the British Sanitary Commission organized to do away with the filth and primitive sanitation that had killed so many soldiers during the Crimean War.

"the necessity of providing for the wants of Jewish soldiers in the hospitals in and around the Capital."[11]

In addition, the congregation faithfully undertook the task of providing burial sites and rites for every Jewish soldier who died in a Washington hospital. A correspondent paid tribute to the members for this act of piety:

> The congregation deserves the acknowledgements of American Israelites for the care and attention they have paid to Jewish soldiers, ill and dying, in the department of Washington. They have looked after the interment of many co-religionists who had no other claim upon them than that of brotherhood.[12]

According to an analysis of war records by the late Robert Shosteck, curator of the B'nai B'rith Museum in Washington, thirty-three Washington Jewish men enlisted in the Union Army, an impressive number compared to the small size of the Jewish community, most of them recent immigrants.

Attendance at synagogue services was augmented during the Civil War by the participation of soldiers, but it was not enough, according to Simon Wolf, who wrote:

> The attendance in synagogue during Passover has been very large. There were but a few soldiers present, owing, I presume, to the difficulty of obtaining passes. The very excellent choir has undergone an orthodox change in the substitution of boys for sopranos, in place of young ladies—a commendable alteration.[13]

Implicit in Simon Wolf's report is a reflection of the differences of opinion on synagogue ritual that would eventually split the congregation, though they remained submerged for the duration of the war. The use of female voices in a choir is clearly forbidden by

Orthodox practice. Wolf approved of the replacement of women singers by men; others disagreed.

With the war's end, in 1865, many of the entrepreneurs and professionals who had been attracted to the District remained in residence, Jews among them. Soldiers demobilized in Washington took jobs with the government and became part of the civil service. The congregation's membership fluctuated with the rise and fall of the Jewish population, ending with a net increase. In his carefully researched study of the census, Robert Shosteck concluded that

> a considerable number of Jewish businessmen, individuals with varied experience and backgrounds, were attracted to Washington after the outbreak of the Civil War. For the most part, this was a highly transient population as reflected in congregational membership rosters and changes in listings and advertisements in city directories during the war years.[14]

### Washington's Jewish Leaders

The Civil War and its attendant tensions projected two Washington Jewish leaders to national prominence: Simon Wolf and Adolphus S. Solomons. Both were called upon to defend Jews who had fallen victim to the upsurge of anti-Semitic prejudice that accompanied the war. They diverged in their religious commitments.

Simon Wolf (1836–1923) became the president of the Washington Hebrew Congregation in 1872 and a leader in the Reform movement nationally. Adolphus Solomons (1826–1910) was a founding supporter and member of the Adas Israel Congregation and a president of the Jewish Theological Seminary Association.

Simon Wolf was born in Bavaria. He migrated to the United States in 1848 and to Washington in 1862, where he practiced law.

In his long and distinguished career, he became United States consul to Egypt in 1881 and national president of the B'nai B'rith in 1904. Because he lived in Washington and was on friendly terms with many high-ranking officials, including, as he stated, every President from Lincoln through Wilson, Wolf saw himself as American Jewry's representative to the government.[15]

During the war, Wolf supported a proposal to build a Jewish military hospital in the capital.

> I am led to these remarks from having had an excellent opportunity to observe the manner the sick are treated in the Hospitals and Infirmary in this place, all of which fall far short of what they should be. . . . A hospital for our people is what we want here.[16]

Nothing came of his advocacy for the project.

Wolf's influence proved especially effective when he succeeded in extracting a retraction from Major General Benjamin F. Butler for the outrageously anti-Semitic statements he made during his brutal occupation of New Orleans. Butler, popularly known as the "beast," made Jews his particular target.

Another ruthless official, Colonel LaFayette C. Baker, chief of the Detective Bureau of the War Department, once arrested Wolf because of his membership in the B'nai B'rith, which in Baker's opinion was "a disloyal organization which has its ramifications in the South . . . [and] is helping the traitors." Wolf had committed the "crime" of acting as attorney for a number of southern Jews arrested in Washington on the charge of spying for the Confederacy. It required the personal intervention of Secretary of War Stanton to secure Wolf's release.

In response to the charge that Jews had evaded service in the nation's wars, Wolf wrote and published a book entitled *The Ameri-*

*can Jew as Patriot, Soldier and Citizen,* "to enforce a recognition of the Jewish people as a militant factor in the upbuilding of the State," and to prove that the Jewish people "have been unfailing in their devotion to their country's cause."[17]

In later years, Wolf's success in winning a landmark immigration ruling affirming that persons dependent on private charities were not liable to deportation as public charges would save thousands of unfortunate Jewish immigrants from deportation. Though he vigorously attacked the anti-Semitic policies of tsarist Russia and Romania, Wolf was strident in his opposition to Zionism. He was among the first to raise the specter of dual allegiance, even questioning the patriotism of Supreme Court Justice Louis D. Brandeis for his statement that "loyalty to America demands that . . . each American Jew become a Zionist."*

Adolphus Solomons, too, was a friend of Presidents and took part in every inauguration ceremony from Lincoln's time to McKinley's. Solomons frequently interceded on behalf of Jews who had reason to see Lincoln. In one instance, he arranged for a New York rabbi, Morris J. Raphall, who felt that slavery had biblical justification, to meet with Lincoln in an effort to secure a promotion for his son. The appointment fell on one of the days that Lincoln had designated for public prayer and national fasting. Solomons recalled that the President said to Raphall, "As God's minister, is it not your first duty to be at home today to pray with your people for the success of our arms as is being done in every loyal church throughout the North, East and West?"

The rabbi responded, "My assistant is doing that duty," to which the President replied, "Ah, that is different." He then wrote

*A definitive biography of Simon Wolf by Esther Panitz, the wife of Rabbi David Panitz of Adas Israel, has recently been published. See her *Simon Wolf: Private Conscience and Public Image* (Cranberry, N.J.: Associated University Presses, 1987)

out a message to Secretary of War Stanton, "The Secretary of War will promote Second Lieutenant Raphall to a first Lieutenancy . . . [signed] A. Lincoln."

"Now, doctor," said the President, "you can go home and do your own praying."[18]

### General Ulysses S. Grant and the Jews

In the midst of the war, there were those who sought to profit from the needs of both sides. When Union forces extended their control over the Mississippi Valley in 1863, a large number of southern planters and merchants salvaged their fortunes by selling much-needed cotton and provisions to their northern occupiers. In a nightmare of profiteering, as one historian described it, gold and silver were smuggled through the lines in exchange for cotton, munitions, food, and medical supplies. "In few was self interest as unalloyed as in James L. Alcorn, Mississippi's future Republican governor, who, after a brief stint in the Southern army, retired to his plantation, smuggled contraband cotton into Northern hands, and invested the profits in land and Union currency."[19]

Brokers enriched themselves by serving as intermediaries; some were politicians in office, others were officers in uniform, and some were Jews. It was the Jewish broker who was singled out for criticism. "If a non-Jew was engaged in disloyal activities, it was only because he was made a tool of by his friends of the Hebrew faith." charged the *New York Tribune*. "Jews were buying up commissions and living in luxury in Washington," wrote the *Cincinnati Commercial* in 1862.

The charges were reiterated both in military barracks and in Congress. Unable to remain silent, the congregation directed a vigorous protest to Senator Henry Wilson of Massachusetts condemning his singling out of Jewish brokers for attack.[20]

The "trading with the enemy problem" derived from the Lincoln administration's premise that it would be mutually advantageous to allow a measured amount of trade to continue between North and South during the war years. This policy was based on two considerations: it was intended to keep the South from establishing trade ties with England and France, which were eager to purchase southern cotton, and it responded to a pressing domestic concern: the northern mills were starved for cotton.

Indeed, cotton was the great corrupter of the Civil War. "Every soldier dreams of adding a bale of cotton to his monthly pay," wrote Charles A. Dana, a former New York editor, in a letter to the Secretary of War. President Lincoln told a friend that "the army itself is diverted from fighting the rebels to speculating in cotton."[21] A Confederate paper charged that "native Southern merchants have outdone Yankees and Jews.... The whole South stinks with the lust of extortion."[22]

For the Confederacy, trade with the North was a necessity to prevent starvation for both civilians and troops. For North and South, trade offered opportunities for enormous gain. Speculators and traders, eager to profit from the needs of both sides, found willing partners in army officers who were also eager to enrich themselves.

The Union Army's commanders, compelled to tolerate a commercial policy with which they disagreed, insisted that the army could not pursue the war while at the same time trading with the enemy. Generals Grant and Sherman were determined to stop the cotton trade with the South. To allow it to continue unchecked, they felt, would serve to fuel the South's military capability and thus prolong the war.

In Grant's perception, Jewish traders were the most obvious if not the most numerous. To Grant's dismay, his own father had brought three Jewish merchants to Memphis to seek trading permits from which he too would profit. Some historians have suggested that Grant deliberately singled out the Jews as scapegoats to divert attention from the misdeeds of his family.

Even though Jews were not the only traders, they were the ones singled out for official condemnation. In November 1862, Grant's headquarters decreed that "no Jews are to be permitted to travel on the railroad southward. . . . they are such an intolerable nuisance that the department must be purged of them."[23]

Worse was to follow. On December 17, 1862, Grant telegraphed General Order No. 11, ordering the expulsion "within twenty-four hours" of "the Jews, as a class," without trial or hearing, from the Department of Tennessee. Any Jew returning after notification of the order was to be imprisoned.*

Supporting Grant's order, the *Washington Chronicle*, published by the Secretary of the Senate, John W. Forney, called the Jews "the scavengers . . . of commerce." The Jews of Washington, again outraged, responded with letters of protest.[24] The *New York Times* captured their sentiments in an editorial which concluded, "Men cannot be condemned and punished as a class, without gross violence to our free institutions."[25]

Widespread suffering in the Jewish community followed the order's enforcement. Forced departures from Tennessee took place in haste and confusion. One family almost left behind their infant child; two dying women were left in the care of neighbors. Others, denied rail transportation, were forced to flee on foot.

Jewish spokesmen and organizations protested to the authorities in Washington. The Missouri Lodge of the B'nai B'rith protested

* A dramatic treatment of this period will be found in William Safire's historical novel of the Civil War, *Freedom*, p. 1165 ff.

"in the name of hundreds who have been driven from their homes, of the thousands of our Brethren who have died for the Union, of religious liberty, of justice and humanity."[26] Three Jewish men from Paducah, Kentucky, sent Lincoln a telegram objecting to "this inhuman order . . . the grossest violation of the Constitution," which marks the Jews "as outlaws before the world."

When they received no response, one of them, Cesar Kaskel, traveled to Washington to intercede directly with the President. On arrival, he approached Adolphus Solomons, who speedily arranged an appointment.

Lincoln, listening intently to Kaskel's report of the cruel impact of General Order 11 on the Jews, could not refrain from injecting a biblical note, "And so the children of Israel were driven from the happy land of Canaan!"

Kaskel, taking his cue from the subtle humor in the President's words, quickly responded, "Yes, and that is why we have come unto Father Abraham's bosom, asking protection."

Said the President, "And this protection they shall have at once."

And so it was. On the same day that he received the protest from the Missouri Lodge of the B'nai B'rith, Lincoln responded in his own hand, writing on the back of the envelope the lodge had addressed to him, "I have today, Jan. 5, 1863, written Gen. Curtis about this. A.L."[27]

The order was revoked by presidential instructions to General-in-Chief H. W. Halleck. Three days later Grant's office transmitted the order of recall.

Seeking reassurance, Henry I. Hart, president of the Board of Delegates of American Israelites, wired Adolphus Solomons asking him to "please ascertain for certain whether General Grant's order concerning the Jews has been rescinded." Solomons responded to Hart, "Feeling happy to have it in my power to attest the promptitude of our Government in countermanding the ill-liberal and unlawful 'order of Genl. Grant.'"[28]

Following the order's withdrawal, a Washington Jewish delegation called on Lincoln to thank him for his intervention. He responded, "I do not like to hear a class or nationality condemned on account of a few sinners."

The infamous General Order No. 11 remains the most sweeping anti-Jewish regulation in all of American history; no single official act was more devastating to the status of American Jews than this harsh edict. While Jews were certainly involved in trade, most of the illicit trade between the two antagonists was being carried on by people who were not Jewish, and some traders who were said to be Jews were, in fact, Christians. People on both sides used the word "Jew" as a pejorative way of describing anyone they considered shrewd, acquisitive, and possibly dishonest. Frequently, the words "Jew" and "trader" were used interchangeably. Little wonder then, that both North and South assigned to the Jew major responsibility for the illicit operations.*

Evaluating the accusation that Jews were profiteers, James M. McPherson wrote in his Pulitzer Prize–winning study of the Civil War, *Battle Cry of Freedom,*

> As in other times and places, people suffering from causes beyond their comprehension fastened on an identifiable minority as scapegoats. There were Jewish merchants . . . and some of them speculated in consumer goods. So did a much larger number of . . . Gentiles. But most merchants–Jewish and Gentile—were as much victims as perpetrators of shortages and inflation.[29]

*Negative evaluations of this kind were so deeply ingrained that Henry Ford, many years later, would refer to moneylenders as "Jews" and was convinced, because of its financial expertise, that the banking firm of J. P. Morgan was Jewish.

Some authorities have suggested that the expulsion order may have been intended not so much to stop speculation in cotton as to remove Jewish competition. As proof, they note that while cotton trading was widespread, only the Jewish traders were marked for expulsion. The illicit cotton trade with the South continued, but without Jewish competition, the wholesale price dropped, allowing a greater profit for the remaining non-Jewish traders.

### The Death of President Lincoln

His position strengthened by several victorious battles, Abraham Lincoln won the election of 1864 over his Democratic opponent, the dismissed former General-in-Chief of the Union Army, George McClellan, and was inaugurated for his second term the following March. His inaugural address, which remains even today a moving and prayerful expression, concluded:

> With malice toward none, with charity for all, with firmness in the right as God gives us to see the right, let us strive on to finish the work we are in, to bind up the nation's wounds, to care for him who shall have borne the battle and for his widow and orphan, to do all which may achieve and cherish a just and lasting peace among ourselves and with all nations.

The war ended with Lee's surrender to General Grant on April 9, 1865. For both sides it had been a costly experience in lives and property. The North rejoiced, but not for long. Five days later, on Friday night, April 14, celebration gave way to bitterness and tears with the assassination of Lincoln by John Wilkes Booth at Ford's Theater. The President died in the early hours of Saturday morning, April 15, in the small back bedroom of Petersen's boarding house across the street from the theater, where he had been carried after the shooting. Petersen's House was near the building which the Congregation had once rented as its synagogue.

One of the nine physicians at the President's bedside was Dr. C. H. Liebermann, a prominent Jewish surgeon, born in Riga, Latvia (then part of Russia), in 1812, and at the time of Lincoln's death, president of the District of Columbia Medical Society. Liebermann is one of the forty-seven persons portrayed in the painting, "The Last Hours of Lincoln." A sample of hair from the area surrounding Lincoln's wound was removed by Liebermann and given to the Surgeon-General, who later conveyed it to the Army Medical Museum. In later years Liebermann was one of the founders of the medical department of Georgetown University and of the District's Children's Hospital. He died in 1886 and was buried in Rock Creek Cemetery.[30]

President Lincoln was shot on Friday night at about 10:15, it was the Sabbath of Passover and Good Friday. In Washington, as in synagogues throughout the country, the joyous mood of the Passover Sabbath was transformed to one of mourning.

In Philadelphia, Sabato Morais received the sorrowful news on Saturday morning. Reflecting his profound affection for Lincoln, Morais had previously sent the President a copy of his sermon memorializing the death of Lincoln's beloved son Willie, which the President had personally acknowledged. Though visibly distressed, Morais refused to inject a note of mourning into the Sabbath service, in keeping with long-standing Jewish tradition precluding public expressions of mourning on the Sabbath.

When the Sabbath ended, however, he publicly expressed his sorrow, mourning "Father Abraham" in an eulogy delivered to his congregation on April 19, 1865.[31] Later, he would take his children to visit Lincoln's grave.

Isaac Leeser, yielding to his congregation's request for words of comfort, set aside the restraints of the Sabbath, but felt that his words were so disconnected that he had to apologize for their apparent incoherence.[32] Leeser was invited to Washington to conduct memorial services at the Synagogue and later reflected editorially on his visit.

> The Editor was called on . . . to deliver an address on the 22nd of April with reference to the death of President Lincoln. Not deeming himself at liberty to refuse the request, he repaired thither . . . and spoke on Verse 3, of chapter 10, of Leviticus.* . . . The Synagogue was about two-thirds full, many Israelites in the city being too much absorbed in business to devote this one day to the service of God in the first place, and to do honor to the memory of the President. . . . Those present, however, proved by the close attention to the service that they felt the importance of the occasion.[33]

Challenged to justify reciting the traditional memorial prayer for Lincoln, a non-Jew, Leeser responded in his memorial sermon:

> It is, indeed, somewhat unusual to pray for one not of our faith, but by no means in opposition to its spirit, and therefore not inadmissible. We pray for the dead, because we believe that the souls of the departed as well as of the living are in the keeping of God. . . . The prayers, therefore, offered up this day for the deceased President are in accordance with the spirit of the faith which we have inherited as children of Israel, who recognize in all men those created like them in the image of God, and all entitled to His mercy, grace, and pardon, though they have not yet learned to worship and adore Him as we do who have been especially selected as the bearers of his law.[34]

His visit to Washington gave Leeser an opportunity to evaluate the state of religious observance in the capital's Jewish community. In the same issue he wrote:

*"Through them that are nigh unto Me I will be sanctified," referring to the deaths of Nadab and Abihu, the sons of Aaron, the high priest.

> As regards the Israelites of Washington, they are generally prosperous; but we deeply regret that the Sabbath rest is so generally neglected by far too many. They speak of reforming this wrong, and we hope that they may have the heart to keep their promises, and that others may soon join them in their good change.

The Jews of Washington were prominent among the mourners for the slain president. The "Order of Procession" for his funeral listed "The Hebrew Congregation," and the firm of Lansburgh & Bro. offered a gift of $500 to "any individual or organization who may be authorized to receive it" for the purpose of erecting a monument to the president's memory.

The *Evening Star*, describing Washington's mourning, called attention to the display in the window of the firm of Philp and Solomons:

> The right window contained a colored portrait of the President and his son Tad. This was the President's last portrait. Both windows were heavily draped with white and black cambric. The balcony was heavily draped and in white letters on black background appeared these words: "Treason Has Done His Worst."[35]

Solomons referred to this portrait of Lincoln in an article entitled "Reminiscences of Abraham Lincoln"[36] in which he described the President's sitting for his portrait.

~ *Adolphus S. Solomons* *Reflections*

As many statements have been made relating to the "last photograph" Mr. Lincoln sat for, I feel assured that the following disposes of the fact:

During the early sixties our bookselling and publishing firm of Philp & Solomons, located at 911 Pennsylvania Avenue in this city, had a large photograph branch in the upper part of the building, under the charge of Alexander Gardner, who was well known for his celebrated *Photographic Sketch Book of the War*, in two oblong folio volumes, in which Mr. Lincoln was a frequent and conspicuous figure in camp and battlefields.

One day, while in his office, I casually remarked that I would like very much for him to give us another sitting, as those we had been favored with were unsatisfactory to us, and would he permit us to try again, to which he willing assented.

Not long afterwards he sent word that he could "come on some Sunday," and a date was arranged, which was the second Sunday previous to the Friday night when the assassin [John] Wilkes Booth, in cold blood shot to death one of the most beloved men God ever created.

At the time named by appointment, he came, and at my first glance, I saw with regret, that he wore a troubled expression, which however, was not unusual at that eventful period of our country's fitful condition, and, throwing aside on a chair the gray, woolen shawl he was accustomed to wear, Mr. Gardner, after several squints at his general make-up, placed him in an artistic position, and began his work.*

After several snaps, during which the President, while making jocular remarks, had completely upset the operator's calculations, I followed Mr. Gardner into his darkroom and learned to my sorrow that he had not succeeded in getting even a fair expression of his mobile countenance, and therefore was much discouraged, which however, was but repetition of former occasions.

I courageously named the result of my investigation to Mr. Lincoln, whereupon he, noticing, perhaps, my disappointment, said to me: "Tell Mr. Gardner to come out in the open"—referring to the

*Mathew Brady, the famed Civil War photographer, observed that Lincoln had so much on his mind that he found it difficult to relax for a photographic sitting.

darkroom—"and you Solomons, tell me one of your funny stories, and we will see if I can't do better."

I complied as best I could, and the result was the likeness as reproduced in these memories.

### President Grant and the Jews

When Ulysses S. Grant sought the presidency in the election of 1868, running against Governor Horatio Seymour of New York, it was only inevitable that his infamous expulsion order would become an issue. Democratic spokesmen urged Jews to vote against the foremost violator of Jewish rights. Republicans, not about to sacrifice their war-hero candidate, insisted that Grant had not been responsible for the order.

Jews who were Republicans defended Grant against the charges of anti-Semitism and some even justified the order of banishment. Simon Wolf, writing in support of Grant, stated, "The order never harmed anyone . . . except those whom we as Jews despise and hold in contempt."[38] Washington's Jews must have smirked when Grant, once elected, appointed Simon Wolf recorder of deeds for the District of Columbia.*

As President, Grant was sensitive to the delicacy of his relationship to his Jewish constituency. He appointed several Jews to public office in addition to Simon Wolf. He sought to appoint Adolphus Solomons governor of the District of Columbia, but Solomons declined on the grounds that his careful observance of the Sabbath would be incompatible with the duties of the office.

In 1872, to register his disapproval of the harsh treatment of the Jews in Russia and Romania, Grant appointed Benjamin Franklin Peixotto, grand master of B'nai B'rith, as U.S. consul in Romania. Peixotto remained in close contact with Simon Wolf and Adolphus Solomons during his tension-filled tour of duty.

*Wolf named his son, born in 1869, Adolph Grant Wolf.

When Adas Israel sought to acquire a location on which to build its first synagogue, its leaders negotiated for a plot of land owned by Grant on 2nd Street between K and I. The site was rejected in favor of a larger one on 6th and G Streets. President Grant was present at the dedication of the first Adas Israel synagogue in 1876, at the invitation of Adolphus Solomons. Mrs. Solomon Metz, widow of the congregation's rabbi, later recalled hearing from a friend that Grant had once attended a wedding at the synagogue.

Historians will continue to differ in their evaluations of Grant's enigmatic presidential tenure. He remains part of the historical experience of the American Jewish community and of Adas Israel.

*~ Rosa Mordecai* *Reflections*

A few Jewish members of Congress and employees of the Government, with a sprinkling of lawyers made up the Jewish population of Washington during the Civil War, when business interests attracted merchants of various kinds to supply the needs of the army.[39]

# 4

## THE SCHISM

On their arrival in the United States, the German immigrants found a country liberal in its legal system, enlightened in its politics, and relatively tolerant of cultural diversity. To the Jewish immigrant, this was a totally new situation, baffling in its tantalizing alternatives between permissiveness and conformity, allowing hitherto unexperienced freedom for variations in religious expression and previously unthinkable opportunities for deviations in ritual practice.

The large-scale immigration from Germany, which had tripled the Jewish population in the United States from 50,000 in 1850 to 150,000 in 1860, ended with the Civil War. The nationalist fervor generated by the war intensified the demand for "Americanizing" reforms. The pull of the environment could not be denied for long.

It was inevitable that the newcomers would begin to search for the right mixture of accommodation to the new and faithfulness to the old. In their new congregation in Washington, the founding members had based their ritual practices on their recollections of the traditions they had brought with them from Germany, but many had also brought with them a sympathetic response to the Reform point of view, which had blossomed in Germany and had already taken hold in the United States.

Changes in synagogue ritual, particularly in decorum and the use of English in worship, were perceived to be the means of adaptation to the New World. The acceptance of innovation did not proceed smoothly; each deviation from familiar procedure elicited vigorous reaction in opposition.

Reflecting the tension between those committed to preserving their traditions and others favoring adapting them to the new country was the furor that followed the efforts of Captain Jonas Levy, the congregation's president, to secure exemptions from the District's Sunday-closing laws for Jewish merchants. In a letter to the mayor of Washington in 1859, Levy asked that Jews be permitted to keep their stores open on Sundays since they closed them on Saturdays in observance of the Sabbath. The request was soon withdrawn, but not before a letter protesting his efforts, signed by "many Israelites," had appeared in the *Washington Star*."[1] A goodly number of the Jewish merchants in the capital did not want to be singled out for special treatment.

The immigrant generation was uncertain about how much adjustment would be permitted and how much conformity would be required. They were unsure of their place in America. For example, delegates to the B'nai B'rith convention in 1868 debated an amendment to their constitution that would have permitted the affiliation of non-Jews. Simon Wolf, later the president of both the Washington Hebrew Congregation and the B'nai B'rith, stated that he favored the admission of non-Jews and that he himself was a member of a Christian association, an option that none of the members who would later be the founders of Adas Israel could possibly tolerate.

Within the congregation, a significant number of members favored retaining the familiar traditions. The schism that eventually resulted in the founding of Adas Israel was first discernible in 1859 during the tenure of Solomon Landsberg.[2] Rev. Landsberg had caused an uproar in the congregation by eliminating one of the psalms in order to shorten the morning service. In angry reaction, several of the more traditionally oriented members resigned and founded a new congregation. They elected Rev. S. Weil as their hazzan and even bought a plot of ground on 7th Street near the District line for a cemetery.

After several months of separation, the two groups yielded to the overriding need for unity; neither faction could afford a separate existence. The traditional element prevailed. Landsberg* resigned and returned to his former home in Baltimore. Weil was elected hazzan to serve the reunited congregation, where he remained until 1867.

During the term of Weil's successor, Rev. Jacob S. Jacobson, the breach emerged once again. Jacobson had sided with the traditional element in the congregation in opposition to reforming either the service or the school curriculum, and thereby had incurred the wrath of Rabbi Isaac Mayer Wise, the pioneer advocate of Reform.

The *Evening Star* reported in 1869 that "an eloquent discourse" delivered by Jacobson at a congregational confirmation service upheld Orthodoxy and "denounced those who are attempting to establish Reform in this Country, and particularly those who are engaged in this work in the City." An enraged Isaac Wise quickly responded with a caustic editorial in his journal, the *Israelite,* noting that Jacobson had "also censored those who violate the Sabbath, transacting business and who violate God's laws for the sake of gain." Wise suggested that it would be best for Jacobson to seek a position in another city, "as he will not be able to breathe Washington atmosphere very long if he exerts his lungs so much in denouncing Reform."[3]

*Landsberg was the father of Gustav, Max, and James, who in 1860 founded Landsburgh & Bros., which began as a dry goods store on 7th and H Streets, and eventually became a major department store. His descendants included Minnie Goldsmith, her son Ralph, Mrs. Eugenia Schwartz, Mrs. Molly Brylawski, Arthur T. Lyon, and Mark Landsburgh.

Soon thereafter, displeased with Jacobson, the congregation invited Dr. Herman Baar, formerly of the Old Hebrew Congregation in Liverpool, England, to become its hazzan. Wise, endorsing the appointment, praised Baar for his "familiarity with both English and German." Furthermore, he wrote,

> The Doctor has considerable literary fame, having delivered a number of scholarly orations and lectures.... Those on the poetry of Schiller and Shakespeare attracted considerable attention. It is high time that the chief city of the nation should have a suitable person to instruct the Jewish people and elevate them to a proper standard. We extend to him the hand of welcome, and offer to the Hebrew congregation of Washington, our congratulations on their choice.

Wise's approval of Baar served to confirm the judgment of those who felt the congregation was heading toward Reform. Baar remained in the congregation only for a brief period and was succeeded or possibly joined in 1869 by Rev. Isaac Stempel, in a relationship that is not entirely clear. While Stempel was designated the congregation's hazzan, Baar was referred to as its minister. This, however, was not in itself a sign of Reform; Adas Israel, too, later referred to its hazzan / rabbi as minister, a reflection of the ecclesiastical influence of the surrounding environment.

### The Separation

Disputes over religious ritual were submerged while the congregation concentrated on refurbishing its new synagogue, the former church on 8th Street. Its completion intensified the urge to institute reforms in ritual to match the reform in the physical structure.

In an attempt to work out a compromise between the traditionalists and the reformers, the congregation adopted new rules of procedure. To placate the traditionalists, the new rules endorsed the continued use of the traditional Roedelheim prayer book, and to appease the reformers, the agreement called for eliminating "unnecessary Selichot," permitting the reading of the *Mi Sheberach* in German rather than Hebrew, and reciting the blessing for the government in English. The texts of these prayers were to follow *Minhag America*, the new prayer book edited by Isaac Mayer Wise. The agreement also called for the participation of a choir.

The new rules did not meet with universal approval. Discussion of further compromise was aborted when the board, in 1869, accepted the gift of an organ from a group consisting of Henry Adler, L. Baar, Isaac Herzberg, Philip Wallach, and Henry S. Blount. The traditionalists were outraged.

In the words of Abram Simon, who became the rabbi of the Washington Hebrew Congregation in 1904,

> Reform was in the air and the congregation felt its bracing and stimulating effect. Changes such as the abolition of "*Kiddush*" in the synagogue, the Chazan's facing the Holy of Holies, the wearing of the funeral praying shroud, and the calling up of Levi, Cohen, and Israelites were accepted without a wrench of soul; the motion to sing hymns in English, to recite aloud the "*Shemoneh Esre*" was readily concurred in but the gift of a melodeon . . . though accepted by the Board, stirred in the congregation a whirlwind of excitement and opposition. To many, the leap seemed too sudden and too great.[4]

While the traditionalists had been prepared to accept certain changes in ritual, they realized that it was no longer possible to hold the congregation to the founding principles adopted in 1852, which they had regarded as immutable standards; once the board accepted the organ, there was no room for further compromise.

Differences in outlook had become apparent within the Washington congregation long before the acceptance of the organ, though neither of the two rabbis who wrote of that period were able to pinpoint the beginnings, much less the point of no return.[5] We can, however, deduce the key issues from letters and from the changes in ritual instituted by the board of the Washington Hebrew Congregation immediately following the separation.

Though Rabbi Simon wrote that board meetings were frequently stormy, the minute books reveal no indication of heated controversy. The separation, as polite as it was inevitable, was achieved without recrimination. "The secession was a blessing in disguise," according to Simon.[6]

The board received letters of resignation from about thirty-eight members of the congregation dated December 31, 1869. The resigning members had dated their resignations to coincide with the end of the congregation's fiscal year as they had paid their dues to its concluding day. The letters in the files of the Washington Hebrew Congregation, simple one-sentence declarations, give no reason for the resignations.

One member did not wait for the end of the fiscal period to resign. As early as May 2, 1869, Charles Freirich, a salesman, residing at 438 4th Street S.W., addressed a letter to the president and members of the Washington Hebrew Congregation, which read, with understated starkness, "Hereby I resign as a member of your congregation."

Among the resigning members, Levi Cohen and Leopold Oppenheimer had been founding members of the Washington Hebrew Congregation. Some had been officers: Jacob Peyser had been the vice-president, Louis Rosenberg, the treasurer, Morris Cohen, the secretary, and J. Jacobson,* the recording secretary. In addition, two of the congregation's functionaries, Simon Mundheim, the *shochet-hazzan*, and Manassas Oppenheimer, the sexton, assumed similar roles in the new congregation.

*Jacobson did not tender his resignation until May 1, 1870.

Authorities differ on the precise number of resignations. Bernard I. Nordlinger states that "more than thirty-five members resigned, including some of the founders, and even the Shamus and Schocath."[7] A letter written by the first president of Adas Israel, Bendiza Behrend, in 1870, gives the number as twenty-five.

The discrepancy may be explained by the fact that some members did not bother to submit resignations; they simply dropped out. Others, probably doubtful that a new congregation could be successfully established, did not immediately affiliate with the new group. Eventually, many of those who had hesitated at the outset later joined the new congregation along with a number of hitherto unaffiliated Jewish residents of the District. The Washington city directory for 1869–70 provides a basis for fixing the number of resignations and affiliations at thirty-eight.

The seceding group withdrew from the original congregation without laying claim to its name or property. According to the brief history of the formation of Adas Israel by the staff of the Jewish Historical Society of Washington, the secessionists, having shared a common investment and a common history, had as much right to the name and property of the Washington Hebrew Congregation as did those who remained.

From the available evidence, however, this question never became an issue. The dissident members simply tendered their resignations to embark on the difficult and uncertain path of founding a new congregation and building a new synagogue at a time when the total Jewish population of Washington, a few hundred at most, was barely enough to maintain even one, let alone two congregations.

### Wise and Leeser

The original congregation served as the testing ground for the opinions of two rabbinic giants, Isaac Mayer Wise and Isaac Leeser, who according to some historians were the two greatest leaders in American-Jewish history.[8] Though neither Leeser nor Wise wanted to see the Washington congregation, or any other synagogue, divided, and both favored communal unity, they struggled with each other to win the congregation's soul. The battle was fought with articles and editorials in their respective journals, and with occasional lectures given in the Washington synagogue.

Through their agreements as well as their differences, as expressed in their lectures, their writings, and the institutions they founded, Wise and Leeser both contributed to the growth and strength of American Judaism. Together they helped to create an indigenous and self-sufficient American Judaism that eventually was able to maintain itself without depending on European institutions. Their lives intersected for over a decade and although they worked together in an effort to unify American Jewry, they diverged in temperament and theology.

### Rabbi Isaac Mayer Wise

Isaac Mayer Wise (1819–1900) was born in Steingrub, Bohemia, and later lived in Prague and Vienna. He studied at various yeshivot and emigrated to New York in 1846. He introduced several reforming innovations in his first U.S. congregation in Albany, New York, but it was in Cincinnati, as rabbi of Congregation B'nai Jeshurun, that he achieved his most notable influence.

Within a few months after his arrival in America, Wise launched his weekly paper, the *American Israelite* and later a German supplement entitled *Deborah.* After moving to Cincinnati in 1854, he organized the Union of American Hebrew Congregations, the Hebrew Union College, and, later, the Central Conference of American Rabbis, all major institutions which have come to be identified with Reform Judaism, though Wise originally had intended them to serve all American Jewry without denominational identification.

Wise was not a radical reformer. Indeed, he was suspicious of extreme Reform because he was aware of what had happened in Germany, where radical Reform had led to large-scale conversion and the weakening of Jewish identity. He favored gradual reforms and a cautious accommodation to the majority culture.

Wise's moderation was reflected in his prayer book, *Minhag America*, which, in its early edition, was largely in Hebrew. Wise had intended *Minhag America* to be the official prayer book of all American synagogues. Despite its Hebrew content, the ideas it expressed and the customs it advocated were too radical for Leeser.

~ *Rabbi David Philipson* *Reflections*

He [Wise] is a man of great, of vast learning, of mighty energy but of a very envious and jealous disposition. He cannot endure that anyone shall stand near him, independent in thought and in action; he must rule; the name the Jewish Pope has been well applied to him. ... When in the time the true verdict will have been passed upon Dr. W. it will read in this wise: a man who did much for Judaism but who made everything subserve his own ambition; he would use every means to crush his opponents.[9]

~ *Rebekah Kohut* *Reflections*

Rabbi Wise seemed to have a genius for creating enmity.[10]

**Rabbi Isaac Leeser**

Isaac Leeser (1806–1868), who had delivered the sermon at the dedication of the Washington Hebrew Congregation's first synagogue, was the recognized leader of traditional Judaism in the United States. Born in Westphalia, he had come to this country in

1824, settling first in Richmond and then in Philadelphia, where the Sephardic Congregation Mikveh Israel invited him to be its hazzan. Leeser later resigned after a quarrel with the board and was succeeded by Sabato Morais, who would also succeed him as the leader of traditional Judaism.

Long before Solomon Schechter, the future head of the Seminary, used the term "Catholic Israel," Leeser spoke of *Kneset Yisrael*, the Community of Israel, which in his view embraced both Reform and traditional congregations, Ashkenazim and Sephardim alike. For Leeser, there were no Jewish religious denominations; only Jews.

> These hateful words—Reform and Orthodoxy—are always at hand when anything is to be done.... We know only Judaism: and if you call it orthodox you do so, not we.[11]

Leeser was deeply committed to a unified and a uniform Judaism. While he agreed with Wise on the importance of decorum in worship, he did not agree that changes in ritual could be introduced without halachic justification.

While German was the chosen language for sermons in the early American Ashkenazic synagogues, including the Washington congregation, Leeser pressed for the use of English in sermons and for instruction. He was the first American rabbi to deliver a weekly sermon in English, for he felt that

> This country is essentially English in its tastes, habits and predilections, and it appears to us absolutely requisite that Jews conform as nearly as possible, consistent with religion, to the manners of the people among whom they live.[12]

Because he had introduced the practice of preaching in English, Leeser was considered a reformer by the more Orthodox rabbis of his time, but others, both traditionalists and reformers, soon followed his example, and before long virtually all congregations were demanding rabbis who could deliver their weekly sermons in English.

Leeser was a pioneer in many areas. His journal, the *Occident,* which he founded in 1843, was the first successful Jewish periodical to be published in America and a rich source of historical material. Single handedly, in order to provide American Jews with a volume of the Bible free of Christological interpolations, he translated the Hebrew Bible into English. He wrote and published educational texts for children and adults. In 1845, he organized the first Jewish Publication Society to make Jewish books available at low cost to the Jewish reader. Recognizing the need for an academy of Jewish learning to train rabbis and religious teachers, he founded Maimonides College in Philadelphia in 1867. Though short lived, it was the first institution of higher Jewish learning in America and was the forerunner of the Jewish Theological Seminary.

Leeser was one of the first to press for a Jewish hospital in Philadelphia opposing those who, instead, favored a Jewish ward or a kosher kitchen for Jewish patients in a general hospital. He and Rebecca Gratz worked together to establish the first Jewish Sunday School in 1838 and the Jewish Foster Home of Philadelphia in 1855.

Even the Jews of far-away China were among his concerns. He urged the Jewish community to send a mission to China and other parts of Asia and Africa to "Judaize" the isolated Jews who still resided there and who were the targets of missionizing Christian groups. He was also among the first to advocate a fund to "protect the poor of Palestine, and to snatch them from the necessity of receiving aid from the missionaries."[13] Even before Herzl, Leeser embraced the conviction that the return of the Jews to a homeland in Palestine was a worthy goal, thus pointing in the direction which would lead the Conservative Movement to make Zionism an integral part of its platform.

The Presbyterian Church, in 1864, at one of its conventions, advocated that Congress proclaim Christianity the official religion of the United States, a prevailing belief in much of the country. Some states maintained that only Christians were permitted to hold public office. Sunday blue laws, and other discriminatory measures were persistant remnants of Colonial days. Leeser faught vigorously in the press and in public forum to remove these disabilities from the law books and from public practice, just as he had earlier joined Captain Jonas P. Levy to oppose the ratification of the discriminatory treaty with Switzerland.

Leeser, together with Sabato Morais and Marcus Jastrow, two other leaders of pre-Conservative Judaism, jointly protested the Thanksgiving Day proclamation of the Governor of Pennsylvania, John W. Geary, who called for giving thanks to God "with Christian humility" and prayed "that our paths through life may be directed by the example and instructions of the Redeemer, who died that we might enjoy all the blessings which temporarily flow therefrom, and eternal life in the world to come." Eventually his protests bore fruit.

Leeser's congregation did not appreciate his involvments on the national scene which, they said, occupied too much of his energies and time. He was in frequent dispute with his Trustees until he was dismissed in 1850 to be replaced by Sabato Morais. Leeser's later years were clouded by poverty, though his friends formed a new congregation, Beth El Emeth, which he led until his death in 1868.

Leeser had tried to achieve a unified position with Wise. At one point, Wise had written to Leeser that he regarded him as "my best friend in this world of flattery and falsehood, since you never hesitate to tell me truly, what you think about."[14] Despite the kind evaluation, the gap between them could not be bridged.

At Leeser's death, Wise, in an editorial eulogy, affirmed that he and Leeser had never been "so estranged that we were not on speaking terms." He praised Leeser, "There is no man in America who will replace him in the Orthodox Camp." Reverting to a previously expressed throught, Wise continued, "He spoke good English but with poor logic. He did not make public opinion but was guided by it."[15] While Wise regretted his loss, he concluded that he could not agree with him.

After Leeser's death, the *Occident* ceased publication and Miamonides College was soon forced to close its doors for lack of leadership and support; the experience was not lost on his colleagues. In tribute to him, Washington's Elijah Lodge of the B'nai B'rith organized the Isaac Leeser Literary Association in February, 1889. Fourteen young men were listed as affiliates; William Prebram was its treasurer.

Leeser and Wise became not only the symbols of the two competing trends in American Judaism in the mid-nineteenth century but their respective leaders as well. In Washington, Leeser must be regarded as the spiritual father of Adas Israel even though he passed away one year before its founding. In the original congregation, those who favored reforming the services followed the guidance of Wise, and those who favored retaining the traditional practices followed Leeser. Despite efforts to bridge their differences, the two groups could not live together under one roof.

Leeser left a persisting influence on American Judaism and established the philosophical ground on which the Conservative Movement in Judaism would later be established.

### External Influences

Adding to the pressures for change was the example of Charleston, South Carolina, where the first Reform congregation had been established in 1824, and the more immediate examples of Reform congregations in New York, Philadelphia, and especially Baltimore.

It was in Charleston that Reform Judaism had first taken root in the United States. Forty-seven members of the Orthodox Congregation Beth Elohim had petitioned the board in 1824 to introduce certain changes in the ritual of worship. Rebuffed, they had withdrawn to organize their own congregation, which they had called the Reformed Society of Israelites. Publishing their own prayer book, they had worshipped with uncovered heads and to the accompaniment of organ music, procedures hitherto unheard of in Jewish practice in America.

Eight years later the seceding group returned to the mother congregation and eventually influenced its philosophy. It was now the traditionalists' turn to secede. Beth Elohim then endorsed the previously rejected reforms to become the first Reform congregation in the United States.*

Closer to Washington, both in proximity and influence, was the first congregation in the United States to be founded as Reform from its very beginning, Temple Har Sinai in Baltimore, established in 1842. When David Einhorn, the most extreme of the early Reform rabbis, assumed its pulpit in 1855, Baltimore became the spearhead of radical Reform Judaism on the eastern seaboard. Because of the close relationship between Baltimore and Washington, it was inevitable that the example of a successful Reform congregation would have considerable influence on the Washington congregation.

### The Aftermath

The partnership that had existed since 1852 was dissolved by amicable separation on the last day of 1869. An exchange of letters between Bendiza Behrend, the first president of the new congrega-

*When the renovated Washington Hebrew Congregation was dedicated in 1898, it considered adopting the name Temple Beth Elohim after the first Reform congregation in Charleston.

tion, and Adolphus Solomons, a prominent Washington resident, establishes that the new congregation had begun to function even before the effective date of the group resignations.

Upon learning of the formation of the new congregation, Isaac Mayer Wise hurled his sarcastic wrath at the secessionists:

> Washington, D. C.—Things are not as bad after all as some people are disposed to presume. Washington bears the name and fame of the "wickedest" place under the moon. But it is all wind and gas. It is not half as bad as the suppositions run. There are, we see, many pious men in that city besides the congressmen from New York. Some of our co-religionists contribute to save the reputation of Washington for piety and godliness, and to this end have formed a new orthodox congregation, consisting of about thirty members from the main congregation, and have already provided a burial place, consisting of six acres of ground. They will meet every Sabbath for divine service, (provided ten male persons shall be present.) "During which day they keep their places of business open," says the Evening Star. Are those men mad? Why do they lend their hands to the destructive and irreligious business of dividing the small number of Washington Israelites into two camps? What good do they expect of the proceedings? What is the thing they call orthodox? Is it a piece of prayer-book or a kind of song over which they quarrel and split? Let's hear of it. If it is an honest enterprise, state your reasons before the broad day-light.[16]

No longer inhibited by the presence of a traditionalist element in their midst, the board of the Washington Hebrew Congregation lost little time before instituting the changes in ritual practice which many had long desired but which they had deferred in the vain hope of achieving a unifying compromise.

In place of the traditional Roedelheim prayer book, the congregation adopted the more liberal prayer book edited by Marcus Jastrow and Benjamin Szold. Later, after Wise addressed the congregation, his prayer book, *Minhag America*, was adopted to replace the Jastrow-Szold volume.

Other delayed reforms were also quickly implemented. In rapid succession, the congregation abolished the wedding canopy (*huppah*, spelled *Hooper* in the minutes), ordered prayers to be recited in English, eliminated the recitation of the Kiddush at worship, and rescinded the imposition of fines for nonattendance at daily services. Soon thereafter the board eliminated the recognition of Kohen and Levi in the order of the call to the Torah. The abolition of the daily services was considered.

For several years after the division, the congregation continued to respect the traditional requirement that worshipers cover their heads at preayers. The first congregation to make this decisive break with the Jewish tradition of worshipping with covered head was Temple Emanuel in New York in 1864; Isaac Mayer Wise's congregation in Cincinnati followed suit in 1874. By 1880, worshipping without head covering became an accepted practice in Reform Judaism. The Washington Hebrew Congregation authorized removing the head covering at worship in 1891.[17]

In many respects, the separation was unique. At other times and places, divisions within congregations were acrimonious, sparked by disagreements over ritual or liturgy and acerbated by ethnic loyalties and personal differences. Most of the early congregational schisms in the United States were the result of the unhappiness of German-Ashkenazic newcomers with the rituals and cultural patterns in synagogues founded and dominated by Spanish-Portuguese Sephardim whose earlier arrival had given them the opportunity to achieve higher social and economic status.

In some places there were even conflicting ethnic rivalries among the Ashkenazim. As an early traveler, I. J. Benjamin II, described the situation in New York,

> The Germans . . . could not endure the English; the Poles could not endure the Germans; so there was soon division and separation in all directions.[18]

Washington, however, was an exception to the usual pattern. There was no Sephardic group in the District, nor was there an English or Polish Jewish community. Both the secessionists and the remaining members were of German origin, with most of them coming from the same Bavarian province. While economic and social-class considerations, the surge for upward mobility, and the desire for Americanization led many German Jewish immigrants to the Reform movement, the birth of Adas Israel shows that some German Jews remained traditional, resisting the pace of acculturation adopted by Reform Judaism.

Unlike many congregational schisms, the separation in Washington was a friendly divorce. The original congregation lent a Torah scroll to the seceding group for the dedication of its first synagogue, and the new congregation was represented at the rededication of the enlarged and now separate Washington Hebrew Congregation. Rabbis from both congregations attended each other's installation services and collaborated in the defense of Jewish rights when necessary.

The differences that caused the separation were based primarily on divergent religious outlooks and differing perceptions of what was required for adaptation to the New World. Ethnic tensions played no role in Washington's Jewish community until the arrival of the East European Jews in the 1880s.

After the break, the two congregations maintained a cooperative relationship. When, however, the Washington Hebrew Congregation joined Isaac Meyer Wise's Union of American Hebrew Congregation in 1873, the year of its founding, the break with Adas Israel was sealed. In retrospect, it was fortunate that Adas Israel came into being when it did, for a few years later, with the beginning of the great influx of Russian Jews, new immigrants settling in Washington found a traditional synagogue awaiting them; a Reform congregation would not have met their needs.

# 5

## THE ADAS ISRAEL HEBREW CONGREGATION

To select a name for their new congregation, the leaders turned to the passage in the Bible relating God's command to Moses and Aaron to instruct *all* of the children of Israel on the observance of Passover: "Speak unto the entire assembly [*adas*] of Israel."*

Having severed their ties with the original congregation, the small organizing group faced the daunting challenge of keeping their new creation alive. Three members, without whom Adas Israel probably would not have survived, played pivotal roles: Bendiza J. Behrend, the first president, Nathan Gotthelf, his successor, and Adolphus Simeon Solomons, the distinguished communal leader.

Three others accepted major responsibilities: Levi (or Lewis) Abraham, a trustee, was a successful pawnbroker; Morris Cohen, the indefatigable secretary, was a clerk in the Post Office; and Simon Goldstein, the prime mover in the building campaign, was a jeweler-pawnbroker. The three trustees who signed the application to incorporate in August 1870 were Levi Abraham, Nathan Gotthelf, and Leopold Oppenheimer.

### The Behrend Family

Bendiza J. Behrend, whose Hebrew name was Binyamin, and who was alternatively called Benedict and Benjamin, was the first

**Adas* is the Ashkenazic pronunciation; the Separdic is *adath* or *adat*. In the new Jewish Publication Society version (Philadelphia 1962), "Speak unto the whole assembly of Israel and say that on the tenth of this month each of them shall take a lamb to a family, a lamb to a household" Exodus 12:3.

president of Adas Israel. He would have been a remarkable person in any generation; in Adas Israel, he was indispensable. Not everyone in the Behrend family followed Bendiza in affiliating with the new congregation. Others are included in this study because their family history offers interesting insights into the early period of Jewish migration and adjustment to the New World. Behrend's family included prolific writers; some kept diaries.

If history is biography, the history of Adas Israel begins in Rodenberg, Hess, Germany, with the birth of a certain Jacob Behr, born in the early 1600s. Jacob Behr (name of wife unknown) begot Bar Behr in 1670 (strictly speaking, "*Bar*" was not a name; it means "the son of"). Bar Behr married Chaya of Hildesheim, and together they begot four daughters and two sons, one of whom, another Jacob Behr, named after his grandfather, married Henneh, daughter of Abraham of Neinberg. They begot seven children, Elsie, Abraham, David, Abram, Itzig, Feibish, and Bar, great-grandchildren of the original Jacob Behr.*

From two members of the latter generation, Itzig and David, we can trace the origins of two founders of Adas Israel, Bendiza Behrend and Nathan Gotthelf. Itzig Behr married Rivka, daughter of Israel of Greppen-brugge. They had eleven children, all of whom adopted the surname Behrend in about 1800, and one of whom, the eldest, Bernard, became the father of Bendiza, the first president of Adas Israel. Bendiza J. Behrend was born in Rodenberg in 1827.

David Behr, Itzig's brother, adopted the family name of Gotthelf. He and his wife brought forth three children, one of whom was Bernhard Gotthelf, the forebear of Nathan Gotthelf, who succeeded his cousin, Bendiza Behrend, to become the second president of Adas Israel.

*See family tree on p. 98.

Itzig Behr-Behrend, born in 1763, wrote in his family history that he took his son Bernhard, born in 1793, to his brother Abraham in Hanover for schooling and education.[1] Abraham was a man of influence, for he and others in his family served as "court Jews," financiers and managers in the feudal court of Hanover.[2] While living with his prosperous uncle Abraham, Bernhard met and later married Eliza Heine, the daughter of Samuel Heine of Hanover. Samuel Heine was the brother of Salomon Heine, who became a banker and philanthropist and one of the wealthiest men in all of Europe, and Samson Heine, the father of Heinrich Heine, the famed German Jewish poet.

Bernhard Behrend returned to Rodenberg to join his father in business in 1815, after having received an honorable discharge and a medal for heroic service to the king during the war for German independence. His marriage to Eliza Heine, in 1825, produced fourteen children, born between the years 1827 and 1844. The family migrated to the United States in 1849 after the failure of Germany's liberal revolution. Bernhard was acutely aware of the political and social problems of his day, and was especially sensitive to the plight of European Jewry. In his concern, he envisioned a remarkable plan for a Jewish homeland which, he felt, would offer a refuge for Jews in distress.

Behrend wrote to Baron Anschel Mayer Rothschild in Frankfurt in 1832, urging him to purchase land in North America as a refuge for "our unfortunate co-religionists" from Germany, Poland, and Italy to enable them to "pursue their religion in freedom and peacefully engage in productive labor." Rothschild rejected Behrend's proposal.

Behrend traveled to Frankfurt in 1845 to meet with Rothschild. Quoting Jewish sources, he argued that unless Rothschild agreed to devote his entire fortune to the cause of Jewish "liberation from slavery," even to giving up his business if necessary, he would not be entitled to share in *olam ha-ba* (the world-to-come), and, furthermore, his wealth would not protect him against the Gentile world's anti-Semitism. Rothschild responded, according to Behrend's notes, that the project was one of *Schtuss* ("foolishness"); "it was God's will that the Jew suffer in *Galuth* [exile], and . . . with God's will, liberation will come in due time."

Behrend also wrote to Dr. Gabriel Riesser in Germany to urge him to form a corporation that would facilitate Jewish settlement in North America. Behrend suggested that the corporation invite his wealthy uncle, Salomon Heine, to become one of its directors.

Riesser's reply, in 1844, acknowledged that Behrend's proposal would help many German Jews, but expressed the fear that since so many of them had already left for America, it had little prospect of success. Indeed, Riesser felt, it might even be harmful to Jewish interests to promote mass colonization.

Whether Behrend was influenced by Mordecai Manuel Noah, who in 1825 had proposed the establishment of a Jewish homeland on Grand Island on the Niagara River near Buffalo, New York, cannot be ascertained.

Behrend's proposal is documented in Zionist archives and in European Jewish publications. In 1935 Henrietta Szold, the founder of Hadassah, wrote from Jerusalem to Behrend's granddaughter in Washington, Mrs. Rebecca Behrend David:

> On my portfolio lies a letter dated May 2nd, 1934 from your Aunt Mathilde. It was written in connection with her sending me a brochure written by her father on Zionism, two generations before Herzl.

Letters in the files of the Jewish Historical Society of Greater Washington reveal a close friendship between the Szold and Behrend families.

In 1832, Behrend's appeal to establish a settlement for Jews in North America fell on deaf ears. Only a few years later, the mass exodus of German Jews to the United States began, and of these migrants, a small segment established the Washington Hebrew Congregation in 1852 and the Adas Israel Congregation in 1869.

As *Der Jude*, a German Zionist periodical, observed in 1923 in an editorial appraisal of the life of Bernhard Behrend, "It was not the time to call and it was not the time to be heard. Bernhard Behrend was well ahead of his time."*

Migrating to the United States in 1849, Bernhard Behrend and his family settled in New York's Sullivan County, where he bought a farm which he scarcely knew how to operate. Unable to support his family on the farm's meager earnings, he was forced to open a small confectionary store. One by one, his children moved from the farm, going first to Baltimore and then to Washington.

Behrend expressed his continuing concern for the future of Judaism in articles submitted to Leeser's *Occident*. In his writings, he voiced his opposition to changes in synagogue ritual. He was particularly opposed to instrumental music in the synagogue and to worship without head covering.

In 1862 Behrend addressed an open letter to Abraham Lincoln, objecting to the lack of concern for the rights of Jewish soldiers as reflected in the order to reduce Sunday duty out of "deference to the best sentiments of a Christian people, and a due regard for the Divine."

Bernhard Behrend passed away on November 15, 1865. He and his wife were buried in the cemetery of the Washington Hebrew Congregation.

*Leo Pinsker's Zionist classic, "Auto-Emancipation" was published in 1882, and Theodore Herzl's "Judenstaat" in 1886. The Zionist Congress took place in 1897. Behrend's proposal in 1832 came earlier.

Bendiza Behrend, Bernhard's eldest son, had preceded his parents to the United States by a few years to join his cousin Nathan Gotthelf in a partnership operating a fancy goods store in Washington. Bendiza married Emma Pribram, a daughter of Solomon Pribram, the first president of the yet undivided Washington Hebrew Congregation.

The congregation's drift toward Reform troubled Bendiza. Uncompromising in his determination to preserve an institution of traditional Judaism in Washington in the face of the Reform challenge, he mobilized like-minded fellow members and led them to establish Adas Israel. Over the next three years, as the new congregation's first president, he guided the disputatious group through the difficult initial period.

Bendiza Behrend died in Washington on June 1, 1884, at the age of fifty-seven and was buried alongside his parents, brothers, and near relatives in the family plot in the Washington Hebrew Congregation's cemetery.

~ *Louis Lipsky* *Reflections*

In December 1832, Bernhard Behrend, a merchant of Rodenberg, in Hess, Germany, worked out a project for the purchase of land somewhere in North America, in order to establish a Jewish Colony there. He submitted plans to Baron Rothschild, the famed banker and philanthropist, and also to Gabriel Riesser (1806–1863), the German political leader who proposed civic equality for Jews.[3]

**The Other Behrends**

Amnon Behrend, one of Bendiza's brothers, born in Rodenberg in 1834, settled in Washington about 1856. He married his first cousin, Sarah Behrend. He and his brother, Elon, were partners in another fancy goods business called Behrend Brothers, located at 443 7th Street N.W. Their advertisements, too, carried the notation "Closed on Saturdays." Amnon served as an officer of the Washington Hebrew Congregation and was one of the organizers of the Hebrew Friendly Inn and the Jewish Foster Home. He died May 9, 1916. Funeral services were conducted at the Hebrew Home for the Aged.[4]

Adajah Behrend, another brother, also born in Rodenberg, was brought to the United States by his father in 1849. In Washington, he became a pharmacist and then a physician, receiving his degree in 1866 from Georgetown University, thus becoming its first Jewish graduate. He later became a member of the faculty of Georgetown Medical School. In later years he also republished and wrote an introduction to his father's book, *Jerusalem.*

Adajah, who married his cousin, Mathilde Behrend, died at the age of ninety-one. The *Washington Post*, eulogizing him on his death on December 28, 1932, wrote that "he had never sent a bill to the many poor families whom he had served as doctor, friend and counselor and that he was also known to bring baskets of food for needy families on whom he was making a professional call." Mrs. John Safer, an Adas Israel member, recalled seeing Dr. Behrend in his home wearing a skullcap as he studied Hebrew texts.

Bendiza's youngest sister, Mathilda (a favored name in the family), was born in 1842 and was seven when she was brought to the United States by her parents. She never married. Exceptionally close to her father and sharing his interests, she was actively involved in the Zionist movement and corresponded with Henrietta Szold, founder of Hadassah.

When Mathilda was ninety-two years old, her picture appeared in the *Washington Post*, showing her casting her vote for delegates to the World Zionist Congress. Rebecca Safer brought the ballot box to her at the Takoma Park Sanitarium, where she was a resident. Mathilde passed away one month after casting her ballot and was buried in the Behrend family plot alongside her mother, Eliza.* [5]

**Nathan Gotthelf**

Nathan Gotthelf, the second president of Adas Israel, was as fervently committed to traditional Judaism as was his cousin Bendiza. As an active member of the Washington Hebrew Congregation, he, too, was disturbed by the increasing drift toward Reform, which led him to join the group that resigned to form the new congregation.

Nathan succeeded Bendiza in the presidency of Adas Israel in 1873 and was called back to the post for a brief period following the resignation of his successor. He held office during a period of severe economic depression when the congregation was scarcely able to remain in operation. More frequently than any other member, he was called upon to act as cantor on Sabbaths, festivals, and the High Holidays; his proficiency obviated the need to employ a professional hazzan.

It was Nathan's determination that led the congregation to establish a school, install a mikveh, and acquire two Torah scrolls. He owned the Torah scroll used by Adas Israel in its early years but ultimately surrendered it to the congregation, which is still in possession of it today.

Nathan paid a visit to his hometown in Germany in 1869. It reinforced his conviction that there was no future for Jewish life in the United States because, in his opinion, it was difficult if not impossible to remain a religiously observant Jew or to rear children in a traditional Jewish atmosphere in America. In his nostalgia and

*Among the living descendants of the Behrend family are Mrs. Julius Goldstein and Mrs. Haskell Small.

idealization of the "old country," he determined to return permanently to the protective Jewish environment that he recalled from his childhood, but it was several years before he could carry out his intentions.

A testimonial presented to him by Adas Israel Congregation at a formal meeting on September 5, 1875, attested that "Nathan Gotthelf intends to remove from our midst at an early date to domicile himself and family at the country of his nativity." The resolution expressed the congregation's sorrow at his departure and offered "its heartfelt wishes for our worthy member's future prosperity in all his undertakings, and that he may continue to live a happy and long life, peaceably and contented, surrounded by all of his family." The resolution, signed by John Boyer, president, Jacob Peyser, vice-president, and Morris Cohen, secretary, lauded Gotthelf for his active leadership and his many contributions to the synagogue.

Nathan Gotthelf, together with his wife and two American-born children, Sarah and Rebecca, returned to Germany, where he resumed his residence in his native city, Hanover. The congregation's wishes for a "happy and long life" were not to be fulfilled. In March 1881, Nathan was struck by the hoofs of a horse which reared while he was hitching it to a carriage he had hired for a family outing. The blow was fatal. A memorial in German expressing Adas Israel's sorrow, dated March 9, 1881, was conveyed to Nathan's widow, Julie, in Scharanbeck, Germany.

Julie Gotthelf and her two daughters, Sarah and Rebecca, remained in Germany. Sarah married Adolph Wolff. Their four sons eventually obtained the precious visas that would allow them to find refuge in Washington, where each of them resumed their family's membership in Adas Israel. Rebecca, Sarah's sister, never married and became one of the six million victims of the Nazi horror.

**Adolphus Simeon Solomons**

Adolphus Solomons, one of the outstanding Jewish residents of Washington in the nineteenth century, was an early supporter and honorary member of Adas Israel and, later, the transition president of the Jewish Theological Seminary Association. Solomons was largely responsible for bringing the congregation and the seminary together.

The long list of institutions which Solomons helped to establish include Washington's first nurses' training school, a free lodging society, and the city's first unified communal charity. He was one of the founders of the American Red Cross and of Garfield Hospital, and an early director of the Columbia Hospital and Lying-in Asylum, now known as the Columbia Hospital for Women.[6]

Adolphus S. Solomons was born in New York City on October 26, 1826, and moved to Washington with his wife and children in 1859. His father, John Levy Solomons, an English-born Jew of Portuguese descent, came to the United States in 1810 to become a member of the editorial staff of two New York newspapers, the *Advocate* and the *Courier*. His mother, Julia Levy Solomons, was born into a pioneer New England Jewish family.

Solomons married Rachel Seixas Phillips, a descendant of a Philadelphia colonial family one of whose members, Captain Jonas Levy, had been the second president of the Washington Hebrew Congregation. She was the cousin of Judge Albert Cardozo of the New York State Supreme Court, who was the father of Justice Benjamin Nathan Cardozo of the U.S. Supreme Court.

In Washington, where he lived from 1859 to 1910, except for an interval in New York from 1891 to 1904, Solomons founded the firm of Philp and Solomons, booksellers, printers, publishers, and stationers. The firm was a major supplier of stationery and office supplies to the U.S. Congress. An annual report of the clerk of the House of

Representatives reveals payments of $33,000 to four stationers, with the Solomons firm receiving $26,102. One order of $50 was for a large framed photograph of the Speaker of the House. The items furnished to Congress included folders, diaries, quill pens, speech envelopes, some of them "extra heavy" to accommodate lengthy senatorial orations, and more expensive gold cases, gold-mounted agate seals, screw-propelling pencils, and sand boxes, probably for use as ashtrays.

The company published several books, including many for the federal government. An advertisement states that the partners were the publishers of all photographs produced by the Gardner Photographic Gallery and the Metropolitan Gallery, thus indicating that the firm competed with the Brady Gallery. Alexander Gardner had left the employ of Mathew Brady, the famed Civil War photographer, in a dispute in 1862, taking with him some of his photographic plates.[7] As indicated in an earlier chapter, the Solomons studio was the setting for Abraham Lincoln's last photograph, taken shortly before his assassination.

The firm manufactured and distributed a "highly improved manifold writer," a "great invention" which enabled one to duplicate letters "in one operation with more ease and greater facility than a single letter with an ordinary pen and ink." Ulysses S. Grant used one of these instruments when he wrote to Robert E. Lee setting forth the terms for the Confederate army's surrender. Solomons's firm also printed the tickets to Andrew Johnson's impeachment trial in Congress in 1868.[8]

Daniel Webster, the Secretary of State, appointed Solomons, who was then only twenty-three years of age, special diplomatic courier to Berlin. Solomons would ascribe his lifelong interest in health services to his visit to the Jewish community's hospital in Frankfurt-am-Main. Distressed that the United States lacked a similar institution, he led the effort to establish hospitals in New York and Washington. In New York he helped found Jews' Hospital, which later became the Mount Sinai Hospital.[9]

Solomons was appointed special agent for the census of 1890 to advise in the collection of "accurate statistics with regard to the vitality and longevity of the Jewish race in this country." During a brief period when Washington was self-governing, Solomons was elected a member of the House of Delegates, which legislated for the District of Columbia under an elected governor; he served as chairman of the Committee on Ways and Means.[10] As previously indicated, he had declined President Grant's offer to name him governor of the District because he had felt that his faithful observance of the Sabbath would conflict with the duties of the office.

As an appointee to the District of Columbia school board in 1886, he opposed Bible reading, prayers, and religious instruction in the public school curriculum. Moral and ethical instruction, he felt, should remain the responsibility of home, church, and synagogue, so that "the thin edge of the wedge of religious discussion and consequent dissension be not forced upon our inalienable right of conscience, and that the blight of 'Church and State' be forever widely separated in our God-given Republic." Solomons notwithstanding, the intrusion of religion in public education would remain a perennial issue for many years.

Upon the death of Samuel F. B. Morse, inventor of the telegraph and the Morse Code, Solomons was chosen chairman of the Committee on Arrangements for the memorial service held in the House of Representatives. He also served on the committee to arrange the funeral of Chief Justice Samuel Chase, who was buried in Oak Hill Cemetery in Washington in 1873. He served on the Presidential Inaugural Committee for the second inauguration of President

Grant in 1873 and was on familiar terms with all of the presidents from Abraham Lincoln to William Howard Taft. On his initiative, a bill was passed in Congress to restore the writing on the original Declaration of Independence, which had become indistinct.

Garfield Hospital, which later was incorporated into the Washington Hospital Center, owed its existence to Solomons. He advocated the establishment of the hospital as a memorial to the assassinated President James Garfield and chaired the effort to solicit funds for its establishment.

Washington's United Givers Campaign had its origin in the unified campaign of the Associated Charities, which was founded in the Solomons residence in 1881, according to a newspaper account.

> A few men and women who had observed the increasing tendencies of pauperism and who had been identified with the former attempts at reformatory measures met at the residence of A. S. Solomons on K Street in April 1881, and realizing the conditions and necessity of better methods of caring for the poor, and protecting the generous contributions of the citizens from being used to demoralize and pauperize, resolved to form an organization under the name of the Associated Charities of the District of Columbia.[11]

"Charity work in Washington was quite disorganized and rather haphazard" the report continued. There were no church-directed charities, and local government charity "seemed to lack intelligent direction."

Among other civic groups in which Solomons played a decisive role were the Society for the Prevention of Cruelty to Animals, Provident Hospital, and a Night Lodging House for homeless wayfarers, whom the press described as "a good class of people [unable] to obtain work—who walk hundreds of miles until they succeed."

Louis Marshall (1856–1929), the distinguished lawyer and communal leader, maintained that the American Red Cross had been founded in the Solomons residence. While this assertion cannot be verified, it remains true that Solomons was one of the original organizers of the society. He was among the fifty-one people who assembled at the home of Clara Barton at 1326 I Street in Washington to approve the constitution of the American National Red Cross. As the new organization's treasurer, he was one of the five signers of its articles of incorporation, dated July 1, 1881. Somewhat later he was elected vice-president of the Red Cross.

Early meetings of the Red Cross were held at the Solomons home with Barton presiding. Under her leadership and with Solomons's involvement, the Red Cross came to the assistance of flood victims in Johnstown, Pennsylvania, and in numerous localities along the Mississippi River.

Solomons undertook several government assignments overseas on behalf of the International Red Cross. President Chester Arthur appointed him and Clara Barton delegates to the International Red Cross Conference held in Geneva in September 1884. His relations with Barton eventually soured because he differed with her on matters of policy and especially in regard to her planned relief effort to feed the hungry in tsarist Russia in 1892. While the image of starving multitudes in the Russian Empire touched the hearts of many Americans, press reports revealed the miserable treatment of Russian convicts deported beyond the Urals for slave labor and the suffering inflicted upon Jews expelled from their homes in Moscow. A *New York Times* editorial cautioned that the Russian government was hoarding grain intended for the starving in order to meet the needs of its army.

Solomons objected to Clara Barton's food relief plan because he felt that "the Russian Red Cross is so in the hands of the officials that it is the same as sending their money to the Government."[12] The disagreement led to his dismissal by the Red Cross. When Barton herself was later removed from office in 1904 as the result of accusations of obstinacy and mismanagement, Solomons was no longer her defender.

Because of his differences with Barton, it was many years before the American Red Cross recognized the role Solomons had played in its formation; his name is omitted from its published history. It was not until April 1989, thanks to an effort initiated by an Adas Israel member, Dr. Gerald Sandler, director of its Blood Bank, that the Red Cross acknowledged Solomons's place in its history at public ceremonies held in its Washington headquarters. On that occasion it accepted a reproduction of a portrait of Solomons, painted by his daughter, Aline Esther, which now hangs on its headquarters walls.

Solomons's home was a cultural center in Washington, as is illustrated by the following letter, written by a visitor to the city in 1862:

> Mr. Adolphus Solomons (of Philp and Solomons) whose place of business in Pennsylvania Avenue is the resort of men of letters (for whose accommodations they have a costly "study" attached to their store) extended us the hospitalities of his house; and we passed a pleasant Sabbath with him and his good family. We were pleased to find Mr. S. doing so well in the capital, especially as he is one of the very few Israelites there who observe the Sabbath.[13]

Another source informs us that "Washington artists frequently exhibit their works in the gallery belonging to Philp and Solomons." Local newspapers referred to the "elegant mansion" or the "handsome residence" whose parlors became the setting for theatrical presentations, including dramas by Shakespeare. The Solomons' daughters frequently took part in the presentations, which were followed by refreshments and dancing.

It may be safely assumed that a mezuzah was affixed to the Solomons' doorpost.

> Our fellow-citizen and co-religionist, A. S. Solomons, Esq. had his new and elegant house on K Street consecrated. Mr. Mindheim, assisted by Rev. Mr. Jacobson, performed the religious ceremonies. . . . Simon Wolf, Esq. toasted the host and family, to which Mr. Solomons feelingly responded. Mr. Mindheim recited a beautiful allegory from the Talmud in honor of the occasion, and in every sense it was enjoyed as a rare treat.[14]

Among the many guests whom Solomons entertained in his home was Charles Dickens. A letter from Dickens to Solomons, dated February 6, 1868, reads in part,

> My dear Mr. Solomons: I was truly touched and affected yesterday evening by the receipt of your earnest letter and your handsome birthday present. I shall always attach a special value to both, and shall make a point of wearing the latter [cuff buttons] on the 7th of February [his birthday] as often as the day comes around to me. Accept my heartiest thanks, and believe, faithfully, your friend, Charles Dickens.

Dickens presented his host with a set of his complete writings inscribed, "Charles Dickens, done at Washington D.C., 6th of February, 1868."

Solomons was chairman of arrangements for the dedication of the new Adas Israel structure in 1876 and was responsible for the presence of President Grant at the dedicatory proceedings. The importance of his role in Adas Israel was recognized in a resolution stating that since this distinguished Sephardi citizen of Washington

> takes a lively interest in the welfare of the Congregation, it is but fair and proper that we show to him our appreciation for such acts; and in connection therewith offer the following: Resolved that he be informed, that proper steps have been taken by this Congregation to reserve sufficient seats at our congregation for himself and family should they desire to visit our Synagogue.[15]

Despite the welcoming resolution, according to the testimony of family members, Solomons did not enjoy worshipping at Adas Israel. He couldn't bear the hazzan's Germanic pronunciation of Hebrew: "*Tau*-rah" rather than "To-*rah*," "Shab*bes*" rather than "Sha-*bat*," grated on his ears.

With all of his involvement in civic and political life, Solomons never compromised his commitment to traditional Judaism. When he was about to move to Washington in 1859, his concern for the lack of a Sephardic synagogue led him to borrow a *ner tamid* (eternal light) from the Spanish and Portuguese Synagogue in New York. With the sacred fixture installed in his home, the family conducted its own Sabbath services. Sensitive to his Sephardic heritage, he could not bring himself to join the Ashkenazic though Orthodox Washington Hebrew Congregation.

Rachel and Adolphus Solomons, together with their eight daughters, Isabelle, Aline Esther, Zillah, Julia, Rosalie, Emma, Alma, Ida, and their one son, Henry, lived at 1205 K Street N. W. A church occupies the site today. While maintaining his residence in Washington, Solomons moved to New York from 1891 to 1904 to administer the Baron de Hirsch Fund, set up to encourage Jewish immigrants to settle as farmers in rural areas of the country and to assist them in their training and resettlement. He returned to Washington for occasional weekends to visit with his daughters and to renew old friendships. He was a widower for twenty-one years.

It was during his New York period that Solomons participated in the reorganization of the Jewish Theological Seminary. He became the president of the Jewish Theological Association in 1901 following the death of its first lay president, Joseph Blumenthal.

Solomons returned to Washington permanently in 1904 when he was seventy-eight years of age. He died at age eighty-four on March 18, 1910. The minutes of Adas Israel record the renewal of his membership[16] and, on his death, the congregation's condolences to his family.

In accordance with his wishes, Adolphus Solomons was buried in the Spanish-Portuguese Cemetery in New York. He was eulogized as one who had dedicated his life "to make our Country the fatherland of those who had been ruthlessly thrust from their birthland," and who "as a true American . . . died . . . leaving to his family and his fellow citizens the heritage of a life usefully spent in the faithful and efficient service of his fellow men."

With their father's death, the surviving daughters moved to a new home at 1604 K Street N.W. The original edifice was still standing in 1989. It was at this address that the last surviving daughter, Julia Solomons, lived out her life until she was moved to California by her niece, Irma Sellars. She died in 1948 at the age of eighty-five.

Cousins and friends in Washington recall that the Kiddush and blessing were always recited at Sabbath dinner in Julia's house. Julia still owned the prayer books willed to her and her sisters by their friend Rosa Mordecai, the first Jewish child to be born in the District of Columbia.

Julia's will conveyed the handsome oil portrait of her father, painted by her sister, Aline Esther, to the Jewish Theological Seminary, where it hangs today. It was a photograph of this portrait that was presented to the American Red Cross in 1989.

The *ner tamid* which Adolphus Solomons borrowed when he moved to Washington was returned to the Spanish and Portuguese Synagogue in New York and today hangs in the chapel adjoining the synagogue building at 70th Street and Central Park West.

A collection of memorabilia of Adolphus Solomons that had lain for decades in an attic trunk came to light in 1974 and was given to the B'nai B'rith's Klutznick Museum. The collection includes precious tableware and period photographs.

Of his family, Henry Solomons, the only son, died at an early age. Only two daughters married. Rosalie married Naphtali Phillips; they had no children. Ida married Daniel L. M. Peixotto and their only daughter, Irma, married Thomas C. Sellars; they had one child, Jean Lawrence. With the latter's death the Solomons line came to an end. Though his name is engraved on one of the outdoor arches at the Jewish Theological Seminary, he is hardly recalled by most of the institutions which benefited from his life.

As much as anyone else, and more than most, Adolphus Solomons was responsible for the founding of Adas Israel in 1869 and for linking its future with that of the Jewish Theological Seminary.

~ *Simon Wolf* *Reflections*

Solomons's home was a center of patriotic activity and he made heavy sacrifices of his personal interest in behalf of the Union cause.[17]

First page of the Behrend Family Tree, prepared by Edgar L. Stromberg, in 1942. The first two presidents of Adas Israel, Bendiza Behrend and Nathan Gotthelf are descendants of this family.

# 6

## IN THE BEGINNING

The newly formed Adas Israel Congregation conducted its Sabbath services in the homes of its members, depending upon those who were more skilled to chant the prayers and read the Torah. Its first and most compelling project was to find a cemetery. As was the case with most pioneer congregations, the need to assure a burial ground for members preceded the need for a permanent place of worship; death could not be denied. A six-acre tract of rural land was soon found on Hamilton Road, later called Alabama Avenue, in Anacostia, the eastern segment of the District of Columbia, which the congregation purchased for $1,000, paying $500 in cash and borrowing the balance.

To serve as a temporary synagogue, the members rented two rooms on 8th Street between Pennsylvania Avenue and D Street. With the approach of their first High Holy Days as an independent congregation, they rented quarters in the Concordia German Evangelical Church on 20th and G Street.[1] Like Washington's two Jewish congregations, the church had been founded by German immigrants. Established in 1833, it was located in Hamburg, the area of German settlement developed and named by Jacob Funk, an early German immigrant. Subsequently enlarged, and renamed the Concordia United Church of Christ, the building remains on its original site today. As a link to its origins, the church bulletin board lists *Die Vereinigte Kirche* as its secondary name.

The members of Adas Israel realized that the new congregation would not prosper in rented rooms. A building of their own, however, was beyond their reach; more members would be required before they could think of a permanent address. The small group could barely maintain their makeshift operation, let alone assume the expense of a building. Yet without more comfortable facilities it would be difficult to attract new members or even to retain the existing ones for long.

The congregation's president, Bendiza Behrend, decided to seek sustaining funds. He began by approaching Adolphus Solomons. Fortunately for our purposes, he was unable to arrange a meeting with Solomons and therefore had to write him. The exchange of correspondence reveals significant details about the congregation's founding and the state of its finances.*

> Adas Israel Hebrew Congregation
> Washington D. C.
> February 4, 1870
>
> A. S. Solomons Esq.
> Dear Sir:
>
> At an informal meeting of the Board of Trustees of the above Congregation, recently founded here on strict traditional Judaism, it was resolved to call on you and solicit your advice, aid and encouragement to our new undertaking, believing you to be in sympathy with the step taken by us, in separating our connections with the Washington Hebrew Congregation, worshipping on 8th Street, between H and I Streets.
>
> Having already failed to see you personally at your place of business, I take this mode to present this matter for your consideration and hope to hear from you at your earliest convenience.
>
> You are, no doubt, aware of the changes and innovations brought about in the old Synagogue, thus depriving us, as true Israelites, to worship our God in the form and manner prescribed, taught and inherited to us by our forefathers.

*Photostats of the original letters will be found in the files of the Albert Small Museum of the Jewish Historical Society of Greater Washington.

We organized about two months ago a new Congregation under the above name, and have temporarily rented two rooms, on 8th Street between Pa. Avenue and D Streets, and fitted same up for a Synagogue as well, as we could for the present. Our congregation now numbers about twenty-five members, mostly in moderate circumstances, but we soon would grow in numbers, as well, as in prosperity, if we only had the means to fix up a suitable place for a synagogue. Our present place of worship we can only keep temporarily, and it is too small at that. We have already bought about 6 acres of land for one thousand dollars, near the National Race Course, for a burial ground, and have already paid five hundred dollars cash on it, and have to remit the balance in two annual installments, with interest. You well know what other moving and incidental expenses are connected with conducting a new Congregation. Now, Sir. We have at present a very fair offer from a certain party, to get a property on lease for the term of six years for the monthly rent of twenty-five dollars, located in the central part of the city but it requires at least one thousand dollars to fix it up in a becoming style for a Synagogue.

Not having the means at our disposal and being small in numbers as yet, I would most respectfully and earnestly ask your views and advice either in writing, or in a personal interview at your earliest convenience.

I have furthermore to state, that in acquiring the land for a burial ground, we were very fortunate in getting a great bargain, as we have rented a part of it for the annual rent of hundred dollars, thus insuring our certain success in our undertaking with the help of God and a little encouragement and aid from generous and liberal hearted friends. Trusting that I have not transgressed upon your valuable time with these lines, and returning you with thanks the Constitution of your School. you were kind enough, to send me, believe, me, Sir.

Yours very truly,
B. J. Behrend

President Congreg. Addas Israel

Solomons responded sympathetically to Behrend's appeal for assistance.

Feb. 13, 1870

B. J. Behrend, Esq.
Pres. of Congr. Addas Israel
Washington, D. C.
Dear Sir:

I am receipt of your valued communication—without date [?] informing me that your Board of Trustees had informally requested you to solicit my "advice and encouragement to your new undertaking" in separating yourselves as members from the 8th St. Synagogue, which has drifted into so called "Reform" practices, and establishing a new Congregation based upon Orthodox principles. You are quite right in assuming that you have my full and hearty sympathy in this righteous movement in defense of the Religion and tradition of the House of Israel: for every Jew is the inheritor of this sacred trust, confirmed upon him by God Almighty Himself, and we have not, if we could, evade the responsibility.

Without attempting to discuss the pretended "Reform" [?] movement both here, and in cities of greater poetentium, I will simply remark that in my humble judgement it might be deemed proper to make certain alterations in our "minhargim" which would prove beneficial to public worship, but until a proper authority is established for making such changes—an authority so learned and pure that its decrees or opinions will carry respect and obedience wherever promulgated—I for one will be unwilling to adopt the ipse dixit of irresponsible parties who, if they know anything ought to know, that no power, human or Divine, have invested them with any such authority. I am not so uncharitable however, to believe that these people intend to commit wrong, but on the other hand I do believe that such is the result of their acts, and therefore, they should be discountenenced by every one who hopes to transmit to posterity the Holy Religion we have inherited from an ancestry dating back through centuries of time.

As you are aware, I have not taken any active part in your Congregational affairs, during my residence in this city. This has arisen, in part, from my habit and the habit of my family of reading our Prayers after the Portuguese Minharg, which as you know, differs essentially from that prevailing here—besides, I have felt that in my humble way I could render as effective service to any co-religionists outside their corporate body as I could within their limits. The same opinion influences me now, and I need not add that I feel it to be no more than my duty, as it certainly will be my pleasure, to assist you to the extent of my limited capacity, in your praiseworthy undertaking.

I have the honor to remain,
A. S. Solomons

Solomons kept his promise to assist the new congregation. He contributed his own funds, and later, when the campaign was launched to build a permanent structure, he secured a contribution from Jacob Schiff, one of the country's foremost Jewish financiers and philanthropists. Schiff would also contribute to building Adas Israel's second building, on 6th and I Streets.

### The Constitution

After a long period of discussion and debate, the congregation adopted a constitution in 1876. Despite the lengthy deliberative process, the constitution did not break new ground; its purpose was to safeguard the past from the encroaching pressures of the contemporary world. Its final form was almost identical with that of the first constitution of the Washington Hebrew Congregation, which itself was largely a compendium of clauses the members recalled from the constitutions of their synagogues in Germany. It was the threat of deviations from this constitution that had prompted the secessionist movement.

To uphold both Jewish tradition and the distinction between Adas Israel and the reforming inclinations of the Washington Hebrew Congregation, the constitution specified that "all prayers shall be read in the original Hebrew language, according to the custom of the Orthodox German Israelite Minhag Ashkenaz," with the exception of the prayer for the government, which could be recited in English "after having been first read in Hebrew."

To fix the mode of worship for all time and make certain that "reforms" would not creep into the ritual, the last article declared that "No alteration, amendment, or modification shall ever at any time be made to those articles of the constitution pertaining to the mode of worship."

Adas Israel was not the only immigrant congregation to hedge its rituals with constitutional safeguards. The constitution of Detroit's Congregation Beth El, organized in 1850, demanded that the "Divine services shall be held according to the German Ritual Minhag and not be changed."

In Baltimore, a group of unhappy members resigned from the Baltimore Hebrew Congregation in 1870 to establish a congregation "where our Prayers will be offered in accordance with the orthodox Ritual, the very same manner of worship, as it was inherited to us by our Forefathers."[2] The group organized Chizuk Amunah in 1871, and their constitution, too, prohibited any alteration in the service without the unanimous consent of the entire membership, further stipulating that any member who so much as offered a motion to introduce a change in ritual would be compelled to surrender his membership.

A comparison of the constitutions of Adas Israel and Chizuk Amunah in Baltimore, also adopted in 1876, reveal sufficient similarities to indicate the probability of collaboration. Adas Israel, the Washington Hebrew Congregation, and Chizuk Amunah all gave their respective governing boards the somewhat pretentious title of "board of managers," a designation not usually bestowed upon synagogue boards.

One may marvel at how a congregation governed by a provision severely restricting changes in ritual could move from Orthodox strictness to the flexibility of Conservative Judaism. Indeed, the restrictions on ritual changes proved to be the downfall of more than one of Adas Israel's rabbis and the harbinger of struggles yet to come.

The articles of incorporation referred to the congregation as the Adas Israel Hebrew Congregation, but the constitution dropped the word "Hebrew." Later revisions returned the deleted word, but for years to come Adas Israel's formal name remained a subject of debate. As late as 1939, the secretary, Falk Harmal, proposed dropping "Hebrew," but the motion failed to carry. The revised constitution adopted in 1954 permitted its elimination without making it mandatory; the two forms of the name could be used interchangeably.[3]

The constitution vested the president with supreme power over the congregation and its personnel, but also with some onerous responsibilities. He was required to "abstain from all secular pursuits on the Sabbath (Saturday) and all other holy days," and was expected to be "present and exercise exclusive control at all religious Services, preserving proper order and decorum, causing to be ejected any disorderly person." Like the European *parnass*, he was granted the power "to impose fines of not less than 50c nor more than $5.00 on members guilty of improper conduct."

While he could designate others to substitute for him "at any Service of the Congregation from which he may be absent," he remained responsible for their conduct. He was further empowered to designate ten members to attend services in a house of mourning, and those so designated were required to attend on penalty of being fined. No deviation from the accepted mode of worship was to be allowed even in a house-of-mourning service.

The corresponding-recording secretary was required to "keep a record . . . of all marriages and deaths occurring in the congregation (noting, in cases of death, number of the headstone) and a list of all the property of the Congregation." A salary could be paid to the secretary, but "in the event of no salary being paid the Sec'y, that officer shall be a voting member of the Board of Managers."

The board of managers was to consist of the officers and two elected members; three, if the secretary received no salary. Meetings were to be held monthly, with special meetings when necessary. Among its duties, the board was empowered to "engage a Balkara [*baal koreh*, i.e., a Torah reader] and additional Chasonim [cantors] for Rosh Hashaunah and Yom Kipper preferring members of the Congregation when practicable." The officiants were required to be those who "live strictly up to the laws of Moses and our Minhag."

The constitution made no provision for engaging a rabbi. The single clergyman it authorized, the hazzan, was expected to combine the duties which congregations today assign to a rabbi and a cantor. Not until 1908 would Adas Israel differentiate between rabbi and cantor in the assignment of duties.

The constitution required that the hazzan be "a competent gentleman . . . thoroughly Orthodox in his profession, fully conversant with, and competent to preach as well as practice our form of worship," and "fully capable of teaching School in the English, German and Hebrew language." His term of office was to be "one year from the date of his election."

The provision limiting contracts for salaried religious officials to one year would prove to be an effective means of controlling the personnel and would remain a standard practice until the 1930s. It would also be a source of conflict.

The heaviest regimen was assigned to the sexton, whose duties combined those of custodian, cantor, Torah reader, mail deliverer, treasurer, financial secretary, and collector of delinquent dues. He was required to attend all weddings and funerals. For every marriage service he was to receive a fee of "not less than one dollar." No fee was to be paid him for attending a funeral, "but he will not be debarred from receiving any present that may be tendered."

The sexton was required to be present at the synagogue "during divine service and at the house of mourning during *Shivah*, when Services are being held there, and report to the President the names of such persons as do not attend after having been notified." He was to receive a monthly compensation of 5 percent of the money he collected, "the amount to be determined by a majority of the members present at the annual meeting in January."

English was to be the language of discourse at the congregation's meetings, except that any member who found it difficult to speak in English was to be permitted to speak in German. Lectures could be delivered in either English or German. Membership was restricted to "any Israelite over 21 years of age who has never been convicted of a criminal offense, [and] any person wedded according to the Jewish laws, whose male children are entered into the covenant of Abraham." Violation of these requirements would lead to trial and expulsion. The latter provision was found in the constitution of the Washington Hebrew Congregation as well. The immigrant generation feared mixed marriages and took steps to guard against it.

Every member of the congregation was entitled to a burial plot measuring 12 by 16 feet, upon payment of $10. Right of burial required maintenance of membership. "Upon the resignation of a member in whose lot no interment has been made, such lot shall become the property of the congregation, and for which they shall give said member ten notes of one dollar each, payable annually in ten consecutive years."

Members were called to the Torah for aliyot on Sabbaths and festivals by alphabetical assignment, and those who failed to attend services after being notified of their designation were to be fined "50 cents for each failure, unless excused by the President." Children under five years of age were not permitted to enter the place of worship.

The constitution outlined an elaborate system of trial for "officers and members who may be guilty of misdemeanor." Charges required the signatures of four members. "The punishment to be inflicted in case of conviction shall be suspension from membership for not less than six months or more than one year, or suspension or expulsion from office. In case of suspension the member suspended shall continue to pay all dues and fines the same as if in active membership." Trial and punishment for misdeeds had been the practice in European synagogues as well; some of them, as in Tykocin, Poland, had a jail attached to the synagogue building.

Seats for the High Holidays were rented to each member. "On the death of a member, his seat shall revert to his widow, but must not be sold or rented by her," a strange requirement since the widow could not in any event occupy her late husband's seat. The requirement, which remains the policy even today, was intended to allow a bereaved family to retain the assigned seat of the deceased so long as a member of the family maintained a membership.

Marriage ceremonies in the synagogue were required to take place between "the hours of twelve noon and sunset." The synagogue had no electricity, and gas illumination was both inadequate and expensive. The president was to be notified in writing of every marriage that was to be performed in the synagogue. "The fees for the marriage of a member, or one of his family, shall be for Chazan not less than $5.00, for Shamus, not less than $1.00." Fees for nonmembers were to be regulated by the board.

A minimum of ten members, one of whom had to be a board member, was required to attend the funeral of a deceased member or of a member's wife or parent. Only one member of the board was required to be in attendance at the funeral of a nonmember. The congregation was expected to provide a carriage or carriages for transportation of the official delegation. The cemetery was located several miles from the synagogue and the area of Jewish residence.

A set of bylaws and an "Order of Business" was affixed to the constitution. "In all deliberative meetings," questions of order were to be decided "in accordance with the parliamentary regulations provided in 'Cushing's Manual.'" The minutes reveal that every meeting of the board and the congregation followed the prescribed "Order of Business" in precise detail.

The signatories to the constitution and bylaws included: L. Hable, chairman; John Boyer, president; Manasses Oppenheimer, Louis Roseman, G. Goldberg, Louis Skoph [sp.?], Morris Cohen, Herman Baumgarten, A. Michaelis, Julius Louis, Max Louis, Jacob Solomon, and Jacob Rich.

# 7

## THE CEMETERY

Isaac Polock, who died in 1813, had been interred in an old burial ground on Observatory Hill, near 23rd and E Streets N.W.[1] There was no Jewish cemetery; there were not enough Jews.

Pierre L'Enfant's plans for Washington city had specified two nondenominational cemeteries so as to bridge religious distinctions. His intentions were never put into practice. The regulations of Congressional Cemetery, founded in 1807, denied burial to any person "known to deny a belief in the Christian religion." Another regulation prohibited the interment of "persons of color."[2] Both of these restrictions were removed in the latter half of the nineteenth century.

Soon after a Catholic cemetery restricted its burials to Catholics in 1808, the boards of the District's other cemeteries imposed sectarian religious restrictions on burial grounds under their management. Mount Zion, a cemetery for blacks at 27th Street near Rock Creek Park in Georgetown, was opened in 1810 by descendants of freed slaves. Another cemetery for blacks was opened in 1829 in North East. Both cemeteries segregated free blacks from slaves.[3]

The death of one of its members, Mr. Melmberg of Georgetown, led the yet undivided Washington Hebrew Congregation to acquire a burial plot in downtown Washington. When, in 1879, the site became inadequate, the now-divided Washington Hebrew Congregation moved the interred bodies to a new cemetery alongside the Adas Israel cemetery and named it *Machpela*, after the burial ground

Abraham purchased in Hebron for the burial of his wife, Sarah. The oldest identifiable tombstone in the Machpela section is that of ten-year-old Albertine Cohen, who died in 1851, her body having moved from its original grave site.

Even after Adas Israel acquired its own cemetery, some of its members retained their family plots in Washington Hebrew's Machpela. Except for his infant son, members of the Behrend family, for example, were all buried in their family plot in Machpela, including the first president himself.

As we learned from Behrend's letter to Solomons, Adas Israel had in 1869 acquired ground for a cemetery on land adjacent to St. Elizabeths Hospital and the no longer existing National Race Track. The District of Columbia directory for 1870 lists "The Adas Israel Cemetery" as "The Jewish Burial Ground, about 1 1/2 miles from the Government Insane Asylum." The cemetery fronted on a street named Giesboro Road for part of its length and Hamilton Road for the rest. Both names were subsequently changed to Alabama Avenue, the street's present name.

The cemetery location, in the southeastern segment of the District, was separated from the other areas of Washington by the Anacostia River, the eastern branch of the more famous Potomac River. The area was originally called Uniontown, but in 1886 Congress ordered the name changed to Anacostia because Uniontown had been preempted as a popular city name in many states following the Civil War. Anacostia was the Latinized rendition of the Indian name for the area. There has never been a Jewish settlement in Anacostia.

Even though racial covenants restricted the area to native-born whites, the most prominent resident of Anacostia following the Civil War was Frederick Douglass, the noted black abolitionist, who had succeeded Simon Wolf as the District's registrar of deeds. The restrictive covenants were relaxed long before they became unenforceable and finally illegal. The federal Freedmen's Bureau purchased a 375-acre farm adjacent to the cemetery to settle some of the thousands of freed slaves who had swelled Washington's black population after the Civil War.

To reach the cemetery, as other parts of Anacostia, one had to cross either a wooden bridge at 11th Street or the Navy Yard bridge. A new iron-and-masonry bridge at Pennsylvania Avenue was opened in 1890. Attending a funeral at the cemetery would take the better part of a day, especially with horsedrawn hearse and carriage.

Adas Israel treasured its cemetery as a precious heirloom. For many years the sale of lots was a major source of operating income for the congregation. Considering the fact that the cemetery remains in use even today, and that only in recent years has the congregation begun to consider the need for additional burial ground, it must be noted that the founders displayed a generous measure of confidence in the future by acquiring a six-acre area far in excess of their immediate needs. They used only a small segment of the expanse, allowing its unused undulations to grow wild. Part of the unused portion was a gravel pit which they quarried as a source of income. A house on another segment of the unused area was rented for additional income. A deep ravine which bisected the cemetery along its length was later filled in to provide more burial space.

On numerous occasions the board considered selling some of the surplus land to Jewish lodges. An offer to purchase a portion of the cemetery came in March 1886 from the Independent Order of the Sons of Benjamin, a local lodge. The president submitted the request in a formal statement to the board, whose discussion the secretary faithfully recorded.

> Gentlemen of the board, a Committee from a Lodge of the I. O. Sons of Benjamin wishes to purchase 1 acre of our Burying Ground.

> Are you willing to sell? Whereupon a majority voted yes.
> The Diagram was produced and it was suggested the price should be stipulated, with the following proviso: Should they select 1 acre on a parallel with the Wagon road,* the price should be set apart separately, and for one acre above the ravine on the hill near the burying ground of the H St. Synagogue,* should also be stipulated and set apart separately.[4]

The first segment, "parallel with the Wagon road," was further described as "near the *metaher* house" (i.e. Purifying house), for which the asking price was $1,200; for the second section, "near the H St. Synagogue," the price was $600. Fortunately, neither section was sold.

Other synagogues and lodges organized by later immigrants, eager to provide death benefits to their members but unable to afford a cemetery of their own, negotiated with Adas Israel for burial rights in the congregation's cemetery. The Columbia Lodge of the Sons of Benjamin, which failed to take up its option to purchase a portion of the cemetery, was told that on payment of $3 per year per member, burial rights would be available to its members without further cost.[5]

In response to its request for burial rights, the Southwest Congregation on 4 1/2 Street was offered the use of a section of the cemetery on payment of $150 for its seventeen members plus $3 per member per year.[6]

The most important benefit that an immigrant congregation could provide its members was support in times of bereavement, illness, or accident. The availability of a cemetery was extremely important to the isolated immigrant Jew. Adas Israel did not evade

*Hamilton Avenue (Alabama Avenue), then a wagon road along the cemetery's front entrance.

*Machpela, the Washington Hebrew Congregation's cemetery.

its responsibilities to the bereaved but did not hesitate to make use of the leverage which cemetery ownership provided.

Members paid a standard fee for burial. Nonmembers were charged what the market would bear. A stranger, Mr. S. Smith, died at the Garfield Hospital in 1890. The board, after thorough debate, agreed to charge $50 for burial "above all expenses incurred, but after considering his assets, $30 was deemed sufficient."[7] The congregation made generous concessions to those who could not afford to pay the full price for burial, especially when the deceased were infants or young children.

The burial of resident paupers posed an increasingly frequent problem for the board. To ease the burden, Adas Israel attempted to negotiate an agreement with the Washington Hebrew Congregation to share the responsibility of burying transients and the destitute. Whether the agreement was put into practice is not recorded.

A fence surrounded the cemetery. In 1875, new hinges were put on the gates, the sign over the gate was painted and lettered, the lots numbered, and assigned lots were registered on a master map.[8] A resident superintendent named either Grayner, Graynor, Graener, Graner, or Groner—the spelling varied with the mood or identity of the recording secretary—occupied a house in the cemetery. When his lease on the house expired on January 31, 1878, he was granted a three-year renewal on condition that the lease be subject to cancellation upon thirty days notice should the congregation decide to dispose of the premises he occupied.

There was no end to the problems surrounded the hiring and retention of cemetery superintendents. Grayner, for instance, decided to resign in November 1886. After nearly four months of exasperating negotiations, Sam Hartong reported to the board in February 1887 that further discussion would be fruitless. The following month, a Mr. Green was hired as superintendent. His duties included digging graves at no extra charge, but he was to be paid an extra fee if called upon to make any improvements. Compensation had been the point of contention with Grayner.

Cemetery maintenance, always a major challenge because of the need to keep the grass trimmed around the tombstones, was rendered even more difficult when, in 1880, the congregation granted permission to "Mr. J. Rich to fence in his lot on the cemetery in a plain manner and so that hereafter members who may desire to do so likewise, may do it in the same manner."[9] Others soon did likewise. In exchange for the permission, Rich paid for the repair of the fence surrounding the cemetery. Many years later, Rich's widow was assured that she was entitled to be buried alongside her husband in accordance with an agreement signed May 13, 1888, for which she had paid $100.[10]

There was no Jewish undertaker in those early days. Indeed, it is doubtful that Adas Israel used any undertaker or even coffins. In 1899, after considerable debate, a *chevra kadisha* (burial society) was formed, with fifteen volunteer participants. A majority of the members present at the meeting were opposed, either because they felt that the society was unnecessary or, what is more likely, because they did not want to be called upon to participate in the rites of preparing bodies for burial.

The original *chevra kadisha* eventually disbanded. A proposal in 1913 to reconstitute the group included a mutual-insurance plan.[11] Participants were to pay a $2 entrance fee and $1 annually as dues for which they would receive certain death benefits.

> Members who pay $1.25 monthly shall receive after death of a child of ten years, the sum of $25.00; at the death of a child of 21 years, $50.00; at the death of a member or his wife, $100.00.

Members who paid $2 monthly would receive higher benefits, from $35 to $200; those who paid $3 monthly, from $50 to $300. A committee was appointed to consider the proposal, and it was later accepted.[12]

In 1913, the board formalized the traditional custom of collecting charity at funerals and during the High Holy Day season. Most but not all of the proceeds were turned over to communal charities.*

The traditionally ordained rites of preparing the body were performed in the *metaher* house at the cemetery. Reflecting his reverence for the procedure, Herman Baumgarten, the secretary, recorded the words for the rites *taharah*, and the *metaher* house in the Hebrew script.

The original house on the cemetery was torn down in 1882 to be replaced by a two-room structure erected at an expenditure of $550. The new house served as a residence for the caretaker as well a site for ritual purification. Mrs. S. Hartong, "in her never ceasing fidelity and philanthropy," furnished the house with a "stove, fuel, and six chairs," for which she was warmly thanked.[13]

Each burial was recorded in the minutes as well as in the cemetery records. Funeral procedures were carefully defined. A guard was to be placed over each new grave "for a reasonable time . . . during the night," and "any expenses to be incurred thereby [would] be charged as necessary to the party who causes such burial to take place."[14]

As in other pioneer communities, the majority of the early burials were those of infants and children. A shocking number of births were stillborn, and an appalling number of children were victims of dreaded childhood maladies. Many young mothers died in childbirth. The earliest tombstones reflect the woeful anguish of the founding generation. The first burials in the new Adas Israel cemetery were the stillborn twins of H. Hammerschlag, a relative of

*In 1913, $7 was given to charity; in 1919, $75 was divided between the foster home, the old-age home, Hebrew Charities, Hebrew Relief, and the Free Loan Association. The balance of $28.62 went to the Sunday school.

the Behrend family, who were interred on June 7, 1870, and the following month, the six-year-old son of Abraham Goldenheimer.

Of the fifty-seven interments between 1870 and 1879, forty-nine were infants or children under ten years of age. Some children lived beyond infancy only to succumb to whooping cough, measles, diphtheria, pneumonia, cholera infantum, or "scarlatina."

The first adult death, in 1872, was a murder victim; the second, in 1873, a patient in St. Elizabeths, the government hospital for the insane. Among adults, there were more than one suicide and numerous accidental deaths caused by runaway horses and collisions: "Jewish woman by the name of Mrs. Sarah Stearman killed by the B and O Ry . . . burial agreed without cost."[15] Particularly poignant were the successive tragedies in the family of Herman Sanger. His wife, Bertha Sanger, was buried on November 30, 1875; his mother, Babette, in October 1876; and his infant nephew, Jacob Sanger, in December 1877. Sanger remarried but lost Gittel, his second wife, only a few years later, in January 1879. Such were the hazards of life in the first decade of Adas Israel's existence.

Beginning with July 1899, newly promulgated Health Department regulations required burial records to list cause of death. The records covering the two decades from 1899 to 1910 document 128 deaths. Nine were suicides, one by gunshot, another by "knife," the others by illuminating gas. There were four accidental deaths; one victim fell from a wagon, another was hit by a train, a third drowned, and fourth died in a fire. Other causes of adult deaths spanned the medical lexicon: asthma, peritonitis, senile dementia, nephritis, cancer, tuberculosis, diabetes, typhoid fever, and hypertrophy of the prostate. One death was attributed to "abortion septicaemia."

The earliest deceased were of German birth. The first recorded death of a person of Russian birth was in 1900, Paulina Levin. One deceased was born in France, three in Hungary, two in Austria, and one, Edward Hartogensis, in Holland. A prominent tombstone at the cemetery's entrance, in granite and perfectly preserved, is that of Aaron Barnett, died January 9, 1900, at age thirty-nine, a postmaster at West Point, Nebraska, of heart failure. He was born in New York City. His parents, Mr. and Mrs. Morris Barnett, their tombstones far more eroded, died in 1908 and 1917, respectively.

President Simon Oppenheimer referred to the cemetery's needs in his 1901 report to the congregation:

> Our cemetery has been greatly improved. During the past year the entire ground has been surveyed and laid off into lots and a new fence has been put up around the entire grounds. A handsome gate of iron and stone is soon to be erected by Mrs. I. Sacks in memory of her parents, Mr. and Mrs. S. Hartong. About 200 trees have been planted in the cemetery which will greatly add to its appearance. But there is yet much to be done. It is absolutely necessary that at least one of the main roads be laid off and gravelled which would cost about $150.00. I would suggest that all members not owning lots would purchase one. In this way we could raise sufficient funds to meet this present demand and further improve our cemetery.
>
> But for the expense of the cemetery there would have been an even larger surplus in the treasury, perhaps for the first time in the history of the Congregation.[16]

In 1908, the daughter of Mr. and Mrs. John Boyer, an early president, wrote to the congregation from her residence in Denver asking permission to remove her mother's remains for re-interment there. The president sought the board's guidance before responding. The board members were not of one mind on the propriety of disinterment, and the congregation at this time had no rabbi to guide them.

> It was on motion of Mr. Wolf who cited a certain paragraph in our higher laws which covers it all, it being this translation of it: That

> whenever you are in doubt about the construction or meaning of any of our laws, consult the state laws. It was therefore resolved to leave the whole matter to the President with full power to act.[17]

This was surely a unique application of the principle of *dina d'malchuta dina*.* Each request for exhuming a deceased would be considered on a case-by-case basis. Permission was usually granted.

Several of the earlier graves were moved in the 1920s to make way for the widening of Alabama Avenue, the old wagon road. In October 1943, the cemetery was again forced to yield a small segment of its front footage to eminent domain, prompted by the further widening of the same avenue. The cemetery lost eleven grave sites to the project; bodies had to be moved. The District paid the congregation $13,000 in compensation.

In 1922, a chapel was erected at the entrance of the cemetery, a gift from the family of Bernard Schlossberg.

### Noteworthy Burials

While every death is important, there have been several noteworthy interments in the Adas Israel Cemetery. Among them was that of Manuel Mordecai Noah, a Washington reporter for the *New York Herald* and the son of the prominent journalist, playwright, philanthropist, Tammany politician, and ambassador, Mordecai Manuel Noah (1785–1851).** Of Portuguese descent and a grandson of the pioneer Jonas Phillips of Philadelphia, the elder Noah was a visionary and proto-Zionist who, in 1825, long before Herzl, launched an attempt to establish a Jewish colony, to be known as Ararat, on Grand Island on the Niagara River, near Buffalo, New York.

*Literally, "the law of the state is the law" (Talmud, Gittin 10b). This principle, enunciated by Samuel, a second-century Babylonian sage, affirms that civil law supersedes Jewish law and was first applied to matters of taxation.

**The elder Noah served for a time as U.S. consul in Tunis. He was removed by President James Monroe in 1815 on the grounds that "the religion which you profess is an obstacle to the exercise of your consular function."

His son, Manuel Mordecai Noah, was born in New York City on December 23, 1828. He moved to San Francisco in 1855, where he became active in Jewish organizations and wrote articles for the local Jewish newspapers. In 1858, he became editor-in-chief of the *Alta California*, a San Francisco paper, and was considered one of the city's most influential Jewish citizens. He left California to settle in Washington in the late 1860s.[18]

The younger Noah died in 1873 at age forty-two. His obituary in the *San Francisco Call* included the information that "he became insane . . . from the excessive use of liquor and opium, and was conveyed to the Government Asylum. . . . The Doctor assigns nervous prostration as the cause of his death."[19]

Adas Israel charged the family $25 for his burial in plot no. 23. Alongside his name in the cemetery records is the sad comment, "Died in insane asylum, Feb. 14, 1873." The board of managers attended the funeral as a group out of respect for Manuel Noah and his distinguished father.

### Murder Victim

"SHOCKING AND MYSTERIOUS MURDER," was the headline in the lead article of the *Washington Evening Star* on Tuesday night, December 24, 1872. The subhead supplied the gruesome details: "The Victim's Head and Face Literally Hacked to Pieces—No Clue to the Perpetrators of the Bloody Deed." Washington's populace had yet to grow accustomed to murder. The crime claimed headlines for three successive days.

In meticulous detail, the news columns described each step of the police investigation that followed the discovery of the mutilated body, sparing the reader none of the grisly circumstances surrounding the murder. The almost bloodless body was found on the night of Monday, December 23, in an alley between 9th and 10th between D and E Streets. An envelope in the pocket of the victim revealed that he was Samuel Rogersky, residing at 1015 7th Street.

Police detectives and neighbors searched the site for clues. The absence of blood from the scene indicated that the victim had been murdered elsewhere and had been dragged or carried to the alley where he was found. The body was still warm. Bloodstains on the snow and ice indicated that the murder had probably taken place in a nearby house.

The following day's headline proclaimed: "MURDER WILL OUT."

An informant who may have been a witness led the police to a house at 10th and E Streets whose occupants were immediately taken into custody. One of the suspects, Margaret Woods, implicated Tom Wright as the murderer. A trail of blood led to the house which had been the scene of the murder. In minute detail, the paper described the house's interior even to noting the remains of the occupants' Christmas dinner found in the cupboard. Tom Wright admitted he was the occupant of the house; he was one of the people who had volunteered to help the police search the area for clues.

The victim was a peddler. Margaret Wood's testimony led the police to find the peddler's pack buried under a pile of lumber. He had come to the house on Monday night to show his goods and to collect 25 cents owed him from a previous sale. Then, as the coroner's inquest stated, "He was sitting in the front room exhibiting his goods, when he was struck a heavy blow from behind and knocked senseless and that other blows followed in quick succession when he was down."

The body had been hidden in a closet. When Margaret Woods came home, she found Tom Wright, her common-law husband, washing the bloodstains from the floors of the closet and front room after having removed the body from the closet and dragged it to the alley where it was later found.

Wright had admitted to his common-law wife that "he had killed that G-d Dutch peddler and only got $5.00." She withheld nothing from the police. At the inquest, carried verbatim in the *Star*, she testified that "on last Friday Tom asked her when that Dutch peddler was coming there again and on being told on Monday, he said, he was going to rob him and get some Christmas money." She responded, "O, Tom don't do that; he looks like a poor old fellow without much money. Go and work for some money."

Margaret Wood's testimony was enough to convict Wright. He turned out to be a troublesome prisoner. In his cell, awaiting trial, he feigned illness. Friends, visiting him, attempted to free him by force but did not succeed. The police described the prisoner as a brazen ruffian who had the temerity to volunteer to assist them in their search for clues to the murder. This was not his first brush with the law.

The victim's body, awaiting identification, was laid out in the rear of the police station on a "slab" made of an old door. The body was claimed and buried, the *Star* wrote, "by a committee of the Society of Adas Israel connected with the synagogue on Pennsylvania Avenue."

### Who was Samuel Rogersky?

The *Star* explained: Rogersky was identified by "Hebrews who recognized the deceased having met him at the Synagogue," as a Polish Jew who had been in the country for only six months and who supported himself by "peddling and hawking fancy goods." He was a lonely immigrant, it was said, who had no family in the District. The congregation met its obligation to a kinsman by assuming the family role.

The congregation's concern did not end with the burial. Over three months later, the members appointed a delegation to call on the U.S. district attorney to claim "such parts of the body of the late Samuel Rogersky as may be in his possession, in order to properly inter them with the body."[20] The minutes delicately omitted the grisly detail that "the head of the deceased, partially severed by the murder, had been retained by the police, perhaps for evidence."[21]

Identification had been made from an envelope in the victim's pocket addressed to a name written in English but in a foreign hand which appeared to spell "Rogersky." Foreign handwriting was difficult to decipher. More careful examination of the address on the envelope revealed that the handwriting had been misread, thus causing the confusion of identity.[22]

The cemetery records, correcting both the newspaper article and the congregational minutes, reveal that on December 25, 1872, one Samuel Roginsky, aged thirty-seven, had become the twentieth person to be buried in the Adas Israel Cemetery. Alongside his name Is the notation: "Killed by assassination of negroe." Such terminology was standard in 1872.

Unlike Rogersky, Roginsky is not an uncommon Jewish name; it denotes someone whose origin was in the Polish city of Ruzhin or Rizhin. While Roginsky may have been a lonely peddler at the time of his death, soon afterwards, either because of his burial there or because they had always planned to join him, other members of the family took up residence in the District of Columbia. They placed a tombstone over his grave with the following legend:

Father<br>In memory of<br>Samuel H. Roginsky<br>March 15, 1836–December 23, 1872

The burials of several other family members are found nearby:

Isaac Roginsky, aged forty-seven, died June 21, 1906.
Louis Roginsky, aged forty-two, died May 16, 1908.
Max Roginsky, aged sixty-three, died March 13, 1913.
Sophia Roginsky, aged ninety, died June 30, 1919.

Max and Sophia (Celia) Roginsky, husband and wife. were the first couple to be married in the synagogue at 6th and G Streets. They were married in the year of its dedication, 1876. Their granddaughter, Rebecca Sachs, died on December 28, 1975.

*Kibbud hamet* (respect for the deceased) required that in the absence of a family, a community must come forward to provide a burial plot and bury the dead with due honor. Adas Israel never failed to accept this responsibility.

**Arthur L. Welsh**

Almost forgotten is the grave of the first Jewish aviator in the United States, perhaps in the world. The tombstone of this pioneer pilot, who was taught to fly by his friend Orville Wright, bears the inscription, "Arthur L. Welsh, Father." Arthur Welsh was born Label Welcher in Kiev, the Ukraine, on August 14, 1881, to Avraham and Dvorah Welcher, who migrated to the United States in 1890 and moved to Washington in 1898.

Welcher joined the Navy in 1901 when he was twenty years of age. In order to avoid the unpleasant treatment which was the common lot of a Jew in the Navy in those days, he enlisted as Arthur L. Welsh, a name which he would use throughout his service career. He retained his birth name in his Jewish associations, which remained considerable throughout his brief life.

Welcher-Welsh was actively involved in the young people's clubs of Adas Israel, where his parents were members. His marriage to Anna Harmel, daughter of Paul Harmel, secretary of the congregation and an early Zionist leader, on October 10, 1907, was the first wedding to be held at the new but still uncompleted Adas Israel Synagogue on 6th and I Streets.

Among Welsh's flying students was General Henry "Hap" Arnold, who later became chief of the Air Force during World War II. A bust of Welsh, together with the prizes he won in competitive flying, are on display at the Smithsonian's National Aeronautical and Space Museum. His name is engraved on a plaque at the Wright-Patterson Air Force Base in Dayton, Ohio, along with the names of the Wright brothers and other pioneer aviators.

Welsh was killed in 1912 in a crash at the College Park Airport in Maryland while testing a new plane for the War Department. The test required the plane to climb to 2,000 feet in ten minutes under full load, which evidently was beyond its capacity. The wings collapsed and the plane crashed, killing Welsh and his co-pilot, Lt. L. W. Hazelhurst.

The funeral took place at the home of Welsh's father-in-law, Paul Harmel, at 466 8th Street S.W. The coffin was draped in a silk tallit. Adas Israel's cantor, Samuel Glushak, officiated. Orville Wright and his sister attended the services. Welsh's only daughter, Aline, was two years old when her father was killed. She moved to London, England, when she was an adult.

The Adas Israel Cemetery records list the cause of Welsh's death with remarkable understatement: "fracture, due to fall."

**Arnold Margolin**

Among the historical figures buried in the Adas Israel Cemetery is Arnold Margolin (1877–1956). Born in Kiev, the son of a sugar manufacturer, Margolin was a Ukrainian lawyer, well known as an attorney in Russian pogrom trials, especially for his defense of Mendel Beilis, who, in 1911, was accused of killing a Christian child in order to use his blood to bake matzot, a case which aroused much of the civilized world, and which was recreated by Bernard Malamud in his novel *The Fixer*.

In 1919, when the Ukraine was briefly independent following the Russian Revolution, Margolin became its diplomatic representative in England, a post he left when he came to the United States to engage in journalism and the lecture circuit. He was admitted to the Washington bar in 1936 and wrote several books. On Friday night, December 2, 1938, Margolin addressed the congregation on the subject, "The Situation of the Jew in Europe." His grave is located alongside the cemetery's main roadway.

**Stephen Theodore Norman**

The granite stone atop the grave reads:

Stephen Theodore Norman<br>Captain, Royal Artillery, British Army<br>Grandson of Theodor Herzl<br>April 21, 1918–November 26, 1946

Few will recall the circumstances leading to Captain Norman's death or the reason for his burial in Washington. Upon inquiry, the British Army refused to release any details about Norman's life or death without permission of next of kin; there are no known next of kin. Some details, however, were obtained from the Central Zionist Archives in Jerusalem through the cooperation of its director, Michael Heymann.

Contributing to the confusion was the fact that the young man's name was not Norman but Neumann. He was the son of Herzl's youngest daughter, Trude, who had married a man named Neumann and had borne a son whom they had named Stephen Theodore. In 1937 Stephen went to England from his native Vienna to enter Cambridge University, where he was active in Zionist societies. It was there that he Anglicized his name to Norman.

With the Nazi occupation of Vienna, Stephen Neumann-Norman lost contact with his parents. At the outbreak of World War II, he enlisted in the British Army, attaining the rank of captain. He visited Palestine in 1945 and 1946 and, according to his own words, was deeply impressed by what he saw.

Norman was sent to Washington as a member of the British Scientific Office Purchasing Commission in 1946. Shortly thereafter, he received a letter from his former governess in Vienna informing him that his parents had died in Theresienstadt, the concentration camp in Terezin, Czechoslovakia. The loss of his parents and, some have said, an unhappy love affair drove him into a deep depression. On November 26, 1946, he left his office in the British Embassy on Massachusetts Avenue, walked a few blocks southward until he reached the Massachusetts Avenue Bridge, and leaped to his death.

In Washington, Stephen Norman had become friendly with Eliyahu Epstein, later named Elath, the representative of the Jewish Agency who became the first Israeli ambassador to the United States. To Epstein fell the sad responsibility of arranging his friend's funeral with Adas Israel.

A few days before his suicide, Norman had asked Epstein to keep a package of papers for him because, so he said, he was returning to England on leave. In the package, which Epstein later opened, were two articles Norman had written describing his impressions of Palestine and revealing the depth of his identification with Zionism. Norman, deeply sensitive, was uncomfortable when being "paraded" as "the grandson of Herzl." Nonetheless, he was proud of his grandfather and was visibly moved when he saw his picture in the Washington office of the Jewish Agency.

The Zionist groups in Washington along with the Jewish War Veterans color guard attended the funeral. Diplomats from the British Embassy and representatives of the British Scientific Office were also in attendance. Norman's coffin was draped with the blue-and-white Zionist colors, the Union Jack, American bunting, and the colors of the Jewish War Veterans. His eulogists included Rabbi Solomon Metz and Mr. Moshe Frelichov, who was acquainted with both Herzl and his grandson.

In his eulogy, Rabbi Metz, who also recited the funeral prayers, stated that Norman was "a casualty of the callousness of the world which has permitted the destruction of one third of our people and is still unmoved by the tragic homelessness of the remnants of Jewry overseas. Though we are overwhelmed by the tragic circumstances of his death, the respect which we pay his remains is also an expression of respect to one of the greatest spirits of our age, Theodor Herzl."

The *New Palestine* pointed out that Norman's funeral took place at the same time that delegates were gathering in Basle, Switzerland, for what would be the last Zionist Congress in the Diaspora.

Herzl's dedication to Zionism had exacted a fearful price from him and his three children, Pauline, Hans, and Trude, Stephen's mother. Herzl died at age 44 in 1904; his wife, Julia, died three years later. Their eldest daughter, Pauline, unstable, became addicted to heroin and died in 1930. In the same year, her brother, Hans, who had never married, committed suicide in Bordeaux. Hans had already shocked the Jewish world by converting to Christianity.

As Moshe Frelichov observed in his graveside tribute, "With the death of Captain Norman, no descendant is left of the great founder of the Zionist movement. The great Herzl now lives only in his great works."[23]

The cemetery records carry the following notation: "Jewish Agency called Mr. Wilner for land, as deceased had no one in this country. Agreed cost $75.00." The Jewish Agency paid the congregation $100 on January 30, 1947.

The Adas Israel Cemetery is history etched in stone, enshrining not only the remains of the founding generations but their aspirations. The granite monuments, covering and transcending the graves, bear testimony to their achievements and those of their descendants.

# 8

## BUILDING A SYNAGOGUE

The founders of Adas Israel had left an established congregation, worshipping comfortably in its own building; now they were wandering tenants, forced to worship in rented quarters. They could not hope to survive as a congregation, much less to attract new members, unless they could offer their members a permanent place of worship at least as comfortable as the one they had left behind.

With the cemetery acquired, it was important to find a permanent synagogue. Bendiza Behrend, in his letter to Adolphus Solomons, identified the first place of worship as two rented rooms at 388 8th Street, between Pennsylvania Avenue and D Street. The congregation leased these in December 1869. Two years later, in 1872, it moved to a loft above a carriage factory at 462 Pennsylvania Avenue, where it remained until February 1876. For the three months prior to the dedication of its new and permanent synagogue structure, the congregation worshiped at 418 11th Street. In the interval between worshipping in rented quarters and dedicating its own building, there were many formidable obstacles to overcome.

The first public mention of a fund-raising campaign for a synagogue building appeared in 1872 in a brief paragraph in New York's *Jewish Messenger*.

> Some of our co-religionists in Washington D. C. have resolved to erect a new synagogue at an early day and are collecting for that purpose.[1]

A two-column report appeared shortly thereafter in the same newspaper, signed by "Semi-Occasional," a pen-name attributed to both Adolphus Solomons and Simon Wolf, stressing the importance of providing Washington with a dignified Orthodox congregation, and describing Adas Israel as "free of debt and paying its own way," while worshipping in a room too small for its thirty-six members and their families. The report concluded that it would be desirable for Washington to possess a truly "Metropolitan synagogue" to meet the needs of those who came on business or as tourists to the nation's capital. To achieve this goal, the members had subscribed $3,000 toward a new building and were now appealing to fellow Jews for assistance. Committee members were listed as: L. Oppenheimer, chairman of the collection committee; S. Goldstein, chairman of the building committee; M. Cohen, secretary; and A. S. Solomons, honorary member.[2] Selig Goldstein, the chairman, began soliciting funds to build a synagogue even though an appropriate site had not yet been found.

The minutes faithfully record the arduous ordeal of maintaining a congregation in rented quarters continually in need of repairs and requiring repeated confrontations with the landlord. In August 1872, the treasurer was instructed not to pay rent for the synagogue premises "until the roof is put in proper condition."[3] Shortly thereafter, the skylight had to be repaired and the rain-stained walls repapered. The endless challenge to keep the inadequate quarters in a reasonable state of repair made the need for a permanent house of worship ever more compelling.

A special congregational meeting was called in December to hear the building committee's report. Several sites had been considered, including one on 2nd and K Streets owned by President Ulysses S. Grant, but the committee recommended "the purchase of a lot situated at the corner of G and 6th Streets, N. W. at an asked price of $2500." The eighteen members present gave the proposal their unanimous endorsement.[4]

Although everyone knew that soliciting sufficient funds to purchase a lot would be difficult, the thought that they had actually selected a site for a building intensified the exhultation at the ceremony dedicating their recently acquired Torah scroll scheduled for later the same day. Despite the congregation's financial straits, the board was determined to continue negotiations. As its members understood only too well, Adas Israel would have little future without a house of worship of its own.

Two months later, Selig Goldstein announced that the owner of the property was willing to accept $2,300 for the lot, whereupon the board empowered the trustees to borrow "any amount which may be wanting to complete the $2,300.00 provided that, for the amount thus to be borrowed shall not be paid a higher than the legal interest."[5] Amidst great excitement, the site was purchased. Fund raising efforts intensified.

Despite Goldstein's energetic efforts, his committee could not raise sufficient funds to cover both the cost of the lot and the cost of initiating construction; their goal had been $3,000. In order to retire their bank loan, the board appointed other committees to collect pledges and to solicit "contributions from co-religionists in the District." Felix Greenapple, one of the trustees, lent the congregation $400, which it would later struggle to repay.

A brief item in the *Jewish Messenger*, again signed by "Semi-Occasional," and headed "AN OMISSION," stated,

> The article you published last week under the caption of "A Metropolitan Synagogue," failed to state a fact which it is the purpose of this communication now to supply, viz, that there already exists in the city a "Reform" congregation, who have a regular place of worship."[6]

This item suggests that "Semi-Occasional" was Simon Wolf, the president of the Washington Hebrew Congregation, rather than Adolphus Solomons, who would have little reason to stress the existence of the Reform congregation, but in all probability both men wrote under the same pen-name.

The same issue reported that "Mr. A. S. Solomons, of the committee for creating a fund to erect a synagogue in Washington D. C. gratefully acknowledges the receipt of the following:

Jacob H. Schiff, Esq., New York......$50.00
J. Corn, Kingston, N. Y. through
S. Goldstein, Esq.,..................$10.00

Jacob Schiff, the noted banker and philanthropist, had responded to his friendship with Adolphus Solomons.

There was a house on the lot the congregation had selected. It was agreed that the shochet, M. H. Sommers, would occupy it "free of charge, under condition he take care of it, and until such time as it may be demanded back for the further use of the congregation."[7]

Fund-raising efforts continued all that summer. It was essential to raise more money before construction could begin. Committees sought support in nearby Baltimore and in more distant Philadelphia and New York. Their efforts were of little avail. Suddenly, in the fall, Adas Israel's fund-raising and building plans came to a halt due to circumstances beyond the congregation's control: the shattering effects of a day known in the economic history of the United States as Black Friday, September 19, 1873.

Uncontrolled speculation in currency and stocks had caused the failure of three major New York banks; the stock market closed down for the remainder of the month. The nationwide recession which followed, known as the Panic of 1873, was unprecedented for the extent of the unemployment and suffering it engendered.

To save paying the property tax, the board decided to demolish the house on the congregation's lot. A member of the congregation,

L. Poppers, agreed to level the house and to fence the lot without cost to the congregation in exchange for salvage rights.[8] While the house was demolished, the land was not sufficiently cleared to satisfy District of Columbia law. The following June (1874), the Board of Health notified the congregation that the lot must be leveled and the weeds removed. With the possibility of raising enough money to erect a synagogue in doubt, the congregation had no alternative but to make the best of its rented quarters despite its unhappiness with the facilities and the landlord. The loft above the carriage factory on 462 Pennsylvania Avenue would remain Adas Israel's address until the members could afford to build.

A special board meeting in September 1874 took steps to reassign and number the seats in the loft-sanctuary so as to eliminate confusion in seating assignments. Each member was assigned a seat, a matching numbered seat in the balcony for his wife, and a similarly numbered burial plot. It was then resolved "that each member must keep the same number as the Lady's seat, and that no officer has the right to change any number of a member's seat without the sanction of the party whose seat has been assigned him in this meeting."[9]

In view of the bleak financial outlook, which made the possibility of a new synagogue more remote than ever, the building committee was discharged with thanks. Having begun its work with zest and hope on March 1, 1872, the committee regretfully surrendered its mandate in 1874. The chairman turned in its records and minutes, including "$18.00 in possession of Mr. J. Rich." Efforts to build a synagogue were officially suspended.

A slender thread of hope for keeping the building effort alive remained in the commitment of a few members who had signed promissory notes as pledges payable over ten years. On the basis of the pledges, some of the members suggested that, despite the recession, the congregation build a *mikveh* (ritual bath) on the lot. The following month, December 1874, Nathan Gotthelf took the lead in soliciting subscriptions for building a *mikveh* that would someday be incorporated into a synagogue structure. It was the need for a *mikveh* that kept the building plans alive.

Washington, along with the rest of the nation, remained trapped in the throes of the depression throughout 1874. Compelled to institute economies, the congregation weighed each expenditure carefully and reduced wages. Even though plans for a new building had only been suspended, not abandoned, many members lost faith in the goal. At the beginning of 1875, some refused to pay their pledges, and others who had already paid them wanted their money refunded. In addition, the congregation was beset by internal disputes. The sexton resigned and there were problems with the hazzan.

It soon became clear that unless there was some progress in planning for the future, the entire enterprise would collapse. The more optimistic members noted that the centennial of the United States would take place in another year. Since the accompanying celebrations would undoubtedly focus on Washington, they reasoned that the enthusiasm and tourism that would be engendered would make it easier to raise funds. A new synagogue would be a significant feature in the commemoration of the nation's one hundredth birthday.

A special meeting in January 1875 resolved to revive the efforts to build a synagogue despite the bleak economic outlook. A rejuvenated committee lost little time in consulting with architects and builders. At the congregation's quarterly meeting in April 1875, the committee reported that the firm of A. Davis and Son had offered to build a synagogue "at a cost (not including gas fixtures and gas) of $7,500.00 taking payments therefore in notes of $50.00 monthly with 8 percent interest per year."[10]

The indefatigable Selig Goldstein, again taking the leadership, called for a nonbinding vote to ascertain the sense of the membership, and challenged the members to prove their commitment by accepting an immediate increase in dues to $1.50 each month, to be increased further to $2.00 per month once construction began. Seventeen yeas and five nays gave way to unanimous consent. Goldstein's driving enthusiasm persuaded the members to revive the building campaign.

Having gained the congregation's support, Goldstein pressed onward. He moved the acceptance of the proposal submitted by the builder on condition that no payment be made until the completion of the building. The congregation approved the motion and authorized the committee to employ an attorney to draw up a contract with the builder. Max Kleinman, listed in the city directory as a draftsman, was engaged to draw up the plans for a suitable structure. Kleinman charged the congregation $20 for his services.[11]

The next month, Goldstein reported that he had secured a $1,000 mortgage on the lot and submitted a bill for $1.75 for expenses. (Money was still precious; small change was anything but petty cash.) Once again, the committee sought funds in Richmond, Philadelphia, and New York. The president, John Boyer, together with Nathan Gotthelf and Selig Goldstein, seeking to aid the fund-raising effort, solicited and received an endorsement from the District of Columbia's commissioners.

Sadly, the economy had not yet recovered, and as a result the drive for funds fell far short of what was needed to begin construction. Momentarily thwarted, but refusing to abandon his efforts, Goldstein scaled down the scope of his building plans to define a more affordable goal. He received permission from the congregation to consult with other builders to learn "at what cost and under what terms a plain one story edifice could be erected on our Lot," and, if satisfactory terms could not be reached, "to consult with the owner of our present place of worship to ascertain in what manner he can improve the premises."[12]

Goldstein placed the alternatives before the board in August: to refurbish their present rented quarters or to proceed with building a more modest structure than originally envisioned. He displayed the revised plans. Despite the shortfall in fund-raising and the grim economic climate, most of the congregation were eager to begin building.

The board decided to continue fund-raising but at the same time made contingency plans to remain in the rented quarters for as long as necessary. Once again the congregation petitioned Mr. Fagan, the landlord, to refurbish the loft and repair the leaking roof. Instead, realizing that a successful fund-raising campaign would eventually lose him his tenants, Fagan retaliated by ordering the congregation to vacate the premises within thirty days. Caught in a difficult situation, unable to build and unwilling to move, the board appointed a committee to negotiate a compromise with Fagan, at least to make "temporary arrangements in regard to the present retention of our synagogue."[13]

The landlord held the upper hand; there was no alternative but to accept his conditions. The High Holy Days were only a few weeks away. For the remainder of the lease, repairs and redecoration would be at the expense of the congregation; moreover, the monthly rent was increased to $25 from the previous $16.66. The year 1875 came to an end with the congregation deeper in debt than before and no closer to realizing its dream of a building a synagogue of its own.

### The Centennial Year

January 1, 1876, a Saturday, ushered in the year of the nation's centennial. Foul weather undermined any attempt at public celebration, but, in any event, little had been scheduled. Contrary to the congregation's assumptions, it was in Philadelphia, the first capital, and not in Washington, that the major commemorative events would take place. The official centennial year opened in Philadelphia with a procession of 100 horsemen and an elaborate exhibition.

The *Evening Star* complained that more should have been planned for Washington. Public buildings should have been illuminated, it wrote, and the Capitol should have been lighted. "The dome of the national building should at least send out its rays on the approach of the New Year."

In Washington, what few ceremonies there were, were modest ones: the bells of the Metropolitan Church pealed 100 times, and the cabinet gathered in the White House to receive greetings from foreign emissaries and representatives of the states.

Still confident that on Independence Day, July 4, Washington would reclaim its rightful place as the center for centennial celebrations, the congregation prepared for the occasion. The country's attention would surely focus on Washington on the nation's hundredth birthday, Goldstein reasoned. The District was bound to be the beneficiary.

There was little time to lose if a building was to be ready for consecration prior to July 4, 1876. The still undaunted optimists had the upper hand, convinced that the centennial year would solve their problems by making it easier to raise funds. Moreover, the dedication of a new synagogue would add a Jewish component to the national birthday celebration.

At a special meeting in February, a unanimous membership determined that "no unnecessary expenses should be incurred in fixing up the hall for Divine Service and that steps be taken for building at once a synagogue of our own on our Lot."[14]

Selig Goldstein proposed accepting an offer from another builder, Mr. J. Williams, to construct a "plain" synagogue without a basement for $2,700. To include a basement would bring the cost to $4,300. Plans and specifications had already been drawn. "What should it be," a confident chairman asked the enthusiastic assemblage, "With a basement or without a basement?"[15]

There was no money for either alternative, but such was the fervor that swept over the gathering that nothing less than a synagogue with a basement would be acceptable. The new building would, of course, include a *mikveh*.

Seeking to convert the enthusiasm to a tangible asset, Goldstein shrewdly called on those present to express their commitment in terms of financial support. The results reflected the extent of the members' wealth. The largest pledge, that of the building chairman, Selig Goldstein, was $25, matched by Levi Abraham. The two were the wealthiest members of the congregation. Another pledge of $20 was announced. Five members pledged $10, and seven, $5 each.

Williams's bid to build a synagogue with a basement was officially accepted. Construction was to begin immediately.

It was further agreed that the absentee members should be solicited and that dues be raised to $2 per month, to take effect on March 1, 1876, provided the congregation "commenced to build a synagogue." The landlord was to be approached once again to seek a month-to-month lease, and should he refuse, the synagogue would move to another rented hall.

As anticipated, Fagan was unbending; he stubbornly refused to accept a month-to-month agreement. An emergency meeting had no alternative but to ratify the temporary rental of another hall at 418 11th Street N.W. and the payment in advance of a month's rent of $30 to the owner, T. E. Waggaman.

In addition, the congregation approved engaging a carpenter to move the synagogue to the newly rented quarters, make minor repairs, and install the seats for a total charge of $18. The secretary was instructed to advertise in the *Evening Star* to announce the address of the new place of worship. It was now February 27, a mere five months from the July 4 deadline.

Fund-raising efforts resumed with frantic determination. Committees were appointed to canvass the city for support. Once again, this time successfully, funds were solicited from the Jewish communities of New York and Philadelphia, resulting in contributions of $300. More from hope than conviction, perhaps in desperation, the secretary was "instructed to communicate to the Trustees of Trinity Church, N. Y. City, our condition, and to ask for a donation in view of the fact that Jews in N. Y. City in 1711 contributed money for building of the Steeple as exhibited in a slip from N. Y. Herald."[16] * There is no record of any response.

Levi Abraham "was instructed to communicate to a certain benevolent party in New York who is reported to be wealthy and charitable and reported to be always ready to either advance or contribute money for building." The "benevolent party" was some one other than the renowned philanthropist Jacob Schiff, who had already contributed $50 at the urging of Adolphus Solomons. Unfortunately his identity cannot be ascertained, since within a few weeks, much to the shock of the community, death overtook Abraham.

In Levi Abraham's sudden death on April 28, 1876, the congregation suffered a severe loss that it could ill afford. Abraham was a prominent leader in the small Jewish community, one of the signatories of a petition to President Grant in behalf of ameliorating the

*According to David and Tamar de Sola Pool, *An Old Faith in the New World: Portrait of Shearith Israel, 1654–1954* (New York: Columbia University Press, 1955), p. 447, seven Jews, one of whom was the minister of Congregation Shearith Israel, donated a total of 5 pounds, 12 shillings, and 3 pence toward the building of the steeple.

lot of Russian Jews.[17] A founder of Adas Israel, and one of its wealthier members, he was also the owner of a precious Torah scroll which he had lent to the congregation. Saddened by his death, the board drew up a resolution of tribute to mark Abraham's contributions to the congregation and extend sympathy to the family.[18]

Sommers, the sexton, as a representative of the congregation, was designated to accompany Abraham's coffin to New York for burial. Selig Goldstein delivered the eulogy at memorial services on the conclusion of the seven-day *shiva* mourning period. The president notified the deceased's brother in Montreal that the congregation would be willing to place a symbol of remembrance to Abraham in the new synagogue for the payment of $50. There is no evidence that the offer was accepted. Nor did the surviving family redeem Abraham's pledge to the building fund.

Despite the disappointment over the loss of Abraham's leadership and pledge, there was no alternative but to continue fund-raising efforts. The rights to the "key" to open the doors of the new synagogue were sold to the highest bidder. The board excitedly acknowledged the gift of "a costly and beautiful mahogany cased revolver" to be raffled off for the benefit of the building fund.

In the meantime, the builder was making rapid progress. Once it was ascertained that the structure would be completed even earlier than the target date of July 4, the congregation notified the landlord that it would vacate his premises on or before June 1. Goldstein's building committee made plans for an elaborate dedication ceremony.

The building was indeed completed in sufficient time to be available for the celebration of the country's centennial. Its total cost, $4,800, was $500 over the bid, but significantly less than the earlier bid of $7,500 submitted by A. Davis and Son. The furnishings from the rented quarters, including the Torah scrolls, the *aron hakodesh* (holy ark), and the benches, were moved to the lower floor of the new building on May 31, 1876.

The congregation was ready to greet the nation's one hundredth birthday in its new building.

**The Dedication**

The dedication service began at 4:00 p.m. on Friday afternoon, June 9, 1876, and continued on Saturday morning. At a total cost of $15, the interior was decorated with flowers and evergreens; flags were draped over each side of the ark. A program book for the dedication was printed in New York. Printed invitations were distributed, along with admission tickets which would be required for entrance. The B'nai B'rith choir had been invited to sing, but was unable to accept.

Matting and carpets were placed at the entrance of the synagogue; the lawn just outside the synagogue's entrance was covered with grass sod. Two small sofas were arranged for seating the President and Vice-President of the United States, who had both been invited by Adolphus Solomons, the chairman of arrangements.

It was agreed that "during Friday evening, June 9, and Shabbes, June 10, no loud praying shall be allowed, and that the Chahzan shall conduct the whole of Divine Service, and that the .... *broiches* [blessings] and kaddish shall not be said in a loud voice." It had been further agreed that there would be no sale of honors or, as they called them, *Mizvahs,* during the Sabbath services, although anyone who wished to offer a gift in appreciation of receiving an aliyah would be welcome to do so prior to the delivery of the dedicatory sermon. Obviously, the congregants knew what was required for a dignified service, even though the standards were seldom observed on other occasions.

Adas Israel owned but one Torah scroll. To add ceremonial majesty, it requested the loan of additional scrolls from the Washington Hebrew Congregation. Unable to spare scrolls needed for its own Sabbath service, the Reform congregation arranged to lend one belonging a member, M. Goldsmith. Additional scrolls were borrowed from Rev. M. Brettenheimer and Mr. Ryttenburg, both of Baltimore, and from the Mount Sinai Congregation in Georgetown, a short-lived offshoot of the Washington Hebrew Congregation.

Rabbi George Jacobs, Isaac Leeser's successor at Congregation Beth El Emeth in Philadelphia, delivered the dedication sermon, and the Rev. Jannover, hazzan of the Henry Street Synagogue in New York City,* chanted the services. In his lifetime, Isaac Leeser had inspired the founders of Adas Israel; after his death in 1868, they looked to his successor for guidance.

Of Sephardi descent, Rabbi Jacobs was born in Kingston, Jamaica, and came to the United States in 1854, settling in Richmond before being called to Philadelphia in 1869, the year of the Adas Israel secession. Like Leeser he was a founding member of the Jewish Publication Society and had aided in the revision of the English translation in the Szold-Jastrow prayer book.[19].

Friday's service lasted three hours. Even before the service began the synagogue filled to its capacity; latecomers were turned away at the doors. President Grant, his son, Ulysses, Jr., acting Vice President Senator Ferry of Michigan,‡ and other prominent citizens

*Probably Congregation Shaarey Zedek, now a major Conservative congregation.

‡Abe Shefferman's version of the congregation's history indicates that Vice President Schuyler Colfax attended the dedication, but Colfax served only in Grant's first term, 1869 to 1873. Another account names Grant's second-term Vice President, Henry Wilson, but Wilson died in 1875, and the dedication took place in 1876. Contemporary news reports indicate that Grant was accompanied by Senator Ferry of Michigan, who was acting President pro tem of the Senate.

were among those present. For Grant it was an opportunity to improve his relations with the Jewish community.

A procession of the congregation's leaders, led by Rabbi Jacobs, solemnly carried the Torah scrolls from the lower floor up the rounded staircase to the sanctuary. Knocking on the closed doors of the sanctuary, the rabbi read Psalm 118, "*Pitchu lee shaarey zedek* . . Open unto us the gates of righteousness, that we may enter through them." The cantor responded, "This is the gate of the Lord; the righteous shall enter therein," and the president of the congregation opened the doors. The procession circled the sanctuary seven times, then approached the ark. As it reached the ark, the *ner tamid* (eternal light) was lit and the Torah scrolls were ceremoniously installed inside.[20]

After offering a prayer for the government, Rabbi Jacobs delivered a sermon which linked the dedication to the nation's centennial celebration. He took as his text the passage "This is none other than the house of God, and the gate of heaven," from the episode in Genesis in which Jacob, driven from his father's house, sleeps in the open wilderness with a stone for his pillow.[21] The same text would be used thirty years later by Rabbi Judah T. Loeb in his sermon at the cornerstone-laying ceremony for the new synagogue at 6th and I Streets in 1906.

After the sermon, John Boyer, the congregation's president, accepted the ceremonial keys, noting that this was the first Jewish house of worship in Washington to be built as a synagogue. (The Washington Hebrew Congregation's building, as mentioned in an earlier chapter, was originally a church.)

According to Simon Wolf, President Grant and the other dignitaries were among those who made contributions when the donation cards were handed out at the close of the dedication service. He observed that this was "the first instance in the history of American

Judaism" that a President and Vice President had attended a consecration service. The press reported: "The congregation is a small one, consisting of regular attendants, who are quite liberal, and with the assistance of many co-religionists here have contributed nobly to the building fund."[22]

Following the dedication, the congregation expressed its appreciation to the guest clergy by presenting Rabbi Jacobs with a silver Kiddush cup for which it had allocated $33.40, and Hazzan Jannover with a gold-headed cane, which had cost $15.

### The Structure

Summarizing the ceremonies in the *Jewish Messenger*, Simon Wolf described the new building.

> On the lower floor is a commodious *shule* room (for daily services), classrooms, and Mikva. Above is the *shule* which is approached by winding stair-cases on each side and which terminate in a vestibule. The finish of the walls is plain white and the wood work is pine and black walnut, oiled.[23]

Many years later, Wolf's meticulous description of the sanctuary enabled the restoration committee to recapture and restore the original appearance of the structure, including its circular staircase.*

The gallery for women surrounding the side and rear walls was supported by simple columns. The sanctuary could seat 150 men and 125 women in the rows of hand-hewn wooden benches, only one of which was returned to its place after being recovered from the church which later acquired them.

The distinctive feature of the synagogue was its *aron hakodesh*, the sacred ark for the Torah scrolls. It was a semicircular wooden bay

*Armed with Wolf's article, Evelyn Greenberg, representing the Washington Jewish Historical Society, was able to guide the architect and the contractor in duplicating the circular staircases during the restoration of the synagogue.

protruding from the exterior of the rear, or eastern, wall of the synagogue and flush with the interior wall. Its position on the eastern wall enabled worshippers to face toward Jerusalem during their prayers in accordance with time honored-tradition. The *aron hakodesh* combined Federal and Victorian details in its design, a classical pediment and Victorian side braces. The furnishings on the *bima* included a reading desk, a semicircular rail, and chairs for the officiants and officers.

Topping the roof was a small cupola to provide ventilation. A wrought-iron fence surrounded the building. A semicircular stone inscribed with the words "Adas Israel Congregation" in Hebrew, and "Erected 5636 (1876)" in English, was set in the pinnacle position high above the central window fronting the entrance. It was this inscription that enabled the historian Evelyn Greenberg to "rediscover" the old structure after it was virtually forgotten in the midst of Washington's neglected downtown area.

The Adas Israel synagogue has been described as an example of early American architecture, its unique combination of Federal and American Jewish folk design reflecting the congregants' desire to blend with the surrounding environment. Evaluating the design, Wolf von Eckhardt, a prominent present-day authority on architecture, observed, "All the more remarkable, if you consider that the synagogue was built at a time when many Jewish congregations began building elaborate temples adorned with Romanesque or Byzantine domes."[24]

Evidence of European influence was uncovered by Evelyn Greenberg when she attended a 1985 conference on liturgical architecture in Jerusalem, where she heard one of the speakers describe the restoration of an eighteenth-century synagogue in the small German town of Michelbach in the state of Wurttemberg. She was amazed to discover from photographs of the German synagogue that it too had a protruding bay for the Torah ark, a clear forerunner of one of the most distinctive features of the Adas Israel synagogue. Greenberg's research of several rural South German synagogues, either too useful or too insignificant to have been destroyed by the Nazis, revealed other details of facade and interior design similar to the design of Adas Israel. Greenberg noted from her study of their U.S. citizenship applications that the majority of the founders of Adas Israel came from Germany's south, the area of Baden, Hess, and Wurttemberg, where several synagogues with protruding bays were located. She concluded that the founders of Adas Israel had transposed from Germany to America not only the religious practices but the architectural designs of their native synagogues, which they were determined to replicate in their new homeland. Concludes Mrs. Greenberg, "They built something similar, yet it emerged a very American and very special Washington building." The design was a reflection of the simple and sincere faith of the early Jewish community in Washington as well as of their determination to blend the style and forms of contemporary American culture with the faith of their ancestors.[25]

On July 3, 1876 the city was fittingly bedecked to celebrate the nation's Centennial Independence Day. There would be fireworks and a mammoth parade. Adas Israel was prepared.

Philadelphia vied with Washington for ceremonial honors. With its Centennial Exhibition, Philadelphia claimed recognition as the nation's first capital. Many Washingtonians took the excursion train to Philadelphia, where celebrations far more elaborate than those in Washington were scheduled. "But," said the *Washington Evening Star*, "enough will be left to make things lively tomorrow."

The *Star* announced that the Rev. L. Stern would deliver the sermon at a service of Thanksgiving at the "8th Street Synagogue" on July 4.

At Adas Israel, Simon Wolf delivered the "oration" at services held in the new synagogue to honor the nation's first hundred years.

**The Movable Sanctuary**

The building on 6th and G Streets served the congregation for thirty years, from 1876 to 1906, when an expanded membership and the shifting pattern of Jewish residence rendered it inadequate. In May 1905, the congregation sold the synagogue together with an adjacent house and lot, which it had earlier acquired, to Steven Gatti for $14,000. Purchased as an investment, the Gatti family leased the building to the St. Sophia Greek Orthodox Church* and later to an Evangelical Church of God.

In 1946, the structure became a grocery and restaurant operated by Michael Kontos. The lower floor, where once there had been classrooms and the weekday chapel, was now the Purity Carry-out Shop. A large neon sign advertised the specialty of the house: barbecued pork. The second floor, which previously had been the sanctuary, was the storeroom. The janitor used the bay of the *aron hakodesh* as a closet to store his brooms and cleaning supplies.

In 1966, the building and its environs were scheduled for demolition as part of an extensive urban renewal program. Energized by the history-sensitive Evelyn Greenberg, the Jewish Historical Society of Greater Washington, with the active support of Adas Israel members, set out to save the old synagogue from the destructive threat of the wrecker's ball.

The group discovered that the building was directly in the path of the new subway being planned by Metro, the Washington Area Transit Authority, which had acquired the entire city block, including the synagogue, as the site for its planned headquarters. Metro authorities refused to consider a proposal to save the synagogue.

*Today, the St. Sophia Greek Orthodox Cathedral on 36th Street and Massachusetts Avenue N.W.

To gain the support of District of Columbia and federal agencies, Evelyn Greenberg submitted a description of the building's history and architecture to the District Fine Arts Commission. On March 17, 1967, the Joint Landmarks Committee of the National Capital Planning Commission and the Fine Arts Commission placed the building on its Washington Landmarks List. The designation alone, though ultimately of importance, was not enough to save the building from demolition.

Mobilized to thwart Metro's plans, the National Capital Planning Commission raised the synagogue to a higher category by listing it in the National Register of Historic Places, elevating it to the status of "a landmark of importance contributing significantly to Washington's cultural heritage." The old Adas Israel thus became only the second Jewish house of worship to be so designated, the other being the Touro Synagogue in Newport, Rhode Island. "The designation caused quite a stir at subway headquarters," reported Evelyn Greenberg. Demolition had to be delayed.

Metro offered to donate the building to a properly constituted guardian but insisted that it was unable to expend funds for its preservation or removal. A joint committee of the Jewish Historical Society and Adas Israel, under the chairmanship of Rabbi Stanley Rabinowitz, met on May 20, 1969, to consider plans for saving the building by moving it to another site. They investigated several sites as well as procedures for moving the building, only to discover that privately owned lots were prohibitive in price, as were costs for shoring up and moving a century-old building. Massive public funding would be required.

After extensive negotiations with District and federal authorities, an agreement to save the building was reached in July 1968, with these terms:

1. The D.C. government would provide a site on a triangular remnant of land left over from freeway construction on the corner of 3rd and G Streets, three blocks from the original site.

2. The City Council would apply for a Housing and Urban Development historic preservation grant to cover half of the cost of moving and restoration; the Jewish community would be responsible for the other half.

3. The building and the site would remain government property but would be leased on a long-term basis to the Jewish group at a symbolic rental.

There were still obstacles to overcome. A ruling held that since the District of Columbia's legal code contained no provision for historic preservation activity, the District lacked the right to give away the land. Moreover, the Federal Highway Administration's Bureau of Public Roads had provided 90 percent of the purchase price of the land and, in principle, was opposed to parting with even a small parcel of land for any use other than highway purposes.

It required an act of Congress to clear away the legal obstacles. Representative Sam Steiger of Arizona introduced H.R. 10366 on April 21, 1969, "A Bill To provide for the lease or conveyance of certain real property in the District of Columbia to the Jewish Historical Society of Greater Washington." The bill, which had the support of the House District Committee, was signed into law by President Richard Nixon in September 1969, the congregation's centennial year.

Eager to proceed with subway construction, Metro complained that Adas Israel was delaying its timetable; it set a deadline for removal, December 1969. On December 18, 1969, the 270-ton building, belted and braced, was lifted onto a 28-wheel, three-section dolly and was pulled through the city streets by two tractors. It moved slowly and majestically down the three blocks to its new setting and, three hours later, came to rest, in perfect alignment, on its previously prepared new foundation.

The seemingly impossible had been accomplished. Mayor Walter E. Washington announced a Department of Housing and Urban

Development grant of $100,000, to be matched by funds from the community. The old Adas Israel would undergo restoration and rejuvenation. The original plans were carefully followed, not from drawings, but from newspaper descriptions. A new ornamental iron fence surrounding the synagogue and its courtyard was designed by the firm of Fred S. Gichner, patterned after the fence surrounding the 400-year-old synagogue on the island of Rhodes in the eastern Mediterranean.

The *mikveh* in the synagogue, built in accordance with traditionally defined specifications, was uncovered when the structure was moved to its new location. It consisted of a wood-framed brick pool with a lead-zinc liner, and was recessed into the lower floor in a rear corner of the building. The planners had ensured privacy by placing a private entrance on G Street with a small antechamber to serve as a dressing room. The *mikveh* continued in use until 1911 even after the building was sold.* It was the need for a *mikveh* that had kept the building campaign alive after hopes for a new synagogue had been virtually abandoned.

Since the building would remain District property, it could no longer be a formal synagogue but could be used for cultural purposes. It was leased for $1 per year to become a Jewish museum. A gift of $50,000 from Albert and Lillian Small endowed the museum, which was installed on the ground floor. Albert Small's father, Isadore, had been a vice-president of the congregation under Simon Oppenheimer, a long-tenured president.

*The *mikveh* was rediscovered early in December 1969 when the building was being readied for its removal to 3rd and G Streets. Its discovery explained a previously puzzling architectural idiosyncrasy: the windows of one part of the lower floor were not aligned with those of the upper story. Evidently the windows had been arranged to provide greater privacy for the users of the *mikveh*. Mrs. Pearl Kipnis, who at age ninety-two was the last surviving person known to have used it, identified the mikveh. She attested to its use as late as 1911. While nothing in the minutes indicates that the mikveh continued to be used after the sale of the building, this still remains a possibility.

The restored building was rededicated on June 22, 1975, ninety-nine years after its original consecration. The second floor sanctuary, now air-conditioned, would be available for cultural events, and even an occasional wedding service. Management is administered by the Jewish Historical Society of Greater Washington.*

*The Committee organized to rescue the building included Bernard Glassman, Evelyn Greenberg, and Samuel Holland, who were later joined by Henry Brylawski, president of the Jewish Historical Society, Leon Brown, Hyman J. Cohen, Esther Coopersmith, Morris Kanfer, Joseph Mendelson, president of Adas Israel, Bernard I. Nordlinger, Donald Wolpe, and Rabbi Stanley Rabinowitz, as well as other members of the Synagogue and the Society who were helpful in the fund raising program.

# 9

## TORAH, WORSHIP, AND STUDY

### The Quest for Torah

Three years after its inception in 1869, the founding members of Adas Israel had only the framework of a congregation but not the synagogue structure it needed to survive; it lacked even the Torah scroll essential to Jewish worship. No longer dependent upon volunteers, the congregation employed a sexton and a hazzan to lead the services and read the Torah, but the scroll from which he read had to be borrowed.

Torah scrolls were not readily available. In the New World, scribes skilled in the art of inscribing scrolls were even more rare than congregations. No synagogue possessed a surplus of scrolls; most of those in use had been brought to America by the migrating families who owned them.

To serve worshippers with dignity required at least two scrolls; three would be better.* Adas Israel was determined to obtain at least one scroll of its own, but until it could raise enough money to buy one, it was forced to depend upon the occasional member who had arrived in this country with a precious European scroll among his cherished possessions.

The congregation borrowed one scroll from Mr. J. Davidson in 1871; a year later, another was borrowed from Levi Abraham. With an appropriate expression of gratitude, the board resolved "that a

*One scroll suffices for the services on most Sabbaths; two are needed for certain Sabbaths and for festival services; some sacred days require three.

guarantee of $150.00 to be signed by the Trustees and the President of the Congregation, be made out by the Secretary and handed to Mr. Abraham for the safekeeping of the scroll."[1]

Meanwhile, the congregation commissioned a scribe in Germany to prepare a Torah scroll. In 1872, Nathan Gotthelf, chairman of the Torah committee, proudly announced to the board that the scroll had arrived and arrangements should be made immediately for its formal reception and dedication.[2]

Gotthelf proposed Sunday, Rosh Chodesh Kislev, the first day of the month of Chanukah, for the formal dedication. A six-person committee proceeded to arrange the dedication, which, it was agreed, would take place at a festive banquet appropriate for such an auspicious occasion.[3] The Torah would cost $165.50.

Anticipating the arrival of the commissioned scroll, Levi Abraham requested that his scroll be returned to him, whereupon, at a special board meeting called for the purpose, it was agreed "that the request be granted and the scroll returned to the loaner with thanks."[4]

Adas Israel's pride at owning a Torah scroll was short-lived, for soon after its arrival the president sorrowfully reported that it was not in a "serviceable condition" and steps would have to be taken, "at the expense of the congregation," to rectify its disqualifying deficiencies.[5] A careful examination had revealed a number of scribal errors, and until they were corrected, the scroll could not be used. A Torah scroll contains 304,805 letters, handwritten on parchment. A mistake in a single word renders the scroll unfit for use.

Nathan Gotthelf, who was now Adas Israel's president, felt responsible for having commissioned the defective scroll and offered to place his own precious Torah scroll at the congregation's disposal. He promised to lend it for congregational use for "as long as he shall remain a member thereof, free of charge, under a guarantee of $100 from the Trustees of the Congregation for its safe keeping."[6]

There was no alternative but to return the defective scroll to the scribe in Germany "from whence it came, for verification and correction." Gotthelf himself took the scroll to Baltimore for shipment to Bremen. In the meantime, the congregation relied on Gotthelf's scroll.

Unfortunately, as the members soon discovered, Gotthelf's membership would not be of long duration. Dissatisfied with the quality of Jewish life in Washington and pessimistic about the future of Judaism in the United States, Gotthelf, founder and second president of the congregation, decided to return to Germany. The congregation could ill afford to lose him, since he was one of its more learned members and frequently served as cantor and Torah reader; moreover he was the owner of one of the only two privately owned Torah scrolls available for its use.

Upon learning of Gotthelf's intended resignation, Philip Peyser offered a resolution to the board: "Whereas this Congregation has for its use but 1 Scroll, and Mr. N. Gotthelf being in possession of 1 Scroll, which it is believed he may not have any use for, be it therefore resolved, that a committee to be composed of 2 members of the Board be appointed to wait upon Mr. Gotthelf, asking him for the loan of such Scroll; and in case of refusal, this committee shall be empowered to procure a Scroll by loan or otherwise."[7]

Pending the conclusion of negotiations with Gotthelf for his "loan or otherwise," Selig Goldstein, the future leader of the building campaign, announced to the board that a friend in Baltimore, Mr. Ryttenburg, was willing to loan the congregation his personal scroll for use until the High Holy Days. Together with Davidson's scroll, this would complete the congregation's requirement for two scrolls.

The situation, however, was far from stable. At the June meeting, Davidson requested the return of his scroll. As yet the negotiations with Gotthelf pertaining to his scroll had made little headway, although Gotthelf reported "progress in regard to the scroll sent abroad and owned by Congregation."[8]

With the return of Davidson's scroll the congregation was left only with Gotthelf's, which would soon be surrendered to its departing owner. Once again, Levi Abraham made his scroll available to the congregation for the limited period of one year with the usual $150 guarantee.

Weary of depending upon borrowed scrolls, the congregation intensified its efforts to acquire a Torah scroll of its own. Finally, in July 1874, it received a letter from a dealer in New York reporting that he had a proper Torah scroll for sale. Following negotiations, the New York dealer, H. Sakolski, "Importer of and Dealer In HEBREW BOOKS at No. 53 Division Street, New York," shipped his scroll to the congregation along with a bill for $100. Such was the price of a Torah scroll in 1874; in 1990, it could be as much as $25,000.

Having been once burned, the officers were cautious about paying for the scroll until they had an opportunity to examine it for possible defects. They informed Sakolski that they were willing to purchase his scroll for $100 and that $50 would be paid forthwith, except that "the balance will be kept back for correctness of the Sephar [*sefer*, i.e., scroll] for a period of six months for which a guarantee will be furnished him by the Trustees, and that he in return has to furnish a guarantee that in case the Sephar be unserviceable that the money already paid will be returned to the Congregation."[9]

Sakolski responded:

Aug. 20th, 1874

Dear Sir,

Yours of the 19th inst. was duly received and in answer beg to state that I can not abide to your proposition namely: to let the Sepher Thora with you for examination for three months. My word is sufficient guaranty that the Sepher is in good order and devoid of any of the errors of which you write.

If you would have asked the conditions at the time of purchase my answer would have been the same.

If you are willing to remit the full cost of the Sepher I am satisfied otherwise I must ask you to send the Sepher back to me with expenses prepaid.

I am

Truly yours

H. Sakolski

P. S. The cost of a good woolen talis is twelve dollars.

After extensive deliberation, the board agreed to buy the scroll for $100, with Levi Abraham pledging his own Torah "as security for the correctness of the Sepher."[10]

Purchased, the Sakolski scroll was joyously dedicated at a banquet to honor its acquisition on October 4, 1874, the eve of Simchat Torah. We have no reason to doubt that this Torah scroll remains in use to this day.

The congregation still awaited the scroll it had returned to Germany for correction; it would then be almost free of the need to borrow others. Finally, a letter arrived from a Rabbi Bainberger in Wurzburg, dated May 11, 1875, informing the congregation that its Torah scroll was *pasul* (unfit for use) and beyond repair. Angered, the congregation sought "to ascertain the whereabouts of Mr. Gruneberg, the Sopher [scribe] who wrote the scroll."[11] The offending scribe was either incompetent or a fraud, probably the latter, since he was not to be found. The money paid him was lost. The congregation, already beset with financial problems, could ill afford either the loss of the funds or of the scroll.

Soon thereafter, Nathan Gotthelf, after thanking the congregation for the gracious resolution of tribute which they had presented to him, tendered his resignation as a member, to take effect on November 1, 1875. As his gift, he returned the "certificate of two shares due him . . . on account of making advance payment for building of the Synagogue." Gotthelf's Torah scroll remained a tempting prize which the congregation was eager to capture. After some private discussion, a special meeting was called "to make arrangements for settlement of indebtedness to Mr. Gotthelf and other matters."[12]

The "other matters" included a loan of $50 which Gotthelf had made to the congregation. Gotthelf generously agreed to accept repayment in monthly installments of $2, and further, offered to sell his precious Torah scroll to the congregation for $80 payable on or before January 1, 1876. Delighted, the board eagerly accepted his generous proposals, subject to ratification by the membership. Pending ratification, the Torah scroll was to remain with the congregation for regular use, with an appropriate guarantee by the trustees insuring the scroll "against loss or destruction, but in case the Congregation will not buy it, or is unable to pay for it on or before January 1, 1876, then the Sephar shall be delivered to him, free of all charge to him, at his future residence in Hanover."[13]

At its next regular meeting, in November, the congregation postponed approving a commitment to purchase Gotthelf's scroll, but agreed to appoint a committee of four to collect funds for its acquisition. In December, the board granted the committee more time to solicit contributions, for in that month, what with expenses of $40 for a stove and pipes for heating, $3 for fuel, and $2 for the promised monthly payment to Gotthelf, not enough money remained to pay Gotthelf for his scroll.

January 1, 1876 fell on a Sabbath and, therefore, no action could be taken to meet the agreed deadline for completing the purchase of the scroll. The next day, at a regular meeting of the congregation, it was reported that only $30 had been collected for the purchase, $50 short of the agreed price. A motion made by H. H. Sommers, the shochet, that the scroll be returned to Gotthelf failed to carry; the congregation was loath to part with something so rare and precious. For reasons known only to himself, Sommers tried repeatedly to thwart the purchase of Gotthelf's scroll.

On motion of Raphael Sanger, the congregation finally approved the purchase of the scroll for $80, as agreed, and informed Gotthelf "that the Congregation will endeavor to raise an additional sum besides the amount thus far collected by subscription as soon as can conveniently be done, and also that the proceeds of a Picnic shall be used to buy the Sephar."[14]

The shochet, Sommers, considering himself an expert Torah reader, tried once again to block the purchase. He moved that the scroll be examined by a "*Bal Masgieh*" (i.e., a mashgiach, or "expert"*). Since Sommers himself had read from Gotthelf's scroll for over a year without uncovering any defect, the board tabled the resolution.

In February 1876, one month after the deadline, the payment for the Gotthelf Torah remained on the agenda as unfinished business: "The Secretary was instructed to communicate with Mr. N. Gotthelf that we will try to raise the additional $35.00 to complete the purchase of his Sephar as soon as possible." An additional $15 had been paid in January.

*The term is usually applied to one who supervises food preparation. In this case it means a knowledgable person.

Two months later came the shock of the sudden death of Levi Abraham, who, like Gotthelf, was one of the more knowledgeable members as well as the owner of one of the two Torah scrolls used by the congregation. In due course, a letter was received from Mr. I. Abraham, the executor of Levi Abraham's estate, who asked that "the Scroll now in possession of the Congregation be returned, to be sent as per his last will and testament to New York City, and that the bill for any indebtedness of the estate shall be presented to the Probate Court." Abraham had bequeathed his precious scroll to the Beth Hamidrash Hagadol on the Lower East Side of Manhattan, and the New York congregation soon requested its delivery.[15]

The Beth Hamidrash Hagadol, literally, the Great Synagogue, once one of New York City's largest and most distinguished Orthodox congregations, had been founded in 1852 by Russian and Polish Jews. It moved to 78 Allen Street in 1856 and still functions today in its original building, although with greatly reduced activity and membership.

Distressed at the threatened loss of both the Torah scroll and Abraham's building pledge, the board appointed a committee, with Morris Cohen, the secretary, as chairman, to call upon Abraham's executor "for the purpose of effecting a settlement relative to the Scroll belonging to the estate of the deceased and the indebtedness due to this congregation."

Cohen reported to the board in July that the committee had met with Abraham's widow and "thought it proper and right to return the Scroll, but no written obligation could be exacted from Mrs. Abraham that she would settle the donations promised by her deceased husband."

The board concluded that it had no choice but to deliver the scroll to the New York synagogue. They felt aggrieved. They had honored Levi Abraham's memory with appropriate memorial services and had sent an escort to accompany his coffin to New York. He had been an active participant in the founding and growth of the congregation and, with evident sincerity, had made a pledge to the building fund. Their attempt to reach a compromise settlement with the widow had been rejected. Angered by her refusal to honor her late husband's pledge, and distressed at the loss of the scroll whose availability they had taken for granted, the board expressed their frustration by adopting a resolution declaring that neither "Mrs. Abraham nor any member of her family in the City, not be allowed to rent or occupy a seat in this Synagogue unless she makes arrangement to settle the promise made by her deceased husband for the donation of certain money for building our Synagogue."[16]

The need to acquire additional Torah scrolls now became more urgent than ever. After Abraham's scroll was sent to New York, the congregation was left with the one purchased from Sakolski and another, acquired but not paid for, from Gotthelf. Little wonder, then, that Torah scrolls were a major item on the agenda at successive meetings.

Over the next few months, an additional part-payment of $15 was sent to Gotthelf. In November 1876, one year after his departure from Washington, Gotthelf found it necessary to write to the congregation "asking for a settlement of the amount due him ($20.00) for the scroll bought of him." At a meeting in January 1877, one year after the congregation had promised payment in full, "The Secretary was instructed to notify Mr. N. Gotthelf that on account of the heavy drainage in our treasury, we ask for an extension of sixty days, wherein we would pay him the balance due him."

The remaining debt owed to Gotthelf was eventually paid, and the Gotthelf Torah remains in the possession of the synagogue today. Additional Torah scrolls were acquired over the years by purchase, gift, or testamentary bequest, until today, Adas Israel, like most established congregations, owns sufficient Torah scrolls to provide for its several auxiliary High Holiday services and even to lend to other congregations temporarily in need.

One Torah scroll was loaned to a new Reform congregation which used it on Friday nights, only to mar its parchment with spilled wine, since it was their custom to recite the Sabbath Eve Kiddush over the open scroll. The board, concerned as much with protecting Jewish custom as with protecting its Torah scrolls, thereupon ruled that Adas Israel would no longer lend its Torah scrolls to congregations that read from them on Friday night,

Two silver-and-velvet-encased Sephardi Torah scrolls from the Eliyahu Hanavi (Elijah the Prophet) Synagogue in Alexandria, Egypt, were acquired as the gift of Mr. and Mrs. Robert Rothstein in 1963. The scrolls had been confiscated by the Nasser government after the Suez invasion in 1956, and had been spirited out of Egypt under mysterious circumstances. Although the Egyptian scrolls are not used during services because the ink has flaked off some of the letters, it has become the custom to display them in the sanctuary on the last day of Passover and on Kol Nidre Eve.*

In 1986, two scrolls were acquired by purchase from an Arizona congregation, which found itself with a surplus of scrolls and in need of funds, at a cost of $8,000 each, substantially more than the $100 paid to Sakolski for the first purchased scroll.

### Worship

In their worship services, the founders of Adas Israel, intent on retaining the forms they recalled from their synagogues in Germany, enshrined the familiar procedures in their constitution for

*A Torah scroll becomes blemished when the ink of the handwritten letters flakes off, thereby rendering a word or a key letter illegible. Lack of use or improper storage contributes to a scroll's deterioration. Relettering, which must be done by a skilled scribe, can sometimes be as costly as commissioning a new scroll.

what they believed would be for all time by restricting the possibility of modification.

It was Manassas Oppenheimer, the first sexton and the president in 1881, who, fearful of the corrosive influences of outside forces, insisted upon the inclusion of the clause safeguarding the ritual against change. According to his son Simon, his father "was conservative to the extreme in his religious views and was bitterly opposed to anything which savored of reform."[17]

The board assigned roles for High Holy Day worship by formal nomination and election. In 1872, Manassas Oppenheimer chanted the morning service "from commencement to *Shacharit*" for both days of the New Year and the Day of Atonement. (The secretary used the English terms to designate the days and the Hebrew script to denote the portions of the service and the role.) Nathan Gotthelf was named to chant *Shacharit* on the first day of New Year and the Day of Atonement, and Levi Abraham, on the second day. Rev. Joseph A. Cohen, the hazzan/shochet, read the Torah and chanted all the other parts of the service. Mr. Sommers was nominated to be the "bal Tekiah" (*ba'al tekiah*, the one who sounds the shofar).

A difference of opinion arose before the holidays that year. Mr. Poppers "protested against the introduction of a choir during divine service." In disagreement, Philip Peyser moved "that the Congregation establish during divine service a choir, to be composed of male grown and youth voices." The subject was tabled. Ultimately, a male choir was introduced.

Each holiday commanded the board's earnest concern. In preparing for Sukkot (Tabernacles), a committee had to be sent to Baltimore on an emergency mission to replace two *etrogim* and *lulavim*.* Passover required an allocation of funds for "scrubbing the

*The *etrog* (citron) and *lulav* (palm branch entwined with myrtle and willow leaves) are an important part of the Sukkot ritual.

synagogue." For Shavuot (Pentecost), precious funds were allocated to decorate the synagogue with the floral greens appropriate to the season.

The board did its best to preserve the dignity and restraint that were characteristic of German Jewish worship. Each year they attempted, though in vain, to control the hilarity associated with the Purim service, regularly adopting resolutions calling for proper decorum during the reading of the *Megillah*. There were repeated attempts to maintain decorum. Rules addressed the need to control the behavior of children: "neither food of any description, carriages for children, and children under 6 years shall not be allowed to enter the building."[18]

Members could be fined 25 cents for "noisy disturbances" during the services. Ushers were appointed "to withhold persons from going in and out of the synagogue" during the reading of the Torah on Simchat Torah. In 1877, Lieutenant J. F. Kelley of the Metropolitan Police was tendered "a vote of thanks for causing to be placed at the Synagogue an officer during divine service for the recent holidays."

Some expressed their unhappiness at the confusion that accompanied the recitation of the priestly blessings; each Kohen chanted at his own pace and, worse, in his own key. Selig Goldstein suggested that a single "*Kauhen* be nominated and elected" to recite the blessings while the other Kohanim would simply echo the responses. The Kohanim were ordered to rehearse the procedure, but the procedure failed the first time it was tried; the other Kohanim objected.

The members persisted in the effort to preserve the familiar customs in every detail. They instructed Mr. Shlomberg, the shochet–Torah reader, on the precise manner in which he was to open the ark for the Torah reading. Even after they hired a trained hazzan, they instructed him on the "proper conduct" of services and the "acceptable manner in which he should wear the Tallit." The first hazzan, Joseph A. Cohen, was told that the congregation questioned "the propriety of his reciting the entire Shema [written in Hebrew in the minutes] prayer orally."[19]

Jacob Voorsanger who was to earn the congregation's respect as its hazzan-rabbi nonetheless would be required to accept instruction on how to comply with the accepted procedures. The president and the vice-president called upon Voorsanger to inform him that when he got to the Kedushah in the repetition of the Amidah prayer, he should first chant "'*Naa-a-a-rizzi-cha*' till '*ve oh mar*' [the first sentence] but the Congregation shall say entirely afterwards the whole '*Keducheh.*'"[20]

The Roedelheim prayer book remained the official prayer book of Adas Israel just as it had been in the in the Washington Hebrew Congregation. Initially, the preferred language of discourse was German, but after the dedication of the synagogue in 1876, English was recognized. The constitution allowed the prayer for the government to be repeated in English. At meetings, members could speak either German or English. Important resolutions and published obituaries were written or printed in German as late as 1890.

Honors on the holidays were assigned by rotation when they were not auctioned. Ritual procedures were enforced by levying fines for minor violations and by the threat of expulsion for a serious breach. Maintenance of the daily minyan was a constant concern. Members were obligated to attend the daily service on a rotating basis. Those who failed to honor this obligation were liable to be denied aliyot for one year. In 1877, this punishment was replaced by a fine of 50 cents for each absence.

Harry Friedman, otherwise unidentified, attended the morning service with such regularity that he was elected an honorary member; they needed him. In 1897, the drop in membership was so severe that Edward Hartogensis moved that "members wishing a minyan at jahrzeit should give 3 days notice to the president who will arrange for 15 members to be present."[21]

To assure the basic quorum of ten for Sabbath morning services, five members were designated to attend in rotation. Because of the small membership and the inevitable conflict between the hours of worship and store keepers' hours, it was necessary to impose monetary fines for failure to respond to the rotating Sabbath morning assignment.

A Bar Mitzvah was an occasion for proud celebration. The first child to become Bar Mitzvah at Adas Israel was the son of B. Burnstine in December 1874. The last child to mark his Bar Mitzvah in the 6th and G Street structure, prior to the move to 6th and I Street, was Joseph Blumenthal, who went on to become the congregation's president in 1961.

A few members of the congregation performed most of the worship roles, such as reading the Torah, chanting the services, and sounding the shofar. Members selected for these functions were expected to be married and Sabbath observers. The Oppenheimers, Manassas and his son, Simon, were especially skilled, as was Nathan Gotthelf. Manassas Oppenheimer was called upon so often that he finally had to announce that he no longer had the strength to conduct the services. The board voted a resolution of thanks to Simon Oppenheimer, who would later become its president, for performing the duties of "Bal Thekeyeh" (*ba'al tekiah*, i.e., blowing the shofar) "so impressively."

Soon after the turn of the century, a local newspaper described the regimen of worship as well as the setting on 6th and G Streets.

> The house of worship proper is on the second story. It is neatly furnished and has a roomy gallery for the women of the congrega-

tion.... The windows are deep and high. Ceremonies are conducted in the eastern end of the hall, and there is a handsome reading desk erected there. The Ark of the Covenant, containing the Holy scrolls, from which the weekly reading of the law is made, is decorated in a becoming manner. A rail and circle of seats enclose the reading desk. Above the Ark of the Covenant is a reproduction of the two tables of the law, as revealed on Mount Sinai. The first words of each Commandment are lettered on each table.

Below is a painting of the priest's hands, held with the palms outward and the thumbs and forefingers touching—after the manner of the ancient Hebrew benediction.

Services are held here on Sabbaths from 9 to 11 o'clock and on special feast days from 9 to 12. Study and worship share the same premises. The basement of the building is used as a schoolroom for the children of the parish and also as a place of worship for the entire congregation on week days. Services are held downstairs every day in the Hebrew week except the Sabbath, when they take place upstairs in the chapel proper, at 6 o'clock in the morning.[22]

~ *Rose Hornstein* *Reflections*

On the High Holy Days, the officers and board members wore formal dress, cutaway coats, striped trousers and high-topped silk hats.

On Rosh Hashanah, the women and girls wore new fall outfits regardless of the weather, and there were no fans or air-conditioning. On Kol Nidre night most of the women wore white. On the afternoon of Yom Kippur there was the auction of the honors. Then, too, it was a custom for the young people to bring flowers to their mothers.[23]

~ *Joseph Blumenthal* *Reflections*

The benches in the shul were hard and the services quite boring. Since I did not understand Hebrew I was continually cautioned to stop fidgeting and be quiet.... I recall the Yom Kippur services with the Kohanim and the *duchanim* falling prostrate on the floor at the *Aleinu*.

Mother had prepared a lunch for brother and me which was left in the care of the janitor to be claimed later when we would walk to the park nearby to eat it. The balcony for the ladies, many fanning themselves with large palmetto fans to keep themselves cool, was occasionally visited by us boys, but we were soon ejected to return back to Dad.

Some members wanted the services and rituals modernized; the diehards fought for the Roedelheim prayer book and the old-type machzor.[24]

### Kashrut

Ritual slaughtering in accordance with the dietary laws has always been a matter of great importance for traditional Jews. Adas Israel's first shochet (ritual slaughterer) was Simon Mundheim, who had previously served the undivided Washington Hebrew Congregation, and whose integrity and qualifications were beyond question. When he retired at age seventy-two, after his hand became unsteady and he felt himself no longer able to perform the procedure properly, it became necessary to find a successor.

The board was hard pressed to find a trustworthy replacement for Mundheim, one who could submit the proper credentials—a *kabbalah* (certificate) attesting that he had demonstrated his knowledge of the laws of kashrut and had correctly performed ritual slaughter to the satisfaction of supervising experts.[25]

In September 1872 the congregation selected Rev. Joseph A. Cohen to serve not only as shochet but as hazzan, teacher, and Torah reader. As Cohen soon discovered, it was impossible to do justice to all of these responsibilities. His duties as teacher in the school interfered with the hours required for slaughtering. Moreover, parents objected when he appeared in class with blood on his clothing. In addition, Cohen had other problems which made him the center of controversy.

The congregation then engaged H. H. Sommers in 1873 and linked him to the butcher shop operated by Jacob Solomon; there were other butchers whom Sommers declined to serve. Solomon, the butcher, asked the members for a commitment to purchase meat from his shop alone so that he could estimate the amount necessary to serve his clientele. All present at a meeting in April 1873 agreed to his request except for three members "who refused to patronize the butcher, on account of the long distance they may have to walk to obtain it."[26] Since there was more than one butcher shop in the community in 1875, the shochet was told that "he is at liberty to slaughter for any butcher he may deem proper."[27]

Before long it became apparent that Sommers could not produce a valid *kabbalah*, which was enough to disqualify him in the opinion of at least half of the board. The other half was willing to rely on him merely on the basis of personal trust. The more meticulous upholders of kashrut prevailed. Sommers was discharged even before the completion of his first year of employment.

To find a shochet who could submit a valid *kabbalah*, the congregation advertised in New York's *Jewish Messenger*. The controversial Rev. Joseph A. Cohen, who earlier had been forced to resign, was to be the judge of the shochet's qualifications. An applicant, Mr. Lazarus, appeared upon the scene in 1874, promising to submit a valid *kabbalah*. After a conditional election, his credentials and election were confirmed in February 1874. Ignoring the sad lesson it had learned during Cohen's incumbency, the board again attempted to combine the posts of shochet and teacher, offering Lazarus an additional $20 per month if he would teach in the Hebrew school. Lazarus wisely declined the offer, but agreed to serve as Torah reader in addition to being the official shochet.

Relations with Lazarus soon deteriorated to the point where the congregation decided to replace him. It found a qualified and suitable candidate for the post in A. B. Shlomberg, who in September 1874 was elected to serve as both shochet and Torah reader for the monthly salary of $15. Shlomberg continued in the congregation's employ until 1877, a record-breaking term of three years.

**The Classroom**

One of Adas Israel's most troublesome problems was that of finding suitable instructors for its school. The responsibility for teaching the congregation's children was usually assigned to the hazzan and sometimes to the shochet. The fortunes of the school and the level of instruction changed as frequently as the change in clergy. Sometimes, when the congregation had no professional clergyman or had one who could not or would not function as a teacher, the school had to close. On occasion, volunteers were pressed into service. Eliezer Hartogensis volunteered to teach in the school during the summer of 1880.

When the school was operating, which was more often than not, members paid a tuition of $1 per month; nonmembers, $2. Children of the poor were admitted without charge. Maintaining the school required constant effort. Fund-raising on its behalf included picnics and "entertainments"; the one on Purim in 1880 was sponsored by "several young gentlemen."

Dr. Nathan Kaganoff offers an overview of the Adas Israel educational system.

> On January 12, 1873, a resolution was passed by the Board of Directors that an independent committee be appointed to look into the affairs of the religious school inasmuch as there was a report that there was a "failing in the number of scholars" and also that the

> school was "irregularly conducted at the time tuition should take place." A week later, a special meeting was held to arrange the affairs of the school, at which time the Committee recommended that certain rules and regulations be adopted "governing the school, the teacher, the parent or guardian, and scholar," and these were accepted by the congregation.
>
> The duties of the teacher required that he submit a monthly progress report on the status of every pupil. He was also to be present in the school ten minutes before classes began and remain until the session ended.
>
> The School Board of the congregation was charged with seeing that the schoolroom was properly heated and ventilated. In addition, the board was to furnish each child with the necessary books at the expense of the parents, and was to report semi-annually to the congregation concerning the progress of the school.
>
> Classes met from four to six in the afternoon from Monday through Thursday and on Saturday from two to four. The latter session was reserved for a review of the important subjects taught during the week preceding. Public examinations were provided for annually with prizes awarded to the outstanding students. In the spring of 1873, at the annual examination, a gold and silver medal were presented to the children in addition to the customary prizes.
>
> All corporal punishment was forbidden; the board reserved for itself the right to expel a child from the school for valid reasons.[28]

It was not until 1887 that the school began to show promise of being a reasonably effective educational enterprise. Thirty-one pupils were enrolled, requiring the purchase of twenty-five primary books and six "*tefillas*," or prayer books. Yet, two years later, in 1889, a resolution of the board stated that "owing to the inability of the Chazan to maintain order and discipline in the Sunday School, and owing to the poor progress the children have made during the last six months, the School Board recommends that the school be closed until further notice."

Despite the report and the poor quality of the teaching, the members demanded that the school continue its operations. In 1898, a committee reported "that there is a very urgent need for a school ... from a religious as well as a financial standpoint. We have noticed that the meager effort of the Ladies Aux. Ass. to maintain a Sabbath School during last season increased our membership. A preliminary canvass reveals 25 scholars willing to start at the rate of $1.00 per month. Once organized it will soon be self sustaining and in a very short time be a source of revenue to the congregation. We recommend that a canvass be made and voluntary contributions solicited."

With the election of Rev. Morris Mandel as hazzan and teacher in 1898, the school began to improve. Mandel, an early graduate of the recently organized Jewish Theological Seminary, was trained to teach in a style that was more attractive to students and parents alike. His "American" standards were especially pleasing to the recent immigrants, who by this time were of Eastern European origin. The ladies auxiliary, ever generous in its support, provided prizes at the end of each school year and refreshments at appropriate occasions, such as Purim and Simchat Torah.

In 1902, another congregation, Ohave Shalom, asked that its children be allowed to attend the Adas Israel school. Now the congregation felt secure enough to set conditions for the admission of children from other congregations; it would accept a group of not less than thirty at the rate of $2 per child per month.

The Adas Israel school around the turn of the century was described in a *Washington Times* article.

> Great windows with huge ironbound shutters painted green open into this school room, giving an abundance of light and air. Rows upon rows of benches are ranged about and a board is fitted to the back of each, forming a desk for the pupils as well as a Bible

rest for their parents. These seats have been used for a number of years, yet this is only an added advantage to the right-minded boy and girl. There is an undeniable satisfaction in using a bench and desk after some one else; it cheers many a weary hour for the schoolboy. It is a feeling akin to that in using some one else's book and knowing that he has had to "grub" over it as well as you; it is something like the spirit of good fellowship which exists between two well-matched companions faring along together on a fine stretch of road.

A set of folding doors makes it possible to divide the room into two or throw it open into one large hall. This is of great service, seeing that it enables the two classes to be taught separately and yet leaves the room in a condition to be readily used as a place of worship on week days.

The Hebrew language is taught from the formation of the letters to Bible reading "in the original sacred tongue," and the school takes pride in its thorough course of grammar, composition, and post-Biblical history. Special attention is given to the order of services on Sabbaths and feast-days, to the reading of the lives and writings of the sages and the benedictions and prayers which should be used in every Hebrew household.

The elemental class is a first years course of instruction in which translation from Hebrew into English and vice versa is taught. The manual used is called the "*Sofoh Chayoh*," and is a book arranged in the form of an American school primer. The use of this manual familiarizes the pupil with a few hundred Hebrew phrases. It is illustrated with pictures of a fascinating type, and varied with short stories. Aside from this, the little children receive instruction in prayers.

The intermediate grade comprises the reading class, where the pupils are taught to join in the congregational service and learn the daily prayers, the Psalms, and other reading matter by heart. At the same time, short lessons from the Bible and the Hebrew grammar are given them.

The advanced class receives a regular Bible course, with notes from Moses Mendelson, H. Weizel, Kimchi, and Abarbanel. It is

> proposed to form a class of the more zealous students and take up the study of Rashi and the Talmud.
>
> Any child whose parents are members of the Adath-israel congregation is admitted free to this Hebrew school. At present the school is somewhat hampered by the lack of accommodations, but it is believed that this defect will be speedily remedied.[29]

Despite the glowing tone of the news article, the school seldom satisfied the members' expectations. Discontent with the school system was a constant in the history of the congregation, and the school administration was continually being "reorganized."

Frequently, teenagers would be pressed into service as teachers. When enough teachers were available, the option of a one-day Sunday school would be offered in addition to the afternoon school. Most of the students were boys preparing to become Bar Mitzvah. Discipline presented a perennial challenge.

*~ Rose Hornstein* *Reflections*

When I was about nine or ten, I went to Cheder at 6th and G. We lived in Southeast Washington, within the shadow of the dome of the Capitol. Street car tickets for rides on trolleys and horse-drawn cars were six for a quarter. My parents were understanding and generous—they gave me a nickel with which I could either ride one way or use to buy a sour pickle, candy, a large pretzel, a bag of hot chestnuts or peanuts from the vendors, and walk both ways, which often was the case. I was never afraid to walk home after dark, through the Capitol grounds, singing Adon Olam or Ein Kelohenu at the top of my voice.

There were times when I was the only girl in the class. Often the boys put me up to throwing the stick the *rebbe* used on them down the sewer near the shul.[30]

# 10

## THE COMMUNITY

In 1800 the District of Columbia comprised three separate municipalities: Georgetown, the original settlement; Washington City, designed on a grand scale by Pierre L'Enfant; and Washington County, an eastern segment. Each had its own municipal government. Separate municipalities were abolished in 1871 in favor of a unified government with a bicameral legislature, the lower house elected by the citizens, the upper house and the governor appointed by the president.

In the mid-nineteenth century, a cluster of Jewish merchants ran clothing and shoe stores on M Street in Georgetown, with many of them living above their stores or residing in the nearby Foggy Bottom area. In addition, there were two other centers of Jewish population and business, one in Southwest, along 4th Street, and the other in Northwest, along 7th Street. The Southwest Jewish settlement in 1865 consisted of twenty-eight Jewish families of German origin; the population decreased after the economic downturn of 1873 and increased to thirty-eight in 1895. By the turn of the century, the Southwest Jewish community had grown to 129 families, almost all of East European origin.

The separation of Adas Israel from the Washington Hebrew Congregation did not put an end to the dissension within either of the two congregations. As a result, several offshoot congregations were founded. These often attracted the heretofore unaffiliated, but they were all short-lived, because the District's Jewish population was too small to sustain them. The dissident groups eventually returned to the congregations from which they had seceded.

With the growth in the District's Jewish population following the Civil War, a new congregation, the Mount Sinai Society, was organized in Georgetown. Lacking both a permanent building and a cemetery, it eventually was absorbed by the Washington Hebrew Congregation.[1] The minutes of Adas Israel refer to a cooperating relationship with the Mount Sinai Congregation in Georgetown in 1876. A group of twenty-three families from a Southwest Washington congregation merged with Adas Israel in 1887.[2]

Relations between Adas Israel and the Washington Hebrew Congregation, still referred to as the 8th Street Shul, were, for the most part, polite and harmonious. The two congregations joined forces in 1874 to petition the District's school board to excuse Jewish children from attending public school during the holidays.[3]

The problem was not resolved. Two years later, Adas Israel received "a communication from the Mount Sinai Congregation of Georgetown dated Nov. 4, 1876 in regard to the several grievances that Jewish children suffer in the public schools." Adolphus Solomons and the recently elected hazzan, Jacob Voorsanger, were appointed to discuss the issue with the school board. The committee invited the collaboration of the "8th St. Synagogue" in dealing with the problem.[4]

Further complaints of discrimination were addressed to the Public School Board in a memorial dated May 10, 1881, asserting that "the Public Schools of the United States must and shall be kept free and intact from sectarian influence."[5] When Adolphus Solomons became a member of the school board, he continued to press for the elimination of religious education from the public school curriculum.

In 1886, to cite an example of the cordial relations between the two groups, the Washington Hebrew Congregation invited Adas

Israel to participate in the dedication of its newly renovated synagogue. Similarly, in 1904 Rabbi Julius Loeb of Adas Israel participated in the installation of Abraham Simon as rabbi of the Washington Hebrew Congregation.

Adas Israel responded warmly to the Washington Hebrew Congregation's invitations to cooperate in its several charity bazaars. In turn, as indicated previously, it sought the collaboration of the Washington Hebrew Congregation in the burden of providing burial sites and funeral services for those who were not members of either congregation.[6]

By 1890 recently arrived East European Jewish immigrants were conducting their own services in rented quarters. In 1894 they dedicated their own synagogue, Congregation Ohev Shalom, which in 1902 sent its children to the Adas Israel school. A second East European immigrant synagogue, the Talmud Torah Congregation, was established in Southwest Washington in 1906; its hazzan was Cantor Moses Yoelson, the father of Al Jolson, the stage and screen star. Several members of this congregation, including Al Jolson's brother, George, later joined Adas Israel.

### Other Organizations

For the German Jewish immigrants, as for the Eastern Europeans after them, the synagogue was the focal point of their community, a place not only for worship on Sabbaths and festivals, but to celebrate significant milestones in life: Bar Mitzvah, marriage, and death. Other needs were served by societies and lodges. The first Jewish social and cultural group to be organized in Washington was the Hebrew Literary Association, which was in existence as early as 1856. Nine years later, in 1864, Isaac Leeser wrote that he was impressed by the activities of the Washington Literary and Dramatic Association, which conducted intellectual and social soirees in a suite of rooms on Pennsylvania Avenue opposite the Metropolitan Hotel.[7]

B'nai B'rith, founded in New York in 1841, organized its first Washington lodge on January 31, 1864, with the installation of the Elijah Lodge No. 50 as part of Grand Lodge No. 3. Isaac Leeser was present at the installation ceremonies of the twenty-three-member group. The Potomac Lodge and the Grace Aguilar Lodge were installed in 1868, the Argo Lodge in 1912. Jacob Rich, Adas Israel's president, attended the B'nai B'rith convention in 1886.

Other organizations were established primarily for mutual support and to provide burial services. There are references to a Deborah Society and a Peabody Literary Society, the latter not necessarily an all-Jewish group. The Harmonie Club sponsored a "Mask Ball" on Purim in 1865.

The roster of community organizations grew along with the population, and Adas Israel members played leading roles in most of them. The United Hebrew Charities was incorporated in 1893 to "assist in relief of needy Hebrews" and "to help newly arrived immigrants make an economic, social and cultural adjustment to Washington." The Washington section of the National Council of Jewish Women was founded in 1895 with the participation of Rosa Mordecai, the first Jewish child born in Washington.

A fraternal group, the Free Sons of Israel, is mentioned as early as 1857. In 1886, another fraternal group, the Independent Order of the Sons of Benjamin, sought to purchase a portion of the Adas Israel Cemetery. Jews were identified with the Masonic order as early as 1853 when Leopold Oppenheimer, Manassas Oppenheimer, and his son, Simon, were initiated together.

The Jewish Foster Home and the Hebrew Free Loan Society were formed in 1908.* The Hebrew Home for the Aged, established

*The organizers included three Adas Israel members: Paul Harmel, Simon Atlas, and Morris Garfinkle.

in 1914, was founded and heavily funded by Adas Israel members. Hadassah was not organized in Washington until 1919. A leading figure in its founding was Mrs. John Safer, a friend of Henrietta Szold, Hadassah's national founder.[8] Adas Israel women later dominated Hadassah's Washington chapter, while women from the Washington Hebrew Congregation were more closely associated with the Council of Jewish Women. Eddie Rosenbloom, an Adas Israel member, took the leadership in establishing the YMHA in 1912. The Young Women's Hebrew Association was organized one year later. Both merged into the Jewish Community Center in 1919.

Aside from the social, cultural, and benevolent activities, communal defense was also an important concern. For this reason, the Adas Israel board recommended in 1877 that the congregation affiliate with the Board of Delegates of American Israelites, the first national organization founded to defend Jewish rights, only to be overruled by the membership, whether because of financial concerns or because of disinterest can only be surmised.[9]

Despite its location in the nation's capital, Adas Israel resisted being drawn into the arena of national Jewish concern; it had too many internal problems. The constant shortage of funds to meet its own financial obligations inhibited the congregation's response to communal needs, although individual members of means made personal contributions. Except for Adolphus Solomons, none of its members had achieved sufficient stature or security to become involved in national political affairs.

### The Civic Community

In starkly simple words, the secretary recorded the cancellation of the board meeting scheduled for Sunday, July 3, 1881.

> No meeting took place today, owing to the unsettled state of members and their excitement caused by the attempted assassina-

tion on the life of the President of the United States, James Abram Garfield, in this city, July 2, 1881.

After only six months in office, James Garfield, the twentieth President of the United States, inaugurated on March 4, 1881, was shot while awaiting a train in Washington's Baltimore and Potomac Railroad station. His assassin was Charles J. Guiteau, a disgruntled office seeker, who was committed to St. Elizabeths Hospital to await trial.

Garfield, in a coma, was hospitalized in his White House bedroom. The congregation added prayers for his recovery to the Sabbath *Mincha* service. The press took notice:

> Our Jewish fellow-citizens of the orthodox wing of the Jewish Church assembled yesterday afternoon in goodly numbers at their unpretentious but neat little synagogue on the corner of Sixth and G streets. The Rev. Dr. Samuels officiated and read in the Hebrew language part of the Psalms of David so cleverly put together that the initial letter of each verse formed an acrostic upon the name of James Abram Garfield.
>
> The usual afternoon service was then read, and Mr. A. S. Solomons, who had been requested at short notice, delivered what he modestly termed a sermonette, and which was characterized by a rich vein of concentrated thought worthy of a much larger number of listeners. He took for his subject "Prayer and Its Relations to Every-Day Life," and in his giving the rationale of prayer made allusion to the good reason the Jews had for appealing to the God of Israel to spare the life of their true friend, who had but a few days before he was assassinated requested his Secretary of State to prepare a dispatch to one of the great powers of Europe, discussing in a broad, liberal way that freedom of conscience which Jews here so fully enjoyed and which they know so little about, with few exceptions, abroad—a dispatch which goes direct to the bottom of things in a truly American way, and which will make European diplomats rub their

> eyes and wonder if they are entirely awake. A fervent prayer by Mr. Solomons closed the exercises. There may have been larger congregations of worshipers assembled yesterday, but surely none were more devout and no more impressive convictions were enunciated than came from the Israelites of Washington.[10]

For weeks and then months, the President lingered, his moments of consciousness delicately balanced between life and death. Doctors were unable to locate the bullet, which had lodged near his spine; X-rays were as yet unknown. Alexander Graham Bell, the inventor of the telephone, used an electromagnetic device of his own devising in an attempt to locate the bullet's position. His efforts were in vain; the steel bedsprings created a field of interference. Garfield died on September 19, 1881, at age forty-nine. A Civil War hero, he had been a popular Congressman from Ohio, and the nation paused to mourn his death.

Adas Israel held a memorial service at which Adolphus Solomons delivered a eulogy for Garfield. In it he called for the establishment of a hospital to bear the name of the assassinated President.

In the days that followed, Solomons pursued his proposal by organizing a committee to solicit support. He announced the project in the *Evening Star* and in a widely distributed letter bearing the signatures of eighteen ministers of local churches, including "Rev. J. Samuels, Hebrew (Orthodox) Church," and "Rev. Louis Stern, Hebrew (Reformed) Church."

On October 5, 1881, Solomons addressed a public meeting convened in behalf of the hospital. "The assassinated president deserved a worthy memorial," he said. The Jewish dimension of his appeal was pointed out by the *Evening Star*, which editorialized,

> It was well known the tragedy occurred upon the Hebrew Sabbath, and the news reached a moral congregation of that people in

> this city at their devotion. Subsequently the idea of a memorial hospital was suggested, and from two small and poor Hebrew congregations, very, and from the church fund, not individual, he presented a check each—one for $50.00 and the other for $25.00.[11]

Solomons's efforts were successful. A hospital was established in a farmhouse where Cardozo High School now stands. As Dr. Samuel C. Busey, a physician-historian, noted in his account of these events, the new hospital was to be nonsectarian, serving all persons without distinction. Busey recalled that Solomons "was desirous to see erected a hospital upon the broadest basis, and which would do credit not only to Washington, but to the whole country."[12]

Garfield Hospital was later merged into the Washington Hospital Center. The congregation's involvement in the drive to establish the hospital was its first corporate commitment to a cause beyond itself.

Finally coming to understand the significance of its location in Washington, the congregation conveyed to Rutherford B. Hayes "its heartfelt congratulations on his election as President of our Republic and [invited him] to be present on the evening of the opening of our Fair now in progress and, if possible, to open it in person."[13]

Nor were the implications of its being situated in the capital lost upon congregations outside Washington. In September 1878, the congregation received a request for support from Memphis, Tennessee, to assist victims of a yellow fever epidemic.

Adolphus Solomons urged the members to extend assistance to the victims of the dread disease, writing, "The contagion is likely to grow worse and to spread;—and my experience of ten years ago, when I was the acting Chairman here of our Relief Society, at the time of raging of the same disease in Memphis, Ten.—that prompt action is worth ten times the effort further on."[14]

The congregation filed the appeal.

A similar response met a request from Beth Elohim in Charleston, South Carolina, after a devastating earthquake and fire, on August 31, 1886, destroyed much of the city and severely damaged the synagogue. The Charleston congregation appealed for aid to synagogues throughout the United States. In Adas Israel "The President laid before the board a movement which was on foot in reference to the Charleston Sufferers, that this Congregation in connection with other Congregations devise ways and means for their relief."[15]

The following month the president reported that "the other Congregation did not act in the matter for the relief of the Charleston sufferers and therefore he thought best not to act alone and had dropped the matter." Apparently, the Washington Hebrew Congregation was also primarily concerned with its own needs.

Preoccupation with its own financial problems continued to exercise a restraining influence upon Adas Israel.

*~ Albert Small* *Reflections*

The neighborhood was our whole lives in those days. The synagogue was the focal point. We went to school at Seaton, and we took music lessons in St. Mary's across the street from our house. We used to help in the family stores two blocks away. I belonged to a Herzl Club in the YMHA at 11th and Pennsylvania but that was about the only time we left the neighborhood.

Seventh Street was a wide street. It had street car tracks. Everyone kept about the same hours. The temple played a very predominant part in their lives. Almost all of the merchants were Jewish.*

*Albert Small was born in 1902 at 725 5th Street. His father, Isidore, operated a hardware store at 713 7th Street. In later years Albert Small and his wife, Lillian, endowed the museum housed in Adas Israel's first synagogue building, as

~ *Samuel Dodek* *Reflections*

At the turn of the century, 7th Street was the leading business street in the city; Connecticut Avenue was yet a residential street. When Adas Israel was on 6th and G and Washington Hebrew on 8th and H, the Patent Office, the Public Library, Carnegie Library, Kann's and Hecht Department Stores were all on 7th Street.

When he was 16, my father, Mayer, went to Palestine with the first Aliyah. His parents sent him there from Berdichev in Russia, where he was born, because they knew that if he remained in his native town, he would be conscripted by the Czar's army. In Palestine, then under Turkish rule, my father worked for some Jewish orchard owners, working along with Arab laborers in the field. But the life was so rugged, the days were so long, and the opportunities were so few, that my father went back to Berdichev. Since he had been living under the Ottoman rule in Palestine he was able to get a Turkish passport. His parents sent him to the United States where he lived for a while with an uncle in Chicago where he met his future wife, Lena Ettinger.

In 1893, he moved from Chicago to Washington, where my father went into business with his brother Hyman. Four years later, he decided to join the United States Army because he felt so grateful for the opportunities he had in this country. He joined the Field Artillery, and one year later, the Spanish-American War erupted. He was sent to Cuba with the Cuban Expeditionary Forces and fought there until the war was over. Upon his return from the war, he continued his business partnership with his brother. Their store, the Dodek Clothing and Furniture Company, was located on Sev-

recounted in an earlier chapter. His reminiscences here are taken from Kathryn Schneider Smith, *Washington at Home: An Illustrated History of Neighborhoods in the Nation's Capital* (Windsor, 1988), p. 50.

enth Street, Northwest. In 1901, after a nine year courtship, my father married Lena. A year later, I was born.*

*Samuel Dodek is a prominent Washington physician. His brother, Oscar, was a successful retailer. Their father was one of two Washington Jews who served in the Spanish-American War. The other was Joseph Ottenberg, who became a baker. This oral history reminiscence is taken from the *Jewish Historical Society of Greater Washington Record* 11, no. 1 (July 1982): 14–16.

# 11

## OLD BUSINESS, NEW BUSINESS, AND PETTY CASH

The minutes covering Adas Israel's first decade were faithfully recorded in meticulous detail by Morris Cohen, the secretary, who worked in the central post office and wrote remarkably correct English for one who was foreign-born. He inscribed the minutes with the classic penmanship characteristic of Old World handwriting. Emerging from his minutes is a portrait of a struggling congregation beset by problems both financial and ideological but determined to maintain its pledge to uphold traditional Judaism in Washington.

The history of Adas Israel may be portrayed in either of two ways: as a series of financial crises, delinquencies in collection of dues and payment of loans, bitter disputes, innumerable resignations, and incidents of shocking pettiness, or, alternatively, as a portrait of a handful of dedicated people determined to establish a synagogue despite overwhelming problems, willing to give sacrificially of self and means in the face of nationwide economic recessions, and firmly resolved to preserve their religious traditions in spite of competition from a less demanding and more successful alternative movement. While the second approach would prevail over the first, neither can be ignored.

For several decades, circumstances compelled each board of managers meeting to address the problem of finding the funds to pay wages, buy fuel, and meet routine expenses. The congregation depended upon the sale of cemetery lots to cover its needs. It had no reserve for the maintenance of graves. Cemetery lots were sold at varying prices with the proceeds absorbed by monthly expenditures. Financially, at least, death served life.

Money, invariably in short supply, made even a modest expenditure of less than one dollar a subject commanding extensive debate. A single dollar from a fee returned to the synagogue by the shochet, Simon Mundheim, evoked intensive discussion and required carefully phrased parliamentary disposition.[1] The purchase of a new checkbook or a secretarial notebook required thorough deliberation and the board's formal approval. It would be unfairly judgmental to ask whether this preoccupation with petty cash evidenced limitation of funds or limitation of scope.

Dissension among the members was acerbated by the congregation's inability to collect sufficient funds to initiate the building campaign which was essential to its survival. The Panic of '73 made even the maintenance of the congregation difficult, let alone its expansion. The treasurer became the scapegoat for the deficits; more than one treasurer resigned his office in bitter frustration. Seeking a solution, Selig Goldstein, the driving force in the building campaign, moved that "hereafter, if the regular monthly dues falls short of the monthly expenses, the deficiency should be assessed to the membership." The motion failed to pass.

Wages were low.* It was assumed that synagogue personnel would receive periodic gifts from individuals at holidays in addition to honoraria for their officiation. The required fee for the "Minister of the congregation" was not less than $5. A minimum fee had to be paid for funeral services. Failure to pay would be brought to the attention of the board under the threat of suspension.[2]

*Rev. Cohen received $50 per month; the sexton was paid $6.25 per month plus commissions.

Dues varied from $1 to $2 per month, an amount comparable to the dues of the Washington Hebrew Congregation.* An unpaid obligation of $5 or more was a ground for suspension, but members could be reinstated by repaying at least half of their indebtedness.

The congregation eagerly awaited the approach of each High Holy Day period knowing that its income would be augmented by the rental of seats. While young children were admitted without charge, members' children under twenty-one paid $1 per seat.

In addition to income from dues and seat rentals, the congregation was the beneficiary of some genuine expressions of generosity. For example, a gift of fabric for a "curtain for the Holy Ark" was formally acknowledged by resolution.

> Whereas it appears that Mrs. Rosalie Rosenberg, the lady of our late member Mr. L. Rosenberg, kindly caused sufficient stuff for the purposes of causing to be made a curtain for the Holy Ark, be it therefore resolved, that steps be taken forthwith to have it made accordingly, and that the President of Deborah Lodge be respectfully requested, to cause the making thereof, the expense to be incurred thereby to be incurred by this congregation, which was seconded and agreed to.[3]

An additional gift of fabric was received from Mrs. Sarah Prince. Mrs. Hartong presented the congregation with a cover for the reader's podium and two spittoons. All were gratefully acknowledged.

Despite its financial straits, the congregation was compassionate. The poor were buried at the congregation's expense. The stillborn and the very young were buried without charge or for a token payment. Holiday seats for the widowed, the unemployed,

*At Baltimore's Chizuk Amanah, a congregation of similar background founded in 1871, the dues were $10 annually.

the stranger, and newly arrived immigrants were offered without charge. Members in arrears "because of hard times" were carried on the synagogue rolls for extended periods. There were resignations. The first recorded were those of Joseph Joseph, on November 3, 1872, and of Jacob Peyser, because he moved to Petersburg, Virginia. The delinquent were suspended, sometimes to be reinstated after settlement of the indebtedness.

Elections were held each January. In 1873, Bendiza Behrend, who had served as president since the congregation's founding in 1869 and did not seek reelection, was succeeded by his cousin, Nathan Gotthelf, whose election was not without challenge. In the balloting, Gotthelf received fourteen votes against four for his opponent, L. Poppers. The other officers were elected without contest, with the secretary, Morris Cohen, recording each designation in pedantic repetition:

> The teller then reported one ballot cast for Vice President, the name of Mr. Jacob Peyser, and the Secretary reported him to be only elected as such for the present year.

The identical formula certified each office. An engrossed resolution was presented to Behrend, the outgoing founding president, for "the ability and fidelity in which he conducted the affairs of this congregation from its establishment to the present date."[4]

Nathan Gotthelf, one of the more learned members of the congregation, chanted the services in the absence of professional clergy. His two terms in office were dominated by the problems of finding a qualified shochet, working out the shochet's relationship with the kosher butcher, and coping with the never-ending financial crisis.

Contention surrounded the administration of Gotthelf's successor, Jacob Rich. He was elected president in 1874 but resigned after six months in office. Three years later, Rich was again elected president only to resign for the second time shortly thereafter. He returned to the presidency for a third time, but died in office. The dissension during this period reflected an underlying schism within the congregation which focused on the relationship with Joseph A. Cohen, the hazzan-shochet-teacher. The bitter dispute came near destroying the congregation.

John Boyer, elected mid-year in 1874 after two presidents had resigned, was forced to call a special meeting of the membership "to endeavor to reconciliate certain members and worshippers now declining to participate in our Divine service."[5]

The bitter dispute had begun soon after the election of Cohen to serve as hazzan, shochet, teacher, and Torah reader for one year, with his term ending September 1, 1873.[6] After his first High Holiday services, in 1872, several board members were so enthusiastic about Cohen's cantorial ability that they moved a resolution of commendation along with the hope that his contract would be extended for another year. The majority objected, not to the commendation, but to any reference to the extension of his contract; it would be a dangerous precedent. Though Cohen had performed well in leading services, the congregation demanded an equally high standard of performance in other areas; they evaluated him by his weaknesses.

Cohen had barely assumed the duties of shochet when he was charged with being unfairly discriminatory for refusing to serve certain members of the congregation. After heated discussion, the board adopted a resolution of reprimand calling upon the president to remind Cohen that he was in breach of contract.[7] Piqued, Cohen declined to deliver the "oration" for the ceremonial festivities to mark the dedication of the Torah scroll. The board had no alternative but to find a substitute preacher for this occasion.

That was only the beginning of Cohen's problems. Inevitably, there was a conflict between his duties as shochet and as teacher. The board attempted to reconcile the conflict by directing Mr. Stern, the butcher, to arrange for slaughtering to be concluded before 2:00 p.m. "so that the slaughtering would not interfere with the religious school hours."[8]

Four months after his election to office, Cohen asked to be released from his duties as shochet because of "poor health," but agreed to continue serving until a replacement could be found. His request granted, Cohen was retained as hazzan, teacher, and Torah reader, at a salary of $75 per month. In addition, he agreed to authenticate the credentials of any shochet applying for the position.

Although Cohen had been commended for the manner in which he had conducted the Hebrew school, as the end of his first year's agreement approached, some members expressed opposition to his retention as teacher. A resolution to invite Cohen to serve another year failed on a minor procedural issue: whether his contract should be discussed at a special meeting to be called for that purpose during the summer or at the year's end along with the election of officers. In compromise, the board asked Cohen to continue his services for the four months between September 1 and December 31, 1873.

Cohen rejected the offer "on account of the wording therein and of irregularity,"[9] insisting that his election should cover one full year, from September 1, 1873 to September 1, 1874. In the course of heated debate, John Boyer declared Cohen to be unsuitable "on account of an alleged breach in not abstaining from eating or drink prior to the finishing of Divine service, at the 2nd day of Rosh Hashoneh of last year."[10] Hardly a violation in today's congregation. Perhaps the secretary confused Rosh Hashanah with Yom Kippur.

After considerable debate, in which the charge of being "unsuitable" was rejected, Cohen was reelected for one year by a vote of eleven in his favor, and five in opposition. John Boyer, who had leveled the charges against Cohen, refused to act as teller.

To replace Cohen as shochet, the congregation elected H. H. Sommers on the condition that he would submit valid certification of his ordination, a *kabbalah*. When Sommers's proof of certification failed to materialize, it was enough to disqualify him in the opinion of many members of the board. Nonetheless, since there was no other candidate, the board decided to retain him despite his lack of a *kabbalah*, whereupon Cohen submitted his resignation as hazzan, which was immediately followed by the resignations of Nathan Gotthelf and the sexton, Manassas Oppenheimer. They objected to the retention of an allegedly unqualified shochet.

The board, seeing no alternative, yielded. It dismissed Sommers. The resignations of the two officers were withdrawn, but the congregation was still without a shochet. In an effort to fill the vacant post, Bendiza Behrend proposed, for the sake of harmony, that the position of hazzan again be merged with that of shochet, and Cohen be asked to assume both responsibilities. The flaw in the proposal was that it did not take Cohen's wishes into consideration; he would not agree.

Cohen was thereupon dismissed, or, as the minutes put it, his previous resignation was now accepted. He was, nonetheless, asked to continue serving as hazzan until after the approaching High Holy Days. After considerable parliamentary maneuvering, it was agreed to retain Cohen for another year and on his terms, namely, that the congregation would engage a shochet who could submit authentic credentials certified by a recognized rabbi or New York yeshiva, or, if necessary, by Cohen himself.

Sommers was asked to vacate the house on the congregation's lot on 6th and G Streets so that it would be available to a suitable shochet.

The entire nation had been suffering from the widespread economic depression that had begun in September 1873, and the congregation's income had been seriously affected. In order to effect economies, the board asked Cohen to agree to a salary reduction from $75 to $60 for the remainder of his term, and, in addition, to once again take on the office of shochet with its emoluments. Cohen firmly declined to accept any reduction in salary and again declined to serve as shochet. Efforts to secure a qualified shochet continued.

A Mr. Freeman served for a brief period. Selig Goldstein, who had attempted to play the role of peacemaker in the dispute with Cohen, recommended that a Mr. Lazarus be named shochet and Torah reader, that Manassas Oppenheimer be invited to serve as honorary sexton without pay beyond the usual commission for collecting dues, and that Cohen continue to serve as hazzan. This arrangement, Goldstein hoped, would bring about "a peaceful solution of all difficulties."

Lazarus deflated Goldstein's comprehensive solution by refusing to serve as shochet and Torah reader. Goldstein, who still "looked for a peaceful solution," introduced a new player, a qualified shochet with appropriate credentials, Rev. A. B. Shlomberg, who was immediately elected to fill the position of shochet and Torah reader for the remainder of the year 1874 at a monthly salary of $15. His appointment proved to be a wise choice; Shlomberg served the congregation for a record-breaking three years.

In January 1874, as if relations between Cohen and the congregation were not complicated enough, charges were leveled against him as a teacher, asserting "bad treatment to the children, scholars of the school, and charges for non-attendance at proper days and hours at school."[11] An attempt to postpone consideration of the charges was defeated by one vote; the board was almost evenly divided between sympathizers and opponents of Cohen.

To complicate matters still further, Cohen then filed a breach-of-contract lawsuit against the congregation, whereupon the board demanded his immediate resignation, which Cohen refused to submit. The board, thoroughly confused about the legal status of their agreement with Cohen, tried in vain to negotiate a financial settlement on condition that he withdraw his legal action and submit a final resignation. To underscore their determination to rid themselves of him, the board voted to advertise for a successor.

The board had failed to reckon with Cohen's friends among the membership, who rallied to his support. In protest, they not only resigned from the congregation, they proceeded to form another. The minutes sometimes refer to the new congregation as *Neveh Israel* (" Oasis or Meadows of Israel")[12] and sometimes as House of Israel (*Bet Israel*).

By April 1874, the effects of the secession threatened Adas Israel's very survival. The thorny issue revolved around the treatment of Cohen. The board saw no alternative but to appoint a committee to seek a compromise. In its appraisal of the situation, the committee recognized that

> two factions exist in our midst, one faction not being possible so far to reconciliate, but another faction, composed of late members of congregation, viz: Messrs. N. Gotthelf, M. Oppenheimer, L. Block, and others, were ready to go with us hand in hand again, provided that Revd. J. A. Cohen, retires in a legal manner, wherein they think he has been illegally disposed of by the congregation.[13]

The committee proposed arbitration of the dispute with Cohen and recommended that Adolphus Solomons serve as arbitrator on condition that the dissidents first return to the congregation as members. The proposal proved acceptable to both groups. Cohen's friends were not pressing for his retention so much as for an equitable severance.

After hearing both sides of the dispute, Solomons ruled that Cohen was to be paid $300 in fulfillment of his contract and was to submit his resignation, and that "late difficulties between members and Rev. Cohen be erased from all minutes and forgotten." Cohen's supporters were to return to the fold and were to be "granted all rights and privileges of membership without payment of $10.00 burial plot fee and the congregation House of Israel was declared dissolved."

Although the secretary concluded his minutes of the meeting with the word *shalom*, written in Hebrew, there was little peace. The president, Jacob Rich, and the vice-president, Jacob Peyser, both opponents of Cohen, resigned; Nathan Gotthelf was again elected president, and John Boyer, vice-president. A motion to extend a vote of thanks to the resigning officers "for the faithful manner in which they performed their duties" failed to pass and was crossed out in the minutes. Solomons, however, was formally thanked for his efforts.

Gotthelf resigned the presidency after one month. Boyer was immediately elected and retained the office after the elections of January 1875. Leopold Oppenheimer, who had signed the Articles of Incorporation, resigned. He had advanced the congregation a loan of $75 which he now wanted repaid. Protracted negotiations for repayment would extend over a year to cause more bitterness. In March 1876, it was agreed to repay Oppenheimer at the rate of $5 per month.

The secretary, Morris Cohen, resigned repeatedly only to be persuaded to return to office after each outburst. The shochet and the butcher required the congregation's intervention to resolve disputes between them. Adding to the turmoil, in July 1875, the president, John Boyer, submitted his resignation, but agreed to remain in office until the January 1876 elections. Despite his threat to leave the congregation after the next election, Boyer finally accepted reelection for another year.

The sexton, Mr. Alexander, was dismissed in 1876. In anticipation of the new synagogue's need for supervision, the board advertised for a "janitor" who would occupy the living quarters in the "basement of our Synagogue and take care of the Mikveh." Two responses were received. One came from the incumbent shochet, the popular Mr. Shlomberg, who, in lieu of rent, would consent to the deduction of $9.12 from his monthly salary as Torah reader and "*Schamuss*," and the other from a Mr. Rabinsky, who was willing to serve as "*Schamuss*" without salary, only commission, and would pay $6 per month rent. By a vote of seventeen to seven, Shlomberg was elected to the post for one year.

Once more, the pedantic secretary, Morris Cohen, submitted his resignation. His successor, I. Abraham, who took office in October 1876, wrote in contemporary penmanship. The emergence of an American influence in writing style was short-lived; Abraham resigned within one month after taking office and Cohen returned to the post. Reasons were not given.

Another major controversy erupted in 1877, this time revolving around Shlomberg, the multi-dutied and popular shochet, against whom charges were leveled. Even before the conclusion of the investigation of the charges, the board refused to remunerate Shlomberg for monies he had spent on supplies, ordering that all supplies should hereinafter be ordered and delivered to the trustees and not to Shlomberg, who was then informed "that he has to obey all legal and lawful orders of the President as well as the chairman, and that he has to show respect to other members of the Committee."[14]

The committee investigating the charges against the hapless Shlomberg found him "guilty as charged, except for the second specification to the first charge." The charges were not enumerated. Julius Louis, chairman of the investigating committee, who was sympathetic to Shlomberg, suggested that "inasmuch as the charges are not highly offensive," the congregation should refrain from imposing any punishment. Boyer, the president, adamantly pressed for punitive action. He was upheld by a vote of thirteen to nine.

After extensive and bitter debate, the board moved that Shlomberg be ordered to vacate the synagogue premises where he lived, but that the congregation would continue his salary until January 1, 1878. The charges against him would be declared null and void if he acquiesced to this arrangement without further protest or appeal.

After a recess of five minutes for private consultation, it was announced that Shlomberg had agreed to sign a document which read:

> I do hereby promise and agree to vacate the vestry rooms and premises of Adas Israel congregation on or before July 1, 1877 in consideration of receiving $15.00 per month until my term of office expires, and of the withdrawal of all charges and everything else connected therewith, and promise to perform all duties of Shamuss to the best of my ability, as ordered or as may be ordered by the officers of the above congregation, on condition that I likewise shall receive my salary as Shamuss, viz: $16.00 per month, and that this agreement shall be in force to December 31, 1877.[15]

The peacemaker was Selig Goldstein. Unfortunately, Goldstein, who was as valuable for resolving disputes as he had been in building the synagogue, passed away two months later, in July 1877. It was the congregation's second loss of an important leader. Levi Abraham was the first.

The congregation memorialized Goldstein's passing. His children, Simon and Morris, announced that, in their father's memory, they would install a new *ner tamid* (perpetual lamp) over the ark, with an appropriate inscription. They would also pay for the lamp's fuel for one year and offer an annual gift on each *Yahrzeit*.

Selig Goldstein's children assumed their father's leadership position. Simon Goldstein was named to the newly created post of chairman of the board of managers. The transition was not without ripples of discontent. A year later, Morris Cohen, the secretary, took advantage of the Goldstein brothers' absence to inform the board that while the Goldstein brothers had placed an inscription above the ark with their father's name on it, the promised new *ner tamid* had not been installed, nor had any funds been received for fueling the existing lamp.

The delicacy of the situation prompted Cohen to wait for a day when the Goldstein brothers were out of the city, before bringing the matter to the attention of the board. A motion to ask them to remove the inscription was tabled. No one wanted to bell the cat. It must have been a stormy meeting, because two members of the board, one of them the past-president, Boyer, were fined 25 cents and 50 cents respectively for "raising disturbances."[16]

The ill-will simmered. At the next meeting, the president, Jacob Rich, submitted his resignation, but after receiving a unanimous vote of confidence, he agreed to remain in office until the next election. Resignations had become a familiar ploy.

Simon Goldstein, evidently aware of the board's unhappiness with the inscription on the ark, announced to the board, in words paraphrased by the secretary, that

> Inasmuch as there seemed to be objections to a certain inscription that he placed over the Ark in our Synagogue to the memory of his departed father, he caused it to be removed, and that in

> place thereof, he caused to be inscribed the Biblical words in Hebrew, "Wherever My Name will be sacredly mentioned, I will come unto thee and bless thee."[17]

This proved acceptable to the board; the crisis passed. Jacob Rich was reelected president without opposition in January 1879 and again in January 1880, only to resign once again in April. He was succeeded by Bernard Rich. The two were not brothers, although they may have been related.*

Not every meeting was torn by disputes and recriminations. As a rule, the board members were bound together by their common concern for the welfare of the congregation. They celebrated each other's birthdays and other happy events: resolutions and gifts were presented to Sam Hartong, the vice-president, on his seventieth birthday, and to Mr. and Mrs. Julius Baumgarten on his fifty-first birthday and their wedding anniversary. President Jacob Rich acknowledged the gift of a clock presented to him on the second day of Chanukah "in very brief and beautiful remarks." The board also used resolutions and gifts to acknowledge the services rendered by its members. On Morris Cohen's retirement as secretary, he was presented "in well chosen language" with a "beautiful Regulator Clock" in recognition of his services, and "on his motion, it was unanimously adopted that the fact of the handsome present given to him be entered upon the minutes of this meeting."[18] Farewell gifts were presented to several members who paid visits to their home-

*On the death of Simon Rich, the congregation published a resolution, in German, in the *Israelite* in Mainz, Germany, conveying condolences to his aged parents in Germany as well as to his "grief-stricken brother and beloved member, Jacob Rich." No mention was made of Bernard Rich. Jacob Rich was a partner in the firm of Gotthelf and Behrend at 819 7th Street N.W. Bernard Rich lived at 1306 7th Street N.W.

towns in Germany. Considering the congregation's financial straits, one might conclude that the board members were quite generous with each other, far more generous than they were with the professional staff.

The repetitive presidential resignations were more the product of momentary anger than of ideological differences, a tactic rather than a philosophy. The rapid turnover in personnel and presidents was a symptom of the turbulence which plagued Adas Israel. During a brief period, five different shochtim served the congregation in rapid succession: Cohen, Sommers, Freeman, Lazarus, and Shlomberg. In one contentious year, 1884, there were three presidents, and in 1880, another three, for a total of eight presidents between 1874 and 1887—

1874, January to June, Jacob Rich;
1874, June to July, Nathan Gotthelf;
1874–77, John Jacob Boyer, resigning in August 1877;
1877–80, Jacob Rich;
1880, April to June, Bernard Rich;
1880, July to October, Julius Baumgarten;
1880–82, Manassas Oppenheimer;
1882–87, Jacob Rich, who died in office in April.

**Julius Baumgarten, Sec'y.**

Julius Baumgarten, elected secretary to succeed Morris Cohen in 1886, inscribed his minutes as if he were a chronicler of historical events, writing in an exceptionally skilled hand and with a magisterial flourish worthy of a state document. Widely recognized for his skill as a calligrapher, he was commissioned to inscribe the Great Seal of the United States Senate. He also engraved the numbers on the pews in two Adas Israel synagogues, on 6th and G Streets, and on 6th and I Streets.

Julius and his brother, Herman Baumgarten, were partners in an engraving firm at 319 Pennsylvania Avenue, N.W. The firm they founded, now owned by the Baturin family of Adas Israel, is still in operation today under the same name.

The board of managers took pains to preserve its proceedings and its records. Prior to his departure for Germany on a long-planned visit, Morris Cohen secured the autographs of the founders of the congregation which he framed and presented to the board in a formal ceremony; it was "received by the President and ordered to be placed in the archives of the congregation."[19] Unfortunately, the document cannot be found; apparently the earlier generations at Adas Israel were more concerned with the preservation of archives and documents than were their successors.

After taking office, Baumgarten asked that the constitution be printed because "the only copy now available is very loose, with amendments improperly written in pencil, and could be lost as actually has been the case and undue alterations could be made by interested parties."[20] With the invention of the typewriter, Baumgarten insisted on using the new invention to record the constitution and other important documents; it was the end of the era of the quill pen.

Baumgarten proved to be as conscientious as his predecessor in recording the minutes. He inscribed a table of contents on the back of the front cover of the third volume, listing important events covering the period from January 1886 to September 1910. His first entry, the trustees' report for 1885, explained that the deficit of $134 was the result of the cost of improving the cemetery and constructing a new house there at a cost of $550. There were fifty-five members on January 1, 1886, twenty-one of whom paid $24 annually and thirty-one $12, with ten resignations or suspensions suffered during the previous year. The congregation still owed $2,800 on its mortgage.

Financial concerns continued to plague the board at each meeting. The original building site, purchased in 1873, had contained a house. It was eventually leveled. Since neither the house nor the lot had been consecrated for religious use until 1876, when the new synagogue was erected, the District of Columbia levied a claim for back taxes. A special meeting on February 20, 1887 had to consider the District's assessment of $239.40 for taxes covering the period prior to religious use. For a deficit-ridden congregation, the assessment was a major hurdle. The board engaged an attorney, at a contingent fee of $100, to plead its case before the District tax authorities. He was successful. The Superior Court reduced the assessment to $62 with interest from 1882.

When an adjacent house and lot became available for $8,500, the board seized the opportunity to enlarge the original site. The 25-foot-front property adjoined the synagogue on the north. With improvements and repairs, the house could be a source of needed income. On January 26, 1891, the trustees, Isaac Levy, Manassas Oppenheimer, and Jacob Hirschfield, were authorized to purchase the premises at 617 6th Street N.W. for $8,500 and to borrow $11,500 at 5.5 percent interest for three years. The house was rented with a six-month lease for $217.65. Annual property taxes were $316.25.

There were five nominees for the presidency at the annual meeting on January 1, 1888. All but Simon Oppenheimer declined. His election was to be the beginning of a record-breaking thirty-six-year tenure in office. At the same meeting, L. Roseman was named sexton; the title of his post was recorded as the "messenger." When Julius Baumgarten took leave to visit Germany, his brother, Herman, was named his temporary replacement as secretary. Julius received a going-away gift of a "satchel."

More dissension: Mr. Scheinberg caused a furor by accusing the respected Raphael Sanger, the former treasurer, of financial mismanagement. An investigating committee concluded that the charges were groundless and soon reported that "Mr. Scheinberg wishes to make an apology and asks Mr. Sanger to forgive him. They shook hands and the committee was discharged."[21]

Sabbath morning services sometimes brought out more than prayerful worship. In October 1896, charges were brought against A. Stein: "At the close of services he did commit a felonious assault upon our officiating chazan by striking him in the face with his fist thereby disturbing the peace and harmony of the congregation and in strict violation of all principles governing the behavior of a gentleman."

The investigating committee reported that "we have attended to that duty . . . also a copy of the charges was handed to the defendant who failed to make his appearance. Subsequently, the defendant was tried in the Police Court for assault and battery upon Rev. Mr. Samuels, and found guilty and fined. . . . On the basis of testimony offered in court, we find him guilty and the charges well founded and recommend that he be expelled from the congregation." Stein was expelled by a vote of nine to two.

Disputes continued: "the President reported disturbances of services by Mr. Korman on the previous Sabbath and it was decided to fine Mr. Korman $20.00 or that he make an open apology to the congregation."[22]

However dedicated he may have been, Julius Baumgarten could not escape the fate of other officers; he too was accused of financial irregularities. In November 1895, Baumgarten was ordered to appear at the next meeting "to repay 8.45$ which remains in his possession from funds collected to repair the graveyard." Again, a committee was appointed to investigate the charges.

In February 1896, the committee members reported on their visit to Baumgarten.

> His records show a balance of the grave yard funds in his possession to be $8.45. His wife called his attention that 19 tickets which he had disposed of were not paid for and he claims he is not responsible for them. Therefore, there only remains in his possession $3.70 which he is ready to pay the congregation. We respectfully recommend to the honorable board that the above statement shall be accepted in good faith.[23]

In March, Baumgarten still had not paid the $3.70. The board threatened to expel him. The following month, when he still had not paid, he was declared delinquent. Baumgarten finally paid in June, and the charges against him were formally dropped. Despite this unpleasant encounter, Baumgarten remained active in the congregation.

Death claimed many of the founders of Adas Israel in the early 1900s. Edward (Eliezer) S. Hartogensis died on January 25, 1903. He was the great-grandfather of Flora Atkin and Eleanor Wolpe, both of them active members of the congregation. *Tachrichim* (burial shrouds) were purchased from Mrs. Hechinger for $2.95.

In December 1900, there is a brief entry: "Mr. Lully resigned from the congregation." Who was Mr. Lully? The name Emanuel Lully appears in the 1852 edition of the Washington city directory. Merno Lully was one of the signers of the petition to Congress to authorize a "Hebrew congregation" to hold property.

Emanuel and Merno Lully were the same person. Lully fought with the Hungarian freedom fighter Lajos Kossuth in the failed attempt to win Hungary's independence from Austria in 1848–49 and then was interned with him in Turkey. When Kossuth went to the United States, Lully and his family accompanied him, settling in Washington in 1851. During the Civil War Lully served in the Kossuth Corps.[24] Merno / Emanuel Lully was the great-grandfather of Mrs. Maurice H. Hacke and Sidney Hechinger, the founder of the chain of hardware stores. One of Lully's children, Rebecca, was the mother of General Mark Clark, of World War II fame.

L. Roseman, the sexton engaged in 1888, who proved to be popular and effective in his office, served the congregation for ten years. His resignation in June 1898, for reasons of health, was accepted with regrets, expressions of gratitude, and the promise of a gift. Jacob Grossberg was elected to succeed him on the condition that he provide a bond of $250.

This was easier said than done. No surety could satisfy the board members. Grossberg's first bond was underwritten by a member of the congregation, Isaac Levy, who withdrew it a few months later. Grossberg then submitted a bond from a Mr. Brooker, but the congregation did not know him and the bond was not worded in a satisfactory manner.

The debate on Grossberg's bond continued for several months. In September, Grossberg complained that the president had rejected every bond he had submitted. The board moved "that Grossberg be given 2 weeks time to submit bond and if not, the position will be vacant. The board has already manifested a disposition of leniency towards our Shammus"[25] Soon thereafter, Grossberg submitted an acceptable bond from the Fidelity Company of Baltimore.

In retrospect, the angry outbursts which spiced the board meetings in the early years may have reflected a displacement of the frustration caused by the difficult problem of earning a living during an economic slump. Just as children who are well behaved in public school sometimes become behavior problems in the protective surroundings of religious school, so the immigrant generation, controlled and decorous in their daily commercial relationships, brought their pent-up hostilities into the board meetings, where, as in a family circle, they could safely release their anger. The board meetings served as a protected arena where strong words could be exchanged, charges filed, fines levied, sanctions imposed, and then, reconciliations arranged and a measure of peace restored.

# 12

## FROM HAZZAN TO RABBI, 1887–1900

Over the years, Jews have called their clergy by many titles: rav, rov, rebbe, maggid, chacham, hazzan, cantor, reverend, rabbi. Each title reflects one facet of the many-sided prism characteristic of the Jewish clerical role. In his own eyes, the clergyman may have perceived himself as heir to the priest, prophet and sage of antiquity. In the congregation's expectations of him, however, his role embraced most if not all of the responsibilities reflected by the titles.

In 1848, for example, the formal agreement between Congregation Brith Shalom in Easton, Pennsylvania, and its hazzan stipulated that he would "fulfill the duties of schochet; conduct school daily for six hours; supervise the mikveh and provide a substitute at his own expense during illness or absence."[1] Little wonder that hazzanim were difficult to find and, once hired, difficult to retain, for invariably it became apparent that no one person could fulfill all of these duties to the congregation's satisfaction.

Authors writing about the clergy serving early American Jewry often place quotation marks around the title "rabbi" as if to suggest that, being unordained, the clergymen were not authentic rabbis, but simply ordinary Jews who were more knowledgeable in Hebrew and more skillful in reciting the rituals than others in the congregation. However valid the characterization, those who acted in the capacity of rabbi performed an essential function and were probably as committed to their calling as their ordained successors.

Communities in the new world needed clergy long before the theological schools that could ordain them were established. In the Christian community in the United States, the earliest clergy were trained by apprenticeship to other clergymen who taught them Bible and the rudiments of theology. The first theological school in America was for Protestants, founded in Andover, Mass. in 1808.[2] The Hebrew Union College, founded in 1875 in Cincinnati, Ohio, was the first seminary for training rabbis in the United States. The Jewish Theological Seminary was founded in 1886.

The earliest formally ordained rabbis in the United States came from Europe with their ordination, the *smicha*, bestowed by Rabbinical heads of Yeshivoth. The first title of rabbi in the colonies was ascribed in 1712 to Abraham DeLucena, an American of Spanish descent who made his living as a merchant shipper. Another merchant "rabbi" named Isaac Touro served the Jews of Newport, Rhode Island, and was called "Jew-Priest" by his fellow citizens. Hayim Isaac Carigal, a native of Hebron, Palestine, who visited Newport in 1773, was a Sephardic Chacham (literally, wise man, the title Spanish Portuguese Jews assigned to their clergy).

The first American-born Jew to serve as "rabbi" of a congregation was the unordained Gershom Mendes Seixas, who in 1768 became the minister of New York's Spanish-Portuguese Shearith Israel, not because he was exceptionally learned but because there were no other candidates. Despite his lack of ordination, his effectiveness proved that the congregation had chosen wisely. Although his Hebrew learning was modest and he could speak neither Spanish nor Portuguese, he spoke English well. Biographers describe him as charming, understanding, sensitive and possessing a delightful sense of humor.

Abraham Rice, the first European ordained Rabbi to settle in the United States, came to Baltimore in 1840 only to resign in 1849 after

## Interments in cemetery of Congregation Adas Israel

| No. | Date of Burial | Name of deceased | Age | Lot | Head Board | Remarks |
|---|---|---|---|---|---|---|
| 1 | June 7. 1870 | Twins. | Still born | 5. | | Born to member H. Hammerschlag. |
| 2 | July 26 1870 | Simon Goldenheimer | 6 1/2 ys. | – | | Son of Abraham Goldenheimer |
| 3 | Augt. 15. 1870 | Frummit Levy | Infant | 22 | | Daughter of member Isaac Levy |
| 4 | Augt. 21. 1870 | Shemajah Levy | " | 22. | | Son " " " " |
| 5 | Septbr. 20. 1870 | Rosa Hecht | 7 month | 27 | | Daughter of member E. Hecht. |
| 6 | March 16. 1871 | Gedaljah Schiller | 1 1/12 ys. | – | | Son of Moses Schiller. |
| 7 | July 14. 1871 | Isaac Goldenheimer | 10 mo. | – | 1 | Infant son of Abrhm. Goldenheimer |
| 8 | Nov. 19. 1871 | Bertha Hartogensis | 7 mo. | – | 2 | Daughter of Edward Hartogensies. |
| 9 | Nov. 24 1871 | Child. | Still born | – | 3 | Born to Herrman Fischer. |
| 10 | Janry. 1. 1872 | Simon Fischer | 2 4/12 ys. | – | " | Born Septbr. 15. 1869 to Herrman Fischer. |
| 11 | Janry 25. 1872 | Lippman Louis | – | 2. | | Infant son of member Max Louis. |
| 12 | Janry 28. 1872 | Gittel Louis | – | 2 | 6 | " daughter " " Max Louis. |
| 13 | Febry. 18. 1872 | Infant child | 3 days | 11. | 7 | Born to member B. Schlossberg. |
| 14 | March. 14. 1872 | Infant daughter. | 20 days | – | 8 | Born to Adolph Heidsman. |
| 15 | March 19 1872 | Sarah Hecht. | 2 1/12 ys. | – | 9 | Daughter of Emanuel Hecht. |
| 16 | March 24. 1872 | M. Walkskey | 2 1/2 ys. | 34. | 10 | Son of member A. Walkskey |
| 17 | June. 2. 1872 | Abrhm. Hirsch | | – | 11 | Infant son of Ignatz Hirsch |
| 18 | Augt. 11. 1872 | Isaac Goldstein | 5 m's. | 19. | 12 | Infant son of member S. Goldstein. |
| 19 | Octbr. 20. 1872 | Estella Cohen | 7 m's. | 8. | 13 | Infant daughter of member Levy Cohen. |
| 20 | Decbr. 25. 1872 | Saml. Koginskey | 37 years | – | 14 | Killed by assassination of negroe |
| 21 | Decbr. 31. 1872 | Jacob Behrend | 2 weeks | 16. | 15 | Infant son of member B. J. Behrend |
| 22 | Febry. 16. 1873. | Manuel Mordecai Noah. | 42 years | 23. | 16 | Died Febry 14 1873 in Insane Asylum. Buried by order of Board of managers on a Lot |
| 23 | May 20. 1873 | Child. | Still born | 26. | 17 | Born to member Jacob Peyser |
| 24 | July 9. 1873 | Salomon Bux | 10 m's. | – | 18 | Infant son of Mendel Bux |
| 25 | July. 16 1873. | Girl. | 3 weeks | 19 | 19 | Daughter of member S. Goldstein. |
| 26 | Septbr. 30. 1873 | Emilie Peyser | 11 years. | 26. | 20 | Daughter " " Jacob Peyser |

Register of first burials in Adas Israel Cemetery, June 1870 to September, 1873.

The first Adas Israel Synagogue structure, 6th and G Street N.W., as it appeared prior to removal from site. The site has historic associations dating back to the Civil War. John Wilkes Booth had used a livery stable across the street; he and the others who planned Lincoln's assassination met in Mrs. Surratt's boarding house, on the next block. Photo courtesy of Jewish Historical Society.

Sanctuary interior of first Synagogue, prior to installation of benches. Rededication ceremonies, June 1975. Photo by Mel Chamowitz.

ving day. The first synagogue on its way from sixth to third on G street, view from the air. Note Aron kodesh protruding from eastern exterior wall.

Moving original synagogue to 3rd and G Street N.W.

Building committee for 6th and I structure standing on the concrete first floor of the building to prove its strength. Note stacked bricks added for weight in background. From right to left: Herman Blumenthal, (*), Isaac Levy, (*), Simon Oppenheimer, Rabbi Julius Loeb, Joseph Hornstein, (*), Bernard Schlossberg, (*), M. Miller, (*). Louis Levy, the architect, Sam Sherman, Arthur Cowsill, the builder, two construction engineers. (*unidentified.) Photo from Washington *Times*, October 8, 1906

The second Adas Israel structure, 1908-1951. Photograph carried inscription, top and bottom, "My Synagog" and "Sixth Street Synagog".

This is your synagog today! The result of sacfices and unselfishness for which we must be ·ateful.

TODAY we have a living, active synagog that looking forward another 50 years and hoping that members and their children will be as loyal and voted as in the past.

WILL YOU HELP ADAS ISRAEL in its progss?

Mr. Oppenheimer had as his vice president during nine years' time Mr. Louis Rosenberg

who is now serving his third year as president. Twelve years a loyal officer and this is his first vacation - a trip to Europe and Palestine!

"Thy going be peaceful
Thy coming be peaceful!"

Front and back of a fund raising appeal card, probably, 1927.

Ground consecration ceremonies at Connecticut and Porter. At podium, Joseph Blumenthal, Speaker Rabbi Albert I. Gordon of the United Synagogue, seated between Joseph Wilner and Rabbi Metz, Septemb 18, 1949. Photo by Steve Zweig.

The Adas Israel Choir, 1933. First row, left to right: Theresa Shefferman, Mrs. Henry Oxenburg, Virginia Gittelman Ponack, Pauline Grossberg, Belle Shefferman (accompanist), Sadie Atlas Koplin. Rear row, left to right: Miss Novick, Dr. Charles Gordon, Clara Wiseman, Meyer Fischman, Cantor Louis Novick, David Gluschak, Eva Gordon, Abe Shefferman (director), Louis Fenik.

Cornerstone ceremonies at Connecticut and Porter, 1950. Foreground: Abe Shefferman; front row: Henry Paul, Sam Lebowitz, Louis Grossberg, (*), Abe Kay, Herman Robbin, Rabbi Solomon Metz, Isadore Turover, Jacob Spund, Edward Rosenblum, Joseph Blumenthal, Louis Rudden, Isadore Alk, (*), Morris Witlin, Henry Gichner (partial).

Second row: Leonore Goldstein, Frances Goldberg, Morris Gewirz, Harry Burka, Stanley Wiener, Daniel Ezrin, Israel Burka, Fred Nessen, Simon Hershman, Morris Levinson, Benjamin April, Samuel Wolfe, Isabelle Gichner, I. Louis Firestone, Ida Wilner, Max Pasternak.

Third and Fourth rows: Herman Paul, David Finkelstein, Nathan Kluft, Stanley Korman, (*), Julius Wolpe, Isadore Peake, Sam Sugar, Fannie Paul, Leon Shinberg, Fred Gichner, Fred Blum, Joseph Mendelson, Alan Wolpe, Herman Goodman, Isaac W. Friedman, Moe Rosenfeld, (*), Morris Fisher.

Rear: (*), David Saks, Rabbi Samuel Weiss, Frank Grad, architect, A. Berman, (*), Joseph Wilner, (*), Isaac Jacobson. (*unidentified.)

The third Adas Israel synagogue dedicated 1951, Connecticut Avenue and Porter Street.

Sanctuary, as it appeared from 1951 to 1969. Paul Lewis is at the podium at dedication of Holocaust Memorial, which he endowed, 1963. Photo by Mel Chamowitz.

Sanctuary, as refurbished, at re-dedication services, 1969. Photo by Monte.

Arthur L. Welsh (Lable Welcher), America's first Jewish aviator, seated in one of the early planes he tested. Photo courtesy of Jewish Historical Society of Washington.

Nathan Gottlelf, the second president of Adas Israel, and Julie Gotthelf, his wife. Photo courtesy of Jewish Historical Society of Washington.

Jacob Voorsanger, Rabbi of Adas Israel, 1876-1877, Voorsanger was the first "trained" clergyman to be engaged by Adas Israel.

Jacob Boyer, president of Adas Israel, 1874-1877. Boyer presided over construction and dedication of first synagogue in 1876.

Isadore Samuels, Cantor, 1908-1909.

Samuel Glushak, Cantor, 1910-1914.

Nathan Colish, Rabbi, 1920-1921. Photo by Bob Loewenthal.

Benjamin Grossman, Rabbi, 1914-1920. Photo by Lenscraft Photos, Inc.

Rabbi Louis Schwefel, 1923-1929.

Theodore Shabshelowitz, Rabbi, 1921-1922.

Solomon Metz, Rabbi, 1930-1951.

Samuel Weiss, Assistant Cantor/Rabbi, 1947-1969. Photo by Henry Gichner.

Adler Shefferman, Cantor, 1914-1925.

Jacob Barkin, Cantor, 1946-1958. Photo by Harris & Ewing.

Raphael Edgar, Cantor, 1960-1972. Photo by Steve Eykamp.

Fred Gichner, president 1929, and Tina Gichner, his wife, Shem Tov Recipient, 1969. Photo by Henry Gichner.

Stanley Rabinowitz, Rabbi , 1960-1986. Photo by Pat Bress, 1986.

Joseph Wilner, President of Adas Israel for 23 years, 1930-1953.

Joseph Wilner presenting citation on retirement of Benjamin Grossberg, sexton of Adas Israel, 1922-1947. Photo by Henry Gichner.

The Sabbath of Chanukah showing the She
Tov Menorah designed by Milton Hebald a
endowed by Dianne and Norman Bernste
With Rabbi Rabinowitz, Cantor Edgar, and Ral
Weiss. Photo by A.M. Bass.

Left to right, Abe Kay, Julius Wolpe, Cantor Barkin, Dore Schary, guest speaker, Rabbi Panitz, Rabbi Harry Halpern guest speaker, Samuel Lebowitz, Stanley Weiner. 90th Anniversary, May 15, 1959. Photo in study of Rabbi Panitz. Note plaster replicas of designs on doors of Aron Hakodesh. Photo by Mel Chamowitz.

Dedication of the Holocaust Memorial, April 22, 1963. Left to right, Luba Tryszynski Frederick, survivor of Belsen, Julius Wolpe, Paul Lewis, donor of the memorial, Joseph Blumenthal, Ambassador Avraham Harman, Myer Feldman, Counsel to President Kennedy, Justice Arthur Goldberg, Rabbi Rabinowitz. Photo by Mel Chamowitz.

Vice President Hubert Humphrey, guest speaker at Human Rights Sabbath, December 10, 1966. Left to right, Milton Baldinger, vice-president, Ambassador Sevilla Sacassa of Nicaragua, Dean of the Diplomatic Corps, Vice President Humphrey, Rabbi Rabinowitz, Samuel Lebowitz, president of the congregation.

Officers of the Congregation, 1953. Rear from left to right: Morris Gewirz, Isaac Jacobson, Joseph Bulman, Abe Shefferman, Julius Wolpe, Stanley Weiner, Henry Gichner. Front row: Rabbi Panitz, Joseph Blumenthal, Isadore Turover, Cantor Barkin. Photo by Mel Chamowitz.

Officers, 1957. Front row, left to right, Henry Salus, Samuel Lebowitz, Julius Wolpe, president, Stenley Wiener. Second row, Morris Gewirz, Samuel Cohen, Abe Shefferman. Photo by Steve Zweig.

Centennial year officers, 1969. Front row, left tc right, Donald Wolpe, Joseph Mendelson, presi dent, Leon Shinberg. Rear rows, Jacob Lish Stanley Wiener, Alex Hassan, Bernarc Fishchgrund, Melvin Cohen. Photo by Me Chamowitz.

Senator Herbert Lehman (center) at Mens' Club Congressional Dinner, Jan. 28, 1953. Joseph Wilner on left, Stanley Wiener on right.

Vice President Richard Nixon at the Mens' Club Congressional Banquet, January 28, 1953. Left to right, Abe Shefferman, Executive Director, Nixon, Phillip Goldstein, Max Goldberg, Stanley Weiner, Mens' Club officers. Photo Steve Zweig.

Guest Speaker: Justice Arthur Goldberg. Left to right, Cantor Edgar, Vice President Joseph Blumenthal, Justice Goldberg, Rabbi Rabinowitz, President Samuel Lebowitz. Photo by Mel Chamowitz.

Rabbi David Panitz succeeds Rabbi Metz in 1951.

The Rev. Martin Luther King visiting Adas Israel where he delivered an address in the summer of 1963. The Rev. Ralph Abernathy, successor to King, is at King's left, Isaac Franck at his right. Trude Feldman, a journalist, is interviewing King.

Tombstone of Stephen Theodore Norman, grandson of Theodore Herzl, Adas Israel Cemetery.

Adolphus Simeon Solomons, (1826-1910) early member of Adas Israel and president of The Jewish Theological Seminary Association. Photograph from a painting by his daughter, Aline Esther, and now hanging at the Seminary with duplicate at the headquarters of American Red Cross. Photo courtesy of Jewish Historical Society.

Prime Minister Golda Meir attends worship services at Adas Israel on the Sabbath of Sukkot, September, 1969. Leading, left to right, Rabbi Rabinowitz, Ambassador Yitzchak Rabin, Prime Minister Meir, future ambassador Simcha Dinitz, following, Rabbi Jacob Garfinkle, Cantor Edgar, and Israeli guard. Photo by Mel Chamowitz.

The Prime Minister addressed the Congregation.

Two venerable leaders, Joseph Blumenthal and Julius Wolpe. (Wolpe's son, Alan, married Blumenthal's daughter, Eleanor.) A presentation to Julius Wolpe on the conclusion of his presidency. Photo by Chamowitz.

Rabbi David Panitz delivering the invocation at Congressional Dinner at the Mayflower Hotel, 1953. On the left, Vice President Richard Nixon, to the right, Stanley Wiener, head of the Mens' Club, Mrs. Nixon and Speaker of the House Joseph Martin.

Rabbi Mordecai M. Kaplan lecturing to the Congregation, 1968. Isaac Franck, director of the Jewish Community Council, bottom left.

Mr. and Mrs. Benjamin Grossberg at 6th and I, in the 1930s. Mr. Grossberg, the long tenured *shamash*, lived to be over 100.

me Minister Golda Meir, flanked by Simcha
itz and Yitzchak Rabin leaving the synagogue
owing services. Security officer in the fore-
und. Photo by Chamowitz.

Chancellor Louis Finkelstein at a relaxed moment after addressing the congregation at its ground breaking ceremony for the synagogue on Connecticut Avenue, 1950.

Mt. Vernon Methodist Church, receiving line after the Thanksgiving Day service which followed the assassination of President Kennedy, 1963. From the left, the Rev. Albert P. Shirkey, minister of the church, President Lyndon Johnson, Lady Bird Johnson, Rabbi Norman Gerstenfeld of the Washington Hebrew Congregation, and Rabbi Rabinowitz who delivered the sermon.

Art Exhibit opening, December 1962. Left to right: Anita Rabinowitz, Dov Safrai of Safrai Galleries, Jerusalem, Lady Ashenheim and His Excellency the Ambassador of Jamaica, Lord Ashenheim. Photo by City News Bureau.

Robert Kennedy addressed the congregation in 1965. Left to right, Jerry Golomb, Mortimer Caplin head of the Internal Revenue Service, and former Attorney General Robert Kennedy looking at a volume of sermons delivered on the death of President John F. Kennedy, Rabbi Rabinowitz, on the right.

a career that was as unhappy as it was brief. Baltimore could also claim the first American-born, university-trained ordained Rabbi in the United States, Rabbi Henry Schneeberger, who served Chizuk Amunah Congregation from 1876 to 1916. Ordained in Berlin, Schneeberger would later join in the formation of the Jewish Theological Seminary and would bring Adas Israel into the Seminary orbit.

The earliest reference to a Jewish clergyman in Washington is found in the news account of a "priest" named Raphael Jones, German-born, who "wrote Hebrew and was acquainted with other languages," and, in 1813, officiated at the funeral of Isaac Polock, Washington's first Jewish resident. Jones, it will be recalled, had been a Georgetown grocer long before the founding of Washington's first congregation.

In seeking a professional clergyman, the founders of Washington's first two synagogues were primarily interested in someone who possessed the skill to pronounce the right words in the familiar way and who knew how to perform the accepted rites at the right time. Of course, he had to be observant of the Sabbath and dietary laws. In short, they were interested in finding someone to fill the role of priest. The desire for a sage would come later, and for a prophet, even later, if at all.

Both the Washington Hebrew Congregation and Adas Israel, like many other early American synagogues, applied the title "hazzan" to their clergymen. The hazzan led the services, officiated at religious ceremonies, read the Torah, sounded the shofar, and instructed children in Bible and the Hebrew language. In some instances, he was required to act as the shochet. Occasionally, he was invited to speak or, as the minutes put it, "to deliver an oration." And for these duties, his remuneration maintained the ancient ecclesiastical tradition that poverty was cleansing to the soul as well as an assurance of a place in the world-to-come.

According to the history of the Washington Hebrew Congregation written by one of its early rabbis, Abraham Simon, the first elected hazzan of the yet undivided congregation was Sam Herman in 1854. Then, in turn, came Mr. Seldner in 1855, H. Mela in 1856, S. M. Landsberg in 1857, S. Weil from 1859 to 1867, and J. S. Jacobson in 1868, all of whom were expected to be "*Hasan, Schocath* and Teacher in Hebrew and German." The brevity of each tenure was a reflection of the state of the "calling" in pioneer days. Dr. Herman Baar was engaged in 1869, prior to the division, but arrived only in 1870, after it had occurred. Rev. Isaac Stempel was engaged in 1870, following the separation.[3]

Stempel's sympathies were with the dissidents who had resigned to form the Adas Israel Congregation, for we find that in October 1870, "Rev. Stempel refused to read prayers in English, refused to light the synagogue properly, and refused to give a sermon, for which a note of censure was adopted by the Board."[4] The president declined to deliver the censure resolution; Stempel retained a sympathetic following within the congregation.

In 1872, Stempel brought suit against the Washington Hebrew Congregation. The dispute was resolved by its president, Simon Wolf. Thirteen years later, in 1885, Isaac Stempel became the hazzan of Adas Israel.

The Adas Israel constitution, adopted in 1876, called for the hazzan to be elected annually. Moreover, reelection could not be taken for granted, for at the end of each one-year term, the hazzan was required to reapply for the post and even to compete against other candidates who might have responded to a published advertisement of the "vacant" post.

With the hazzan/rabbi so dependent upon congregational whims for his continued employment, never certain of reelection, and without tenure or security, the lay leaders were able to exercise effective control over his behavior. This provision would plague hazzan, rabbi, and congregation for many years and provides a significant explanation for the rapid turnover in the professional staff. One-year terms without tenure would remain the policy of Adas Israel for over eighty years, from its beginning until the decade of the 1940s.

The minutes of Adas Israel refer to the hazzan as "Reverend Mr.," "Reverend Doctor," or "Reverend Gentleman." In some instances he is referred to as "minister," a practice that was not unique to Adas Israel.

The prestigious Orthodox Congregation Kehillath Jeshurun in New York called Rabbi Mordecai Kaplan, who served them from 1903 to 1909, not rabbi but "minister," a reflection of its feeling that seminary ordination did not confer an authentic title.[5]

Adas Israel resisted using the title "rabbi" even for one who was formally ordained. Rabbi George Jacobs of Philadelphia, invited to consecrate the new Adas Israel synagogue in 1876, was referred to as the "Reverend Doctor."

The first Adas Israel clergyman to be referred to as "rabbi" was Morris Mandel in 1898, and then only in passing. His successor, Julius Loeb, though ordained, was assigned the rabbinical title not in the minutes but in a newspaper article in 1903. It was many years before Adas Israel used the title "rabbi" for its clergy.

From its founding in the winter of 1869 until September 1872, Adas Israel did not employ salaried clergy. Initially, only two persons served for wages: Simon Mundheim as shochet and Manassas Oppenheimer as sexton. To lead the congregation in worship, read the Torah, and sound the shofar, the congregation relied upon several skilled members as well as its two salaried officials.

On Mundheim's retirement, the congregation elected Rev. Joseph A. Cohen to serve as "Chahzan, Bal Korah, and Schochat."[6] When it turned out to be impossible to replace Cohen at his salary, the congregation decided to struggle on without a paid hazzan. Again, members conducted the services. For two years, the board assigned responsibility for the Sabbath services by monthly rotation, restricting the assignments to those who were "married and who strictly keep Shabbes and all holidays."[7]

Once the congregation moved into its new synagogue on 6th and G Streets in 1876, the members realized that it was essential for them to employ a professional hazzan. To attract the "right person," the board agreed to pay a salary of as much as $1,000. The members were well aware that the Washington Hebrew Congregation had enjoyed the services of a well qualified Hazzan and teacher since 1872, the unordained Louis Stern.

An advertisement in New York's *Jewish Messenger* brought several responses. The search came down to two candidates, both of whom were invited to preach trial sermons. One was a Mr. Gershon, the other, Jacob Voorsanger.

By secret ballot, on August 27, 1876, "Mr. J. Voorsanger was duly elected as Chahzan, Bal Kaurah, Hebrew Teacher and lecturer."[8] Voorsanger received sixteen votes to Gershon's two. His salary was not the optimum $1,000, but $900 per year.

The board had chosen wisely. We know nothing about Gershon, but "Mr." Jacob Voorsanger was destined to have a distinguished career in the American rabbinate. He possessed many skills and proved to be an effective religious leader.

### Jacob Voorsanger

We know more about Voorsanger than we do of his unordained predecessors or successors because he left behind a considerable body of sermons, articles, and letters and also because his successor in his San Francisco pulpit, Rabbi Martin A. Meyer, wrote his biography.

Born in Amsterdam, Holland, on November 13, 1852, the year of the founding of Washington's first congregation, Voorsanger came to the United States in 1873.[9] His first position was that of hazzan of the Bene Israel Congregation in Philadelphia, founded by Jewish immigrants from Holland. Out of his modest annual salary of $400.00, he "engaged a teacher of elocution" to help him in his English speech.[10] By the summer of 1876, the Philadelphia congregation could no longer afford to pay his salary.

From the dying congregation in Philadelphia, which soon disbanded, Voorsanger came to Adas Israel shortly after the dedication of the synagogue on 6th and G Streets. Although he was only twenty-four years of age, the congregation's elders expected him to be a duplicate of the *hazzanim* they remembered from the old country. And Voorsanger succeeded. The congregation referred to him neither as rabbi nor as cantor, as shown by the regulation adopted soon after his arrival:

> The Minister of the Congregation shall be authorized to perform all marriage ceremonies to all parties applying therefor at a fee not less than $5.00 provided such parties have previously obtained consent from the Board of Managers of this Congregation.[11]

Soon after his arrival in Washington, Voorsanger had the good sense to visit one of the city's leading Jewish citizens, the past president of the Washington Hebrew Congregation, Simon Wolf, who would recall that Voorsanger "introduced himself as the new chasan of the orthodox synagogue, corner of Sixth and G Streets, N.W."[12]

However impressive Voorsanger may have appeared, it was still necessary to mold him into the accepted format of Adas Israel. Manassas Oppenheimer, the sexton, called upon the officials to "instruct the chahzan how in what manner he shall wear his *Talish.*"[13]

Adas Israel's constant need for funds gave Voorsanger an opportunity to display his leadership ability. To meet its budget, the congregation had decided to sponsor a "fair," which was scheduled for March 1877. To the amazement of all, Voorsanger volunteered to take charge.

He assumed responsibility for the project with conscientious diligence, soliciting members for support and encouraging their participation. People responded to his enthusiasm. The results were impressive. Proudly, Voorsanger reported to the board in his capacity as "Honorable Secretary of the Committee on giving the fair," that the fair had earned a net profit of $921.

The congregation was impressed; never had one of its fund-raising efforts brought in so much money. As an expression of appreciation, the board adopted a resolution of commendation and gave Voorsanger a gift of "one set of parlor furniture and a small table at a cost of $47.00 which they sent before Pesach to the Rev. Gentleman's house."[14]

Adas Israel's clergy were not permitted to attend board meetings unless invited to be present for a specific purpose. Voorsanger, already on the premises, was invited to enter the meeting room, where he was presented with the gift along with a letter thanking him for his zeal, "to which the Rev. Gentleman, in fitting terms, replied, thanking the congregation for the kindness manifested and accepting with thanks the gift not merited on his part. The Rev. Voorsanger then withdrew."

This idyllic picture of a harmonious and mutually beneficial relationship, marred only slightly by the congregation's disputes with the shochet, was not of long duration. Financial problems interceded. On July 1, less than a year after Voorsanger's arrival, the board was told that $25 had been advanced to him at his request prior to Passover and had not been repaid. Therefore, it was felt, the amount should be deducted from his salary. Three board members, Jacob Rich, Julius Louis, and Philip Cohen, felt the unkindness of the resolution strongly enough to ask that their names be recorded in opposition.

The congregation's leaders sensed that they would not be able to retain Voorsanger for another year. In August 1877, even before the expiration of his term, the board resolved that should Voorsanger resign, the next hazzan would be paid only $600. Sure enough, at its meeting later that same month, the board received and accepted Voorsanger's resignation, to take effect on September 1.*

From Washington, Voorsanger went to Providence, Rhode Island, where he served the Sons of Israel and David Congregation for one year, 1877 to 1878. Founded as an Orthodox synagogue in 1854, the congregation had become "moderate Reform" in 1877. This was Voorsanger's first experience with a non-Orthodox congregation, and it evidently made a deep impression on him, for we find that he attended the convention of the Union of American Hebrew Congregations in 1877.[15] Soon thereafter, he identified himself fully with the Reform movement.

It was in Houston, Texas, where Voorsanger served Beth Israel Congregation from 1878 to 1886, that the title of "rabbi" was first

*Money probably paid a big part in Voorsanger's decision to leave. In 1876, when he was being paid $900 a year at Adas Israel, nearby Baltimore's Chizuk Amunah was paying Rabbi Henry Schneeberger $1,200 a year, while in 1873, Baltimore's Oheb Shalom had paid Rabbi Benjamin Szold $4,500.

applied to him. In Houston, sensitive to the isolation of the Jews in the surrounding small communities, Voorsanger urged the appointment of circuit preachers, writing:

> Religion is now a dead letter with the majority of Israelites living in towns and villages; business, and nothing else, engrosses their minds, and their children are generally, nay totally, neglected.[16]

Despite his foreign origin, Voorsanger was an effective orator who, during his first fifteen years in the United States, had mastered English by carefully writing out every word of his speeches and sermons. Later, as his confidence came to match his fluency, he was able to speak without written texts.[17]

By the time he reached Congregation Emanu-El in San Francisco, where he served first as an assistant to Rabbi Elkan Cohn and subsequently, upon the latter's death in 1889, as the senior rabbi, Voorsanger was regarded as "one of the most talented and powerful Jewish preachers in the country."[18]

In San Francisco, Voorsanger also was professor of Semitic languages and literature at the University of California and a lecturer at Leland Stanford University. In 1895, having already edited the *Jewish South* while in Houston, and the *Sabbath Visitor* in Cincinnati, he founded and became the editor of his own weekly, the *Emanu-El*. His published works also include a book entitled *Moses Mendelssohn's Life and Works*.[19]

Voorsanger was well suited to Adas Israel during the period he spent there, for as his biographer, Martin Meyer, wrote of him, he "was never happier than when he could occupy some orthodox pulpit, in circles where it could be understood where he would be able to deliver himself of a modernized *Derashah* [sermon]. On such occasions he fairly revelled in the abundance of the riches which he brought forth out of the vast store-house of Jewish literature."[20]

It is doubtful that Voorsanger's tendency toward Reform or skill as a preacher in English were manifest during his brief tenure at Adas Israel. His antipathy to Orthodox traditions became evident after he left Washington. In his "Reminiscences," published in the *American Hebrew*, he revealed his contempt for Orthodox Judaism, describing it as "tinged with all the feudalism of the Middle Ages," and concluded his essay with a ringing affirmation of his faith that Judaism, "stripped of its oriental attributes will follow historical lines which are deeply grafted upon the destiny of the Jewish people."[21]

To Voorsanger, kabbalism (mysticism) was the "garbage of science, the distillation of all the aberrations that disfigure our literary and intellectual history."[22] He was no less hostile to Zionism which, he charged, masked the spiritual greatness of Judaism; he opposed the first Zionist congress which was held in Basle in 1897.

His intense dislike of orthodox traditions led him to be critical of the East-European Jews, whose migration had begun while he was yet in Houston and who, to his mind, were "Jews who mumbled their prayers, concerned themselves with clean pots and pans and this food or that, and failed to take their heads out of the Talmud."[23]

Voorsanger died on April 27, 1908, at the Hotel Del Monte in Monterey, California, where he had been vacationing. One of his close friends, noted that the name Voorsanger, in Dutch, is a euphemism for "chazan" or "cantor."[24]

One may wonder if it would have made any difference in the development of Adas Israel or in Voorsanger's career had Adas Israel been able to retain his services for more than one year. Unfortunately, his writings do not include any reference to the year he served in Washington nor can we reconstruct any trace of his influence on the congregation. It is reasonable to hope that Voorsanger's experience at Adas Israel did not condition his attitude toward the Orthodox tradition. From all accounts, the year in Washington was beneficial to both hazzan and congregation.

In 1983, two researchers, writing in the publication of the Western States Jewish Historical Society, challenged Voorsanger's right to call himself "rabbi" and the extent of his Jewish education in Holland, noting that they were unable to find any record of his ordination or of his attendance at the Jewish Seminary in Amsterdam. They asserted that his Jewish training was limited to high school level at a Hebrew day school, where, they wrote, he studied for seven years, from age twelve to nineteen. Nor could they substantiate the claim which others had made that Voorsanger was the descendant of several generations of German Rabbis. His father, Wolf Voorsanger, they wrote, had been a diamond cutter in Amsterdam.[25]

They did not deny that he had been an assiduous student who had acquired considerable rabbinic knowledge. Rabbi Stephen S. Wise had noted that Voorsanger "grew with the years" and that he was a Talmid Chacham. Rabbi Emil Hirsch of Chicago, a distinguished Reform Rabbi, who may have been aware of Voorsanger's lack of formal university or rabbinic training, nevertheless had affirmed that Voorsanger had achieved the status of rabbi by his own efforts:

> Voorsanger was, to a large extent, a self-made man . . . the superstructure he reared was essentially the result of studies pursued by himself, and that, too, in the scant hours of leisure which busy life as an active minister afforded.[26]

According to his biography in two Jewish Encyclopedias, Voorsanger had received his rabbinical education at the Jewish

Theological Seminary of Amsterdam, and, later, received two honorary degrees from the Hebrew Union College in Cincinnati, Bachelor of Theology in 1895 and Doctor of Divinity in 1903.

The researchers conceded that Voorsanger's achievements justified his honorary degrees; they only questioned his claim to formal ordination. The critism ignores the fact that in early American-Jewish history more than one "rabbi" served the Jewish community without benefit of formal ordination; they were either self-taught or apprenticed to others. Knowledge and skill in ritual were sufficient to ascribe an authority akin to ordination; only the shochet had to display formal credentials of ordination. Challenges to Voorsanger's qualifications notwithstanding, there is no reason to question the accuracy of the appraisal of the *Encyclopedia Judaica* which wrote of him that he was "well versed in Jewish literature, an energetic worker, and an able preacher and writer."[27]

### From Hazzan to Hazzan

With Voorsanger's departure in 1877, the congregation decided to engage a temporary replacement to chant the services for the forthcoming High Holy Days rather than to select a permanent successor from the two candidates who had applied for the post. Neither of the two applicants would accept the temporary assignment for the $75 offered by the congregation, and efforts to raise the stipend to $100 failed to gain the board's approval.

Immediately following the holidays, the congregation redoubled its efforts to secure a permanent hazzan, offering a salary of $500 with the use of the congregation's house rent-free or $600 without it. From among the two responding candidates, the congregation selected Rev. Adolph Boernstein to serve as "Chahzan, bal Korah, and Hebrew Teacher, at an annual salary of $500.00 . . . besides the free use of the dwelling connected with the synagogue, free fuel and gas and all perquisites," for one year beginning November 1, 1877.[28]

With Boernstein's arrival, the congregation was forced to face the unpleasant realization that it lacked the funds to pay him his first month's salary. Selig Goldstein advanced the newly elected hazzan $50 so that thereinafter he could receive his salary on the first of the month rather than at the end.

It soon became apparent that Boernstein could not support himself and his family on an annual salary of $500, whereupon the congregation agreed to increase his compensation to $800 per year on condition that he vacate the synagogue's dwelling, making it available to the sexton, who had agreed to serve without salary beyond free-will offerings and commission for collecting dues, if he were given free use of the house.

Boernstein survived his first year, although at its conclusion he had to apply for the position afresh and in writing even though there were no other candidates. He was reelected for the second year, 1879, at the previous salary of $800, "payable in equal payments of $66.67 every month in advance on or before the Sunday of each month."

The congregation's precarious financial situation continued throughout 1879. Without the motivation of a building campaign to stir them, the members appeared to lose spirit. The trustees informed the annual meeting in April that many members had resigned, only four had paid their current dues, and delinquencies totaled $130.

A bright spot in the report was the announcement that the "ladies proved themselves on the occasion as worthy daughters of Israel, for hardly had these members left us then the ladies formed themselves into a club, promising to aid us and to contribute their mite monthly."[29] * The women's group donated $40 as its initial offering.

*The "club" was the ladies' auxiliary, the forerunner of today's sisterhood.

The trustees then addressed the congregation's indebtedness.

> The indebtedness of the Congregation, which thanks to God is not increased, is nevertheless not so much in the decrease as we would like to see. . . .
>
> Our Chahzan, Rev. Boernstein, proposed to give a Concert for that purpose, but fearing it would not pay, we abandoned the idea.

Boernstein, disturbed by the congregation's precarious financial predicament and unhappy with his situation, sought and received permission for a "brief vacation." The board became angry when it learned that he had used his leave to officiate for a congregation in Philadelphia. It immediately appointed a committee to consider whether Boernstein should be impeached for breach of contract. The appointment of the "impeachment committee" was a bluff since the board recognized it could not retain the hazzan's services beyond the term of his contract which, in any case, was due to expire within nine months, on the first of January, 1880. To save face, the board gave the committee nine months to render a report; it was a way of avoiding a confrontation while maintaining the board's dignity.

On July 18, 1879, prior to the contract's termination date, Boernstein informed the congregation that he had been elected hazzan by a Philadelphia congregation as of September 1. The board had no alternative but to accept the resignation, but urged him to remain at his post until August 31.

Realizing that the congregation could no longer function with volunteers alone, the board advertised for a successor, who, again, would be expected to serve as "Chahzan, Bal Korah and Teacher and, if possible, Schochet . . . at an annual salary not to exceed $600.00."[30] There were two other conditions: applicants for the post would be required to chant the services "on two occasions," and the congregation would not pay for the candidate's trial visit to Washington.

A candidate soon appeared in the person of Rev. Isadore W. Samuels, who was immediately elected to complete Boernstein's unexpired term of service, from September 1 to December 31, 1879, as "Chahzan, Bal Koreh, and Hebrew Teacher at an annual salary of $600.00."

At the expiration of his four-month term, Samuels applied for reelection but found he had to face the competition of Rev. Brill of Richmond, Virginia, who had also applied for the position at the stipulated salary of $600. Finding themselves in the luxurious position of having a choice between two applicants, the board announced that the salary would now be $500, whereupon Brill withdrew his application. Samuels then agreed to serve at the lower figure.

As was the case with his predecessors, Samuels's tenure was anything but serene. In March, he asked for a week's leave. In April, unspecified charges were leveled against him by one of the members. In December, the congregation advertised in two Jewish newspapers that "an election of Chahzan etc. will take place on the first meeting in January next."

In January 1881, the board announced that there were three candidates for the advertised post: Rev. M. Salter of New London, Connecticut, Rev. M. Cohen of Philadelphia, and the incumbent, Samuels. The two Oppenheimers were asked to officiate at services for the four Sabbaths in January, and the cantorial applicants were to be invited "to come for trial, provided no expense to the congregation is thereby involved."[31]

Samuels could count on a small number of followers who remained loyal to him despite, or perhaps because of, the dissension that had accompanied his tenure. His friends moved to retain his services but failed to prevail. The board agreed, however, to employ him on a temporary basis at a remuneration of $5 per week, with

Manassas Oppenheimer to officiate whenever he was not available.

The proposal failed to take Samuels's feelings into account. He refused to meet with the committee sent to negotiate with him and "therefore, he left his residence temporarily for the purpose of not being met."[32]

The congregation faced an impending crisis. No one was on hand to officiate at the approaching festival of Purim. Without a hazzan it would be impossible to chant the *Megillah*, unless Oppenheimer agreed to do so, and he was reluctant to fill the breach because he felt strongly that a permanent hazzan should be employed. By withholding his services he hoped to force the board to engage one.

The board refused to yield. Eventually Oppenheimer assented to chant the *Megillah*. He was given a Kiddush cup as a token of the congregation's appreciation, a gift which no doubt cost more than the $5 they would have paid Samuels.

The *Jewish Messenger* carried the congregation's advertisement for a hazzan at a cost of $3.60. Oppenheimer was pressed into service for Sabbath worship, but announced in July that "it would be hardly possible for him to hereafter officiate at the Synagogue and that it is necessary for the congregation to engage a Chahzan." A motion to delay was rejected; the president was empowered to "procure a Chahzan now from Baltimore, but no expense shall be incurred except travelling costs for the gentleman's coming here for a trial."[33]

When the president's efforts proved to be unsuccessful, and realizing finally that a hazzan was indispensable for the forthcoming High Holidays, the board was more receptive to Samuels's offer to return to his vacated post on the congregation's terms. He was then elected to serve for the "unexpired term from September 1, 1881 to January 1, 1882, and for four months thereafter to May 1, 1882, at a monthly salary of $25.00."

A suggestion by Oppenheimer that Samuels's monthly salary be increased by $5 was "reluctantly" rejected by the board in March 1882. The hazzan was, however, presented with a $5 "donation for Purim."

In 1885, Rev. Isaac Stempel, who had formerly served as hazzan of the Washington Hebrew Congregation, and had been sympathetic to the group that withdrew to found Adas Israel, was elected by Adas Israel as its hazzan. He applied for reelection in 1886 and was granted one additional year. Even though he was commended for the "admirable manner in which he had conducted the High Holyday services" the board refused to retain him beyond the two years he had served. In appreciation for his services, it appropriated $30 to purchase a tallit for Stempel and a gold-headed cane for an assistant hazzan, Mr. Tanzer.

By the late 1880s the number of East European Jews in the congregation had increased. In preference to Stempel, favored by the German Jews, they looked to a new applicant, Philip Bernstein. Adding spice to the process of choosing between the two candidates, the German Jews who opposed Bernstein circulated rumors "touching upon his character." Despite the slander voiced by the opposition, Bernstein was elected over Stempel by a vote of twenty-six to five. It was the beginning of the revolt against German domination of the congregation.

Stempel, now a victim of the emerging ethnic rivalry in Adas Israel, wrote to the congregation, "I herewith respectfully request you to import to me a testimonial for having served for two years your congregation as Preacher, Reader, Teacher, and Bal Korah."[34] His request was granted but his application for membership was rejected. Members were not eager for him to remain in the congregation.

Stempel's successor, Philip Bernstein, inherited a divided congregation; his opponents would not forgive him for having displaced Stempel. Herman Baumgarten, spokesman for the German element, persisted in pressing charges against Bernstein, submitting a petition which read, "We the undersigned deem it our duty to prefer charges against the Rev. Philip Bernstein for conduct unbecoming a Gentleman and Minister and ask the same to be investigated. Signed, Herman Baumgarten and Gottlieb Spitzer."[35]

Mr. Lewis objected to the charges on procedural grounds: the petition had been written in pencil. Lewis's strategy was to buy time and burden the investigation with technical obstacles. The president ruled that a pencil was a valid writing instrument and appointed Simon Oppenheimer to investigate the charges, which were to be submitted to three-man arbitration.

In April 1888, concerned about his future and fearful of opposition, Bernstein asked the board for some indication that he would be retained at the conclusion of the current agreement. The board responded that it was unable to predict the outcome of the elections for hazzan, which would not take place until June.

The June elections were indeed heated and had less to do with the hazzan's ability than with his ethnic background. There were five applicants for the post in addition to Bernstein: T. Salzman of Baltimore, A. Applebaum of Danville, Pennsylvania, W. Berger of Rondout, New York, William Wintrop of Philadelphia, and J. Lublinsky of Pottsville, Pennsylvania.

Baumgarten moved "that where an applicant for the position was under charges, his application could not be considered until those charges were disposed of." The minutes reflect the heated nature of the discussion.

> After considerable quibbling over this question, the Sec'y. p. t. requested the floor in order to harmonize the turbulent feeling,

> which was accorded to him. He stated that as prosecuting witness in the charges pending against Rev. Bernstein, he would, if the Committee on charges retire with him, enable them to bring in their report, and thereby remove the obstacle against Mr. Bernstein's candidacy. This announcement was greeted with applause, and on motion that the committee on charges retire and bring in their report, it was carried. A recess was then taken for five minutes.
>
> Mr. Lewis, of the Committee on charges, reported that inasmuch as Mr. H. Baumgarten the plaintiff in the case against Rev. Mr. Bernstein, had withdrawn his charges, the Committee would suggest that the Committee be discharged, which was adopted. Mr. Greenapple then moved to go into an election of chazan, teacher, and bal korah.[36]

With fifty-four members present, Bernstein was reelected with twenty-six votes in his favor but with twenty-three abstentions. A motion to expunge all reference to charges against the hazzan was adopted, whereupon "Mr. Bernstein in a feeling manner promised to do his duty and strive to maintain the dignity of the office and thanked the members for their favorable action in his case."

Peace would remain elusive.

In October, further charges were leveled against the hazzan touching on his "character." Julius Baumgarten again moved to appoint an investigation committee.

> The President tried in vain to appoint a committee but disorder prevailed to such an extent that the President handed in his resignation, which, however, was laid on the table.
>
> Mr. Greenapple, Mr. Isaac Levy, and Mr. P. Rich would continuously speak in favor of the Chazan. Several attempts were made to ask the Chazan to resign but all to no avail. Finally, Mr. Horn withdrew his charges, contrary to the protest of the Sec'y and took the charges from the table. After a great deal of debating, the Congregation adjourned.[37]

One month later, unable to dislodge the hazzan on the basis of his performance as cantor, Herman Baumgarten now expressed unhappiness with his administration of the school. "Owing to the incapacity of the Chazan, he was deprived of his privileges of sending his children to school." Baumgarten pressed for reorganization of the school board. In January, the school was closed "for lack of progress."

Bernstein continued to be hounded by opponents whom he could not satisfy. His problems were not limited to dissatisfaction with his cantorial or pedagogic ability nor to his East European origin; they included unhappiness with his management of his personal affairs. When his salary was attached by court injunction, the hazzan's supporters surrendered. They privately agreed to pay him $200 if he would resign. The board succeeded in obtaining his resignation in March 1889 for only $180, the equivalent of three months salary. And thus ended the unfortunate saga of Hazzan Philip Bernstein.

Unable to secure an immediate replacement, the congregation again invited the ever-accommodating Isadore Samuels to serve on a temporary basis while continuing the search for a permanent replacement. Mr. Kalman of Philadelphia was invited to serve for one month but was dismissed after one week because he did not "possess the required qualifications." He was paid $10.

"Rev. Mr. Mendes recommended Mr. Mosesohn of New York and Herman Baumgarten volunteered to interview him on a forthcoming trip to that city."

Finally, weary with the search, the congregation settled on Leopold Heiman, origin unknown, first for four months, and then for one year as of January 1, 1890, at $600 per year. His election was uncontested.

Heiman reopened the school and one month later asked to appear before the board ostensibly to render a report on its progress, but before concluding he stated that "it was impossible to get along on his salary." Herman Baumgarten concurred but insisted that the request was unconstitutional and demanded that a special meeting be called to consider the hazzan's request. The meeting took place on January 12. The hazzan's wages were increased by $10 per month.

Except for the hazzan's complaint about the poor behavior of the children in the school, all went reasonably well until July 1890, when Mr. Lewis (who believed that a petition drawn in pencil had no validity) "entered a verbal complaint against the Chazan owing to his non-attendance at Minyan, and otherwise being negligent in the discharge of his duties."[38]

By December it was clear that Heiman had worn out his welcome; he was notified that "there was no possibility of his re-election." The board granted him a month's leave with pay to find another position. Once again Samuels, the faithful standby, was called back at $5 per week.

The congregation advertised for a successor. Emanuel Rosenzweig responded and "after lengthy debate" was elected for three months for $75 monthly. One could conclude that the "lengthy debate" centered around the increase in the new hazzan's wages to $75 from the previous level of $50, because following the hazzan's election, the financial secretary, Sol Lewis, resigned his office.

Rosenzweig, reelected the following year, served from 1891 to 1894. He was expected to teach two hours each day except Friday and had to be reminded that he was neglecting the school. The congregation found it difficult to pay his salary; nor was it content with his services. In April 1894, it notified Rosenzweig that his contract would not be renewed and paid him $108.52 in back salary in addition to $75 as severance.

President Oppenheimer, taking the board's approval for granted, again engaged Samuels as a temporary replacement at $10 per month. Samuels was requested to attend Mincha services on the Sabbath.

Weary with temporary replacements and the succession of ineffectual and apparently untrained clergymen, the congregation finally agreed to turn to the Jewish Theological Seminary, which had recently opened its doors, to seek a formally ordained and educated rabbinic personality who would be expected to assume responsibility for Adas Israel's total program.

# 13

## THE SEMINARY AND THE SYNAGOGUE

Four loosely organized philosophic approaches defined American Judaism in the mid-nineteenth century: the Orthodox, the moderate Reform led by Isaac Mayer Wise, the extreme Reform led by David Einhorn, and the "Historical School" led by Isaac Leeser, who passed away in 1868 to be succeeded by Sabato Morais. The Conservative Movement was an outgrowth of the Historical School, a descriptive term for a group that held, in the words of Dr. Moshe Davis, its historian, that "even while affirming the imperative of change and adjustment, the entire Tradition and Jewish experience would have to be explored and studied before specific innovations could be made."[1]

Although the two most influential religious leaders of the period, Wise and Leeser, agreed on the need for a college to train rabbis for American synagogues, they strongly disagreed on its religious orientation. Wise had organized Zion College in 1855, but it turned out to be little more than an elementary school. In 1865, two New York Reform rabbis founded the Emanu-El Theological Seminary; it was openly Reform in its approach.

Not to be outdone by the reformers, Isaac Leeser, in 1867, enlisted the aid of a group of wealthy laymen to launch Maimonides College in Philadelphia with an impressive faculty that included Sabato Morais, Marcus Jastrow, and others who would later be associated with the Jewish Theological Seminary.

Reacting derisively to the announcement of the founding of Maimonides College, Wise questioned the credentials of its professors, challenging the ability of Morais, Jastrow, and Leeser to teach homiletics, theology, or Hebrew philosophy. "What kind of an animal is this?" he asked rhetorically. He answered his own question: "Quackery, humbug."[2]

Leeser upheld tradition:

> It is not progress that we deprecate, but novelty, termed reform. . . . Men not noted for their piety or their devotion to Judaism destroy and do not build up. Reform . . . is an expression of the desire . . . to assimilate our worship to that of Christians. . . . If there must be change, let there be assembled God-loving and God-fearing Jews, whose learning, virtues, integrity, and labors commend them as fit representatives.[3]

Initially, the Hebrew Union College, which Wise founded in 1875 to train rabbis of all persuasions, had the backing of several rabbis who would later support the Jewish Theological Seminary, including Marcus Jastrow, Benjamin Szold, and even the seminary's first president, Sabato Morais. Wise had assured them that he had no intention of turning the College into a Reform institution. After examining its student body in 1877, Morais had written approvingly of the Cincinnati college, which, he said "may unequivocally be pronounced an object deserving of the support of all Israelites."[4]

Marcus Jastrow served on the committee to set admission and degree standards for the Hebrew Union College. Benjamin Szold served as an examiner for the school in 1883 and accepted an honorary degree one year later. In their cooperation with the college, the three leaders of the Historical School may have hoped either to influence its philosophy or at least to stem its extremism; they clung to the hope that the differences in ideology could be bridged by compromise and understanding.

The nondenominational premise on which they had based their hopes was shattered by the banquet held in Cincinnati in July 1883 to honor the first graduating class. The menu included littleneck clams, soft-shell crabs, shrimp, and frogs' legs, plus beef, ice cream, and cheese.[5] Infuriated, the traditionalists stormed out of the hall.

In reaction to the ensuing storm of protest, Wise, instead of apologizing, castigated the dietary practices of Judaism. His sneering contempt for the Jewish dietary laws and for those who upheld them enraged the traditionalists and disillusioned many who initially had been responsive to the idea of a nondenominational college. Wise's contemptuous reaction strengthened the convictions of those who felt there was no alternative but to organize another institution for the training of rabbis. Sabato Morais would be their leader.

### The Pittsburgh Platform

The Pittsburgh Platform, which has been called the charter of the Reform Movement, issued in November 1885, confirmed Reform Judaism as a distinct and separate denomination. To the Historical School, its most jarring provisions were those that rejected *kashrut*, rituals, and Jewish settlement in Palestine. Already shocked by the Trefe Banquet, as the infamous dinner at Hebrew Union College was dubbed, and repelled further by the terms of the platform, Szold and Jastrow withdrew their support from the Union of American Hebrew Congregations and the college and tried to induce their congregations to withdraw with them. In this endeavor, neither was successful.

Angry reactions to the Pittsburgh meeting raged in pulpits and the press. Editorial after editorial, page after page, letter upon challenging letter filled every Jewish paper and periodical. To the editorials in the *American Hebrew* attacking the platform, Wise responded with vitriolic sharpness, declaring the reformers to be the true orthodox of Israel and their opponents inconsistent fools and hypocrites because they themselves did not follow all of the 613 precepts.[6] A European Hebrew publication, *Hammagid*, termed the Reform conference *asefat harah banim*, punning the Hebrew word for "rabbis," *rabbanim*, with *rah banim*, "evil sons."

In the Jewish press, the antagonists were the Conservative *American Hebrew* and the Reform *Israelite*. The editorial debate spilled over into the nation's daily press.[7] Even Felix Adler, the former rabbinical student who had founded the Ethical Culture Society entered the fray in opposition to Reform: "They get rid of a good thing and replace it with nothing."[8] The debate intensified the drive to establish a new seminary.*

Even before the Reform meeting in Pittsburgh had taken place, two prominent Jewish papers, the *Jewish Record* in Philadelphia and the *American Hebrew* in New York, had issued a public call for the establishment of a new non-Reform rabbinical college. In his Chanukah sermon in 1884, Sabato Morais, whose congregation had never been part of the Reform Union, called for a new college. In the wake of the Pittsburgh Platform, the Historical group was compelled to define its own philosophy and to become less a school of thought and more a formal movement.

### The Seminary

Advocates of the effort to establish an "eastern seminary" solicited support in a widely distributed circular which bore the signatures of Sabato Morais, Alexander Kohut, H. Pereira Mendes,

*Among the prominent laymen who voiced their opposition to Reform were Cyrus Adler, Solomon Solis Cohen, Aaron and Harry Friedenwald, Mayer Sulzberger, Simon Roeder, Adolphus S. Solomons, Joseph Blumenthal, Edgar Phillips, and David Riza.

A. P. Mendes, Frederick de Sola Mendes, Bernard Drachman, and Henry W. Schneeberger.

The rabbinic leaders, disillusioned with the leadership of Isaac Mayer Wise and shocked by the excesses of the Reform group, proceeded to carry out their plans despite the absence of a supportive framework. Public announcement of the founding of a seminary came on January 31, 1886, emanating from an organizational meeting held in the trustee room of the Shearith Israel synagogue in New York City. The group of twelve rabbis and three laymen, altogether representing eleven congregations, adopted a resolution submitted by Rabbi A. P. Mendes of Newport, Rhode Island, calling for the establishment of a seminary to train teachers and leaders for the coming generation "in sympathy with the spirit of Conservative Judaism."

The organizing group called itself the Jewish Theological Association, and the school, the Jewish Theological Seminary of New York. The association adopted a constitution which defined the purposes of the group as "the preservation in America of the knowledge and practice of historical Judaism."[9] Sabato Morais was elected chairman and Henry Pereira Mendes secretary. Among the organizers was Rabbi Henry Schneeberger, who assumed the responsibility for bringing Adas Israel within the seminary orbit.

Henry William Schneeberger, the rabbi of Baltimore's Congregation Chizuk Amunah from 1876 to 1916, was the first American-born ordained rabbi in the United States. He was born in New York city in 1848 and received a Masters Degree from Columbia University and his rabbinical ordination from Rabbi Israel Hildesheimer in Berlin in 1871.

The participants at the meeting differed on the name to be given the institution as well as on the use of the term "Conservative Judaism." Neither were they of one mind in defining their religious ideology. Consistent with his thinking, Morais wanted to call the new school the Orthodox Seminary, but Alexander Kohut persuaded Morais to abandon the sectarian name and instead to name it the Jewish Theological Seminary, because, as he stated, "we imperiously need a seminary which will have no other ambition, no other title than that it be purely and truly Jewish. We do not desire it to be destined for a sect, whether reform, conservative or orthodox."[10]

In compromise, the new association used the term "Conservative Judaism" in its organizational resolution but retained "Historical Judaism" in its constitution. The two terms were to remain linked for a few more years; ultimately "Historical Judaism" would fall into disuse.

In opposition, Wise insisted that neither the signers of the circular nor the recipients were "genuinely orthodox." He argued,

> We would like to see a genuine Yeshiva . . . with long bearded rabbis, little cunning black eyes glittering forth from under their high foreheads, covered with black caps, expounding the Talmud as the book handed down orally from Heaven. . . . This merely opposition Seminary . . . under the auspices of men who are themselves *Poshim* [sinners] in the eyes of the genuines hardly deserves support.[11]

The traditionalist wing of the seminary's founders was counterbalanced by a liberal group made up of Alexander Kohut (1842–1894), Benjamin Szold (1829–1902), and Marcus Jastrow (1829–1903). Both Szold and Jastrow traveled on the Sabbath when necessary. Szold was known to recite grace at meals without head covering, although he insisted on worshiping with covered head at synagogue services.

While the liberal rabbis in the group did not influence the formation of Adas Israel, they exerted a discernible influence on the seminary and many of its graduates; they also helped create the climate which would enable Adas Israel as well as the seminary to move from Orthodoxy to Conservative Judaism.

**Beginnings**

Reasoning that one cause for the failure of Maimonides College had been that Philadelphia Jewry had lacked the resources and population to maintain a Jewish college, Morais determined to place the seminary in New York, where it would be in a better position to benefit from the support of what was even then the largest Jewish population in the country, even though the distance of the proposed seminary from his own residence in Philadelphia would work a hardship on his already overburdened energies. Morais asked New York's Sephardic Congregation Shearith Israel, then located on 19th Street, to house the seminary in its vestry room.

Morais commuted to New York each week and depended on Kohut to raise the funds and carry out the administrative functions necessary for the seminary's operation. Under Morais's influence the newly established seminary attracted the participation of Dr. Cyrus Adler of Philadelphia and Washington, who would later assume an important role in its leadership and that of the Conservative Movement.

Eight candidates for admission responded to newspaper announcements of the seminary's entrance examinations. All were American-born children of immigrants. Opening exercises were held in New York City's Lyric Hall on January 2, 1887, with addresses offered by Sabato Morais, the president of the faculty; Alexander Kohut, professor of Talmud; and Joseph Blumenthal, chairman of the board of trustees.

It was Alexander Kohut more than anyone else who, in his address, defined the purpose of the school and the ideology of the movement.

> This spirit shall be that of Conservative Judaism, the conserving Jewish impulse which will create in the pupils of the Seminary the tendency to recognize the dual nature of Judaism and the Law . . . and acknowledges the necessity of observing the Law as well as of studying it.[12]

Classes met in one of the rooms of the Shearith Israel building on 19th Street. When the number of students increased, the school moved to the Cooper Union. Benjamin Szold had been invited to join the faculty but declined because it would have necessitated his giving up his congregation in Baltimore.

The seminary's founders immediately set out to garner the support essential to the new institution's viability. They established membership categories for individuals and congregations, and launched an effort to seek the affiliation of both.

Rabbi Schneeberger of Baltimore wrote to Adas Israel asking to be invited to speak to them on seeking "the cooperation of the Congregation in the project of building a Seminary for the education of Jewish Rabbis in the City of New York."[13] Schneeberger was not a stranger to Adas Israel. He had lectured there in 1878. Adas Israel had sent him a resolution of thanks.[14]

Adas Israel responded to the "Rev. Gentleman" that the facilities of the synagogue would be available to him "at any time he may feel disposed to come." Schneeberger then informed Morais of his plans to speak in Washington and asked that promotional material be forwarded to him for distribution. He spoke at Adas Israel on March 28, 1886, delivering what Oppenheimer, the president of the congregation, described as "an eloquent lecture," adding his regrets "that the attendance was not larger." Reporting back to Morais, Schneeberger wrote:

> My long proposed visit to Washington took place yesterday. I had a fair audience. I was not surprised of such, because the president

> of the congr. in a letter some time ago complained of the indifference and lukewarmness of its members.
>
> I gave them some healthy admonition regarding school and synagogue and spoke most emphatically on the Seminary and its purposes. I had the appeals circulated and hope to meet with some beneficial results.[15]

The seminary and Schneeberger persisted in their efforts to enlist Adas Israel's support. "Several communications from the Jewish Theological Seminary in N.Y. were read and filed."[16] While there is no record of congregational endorsement, individuals must have offered some support, because years later the relationship with the seminary would be cemented by Adas Israel's selection of one of the seminary's scarce graduates to serve as its rabbi.

**Depression**

The last decade of the nineteenth century was burdened by searing depression; the gloom was worldwide. In Europe it was a decade of shocking anti-Semitism underscored by the Dreyfus affair in France. In promising contrast, it was also the decade of Theodor Herzl and the First Zionist Congress.

Washington was not exempt from the depressed state of the world's economy. Reflecting the situation, Adas Israel suffered loss of membership and increased difficulty in collecting dues. It had been served by a series of hazzanim whose only function was to chant the services. The congregation continued to depend upon the sale of cemetery plots to meet its budget. Worse still was the loss of enthusiasm that resulted from repetitive frustrations; meetings were canceled for lack of quorum, and when conducted, the agenda was a litany of financial woes.

Equally foreboding was the despair that had descended upon the Jewish Theological Seminary. Sabato Morais, the seminary's founder and first president, had passed away in 1897. The devoted president of the board of trustees, Joseph Blumenthal, who willingly and frequently had covered its monthly deficits from his own funds, passed away shortly thereafter. A $6,000 gift from Baroness de Hirsch, obtained by Morais with the intercession of Adolphus Solomons, had long been expended.

Isaac Mayer Wise passed away in 1900. With the death of the two rabbinic leaders, Morais, the champion of tradition and founder of the seminary, and Wise, the champion of Reform and founder of the Hebrew Union College, it was proposed that the two institutions merge into a single unified and broad-spectrum college for rabbinic studies. The *American Hebrew* invited a symposium on the subject which appeared in its issue of May 25, 1900.

Two Washingtonians participated. Simon Wolf, past president of the Washington Hebrew Congregation, wrote in favor of the merger. Cyrus Adler, vigorously opposed, stated "that the positive and probably irreconcilable views animating the leading spirits of the two institutions render even the consideration of this subject a waste of time."

Louis Dembitz, an uncle of Supreme Court Justice Louis Brandeis and an early supporter of Reform Judaism who had turned to the seminary after the Pittsburgh Platform, offered an amusing reaction to the proposal by asking, "What kind of a commencement supper would be served?" a light-hearted allusion to the calamitous nonkosher Banquet served by the Hebrew Union College at its first graduation. The proposal to merge came to nought.

Despite the loss of its founder and the prevailing mood of despondency, the Jewish Theological Seminary pursued its commitment to prepare students for the American rabbinate. The students, of modest means, faced the serious problem of supporting themselves. Most came from immigrant homes in the ghetto of the Lower East Side. They could not afford to pay tuition; the seminary had to provide them with financial stipends and even proper clothing. To support themselves, students took jobs as teachers at schools on the Lower East Side where the pupils were the children of newly arrived Russian Jewish immigrants. Some conducted Sabbath services, including those at the YMHA and the Guardians' Orphan Asylum. Nonetheless, some students were forced to drop out because of financial problems.

After eight years of instruction, only one student was deemed ready for ordination. At the seminary's first graduation exercises in 1894, Joseph H. Hertz became its first ordained rabbi. He was elected to serve a congregation in Syracuse, New York. Later, he would be called, in turn, to Johannesburg, South Africa, and New York City before becoming Chief Rabbi of the British Empire in 1913. Hertz's widely used edition of the Pentateuch and Haftaroth is still used in many congregations.

The second graduating class, in 1895, ordained Henry Speaker and David Wittenberg as rabbis and Emil Friedman as hazzan. The third graduating class, in 1898, ordained two rabbis, Bernard M. Kaplan and Morris Mandel. Kaplan served first in Montreal, moved to Sacramento, California, in 1902, and three years later became the rabbi of Congregation Ohabey Shalom in San Francisco, where he remained from 1905 to 1915. Upon the death of Jacob Voorsanger, Adas Israel's former hazzan, he became the editor of the *Emanu-el*, which had become the most important Jewish weekly on the West Coast.[17]

His classmate, Morris Mandel, became the first seminary-ordained rabbi of Adas Israel.

Mandel's election followed a visit to New York by Adas Israel's president, Simon Oppenheimer, and secretary, Julius Baumgarten, who travelled to New York not to select a rabbi but to attend a meeting called by the seminary to form a national organization of non-Reform congregations. Adas Israel responded to the Seminary's invitation.

> A Communication received from the Orthodox convention to be held in the city of N. Y. on June 1, 1898 and asked this congregation to send delegates. On motion of the secretary two delegates were nominated and elected. The delegates were President Simon Oppenheimer and Secy. Julius Baumgarten, who are to pay their own expenses. The gentlemen accepted their office amidst applause.[18]

The "Orthodox convention," at which fifty congregations were represented, was held at Shearith Israel on 70th Street and Central Park West; the organization founded by the delegates was the Union of Orthodox Jewish Congregations of America. Its ostensible purpose was to promote the cause of Orthodox Judaism. In reality, it was intended to provide a membership basis for the seminary and a vehicle for the seminary to assert its leadership over the increasing numbers of Russian Jews and their congregations. The Orthodox Union was to have the same relationship to the seminary as did the Union of American Hebrew Congregations to the Hebrew Union College. Adas Israel was a charter member of the newly organized Orthodox Union which later became what it is today, the official organization of Orthodox congregations.

Soon after he and Baumgarten returned from New York, Oppenheimer called a special meeting ostensibly to prepare for the forthcoming High Holy Days. In the course of the meeting, he recommended the engagement of a rabbi, "a Mr. Mandel of New York as a gentleman having the requisite qualifications and who comes highly recommended."[19] The resolution met with immediate resistance.

> Mr. Isaac Levy objected. It is more important, he declared, first to elect the High Holiday cantors and to confirm reelection of the sexton, Mr. Jacob Grossberg. His objection was sustained. Undaunted, Mr. Oppenheimer persisted in his recommendation in the face of continued objections.
>
> Mr. Lewis wished to know what functions Mr. Mandel was to perform, whether Rabbi or Teacher? The President answered that he was a Rabbi and teacher both. Mr. M. Roginski objected to having a Rabbi. Mr. Isaac Levy also opposed the election of a Rabbi. After a lengthy and lively debate, Mr. Roginski moved the salary of Mr. Mandel be $50.00 a month and that he be elected for 4 months or the balance of the year. Motion carried.[20]

Mandel was elected by Adas Israel in 1898, becoming its first American-ordained rabbi. The board allocated $10 to cover the expenses of his trial visit. In debating his employment, the congregation applied the title "rabbi" to its clergy for the first time, if only indirectly. The opposition to electing a rabbi reflected the growing East European Jewish influence in the congregation. East European Jews were accustomed to a *stadt rav*, a communal rabbi who served as ritual arbitrator for all the synagogues in a community. The custom of employing one rabbi to serve a single congregation had originated in Germany and seemed a frivolity to the East Europeans, who, though still a minority in 1898, could no longer be ignored. Though they opposed Mandel's election as rabbi, he might well have been acceptable to them as hazzan or teacher.

**Rabbi Morris Mandel**

Morris Mandel graduated from the City College of New York in 1898 and was ordained by the Jewish Theological Seminary in the same year. He had entered the seminary in 1890 for an eight-year course of study. In September 1896, he served as student rabbi for the High Holidays at the penitentiary on Blackwell's Island.[21] That same year he was elected president of the seminary's English Language Literary Society, and the following year, he delivered a "well-received lecture" in memory of the Vilna Gaon.[22] He also served as treasurer of the Hebrew-language Morais Literary Society.[23]

The meetings of the English Language Literary Society, which would later be renamed the Blumenthal Literary Society to honor the memory of the seminary board's first president, featured "poetry readings, musical selections, and debates on a whole range of Jewish and general topics ranging from the Boer War to Zionism and the value of Hasidism."[24] Both the English-speaking Blumenthal Society and the Hebrew-speaking Morais Society would later be combined into the student organization called the Morais-Blumenthal Society.*

Mandel was one of the speakers at his seminary graduation exercises on June 15, 1898, along with Dr. Henry Pereira Mendes, of New York's Sephardic Shearith Israel, who would later deliver the sermon at the dedication of Adas Israel's second synagogue building on 6th and I Streets. The seminary's first graduate, Rabbi Joseph Hertz, who at the time was still serving the Adath Jeshurun Congregation in Syracuse, New York, was the other commencement speaker.

A group photograph of the seminary's student body in 1897 pictures Mandel together with his professor, Joshua A. Joffe, and his classmates, Mordecai M. Kaplan, Herman Abramovits, Charles Kauvar, Elias Solomon, Alter Abelson, and Julius Greenstone.[25] Mandel was one of the six seminary alumni who came together on June 17, 1901, at the home of Rabbi Menachem Eichler in Philadelphia, to form the Jewish Theological Seminary Alumni Association, the forerunner of today's Rabbinical Assembly.

*Rabbi Stanley Rabinowitz was president of the Morais-Blumenthal Society in his senior year at the seminary, 1942-43.

The importance of Mandel's election by Adas Israel was not allowed to pass unnoticed by the seminary, which had come to understand the public relations value of installing one of its graduates. The festivities that had followed the seminary's first graduation in 1894 had been extended to include Hertz's installation. On the morning after commencement, Hertz, his father, and four seminary representatives had traveled to Syracuse, where Hertz had been installed as rabbi of Congregation Adath Jeshurun. The weekend in Syracuse had resulted in the organization of a Seminary Association in that city.

This example explains Oppenheimer's announcement to the board of Adas Israel that "the rules of the Jewish Theological Seminary Association require the Installation in Office of any of their graduates and as our Minister, the Rev. Mr. Mandel, is one of their graduates it would be necessary that an invitation to the President of the Association should be sent from this Congregation inviting the President to come here and install Mr. Mandel in office." Dr. Bruckheimer, the tenant of the congregation's recently acquired house, moved that the invitation be sent.[26]

Since the demand for modern trained rabbis far exceeded the supply in 1898, why was one of the only two graduates of the Jewish Theological Seminary assigned to Adas Israel, at the time a relatively weak congregation?

Two reasons may be offered in explanation. First, the seminary was eager to place its few graduates in areas which would expand its influence and broaden its membership base. It had been founded by a coalition of Sephardic and German Orthodox rabbis and congregations, and its leaders felt more congenial with congregations that were either Sephardic or, like Adas Israel, German in origin; they felt that the seminary would gain more support from congregations with which they shared ethnic identity. Adas Israel fitted that model.

Second, the seminary was responsive to the influence of its leaders, two of whom, Adolphus Solomons and Cyrus Adler, had significant links to Washington and Adas Israel. Both of these men understood the potential benefits of placing a seminary graduate in Washington. This would not only anchor Adas Israel to the seminary movement but would provide a stronger alternative to the Reform movement in the nation's capital. Rabbi Mandel's assignment to Adas Israel was the result.

### The New Century, 1900

The new century awakened a more optimistic mood in the congregation. Cushioned by the federal payroll, the District of Columbia was one of the first areas in the country to show signs of recovery from the prevailing economic recession. Many of the founders of Adas Israel had now become more secure in their business operations; a second generation had begun to emerge. With the arrival of the Eastern European Jews, Russian, Polish, and Lithuanian, the congregation gained in both numbers and strength. The presence of the Reverend Doctor Mandel, as he was referred to in the minutes, also contributed to the more confident mood.

Mandel's arrival in 1898 transformed Adas Israel and especially its school, which until then had operated intermittently, and had frequently been forced to close "owing to the poor progress the children have made." The members demanded that the school be reorganized and insisted that it function on a more regular basis.

Mandel administered the school far more successfully than any of his predecessors. No longer threatened with closing, the school thrived; enrollments increased and the congregation's membership more than doubled. It was soon necessary to hire an assistant teacher.

Before the conclusion of four months of Mandel's first contract, the president called a special meeting to recommend its extension;

Mandel's success made it a foregone conclusion. The members expressed an enthusiastic endorsement of Mandel's efforts. Mr. Lewis, who at the outset had expressed some doubts about engaging a rabbi, rose and "advocated in very eloquent remarks the nomination and election of Mr. Mandel, the present incumbent, at a salary of $60. per month,"[27] an increase of $10 per month.

Other former opponents of engaging a rabbi now acquiesced to Mandel's retention but argued against any increase in salary. Baumgarten, the secretary, urged "in a spirit of gratitude towards Mr. Mandel the small increase stating that he would far prefer to vote an increase of $25.00 per month but would settle for $10.00."

Oppenheimer, the president, argued for the salary increase, insisting that the congregational budget could easily afford it. Unfortunately, the memory of poverty was not easily overcome, nor was the original opposition to engaging a rabbi. Finally, after lengthy debate, Mandel was unanimously reelected but with "an almost unanimous rejection of the increase." His salary would remain $50 per month.

That summer, Mandel requested and received permission to take a two-week vacation. He was retained in 1900, but only after he had submitted a written application. Once again, there was a debate on his salary. Mr. Goldsmith moved that it be increased from $600 annually to $900. Others proposed a compromise of $800. Finally, Mandel was retained at an annual salary of $720.

The following year, 1901, in a glowing report, Oppenheimer credited Mandel for the congregation's progress.

> ... Membership of 141 all in good standing, an increase of 81 since Jan. 1899, just two years. Through the efforts of our worthy minister, the Rev. Dr. Mandel, our Hebrew School has been elevated to a high standard and can compare favorably with the schools of other congregations. There has been a steady increase in the number of pupils since Dr. Mandel has been in charge; from the 10 or 12

> children who attended in the beginning there are now 80 children enrolled as pupils, and through the maintenance of our Hebrew school our membership has also been materially increased. Such an important factor in a congregation as a school should receive the individual attention of its members and I would earnestly urge each and every one to make a personal visit to the school occasionally.[28]

### The Seminary's Plight

The Jewish Theological Seminary, at the turn of the century, had yet to emerge from its crisis; its situation was more precarious than ever. It appealed to congregations for financial aid. In response, the Adas Israel board voted $25 from the treasury and authorized Mandel to represent the congregation at the convention of the Seminary Association to be held in New York in March 1900. His presence at the convention marked the beginning of Adas Israel's official affiliation with the seminary movement.

By 1902 the number of congregations affiliated with the seminary had fallen from a high of twenty-five to a mere ten, and its income had dwindled to the point where faculty salaries were regularly in arrears. The seminary's only asset was a dwelling at 736 Lexington Avenue which had been converted into a college building and dormitory. Its future hung by a slender thread strained by the burden of debt and doubt.

Two men, Adolphus Solomons and Cyrus Adler, played important roles in rescuing the seminary. Their relationship had begun in Washington and was cemented by their common affinity to Sephardic aristocracy, Solomons by birth and Adler by association with Sabato Morais and his Sephardic congregation. Both were affiliated with Adas Israel.

### Cyrus Adler

Cyrus Adler was born in 1863 in Van Buren, Arkansas, and died in New York City in 1942. His mother, Sarah, was a Sulzberger, one of the most respected families in Philadelphia. His wife, Racie Friedenwald, was the daughter of a prominent family that had left the Baltimore Hebrew Congregation in protest against its its introductions of reforms to found the Chizuk Amunah congregation. The first rabbi of the "Friedenwald shul," as it came to be popularly known, was Henry Schneeberger, who, as stated previously, had introduced Adas Israel to the seminary in 1886.

Cyrus Adler settled in Washington in 1894 when he assumed the post of Librarian and Assistant Secretary of the Smithsonian Institution. Until his marriage to Racie Friedenwald, he lived in rented rooms where, because of his observance of kashrut, he prepared his own meals. Adler's friends, Adolphus Solomons and Oscar Straus, who later became Ambassador to Turkey, were concerned about his health and his irregular eating habits.

Adler's biography revealed the solution to his problem.

> The difficulties of my Jewish diet were overcome by my being supplied with a cook who had been brought up in the Solomons household, an act of generosity which a later age would have regarded as most unusual."[29]

Engaged to marry, he wrote to his fiancée,

> This morning I walked down to the Cosmos Club and found your Friday's letter at 9:30 so you see a special delivery stamp is not necessary for the Club. . . . I have not forgotten the prayer book but cannot send you one till I get to Philadelphia or New York. I find that these I have here are without translation. . . . but I can readily get one of the Singer prayer books and send it up.[30]

The prayer books at Adas Israel were the traditional *siddurim* which, of course, were in Hebrew.

Elected to the board of the prestigious Cosmos Club in Washington, Adler took his reponsibilities seriously. He proposed several architectural changes in the club's building, then located on Madison Place alongside the Dolley Madison House, including suggestions to enlarge the accomodations for the scientific societies associated with the Club.[31]

Upon his marriage, Dr. Adler brought his wife to Washington where they resided at the Mendota Flats Apartments "on the outskirts of Washington and overlooking Rock Creek Park."* In his membership application to Adas Israel, Adler listed his office address as The Smithsonian and his home address as 2220 20th St. N.W., the Mendota Flats.

Adler had achieved earlier prominence as commissioner of the World's Columbian Exposition in Chicago in 1894. Invited to join the Smithsonian Institution as an executive, he at first declined, telling the Secretary, Professor Samuel R. Langley, that he could not accept the post because "I was a Jew and did not work on Saturday, and I knew the office would have to be open." Adler also warned Langley that, as a Jew he "would not travel on Saturday." Langley responded, "Well, I was brought up in New England and won't travel on Sunday, so we'll keep two days a week." Langley, whom Adler felt was more responsible for man's first air flight than the Wright brothers, became a close friend of the Adler family.

Adler was the first person to receive the doctor of philsophy degree in Semitics from an American university, Johns Hopkins in Baltimore. He was recognized for his work in Asiatic and Oriental studies. He was one of the founders of the Jewish Publication Society

* "It was very comfortable and provided us with sufficient wall space for books. We had very happy years there, and in this little apartment our daughter was born." (Adler).

in 1888, and convened the meeting for the founding of the American Jewish Historical Society in 1891. He was its first secretary and later its president.

Adler worshipped at Adas Israel throughout his stay in Washington, but did not formally become a member until 1907. A letter addressed to him by the secretary of the congregation reads:

> It affords me pleasure to inform you that at a regular stated meeting of the board of the Adas Israel Hebrew Congregation held May 5, 1907, you were unanimously elected a Member of the Congregation. The Congregation meets in regular session 4 times in the year when you will be invited to attend. The board of managers meet the first Sunday in every month.
>
> I am dear Sir,
> very deeply yours,
> J. Baumgarten,
> Secretary

**The Rescue**

Adolphus Solomons, while maintaining his Washington residence, lived in New York between 1891 and 1904, having moved there to manage the Baron de Hirsch Fund. His presence in New York made him an ideal choice to fill the vacancy caused by the death of Joseph Blumenthal, head of the seminary's board of trustees, especially since he was on good terms with Jacob Schiff and other wealthy New York Jewish philanthropists.

Solomons's connection with Schiff proved to be crucial in the series of events that saved the Jewish Theological Seminary. As Adler later wrote that "it was primarily Solomons who brought to Schiff's attention the need for making a stronger institution of the Seminary."[32]

Schiff invited a few friends to meet with him at his home in order to discuss the seminary's problems. Soon thereafter, another gathering was arranged to take place at the home of Isidor Straus, head of Macy's Department Store, who was to lose his life in the sinking of the Titanic. In a variation of his recollections, more dramatically described, Adler wrote that it was he who planted in Schiff's mind the proposal to rescue the seminary.

In his history of the Seminary, Robert Fierstien, reasons that it was Adolphus Solomons rather than Adler who was the prime mover of the seminary reorganization plan because Solomons was the President of the Seminary Board of Trustees at the time and because Solomons had forged close relationships with the Jewish men of wealth whose cooperation would be necessary for the seminary's rescue.

Solomons understood that the seminary's future was linked to its ability to provide rabbinic leaders for the country's growing number of East European Jewish congregations, but that since the newly arrived immigrants were not people of means, it would be necessary to obtain the support of wealthy backers even though they were of German background and affiliated with Reform synagogues. These wealthy German Jews would be receptive to rescuing the Seminary, Solomons felt, because of their concern for Americanizing the new immigrants who surely would not respond to the Reform movement. The wealthy philanthropists, led by Jacob Schiff, were indeed receptive to funding the Seminary but only on certain conditions; they demanded a new board of trustees, new bylaws, and a new chief executive.*

To head the seminary and its board, no one but Adler would satisfy the philanthropists. They were impressed with his scholarly

* Jacob Schiff seldom made gifts without extracting prior conditions, noted Stephen Birmingham, in *Our Crowd* (New York: Harper and Rowe, 1967), p. 184. His gifts to Adas Israel, secured by Adolphus Solomons, $50.00 in 1876 and $250 in 1906, were notable exceptions.

reputation, his easy relationship with the civic community and especially with the fact that he was American born.* They also insisted on Louis Marshall as chairman of the board of directors.[33]

Adler acceded to the conditions set by the philanthropists but exacted one of his own: Solomon Schechter. As he wrote to Solomons, "I should not be willing to take up this work without the assurance that Professor Schechter will accept the position as head of the faculty with the title either of President or Dean as he prefers."[34] Adler clearly saw his position at the seminary as a temporary one.

Sabato Morais had wanted to bring Solomon Schechter, a Reader in Rabbinics at Cambridge University in England, to the Seminary as early as 1888.‡

Schechter was widely recognized for his scholarly achievements. Efforts to woo him had led to bringing him to the United States in 1895 to deliver a series of lectures in Philadelphia and Baltimore where he had been warmly received.

Schechter had agreed to accept the post of President of the Seminary faculty in 1899 two years after Morais' death and well before the fund raising gathering at the home of Isador Straus. but it would take two more years for the Seminary to secure the financial foundation necessary to assure Schechter's security in the new position.[35]

Adler would not accept the leadership of the seminary nor could Schechter leave Cambridge without an endowment fund sufficient to insure the seminary's future, which only the wealthy German Jewish philanthropists could provide. The philanthropists

*Adler would select a colonial American design for the new Seminary building on 122nd Street and Broadway.

‡Alexander Kohut had travelled to London in 1888 "to invite Professor Schechter to come to America as the head of the faculty of the Jewish Theological Seminary as arranged by Sabato Morais, Jacob H. Schiff and himself." (Fierstien, p. 130, quoting Rebecca Kohut.)

agreed that Schechter was the ideal choice to succeed Adler as head of the seminary. As they saw it, he would train the rabbis who would Americanize the immigrants from Eastern Europe and "replace their Polish with polish."

Adler agreed that changes in the membership of the Board of Trustees were essential. He arranged with Samuel Langley, head of the Smithsonian, to relinquish his duties as custodian of the Smithsonian Deposit at the Library of Congress but to retain the title and duties of the Librarian of the Smithsonian which would enable him to divide his week between New York and Washington.[36]

Willingly or not, perhaps reluctantly, Solomons acceded to the conditions laid down by the philanthropists. They, on their part, agreed to contribute generously to the reorganized institution. Solomons and Adler secured financial support for the Seminary from the widow of Baron de Hirsch while Jacob Schiff pledged $100,000 for a new Seminary building and an additional sum for an endowment, as well as funds to support "superannuated rabbis." The new Seminary building would be built on 123rd street between Broadway and Amsterdam Avenues, in New York's Morningside Heights, an intellectual enclave that included Columbia University, Barnard College, and the Union Theological Seminary.

On April 14, 1902, an agreement was signed merging the Jewish Theological Seminary Association into the reorganized Jewish Theological Seminary of America. Signing for the party of the first part, the Association, was Adolphus Solomons, and for the party of the second part, was Cyrus Adler, both members of Adas Israel.

The transfer of power shunted aside the previous board of directors and was not completed without some resentment on the part of the deposed. A letter from Adler to Schechter revealed that Solomons' predecessor, Joseph Blumenthal, had not been amenable to the reorganization plan and that "the gentlemen who had large sums of money . . . would not give them . . . as long as Mr. B was at its head."[37] Blumenthal, an observant Jew, had objected to surrendering the Seminary to domination by Reform Jews.

**Solomon Schechter**

Solomon Schechter (1847–1915), born in Rumania, was educated in Germany and ordained in Vienna. As reader in rabbinics at Cambridge University, he made a monumental contribution to Jewish scholarship with his exciting and dramatic discovery of the horde of ancient Hebrew texts in the Geniza (depository of sacred texts) in a secret attic of the Ben Ezra Synagogue in Fostat, Egypt, a find as significant in its day as the discovery of the Dead Sea Scrolls in recent times.

Schechter's idea of "Catholic Israel" as the validating body for the viability of Jewish customs would remain his most enduring legacy. The concept, which became one of the key principles of Conservative Judaism, affirmed that the center of authority for the interpretation of Jewish tradition, custom, and law inhered not in any ecclesiastical hierarchy or authority but rather in "the collective conscience of Catholic Israel as embodied in the Universal Synagogue." However revolutionary the concept appeared to its detractors, its application was not a break with the past. Its halachic basis flowed from the talmudic principle "Go see what the people are doing,"[38] which implied that any law or custom no longer observed by widespread masses of Jews must be regarded as outmoded regardless of its origin.

In 1902 Schechter arrived in New York to take over the reorganized seminary while Adler succeeded Solomons as president of the board of trustees, dividing his time between the Seminary and the Smithsonian. At the seminary, Adler was a mediator between opposing positions. He reconciled Reform-minded trustees with a virtually Orthodox faculty. As his biographer wrote, he was as committed to decorum and modernity as any Reform Jew but was thoroughly traditionalist in his own Jewish practice.

Jacob Schiff transferred his generous support of the seminary to the newly organized American Jewish Committee in 1906 because he disapproved of Schechter's public affirmation of Zionism. In 1908, Adler left the Smithsonian to become the first president of Dropsie College in Philadelphia. Because he would no longer be living in Washington, he gave up his membership in Adas Israel. His letter of resignation was read to the board. "The Secy was requested to answer the Dr. accordingly."[39]

Adler succeeded Schechter as president of the Seminary on Schechter's death in 1915, a position which he held until his own death in 1942, when he was succeeded by Dr. Louis Finkelstein.* It was Adler who, in 1930, recommended Rabbi Solomon Metz to Adas Israel.

~ *Cyrus Adler* *Reflections*

On upper Broadway, at 106th and 107th Street, there was a spacious old-fashioned house to which there were attached very fine stables. This was the dwelling place of Isidor Straus. (He and his wife perished on the Titanic, and in their memory a park was dedicated, known as the Straus Park, just opposite the site of their home.) In 1901, I was living in Washington and, at that time, was invited to a man's party at the home of Mr. Straus.

There was a small group standing together and they were speaking of Jewish education. I said, possibly in an off-hand and breezy sort of way, as young men are likely to do, that the Jewish

* Rabbi Louis Finkelstein retired in 1972 and passed away on Nov. 28, 1991.

community in New York, which was destined to be the largest Jewish community in the world, was allowing its only institution of higher Jewish learning to perish, and I told them something about the precarious situation of this Seminary. Mr. Schiff, who was a man of quick decisions, said to the men standing around: "Dr. Adler is right," and a few weeks later I received a letter from him, asking me when I was coming to New York next time, so that he might invite a few men to meet with us. Among these men, I remember, were Leonard Lewisohn and Mayer Sulzberger, joined the next day by Daniel and Simon Guggenheim.[40]

### Mandel at Adas Israel

Despite the praise he had received from Simon Oppenheimer, the congregation's president, at the annual meeting in January 1901, a move to increase Rabbi Mandel's salary to $75 per month was rejected in favor of "making it $60.00, the same as it was."

Unhappy with his personal and professional progress, Mandel submitted a letter of resignation in March. It must have been written in a moment of despair, for soon afterwards he had second thoughts on the wisdom of resigning. At a special meeting on April 7, called to consider the situation, Julius Baumgarten, the secretary, who had favored Mandel from the first, asked the board, on the rabbi's behalf, to withdraw the resignation. He was supported by Mr. Hartogensis, but to no avail. The board insisted on accepting Mandel's resignation and moved to go back to the days of securing a "Chazan, Balkorah and teacher."

The *American Hebrew*, in its account of Mandel's resignation, reprinted the substance of an interview he had given to a reporter for the *Washington Star*.

> I have found it impossible to persuade the members of the congregation to follow certain of the principles of our religion, without

> which they would not be Orthodox Hebrew. I have attempted to obtain among the members of the congregation a proper observance of our Sabbath, but they keep their stores open on that day just as well as upon other days of the week, quite as much as ever. Various other matters of observance it is absolutely impossible to persuade them to observe, and it seems that my labor are gone for nothing.
>
> I have also tried to build up a Jewish school, in which rudiments of the Hebrew tongue should be taught, and also the principles of religion. To this school, which I consider one of the most important things in the church work, though I have labored for it constantly, there is no assistance given, or any encouragement. Families do not send their children. All of this is quite harassing to face, after you have been working for years on a small stipend, hoping that surroundings would be helpful and congenial.[41]

Oppenheimer, defending the congregation against Mandel's charges, responded:

> The Adas Israel Church is no different now in point of observance from what it was when Rabbi Mandel came, and there is more interest shown in the services and the school. When he came to the church from his seminary, he knew just what the conditions were and just what problems he would have to face. He may not have realized sufficiently what they were. I do not think he should have any reason to be discouraged about the attendance at the religious schools. At the time it closed I think it had about 75 or 80 members. That, as an increase from 40 in two years and a half, ought to encourage any man. The congregation, in regard to its Orthodoxy, is quite on a level with any Orthodox church in the country. Most rabbis of experience would realize that, as far as observing the old Hebrew rules is concerned, we go as far as anyone, and as far as it is possible in this country. The majority of us observe the dietary laws, and laws less binding upon us even than those.

The *American Hebrew* writer observed that other members of the congregation "have stated that the disagreement was all one of salary."

Mandel wrote to the board requesting a letter of recommendation, and the secretary was instructed to write one. On this unfortunate note, the three-year relationship of Rabbi Mandel and Adas Israel came to an end.

After leaving Washington in 1901, Mandel was engaged by Congregation Keneseth Israel in Allentown, Pennsylvania, where he served until 1909. Today Keneseth Israel is affiliated with the Reform Movement.

# 14

## FROM G TO I STREETS

Rabbi Morris Mandel's success during his three-year tenure at Adas Israel had created a new problem for the congregation, lack of space. The synagogue on 6th and G Streets had served well since its dedication in 1876, but twenty-three years later, the growth in membership and school enrollment exceeded its capacity; moreover, the center of Jewish residence had shifted to upper 7th Street and to lower 14th Street. The new century demanded expansion and relocation.

At a special meeting held on October 8, 1899, still within Mandel's tenure, Oppenheimer posed a serious question to the members: should they seek a site for a new structure on the assumption that the present property could be sold for at least $25,000? The meeting endorsed a proposal to build a new synagogue as soon as possible and agreed to initiate a building fund by raffling a piano. As a first step, they collected $28 in contributions of $1 each toward the purchase of the lottery prize. (A revolver in a mahogany case had been the prize in the lottery for the benefit of the first building campaign twenty-five years earlier.)

With Mandel's departure in 1901, the leaders felt they would not be able to raise funds for a new building unless they first engaged another rabbi. To return to the days of the poorly trained combination of hazzan, Torah reader, and teacher would surely displease the more sophisticated of the members. It was important to find a successor who would appeal to both the founding group, German in origin, and the Yiddish-speaking newcomers whose numbers had increased, which meant someone who could deliver sermons in Yiddish as well as English. German was no longer a requirement.

Such a candidate presented himself in the person of Julius T. Loeb. Once introduced to the congregation, on August 6, 1901, he was elected by acclamation as "Rabbi, Chazen, Balkorah and Teacher," at a salary of $1,000.

**Rabbi Judah T. Loeb**

Born Yehudah Leb Tukchinsky in Brest, Russia, on April 23, 1869, Julius Loeb, as he later called himself, came from a distinguished rabbinic family. His younger brother, Yechiel Michel, a son-in-law of the Ashkenazic chief rabbi of Palestine, Samuel Salant, was the head of Yeshivat Etz-Chayim in Jerusalem. Introduced to the Talmud while still a child, Yehudah-Julius had studied with his stepfather, Rabbi Josiah of Nesvig. He had also attended one of the tsar's government schools, graduating in 1885.

Loeb was ordained at the well-known Brisk Yeshiva, which he attended from 1886 to 1889, and emigrated to the United States in 1890. On arriving in New York, according to his biographer, he registered in the preparatory department of the Hebrew Theological Seminary.[1] No institution by that name existed or exists in New York. Neither the Seminary nor the Isaac Elchanan Yeshiva, the only other New York institution at the time that might have been described as a seminary, can verify the biographer's claim, but in all probability Loeb audited classes in the preparatory department of the Seminary in order to improve his rudimentary knowledge of English. There would have been no need for him to register in any rabbinical school since, as an ordained rabbi, he was already well versed in rabbinic texts.

Once he felt competent to serve an American congregation, he changed his name to Julius Loeb (despite the midrashic admonition disapproving of the Roman name Julianus). His first post, where he remained for five years, was Congregation Bikkur-Cholim in Brooklyn. He spent the next three years in Nashville, then returned to Brooklyn to serve Congregation B'nai Jacob, because, as he stated in an interview, he did not enjoy the Tennessee climate.

Loeb came to Adas Israel ten years after his arrival in the United States, residing at 16th and I Street N.W. with his wife and five children. He was Washington's first *rov*, the title ascribed to a yeshiva-trained, traditionally ordained rabbi. Loeb's strength lay in his ability to deliver sermons in Yiddish "for the benefit of the older Hebrews of his congregation who are not familiar with any other tongue than their own."[2] He also took the school in hand, completely reorganizing and enriching the curriculum.*

The assassination of President William McKinley on September 14, 1901, which occurred only a few weeks after Loeb moved to Washington and shortly before the High Holy Days, gave his first holiday sermons an unexpected and exciting relevance that impressed the congregation and propelled him into sudden prominence.

In April 1903, during the Easter/Passover season, two pogroms took place in Kishinev, Bessarabia, organized by local anti-Semites with the collaboration of the Russian authorities. Forty-seven Jews were killed, 345 injured, and almost 3,000 families were driven from their homes. Jews throughout the Western world responded with relief efforts and protests. In Washington, a mass meeting took place at the Columbia Theater on June 5, 1903. District Commissioner H.

*Abe Shefferman, executive director, credited Loeb with the school's rapid growth and increased prestige during the years 1901–1907.

B .F. MacFarland together with a procession of local ministers expressed the city's outrage.[3] Adas Israel and Rabbi Loeb participated in the meeting at the Columbia Theater. Jacob Voorsanger, Adas Israel's first rabbi, addressed a similar protest meeting in San Francisco.

Judah Loeb had a feeling for public relations; he frequently submitted letters and articles on Jewish themes to the local press. While zealously protecting his Orthodoxy and hardly sympathetic to reforms in or out of the synagogue, he had an overriding sense of community. His disapproval of Reform did not prevent his participation in the installation of Rabbi Louis Stern at the Washington Hebrew Congregation in 1904.

*~ Rose Hornstein* *Reflections*

I can recall several protest meetings. One was a meeting to protest the pogrom in Kishinev and one about the Dreyfus case in France. At a meeting in 1901, bonds in the Jewish Colonial Trust Company were sold, to raise money for Palestine. The bonds were one pound. The value of the pound at that time was about $5.00.*

*~ Joseph Blumenthal* *Reflections*

My first recollection of the synagogue goes back to 1899, when I was six years old. My grandfather Hartogensis walked me from my

*From Rose Hornstein's recollections at the centennial meeting, November 1969. The mass meeting demanding the exoneration of Captain Alfred Dreyfus in France took place in 1904. The Jewish Colonial Trust was incorporated in London in 1899 as an instrument for the economic realization of Zionism, with an authorized capital of 2 million pounds. It was not until 1902 that sufficient shares were sold, at 1 pound each, to reach the statutory minimum of 250,000 pounds.

home at 7th and S Streets N.W. to the shul at 6th and G Streets N.W. We lived practically at the north boundary of the city. Seventh and Florida Avenue N.W. was the fire limit and was the end of the cable car and the turntable for their return trip. The shul was located practically at the center of the city; the southern end was 7th and Pennsylvania Avenue N.W. and the canal. Beyond that point was the Island. A number of our members lived and had their business on 4 1/2 and 6th Street S.W. on the Island.

It was before the telephone and before President McKinley. The pushcarts with lemons, fruits, and notions did a thriving business and were mostly run by immigrants, Jews, Italians, and Greeks. There was also the Hoky-Poky Ice Cream man and the organ grinder with his monkey begging pennies.

The filtration plant was being completed about this time, and soon we no longer had to rely on the pump for our water. Modern grocery stores were still unknown, and the milkman with his horse and cart dipped the milk from his cans into our pitcher at the curb. Gaslights in the home and on the streets provided illumination. I remember the lamp lighter who made his daily rounds with his ladder to turn the streetlights on and off. Very soon the telephone came into existence. I remember the telephone booth and the corner store.

It wasn't long before I was enrolled in the Hebrew school. Rabbi Julius Loeb was also our teacher, and he walked up and down pointing with his ruler. One day, when it became my turn to read, my teeth were stuck together with a piece of taffy I had smuggled in and I promptly received a smack on the knuckles from his ruler. He also confiscated what was left of my taffy.*

*From Joseph Blumenthal's recollections at the centennial meeting, November 1969.

## The New Century

President Simon Oppenheimer notified the congregation in 1901 that its mortgage had been reduced to $1,100; the time had come to reactivate plans for a new synagogue to meet the challenge of the new century. The president stated:

> Our present house of worship is entirely too small for our ever increasing membership; we must put forth all our efforts for a new home for the congregation. As you all have the interest and welfare of our beloved congregation at heart, you each will do your utmost to realize our hopes, and let us join in thanks to Almighty God for the blessings that have been showered upon us.[4]

The congregation's needs and activities had grow along with the size of the membership. In 1902, a young people's club was organized. When the seating capacity of the synagogue proved to be inadequate for the High Holy Day services, a hall had to be rented for the overflow. Moreover, time and wear had left their mark on the synagogue. Its deterioration heightened the importance of raising funds for a new synagogue in a new location.

Rabbi Loeb brought fresh enthusiasm to the fund-raising efforts. A gathering on May 8, 1902, produced pledges totaling $1,611. The largest pledges were received from Simon Oppenheimer, $500, and Isaac Levy, $200; other pledges ranged from $10 to $50. The Sunday edition of the *Washington Times* noted,

> Another project of the rabbi, which is very dear to his heart, is the building of a new and larger synagogue for the congregation of the Adath-Israel. At present the building on Sixth Street is too small to accommodate all the people on feast days and solemn festivals. Many of his flock are obliged, for this reason to absent themselves from their own synagogue on such occasion and go to the larger

> ones of the city. Rabbi Loeb feels this keenly, and he has been working steadily since his connection with the Adath-Israel to the end that sufficient funds may be saved to buy a suitable lot and erect a new synagogue.[5]

A subsequent meeting pledged $2,345, a generous sum for those days, reflecting the members' new and unaccustomed prosperity. Oppenheimer, together with Simon Atlas and Louis Rosenberg, sought a buyer for the synagogue building.

With a new site already in mind, and the building as surety, the congregation borrowed $10,000 in order to be prepared for any likely opportunity. In May 1905, it found a buyer for the synagogue building—the Gatti family, investors in downtown property.[6] They were willing to pay not the $25,000 the congregation was asking but $14,000; of this, $4,000 would be in cash, and the buyer would assume the trust of $10,000 which the congregation had previously negotiated. The sale included the synagogue and the adjacent house, 617 and 619 6th Street. Furniture and benches were not included.[7] There is nothing in the minutes about the mikveh, despite the claim that it continued to be used until 1911.

Soon after these events, in July 1905, the trustees reported that they had purchased a new lot at 6th and I Streets.[8] Louis Levy, a Baltimore architect, was engaged to draw the plans at a fee equal to 2.5 percent of the building's cost. Meanwhile, its synagogue sold, the congregation returned to rented halls for services, paying a monthly rent of $65.

Despite the lack of sufficient funds and the difficulty of borrowing more, construction began on May 24, 1906. Even as the building progressed it was evident that the congregation would be unable to meet its obligations to the contractor, Arthur Cowsill, who had agreed to wait for full payment until the building was roofed.

The congregation attempted numerous strategies to raise the necessary funds: raffles, assessments, and solicitations within and beyond the membership. It asked members to lend it money at 6 percent interest; it issued notes which it registered and discounted at a bank. *Pushkes* (charity boxes) were installed in homes; members were asked to contribute 1 cent per family member daily.

Albert Small proposed soliciting assistance from Washington's other synagogues. While no response was forthcoming from any of them, $342.35 was received from the Rebecca Lodge and $150 from the Council of Jewish Women. To satisfy the contractor's demands for payment, the board negotiated additional loans from the more affluent members of the congregation which it discounted at the bank.

At the end of his second year, Loeb requested and received a $200 increase in his annual salary of $1,000. Adolphus Solomons, who had resumed full-time residence in Washington in March 1906, joined the fund-raising effort, successfully approaching his friend Jacob Schiff, from whom he received a gift of $250.

In the meantime, the rabbi had to be admonished. A board meeting moved that "Dr. Loeb be notified that duties of Chazen are to attend all funerals of members without fee unless voluntarily offered."[9]

## The Cornerstone

The builder, Arthur Cowsill, and the architect, Louis Levi, employed a new method in constructing the floor of the new structure, substituting reinforced-concrete columns and girders for the customary iron columns and supporting floor beams. In a formal ceremony on October 24, 1906, the strength of the concrete floor was put to a spectacular public test by loading its 47-foot span with an assembled group that included the building committee, the engineers, several interested spectators, and seventy-two courses of heavy brick.

This proved, according to the *Washington Times*, that the "congregation may feel sure in worshipping in this new building, that there is no likelihood of the floor not supporting them."[10] The District's computing engineers affirmed that "the test was most satisfactory. The floor slab did not deflect, while all this weight was on it, one sixty-fourth of an inch."[11]

The formal ceremony for laying the cornerstone of the new building took place on November 22, 1906. Rabbi Loeb, Simon Wolf, and District Commissioner H. B. F. MacFarland delivered addresses. Rabbis Abram Simon and Louis Stern, both of the Washington Hebrew Congregation, offered the opening and closing prayers, respectively. Messages were read from President Theodore Roosevelt and Secretary of the Navy Charles J. Bonaparte.

The cornerstone was carefully lowered in place and "declared level and plum and a credit to the craftsman, whereupon corn, wine, and oil, symbols of the craft, were poured upon the stone by the Masonic Grand Master, Walter A. Brown."[12] Placed in the cornerstone was a box either of copper or of lead, depending upon which newspaper one reads, containing copies of the U.S. and Adas Israel constitutions, that day's Washington daily papers, current issues of Jewish newspapers published in the United States, coins minted in 1906, a membership list of the congregation, the yearbook of the Council of Jewish Women, a copy of the Masonic code, the Masonic calendar for 1906, a copy of the *Evening Star* of September 10, 1898, carrying an account of the dedication of the Washington Hebrew Congregation's 8th Street building, and a copy of the *New York Herald* of Saturday, April 15, 1865, with its accounts of the assassination of Abraham Lincoln and the fall of Richmond.

In his address, Commissioner MacFarland complimented the Jews of Washington for their "good citizenship and willingness to perform all their civic duties." In a deferential sweep through history, he noted that America's Jews "have faithfully kept the obligation they took when they first landed in New York under the old Dutch government, to take care of their poor, and no one else has had to share that burden with them. . . . People who have been themselves the victims of misrepresentation will not wrong others by unfairness."[13]

Simon Wolf, in his address, recalled that thirty-five years previously, President Ulysses S. Grant had been present at the ceremonies accompanying the laying of the cornerstone for the first building. Wolf expressed the wish "that the reformed and orthodox Jews should stand together, undivided." He referred to the Masonic ideal "which recognized no particular religion nor creed but only the quality of the man," a favorite theme in Wolf's thinking which he repeated on numerous occasions.

Rabbi Loeb's sermon drew upon the Torah portion for the approaching Sabbath, which described the episode of the patriarch Jacob alighting on a stone-pocked landscape where he stopped to rest on the night of his lonely journey.[14] With a stone for his pillow, Jacob slept, and dreamed of a ladder on which angels of God were ascending and descending. To Loeb,

> This mysterious legend offers a solution to the seemingly unending problem of dissenting creeds. John Ruskin was right in his assertion that the stone lives its life, dies its death, and affords its lesson to the world in much the same manner as all the rest of us.
>
> The stone denotes a pillar of worship, an altar of sacrifice, and a memorial of great events. Since it suggests strength and durability, it is a monument to the imperishable, a connecting link between time and eternity, an inspiring symbol to the Jew and the Gentile, the Christian and the Mussulman, the Buddhist and the Brahman.[15]

The account in the *Washington Post* concluded with the statement that Loeb merited "a great deal of credit for the progress made on the structure . . . as did . . . the members of the building committee: Simon Oppenheimer, chairman; Isaac Levi, Julius Baumgarten, Jacob Small, B. Schwartz, N. Horn, Herman Blumenthal and Fred Gichner."[16]

The building's progress outpaced the fund-raising essential to its completion. Suddenly, for some inexplicable reason, Rabbi Loeb submitted his resignation. He would no longer participate in the fund-raising campaign, nor would he see the building through to its dedication. Shocked, the congregation insisted that "in the absence of any official resignation in writing, to send for Mr. Loeb for explanation."[17] Loeb then informed the board that "he would like to sever his connections with this congregation to commence August 1 next."

Many on the board refused to regard the resignation as final, but when Loeb informed them that he had already accepted a position with Congregation Bes Israel in Atlanta, Georgia, there was no alternative but to release him and order the payment of his monthly salary to the day of his departure, August 15. And then "Mr. Loeb did bid adieu to the board and departed."[18]

### Loeb's Career

Loeb remained with the Atlanta congregation for twelve years. During World War I he served as chaplain at Camp Hancock, in Augusta, Georgia, and at Camp Crane, in Allentown, Pennsylvania. In 1919 he returned to Washington to serve the Orthodox Congregation Ohev Shalom on 5th and I Streets, one block from the structure he had helped build but had failed to dedicate. One of his first duties at Ohev Shalom was to officiate at the burial of his son, Joseph, a World War I casualty, who had died from the lingering effects of poison gas.

After leaving Ohev Shalom, Loeb remained in the District to serve the Southeast Hebrew Congregation. "A man should work as long as God grants him life and health," he observed. In his later years, he served the synagogue of Washington's Hebrew Home for the Aged.

Loeb saw himself as a *stadt-rav*, a communal rabbi in the tradition of the European shtetl. Those who remember him have described him as a gentle person, insecure in his self-appraisal and restless in his interests. He was a driven soul.

Loeb died in Washington in December 1942, at age seventy-three. Funeral services were conducted by Rabbi Solomon Metz at Adas Israel with interment in the Adas Israel cemetery, where his four-year-old son had been buried in 1906. His wife, Rose, would be buried alongside him a few years later.

A newspaper obituary described Loeb as "a staunch defender of traditional Judaism and a religious and civic figure in Washington for nearly four decades."[19] Statements issued by District of Columbia Jewish organizations portrayed him as "one of the builders of the Washington Jewish Community and its institutions." At the time of his death he resided at 3627 13th Street N.W.

### The Dedication and a New Rabbi

Upon Loeb's departure, the secretary was instructed "to communicate with the Chasan who had advertised in the Standard and also to place an advertisement there." Meanwhile, the congregation engaged Rev. H. S. Lebovitz as hazzan to conduct all services during the month of September including the High Holy Days, for the sum of $200 plus expenses. Once again, the faithful Isadore Samuels was engaged as a standby hazzan beginning in December at a fee of $20 per month. At the same time, the board asked the seminary to suggest a successor to Loeb. One would soon be forthcoming, but in the meantime, the synagogue building had to be completed.

To meet the congregation's obligations to the contractor, the board authorized the trustees to secure a bank loan of $5,000. Fred Gichner promised to obtain another $1,000. Adas Israel was in dire need of money. In all probability, it was the unremitting stress on fund-raising that had led to Loeb's decision to leave.

The ground floor of the new synagogue was ready for use in September 1907. The contractor, pressed for permission, allowed it to be used for meetings despite the fact that he had not been paid. The board meeting on October 7, 1907, took place in the new building's vestry room. It was felt that meeting in the half-completed structure would stimulate greater generosity.

The synagogue's dedication was set for 2:30 p.m. on Sunday, January 5, 1908. It was a significant event in the community, described in detail by all the Washington papers—the *Herald*, the *Post*, the *Times*, and the *Evening Star*—in their editions of January 6.

Rabbi H. Pereira Mendes* of New York's Spanish and Portuguese Congregation Shearith Israel, delivered the dedicatory address. Born in 1852 in Birmingham, England, of a distinguished Sephardic rabbinic family, Mendes had helped Sabato Morais establish the Jewish Theological Seminary in 1886, becoming its professor of history. On Morais's death, he served as acting president of the faculty until the arrival of Solomon Schechter. Mendes, who died in 1937, was a recognized figure in American Jewry; his presence added luster to the dedication service.

The *Washington Post*, noting that the building had been completed at a cost of $90,000, described it as one of the finest in Washington.

*Henry or Haim or H.P. Mendes preferred not to use the name Henry.

It is built of light gray vitrified brick, with handsome terra cotta trimmings and unglazed red tile roof. There are five domes, a large one in the center, forty feet in diameter, and smaller ones in each corner. The style of architecture is a combination of modernized French and Byzantine. The trimmings over the entrances are rich in decorative effect and harmonious in their proportions.*

The chief feature of the interior is the large central dome, the ceiling of which rises 69 feet above the auditorium floor. Cathedral style is used in the interior, the large and small arches rising in graceful bows to meet each other. The glistening white enamel of the panel work and the rough white sand work of the walls made the richly colored stained glass windows, of which there are more than a score, stand out in striking contrast.

The large stained glass rose window on the Sixth street side of the synagogue is unique in Washington.‡ Two large golden candelabra, presented by Simon and Gustave Oppenheimer, in memory of their parents, stand on the altar. A perpetual light at the shrine was donated by Mr. Louis Steerman.

The basement of the building consists of one large room, 75 x 75 feet in size, which can be divided by folding doors into four small rooms. The seating capacity of the main floor of the church is about 800, while the gallery will hold an equal number.

The *Post* termed the dedication "an epoch in the history of the Washington Jewish community," and reported that "1,200 prominent orthodox Hebrews, many from different parts of the country, attended the dedicatory exercises.

From the time that the ancient rite of lighting the perpetual lamp was performed until the cantor, Rev. H. Glass, of Baltimore, Md.,

*"Adas Israel in Washington, D.C. with its saucer-dome on a drum and four corner domes, was one of a considerable number of central-planned synagogue buildings which had become standard." Rachel Wischnitzer, *Synagogue Architecture in the United States* (Philadelphia: Jewish Publication Society, 1955).

‡The large rose window was returned to Adas Israel in 1989 and remains in storage for future placement.

assisted by the choir, sang the last hymn, "Blessed Be He Who in His Holiness Gave the Law to His People Israel," the dedicatory rites, as instituted thousands of years ago, were observed, not only in the blessing of the temple, but in the singing of the sacred songs by the cantor, and in the responses of the choir. The opening of the door, the entering of the temple, the carrying of the sacred rolls, and the lighting of the perpetual lamp were but a few of the ancient rites observed yesterday.

The platform was lighted by the perpetual lamp and two candelabra of twelve candles each, and the handsome auditorium was crowded when Rev. Dr. Abram Simon offered the dedicatory prayer. The regular afternoon service was then carried out with a sermon by Rev. H. P. Mendes of New York, one of the most eloquent rabbis and Talmudic expounders in the country.

Rev. Dr. H. W. Schneeberger, of Baltimore, exhorted the congregation to strive for the success of their religion in Washington. He urged the members to assist in every way the founders of the temple assuring them their recompense would be great.

The congregation while not the largest in the city is constantly growing and numbers many of the most influential Hebrews of Washington among its members. The synagogue has no rabbi at present. Rabbi Loeb under whose direction the cornerstone was laid several years ago having removed to Atlanta, Ga., last summer. It is understood that a new rabbi will be selected in the near future, a large number of candidates for the office being now considered by the committee.

The *Washington Herald* carried a lengthy excerpt from Rabbi Mendes's sermon.

This synagogue, situated in the chief city of the youngest and greatest nation of the world, has been consecrated with more importance than is usually associated with events of this kind.

The first altars, synagogues, or places of worship, were built by Father Abraham, in order that he might preach the Word of God and make the people understand that they had a Superior Being watching over them. This God was not only God of the Jews, but a God for the world.

Moses, when he stood before the burning bush, did not address God as the God of the Jews, but he called Him the God of all mankind. So, too, all the patriarchs of the Hebrew race. . . . A synagogue, therefore, should be a place of worship for all mankind, and not alone for the Jew. Every Gentile is welcome to enter the portals of this synagogue and pray to the God of Mankind.

The synagogue is only the casket; the jewel it contains is the Bible. Through the Bible the world of thought has been revolutionized and man has been enabled to step forth from chaos to progress. The corner-stone of America's greatness is the Bible. . . . Empires like Babylon fall, the Bible and the synagogue still exist.

Do not the martyrs who gave up their lives in Russia, because they refused to give up their synagogues, inspire us to be faithful and loyal to Judaism? Great will be the blessing to this country when it shall appreciate the meaning of the orthodox synagogues. They stand for righteousness and justice.

The press listed the names of the various committee members:

Reception committee: Jacob Schwartz, B. Schechter, Max Rosenthal, H. Schrott, Charles Stein, J. Schlossberg, Falk Harmel, Max Cohen, Elihu Horn, William Levy, and George Levy.

Officers of ladies' auxiliary: Mrs. Simon Oppenheimer, president, Mrs. H. Schlossberg, vice-president, Miss Dora Steerman, secretary, Mrs. D. Rosen, financial secretary, Mrs. W. Schlossberg, treasurer.

Building committee: Simon Oppenheimer, chairman, Julius Baumgarten, secretary, Fred S. Gichner, treasurer, and Isaac Levy, Herman Blumenthal, D. Goldsmith, N. Horn, I. Small, Jacob Shapiro, Ben Schwartz, and I. Rosenfeld.

Once dedicated, the new synagogue building brought the congregation a fresh measure of strength and dignity. Over the next several years Adas Israel grew in membership and in the breadth of its activities. Yet the old problems continued to plague the members: tension between proponents of tradition and those demanding change, conflict between dedicated lay leaders and the professional clergy, the need for an effective Hebrew school and resistance to the requirements for maintaining one, and the usual tensions inherent in trying to satisfy the often conflicting demands of the congregants with the limited means available.

The financial situation, precarious even in the best of times, was further complicated by the several economic recessions which plagued the country from time to time, making it difficult to meet the payments on the new building's mortgage. Finding ways to meet the operational expenses consumed much of the board's energies. Adding to the difficulty were two new elements: the demands of the growing number of recently arrived East European immigrants, and a new and independent rabbi with fresh ideas.

After Judah Loeb's precipitous resignation in 1907 even before the completion of the new building, it was with some relief that the board received a letter from the "Rev. Mr. Egelson." He had been prompted to write to Adas Israel on the recommendation of the seminary, where he had been ordained. The secretary was instructed to "communicate with him with a view to his coming here for trial." The congregation could no longer afford to be without a modern, professionally trained leader.[20]

Louis Isaac Egelson, American-born, would become the first seminary rabbi to serve in the recently dedicated Adas Israel synagogue on 6th and I Streets N.W. The congregation quickly elected him as its "Rabbi and Teacher" at an annual salary of $1,500 on February 16, 1908, and, at the same meeting, elected J. L. Gargunski of Baltimore as "Chazzan" at an annual salary of $900. Both agreements were to terminate at the end of one year, on December 31, 1908.

The election of Egelson and Gargunski in 1908 was the first time that a team of rabbi and cantor had been engaged together, with their respective roles defined and differentiated, a pattern that would henceforth remain the practice. As usual, the election had not been without debate or concern for costs. "To defray the salaries for the 2 gentlemen, a volunteer subscription was opened." Those present pledged $353.50 in sums ranging from $1.50 to the $50 each pledged by Simon and Gustave Oppenheimer.

*~ Hymen Goldman* *Reflections*

I was born on January 28, 1888, in a little village that lies between the town of Chotin and Lepkon in Bessarabia, a region that at various times in its history has belonged both to Russia and to Rumania; it was Russian at the time of my birth. I came to Washington on January 6, 1906, (at the age of 18)....

I hated life in the city: the heat, the low altitude, the mosquitoes, and the cobblestone streets. I could not sleep at night because of the heat and the noise from the cobblestones with which the street were paved.... One day [in 1907], I went to Fort Myer, the cavalry post near Washington, to see the Wright brothers demonstrate the flying machine they had built themselves. (The plane crashed; one of the brothers broke his leg.)

When I came to Washington in 1906, there were two separate groups. They were segregated, like the whites and the blacks. Most of the German Jews felt that it was beneath their dignity to mix with the eastern European Jews. They felt that since they had come to America first, they should be the benefactors of the newcomers, but that did not mean social equality. The Hebrew Relief Society and the Jewish Foster Home were organized by the German Jews to help the poor Russian Jews....

I was taken to the Adas Israel Synagogue on 6th and G Streets. The services were liberal Orthodox. I was brought up in an Orthodox atmosphere and enjoyed the services. The synagogue then moved to Sixth and Eye Streets, where I attended services but only half heartedly. I felt that there was something missing. People did not come to pray. Some brought along their newspapers, or the racing sheet. The women, although they were not as yet sitting with the menfolks, came there to display their new dresses and spent most of the time on the street outside the synagogue. The whole atmosphere made me very unhappy.

My partner, who was a radical, ridiculed me for belonging to a synagogue. He did not belong to one, but many years later he became a member of Adas Israel. It had become fashionable for a Jew to be a member of a synagogue; or maybe it was because membership entitled you to a cemetery plot.

The principal Jewish industry in Washington at that time was the small corner grocery store, 90 percent of which were owned by Jews. There were only three synagogues and one reform temple. Every synagogue was supposed to have some kind of Hebrew school, and the rabbi was supposed to be the teacher. We had some highly learned rabbis, but it was not appropriate that they teach children the aleph bet. It was actually an insult to a man like Rabbi Loeb, who was very learned, to require that he go down in the basement of the synagogue to teach the Hebrew alphabet to half a dozen children. In addition, the Jewish families were scattered all over the city and it was impossible to bring the children to Fifth and Eye Streets or to the Adas Israel Synagogue at Sixth and Eye for a couple of hours of Hebrew education after they had attended classes all day at the public schools.

The Jewish parents, if their children were interested in some Jewish education, and most of them were not, had to resort to a traveling Jewish teacher, a so-called rabbi. These teachers were new immigrants from Europe who were too old or too poor to have a grocery store. They could not speak a word of English, and the children could not speak Yiddish. So you can imagine what happened.

One of the biggest problems was that these grocery shopkeepers would stay in a location for three or four years and as soon as they accumulated a little money, they would sell their store to a new immigrant and move to a larger store in another location. Naturally, in this new neighborhood there was a different traveling rabbi. On his first visit to get acquainted with the new pupil, he would say to the parents: "Why, your son does not know anything. He will have to start all over again." This was a calamity, especially if the boy was approaching the age of bar mitzvah. The rabbi had to work overtime to teach the boy the blessings and especially to make a speech. . . .

Attempts to organize a city-wide Hebrew school would fail. Until the Jewish Community Council was organized and the arrival of Dr. Isaac Franck, very little was accomplished in the field of Jewish education.*

*Hymen Goldman, an early member of Adas Israel, became a successful businessman and a prominent civic leader. These excerpts are taken from his memoirs, *I Could Write a Book* (Washington, D.C.: Privately published, 1974).

# 15

## THE RUSSIAN JEWS

In 1869, the year of Adas Israel's birth, the government of tsarist Russia issued an edict expelling Jews from the border region of Bessarabia. The edict, which uprooted over 20,000 Jewish families, was but one of a series of oppressive laws embittering the lives of Russia's Jews.

The expulsion order aroused the ire of Jews throughout the world. In Washington, both B'nai B'rith and the Board of Delegates of American Israelites lodged formal protests against Russia's action. The B'nai B'rith petition was signed by Simon Wolf, N. Adler, Jacob S. Jacobson, and two members of Adas Israel, Adolphus S. Solomons and Lewis (Levi) Abraham. The signers met with President Grant on November 30, 1869. In response to their urgings, he dictated a letter to be forwarded to the Russian government.[1]

Worse was to come. The bomb which took the life of Alexander II, "the tsar of all the Russias," in March 1881, set in motion a wave of pogroms in more than a hundred Jewish communities, followed by still more restrictive laws aimed at eliminating Jews from Russia's economic and civic life. The era of savagery which blanketed the Jewish Pale of Settlement produced the inevitable consequence of panic: flight.

Thousands of Jews fled, frantically seeking a refuge. Many of them, fortunate enough to raise passage for the transatlantic voyage, poured into the United States, landing at one or another of the several ports dotting the northeastern coast.

By 1891, Jews were arriving in the United States at the rate of 100,000 each year. The Kishinev pogroms in April 1903 produced an even greater flow of refugees, augmented still further as a result of the suffering which accompanied the Russo-Japanese War in 1905. All told, persecution and oppression brought 2.5 million Jews from Eastern Europe to America in the half century from 1880 to 1930.

As much as American Jews commiserated with the plight of their Russian coreligionists, there was a gap between their sympathy and their apprehension at the implications of the huge number of arrivals seeking refuge in the United States. While the American Jewish community mobilized to receive the hapless and forlorn refugees, not everyone was prepared to welcome them. Indeed, there were Jewish communal leaders and rabbis, including the rabbi who had once served Adas Israel, Jacob Voorsanger, who openly and loudly advocated closing the immigration gates to the wretched refugees. Voorsanger, known for his hostility to Orthodoxy, opposed admitting the Russian Jews to the United States because "he feared that non-Jews could not distinguish the North American Israelites from their Yiddish members."

Outraged, Sabato Morais appealed to the American Jewish community to help the fleeing impoverished Jews. "The only hope for the Jews in Russia is to become Jews out of Russia," he cried. Following his courageous initiative, members of the Historical School and their synagogues were among those who came to the aid of the refugees whom Morais regarded as "martyrs to the faith whom the Almighty had spared in their hour of trial."[2]

The large influx of Jews challenged the equanimity of the established order. As the result of the massive immigration, the relatively homogeneous American Jewish population became a diverse and deeply segmented community marked by subdivisions based on differences of dialect, diet, place of origin, economic status and social class.

In the pattern of their German predecessors and for the same reasons, the new immigrants turned to peddling. Despite the hostility, which their German predecessors had largely avoided, many East European Jews eventually became successful merchants. Tailors, especially, in great demand, were successful in obtaining employment, although frequently in sweat shops. The bulk of the immigrants, however, had no vocation. Their established Jewish brethren received them with a mixture of concern, pity and annoyance.

The Russian Jews differed from the German Jews in many significant ways. Their food, dress, and appearance differed from that of the earlier arrivals. They spoke Yiddish, a language earlier arrivals considered less elegant than German. Consequently, many German Jews regarded the East European newcomers as a threat to their own delicately elevated status. "We belong to the minority, and the minority is always judged by its lowest representative," was the opinion of an outspoken German immigrant.[3]

The Russian Jewish immigrants, in turn, resented the condescension of their "upper-class" coreligionists. In the large cities where they settled, the new immigrants formed religious and social associations, just as their German predecessors had in earlier years. The religiously observant among them either rented rooms to form their own congregations or joined existing ones. They rejected Reform synagogues not only because of their nontraditional forms of worship, but because the Reform Jews, predominantly of German origin, seemed strange to them.

A woman in Baltimore wrote to her son that in one of his Passover sermons, Rabbi Schneeberger had castigated the recent arrivals because "they have so many little Schules and not always in the best neighborhoods. He thought they ought to go to our Schule and that we should not be unkind to them and if they wanted to come in, we should let them in."[4] His criticism could apply to the Russian Jews in Washington as well.

The non-religious among the immigrants, socialists and bundists, rejected affiliation with any synagogue, preferring their own secular social groupings.

### The Effect on The Seminary

The seminary perceived the Russian Jews as both challenge and opportunity; the challenge was to Americanize them; the opportunity, to augment the movement's base of support. Addressing the challenge, Rabbi Henry Morais, the son of the late founder of the seminary, who had died the previous year, advised the Seminary Association Convention in 1898,

> Those [Russian] congregations will be either the fame or the shame of American Judaism. They can make the American Judaism of the future equal to the Golden Age of Spanish Judaism . . . or they will, by uncouthness, or by infidelity, . . . feed the prejudice against us in this country. . . . Our own interests require that they shall be supplied with ministers who shall be acceptable to them."[5]

At the same convention, Rabbi H. Pereira Mendes addressed the opportunity: "American Judaism will be profoundly influenced by Russian Jews, who are establishing hundreds of congregations in the United States."[6]

In truth, the Seminary desperately needed the mass support which only the Russian Jews could supply. The Sephardic sources of membership had dried up. German immigration had ceased and, in any case, had largely turned to Reform. The Russian Jews were the only remaining population group available to the seminary and to its congregations. To secure their affiliation, it was essential to bridge the culture gap separating them.

The Russian Jews in New York were not receptive to the seminary's approach. They looked with suspicion upon their representatives, first, because the seminary people were "uptown" and the Russian community, "downtown" and, second, the seminary spoke English and the new immigrants, Yiddish. The orthodoxy of the seminary was regarded with suspicion by the pious East European Jews who were accustomed to a yeshiva not a seminary.

The seminary faculty had led in the organization of the Union of American Orthodox Congregations in the hope of attracting the East European congregations only to discover that the Yiddish speaking downtown Jews had succeeded in capturing the organization. At the Union's convention in 1900, the guest speaker was the "Slutzker Rov," Rabbi Jacob Willowsky, who felt that to speak English in a synagogue was akin to turning it into a church.

The Slutzker Rov, also known by his acronym "Ridbaz", was the recognized leader of the immigrant Orthodox community. When he asserted the right to deliver a sermon in Yiddish at the High Holiday service at Yorkville's Congregation Kehilath Jeshurun, Mordecai M. Kaplan, the resident rabbi, was told not to preach his sermon. The Ridbaz felt that with the English sermon there was "no hope for the continuance of the Jewish religion"

Orthodox, Yiddish-speaking immigrant leaders such as J. D. Eisenstein, a writer and grand-father of Rabbi Ira Eisenstein, the future leader of the liberal Reconstruction Movement, could not forgive the seminary for employing men like Kohut, Szold, and Jastrow, whose Jewish observance was suspect, or attracting the participation of non-observant laymen. They were shocked to learn that, during the 1902 Seminary commencement exercises, some professors sat with uncovered heads with one of them even pronouncing the name of God while bareheaded.

The affiliation of congregations dominated by East European Jews would indeed save the Seminary movement from collapse; in the process the Seminary would be transformed—as were its affiliated congregations.

### The Effect on Adas Israel

The East European Jews migrated to Washington in search of jobs or business opportunities just as the German Jews had done before them. The city, which had avoided Ashkenazic-Sephardic tensions, would now experience German-Russian tension and rivalry.

The beginnings of the trickle of East European migration to Washington was discernable as early as 1885. Immigrants who turned to the traditional synagogues brought them strength of numbers and the skills and knowledge derived from their traditional Cheder and Yeshiva backgrounds.

The East European newcomers, like the Germans who had preceded them, joined together not so much to discover new worlds but to retain memories of the old; they formed landsmanschaften and home worship circles defined by region of origin. Continuity of ritual and worship eased the trauma of migration and resettlement; they derived comfort from their social kinship. They preferred to organize their own synagogues where prayers could be expressed in accents and modes familiar to them. Two significant needs, however, they could not provide: a Hebrew school and a cemetery. They lacked the means to acquire them. Adas Israel would profit from these needs; the Washington Hebrew Congregation could not attract them.

By 1900, there were 3500 Jews in Washington, enough to form new congregations and to strengthen existing ones. Newly organized congregations, Voliner Anshe Sfard and Talmud Torah in

Southwest, Ezras Yisrael in Northeast, Ohev Shalom in Northwest, and Kesher Israel in Georgetown, attracted newcomers who hailed from their own particular regions of Eastern Europe. In 1903, Rev. Reuben Graffman became the "Chazen, Shochet Oifess, Mohel, Teacher, and Choir Leader" of Congregation Ohev Shalom at an annual salary of $550.00.

The immigrants who joined Adas Israel added an ethnic dimension to the unresolved tensions within the Congregation and further accentuated the distinction between it and The Washington Hebrew Congregation. Adas Israel was as eager for the support of the new arrivals as was the Seminary. Without new members, Adas Israel could not hope to meet its current expenses, much less expand into a new structure.

The members of Adas Israel actively solicited both individuals and groups, offering the new arrivals reduced dues to attract their affiliation, despite the opposition of some of the German members, who objected more to the reduction in dues than to the new alliances. When the Board lowered its dues for new members from $2.00 per month to $1.00 per month and waived the usual initiation fee, some members, even founders, deliberately resigned their membership, only to re-apply for admission as new members at the reduced rate.

By 1885, four years after the great wave of Russian immigration began, Adas Israel's German members found themselves sharing the congregation with an increasing body of Russians. In 1887, the secretary reported that "a number of gentlemen and members of another congregation wishing to join this congregation ask upon what terms."

Soon thereafter a committee reported to the board:

> Gentlemen, We the undersigned committee appointed to confer with a similar committee of a sister Congregation with a view of

consolidating with this Congregation beg leave to report that we attended to that duty and met the Committee of gentlemen appointed by the other Congregation and after interchanging our respective views, it was agreed that we recommend the admission of those 23 gentlemen on the following basis: 1, that they be admitted under the one dollar clause. 2, Whatever property they possess it is left optional with them to keep or present the same to the Congregation, and that they strictly comply with the rules and laws governing a one dollar member, and that no concession is made to them on account of their number or otherwise, and it is agreed that the Committee sign this report. Very Respectfully,

S. Lewis, Julius Baumgarten, R. Sanger, Isaac Levy, F. Greenapple.[7]

The following were then accepted as members: Louis Garner, F. M. Goldsmith, Isaac Shainberg, L. Sterman, P. Levy, J. Goldstein, Jacob Aaron, H. Landy, A. Cohen, S. Rosenthal, A. S. Levitsky, Jacob Levy, S. Cohen, K. Mosshikow, J. Bildman, P. Cohen, G. Goldberg, A. L. Saltzstein, A. Wainstein, S. Schlomberg, Isaac Levy, William Gardner, S. Goldblatt. The new members were of East European origin.

One eager new member, once admitted, willingly paid the regular $2 monthly dues only to request and receive a refund when others in his circle were admitted at the lesser fee, a refund which aroused the ire of several board members. When a group of twenty-one applicants was admitted to membership in April 1895, the secretary, Julius Baumgarten, was so angered at the discounted dues that "he withdrew from office for the day."

As the number of East European Jews in the congregation increased, so did their demands and, in reaction, so did the resistance to granting them. Particularly vexing was the problem of selecting a cantor. Hazzan Isaac Stempel, who originally had been employed by the still-united Washington Hebrew Congregation and had been engaged by Adas Israel in 1885, was an early victim of the ethnic conflict.

Stempel, who chanted the services in the manner familiar to worshippers of German origin, had the misfortune of standing for reelection at a time when the preferences of the Russian immigrants were beginning to be expressed. German and Russian Jews pronounced Hebrew differently and were accustomed to different styles of worship and melodic modes. Each year, Stempel's retention met with increasing opposition from those for whom the German style was foreign. His supporters were thwarted by the parliamentary maneuvering of his opponents, who blocked motion after motion, year after year, to extend his contract beyond a month-to-month agreement.

Stempel's supporters persisted in the effort to give him a full year's contract. In the course of heated debate, Herman Baumgarten, exasperated at the delaying tactics of Stempel's opponents, asked aloud, "What is the cause of this opposition to Mr. Stempel?" Whereupon the treasurer, Raphael Sanger, also of German origin, shouted aloud, "Because Mr. Stempel is no Pollack!" Sanger was fined $5 for this insulting outburst. After the embarrassing encounter, the vote on Stempel's retention resulted in his rejection, with seventeen opposing him and fourteen in his favor, revealing the extent of the division that had arisen on the board.

Before long, Yiddish was being spoken at board meetings as frequently as English and far more frequently than German. On one occasion, Baumgarten, meticulously faithful to detail, ignored idiomatic meaning to record the words of a board member with literalist pedantry, as follows: "Mr. L. Cohen asked the unanimous consent to address the members or a majority of them in their own language which was granted,"[8] a sentence which is more intelligible in its Yiddish original, *"Ich vill reden a sphrach vas alleh ken varstehn"*

("I want to speak in a language which everyone can understand"), meaning, as a Yiddish idiom, "I want to speak emphatically!"

While funeral notices, associated with an older generation, continued to be published in German well into the 1900s, Rose Hornstein recalled that at the turn of the century, business meetings of both the congregation and the ladies' auxiliary were conducted largely in Yiddish.

Although the congregation could not have survived without the new members, its older members were clearly ambivalent about their presence. They aggressively sought to recruit the newcomers but resisted yielding power to them.

Applicants for affiliation had always been required to submit to a vote of the board as part of the admission process, as though the synagogue were an exclusive lodge. In almost every case, the vote on admissions was perfunctory; applicants were seldom challenged or rejected. As more and more East Europeans began applying for membership, whether in groups or as individuals, challenges to affiliation became more frequent; there were even instances in which applicants were rejected.

In 1902, East European Jews formed the largest immigrant group in Northwest Washington. They flocked to a thriving downtown community where the predominantly East European Chai Adom Congregation had been founded in 1886. One year later it changed its corporate name to Ohev Sholom, and in 1906 purchased the Assembly Presbyterian Church at 5th and I Streets, replacing the steeple of the picturesque wooden church with a dome. Three major congregations were now located in the same neighborhood: Washington Hebrew was on 8th Street, Oheb Shalom on 5th, and Adas Israel on 6th Street, one block away.

Despite their physical proximity, there was considerable social distance between the ethnic communities and their synagogues.

The residential self-segregation of the German and East European Jews persisted for many years. The German Jews lived around 8th and 9th Streets, upward of K, and the East European Jews on 7th Street. The German Jews were the first to leave the downtown area. The Gichner and Wilner families, both leaders of Adas Israel, were among the first East European Jews to move to a German dominated Jewish residential area in the upper Northwest, Cleveland Park, where Adas Israel's present building would be located.

While the leadership of Adas Israel remained vested in the founding German group until 1924, many of the leaders' children and grandchildren found reason to affiliate with the Reform Washington Hebrew Congregation. Some of the older generation maintained dual membership in Adas Israel and the Washington Hebrew Congregation—"for the sake of the children," they would explain in justification. The process of acculturation which transformed Adas Israel from German to East European eventually led it from Orthodoxy to Conservative Judaism.

~ *Iphigene Sulzberger* *Reflections*

My grandfather (Rabbi Isaac Mayer Wise) had many followers, and his new approach to Judaism might well have overcome the old in this country had it not been for the great influx of Jews from Eastern Europe. Those immigrants were practically medieval in their religious practices.[9] *

*Iphigene Sulzberger, the granddaughter of the founder of Reform Judaism in the United States, was the daughter of Adolph Ochs, the first publisher of the *New York Times*, the wife of Arthur Hays Sulzberger, its second publisher, the mother-in-law of Orvil Dryfoos, its third publisher, and the grandmother of its present publisher.

*~ Leon Shinberg* *Reflections*

I was born in 1904 in Piriaken, a small village in the Ukraine in Russia. Piriaken had a downtown area with two synagogues and dirt streets. In the winter the streets were covered with snow. We'd make a sled by putting water in a big washtub and freezing it. Then we'd take the frozen block of ice out of the tub and go sliding down the hill on it.

We lived in a one-room house with a thatched roof, clay floor, a big fireplace and no plumbing. We slept on top of the fireplace. This house was in a yard that was part of a little farm that belonged to Russian peasants. It was customary for Jews to live with Russians for protection.

In Piriaken, there was a garrison of the Czar's Cossacks. They wanted a pool table made for their club and asked my father, a cabinetmaker, to make it. Not only did he make it, but he also developed a relationship with these Cossacks. He developed a skill in playing billiards, and he would be invited to play billiards with them, even though they knew he was a Jew. This was absolutely verboten. The Cossacks would take my sister and me on their horses and go riding around the village.

In 1905, my father participated in the Russian Revolution in an effort to overthrow the Czar's government. The revolution failed, and many people were punished. My father was in possession of some weapons and documents which he hid successfully in my crib because when the police came and searched our house, they didn't find them.

My father emigrated to the United States in 1909; in 1912, he sent for my mother, my sister and me. The farewell was a terrible experience. We had been living with my grandparents, and my mother had a married sister who, with her family, lived in the same town. We left on a Sunday morning, and we knew that we would never see each other again. It was a living funeral.

We arrived in Philadelphia on Labor Day, 1912. My father was supposed to meet us, but his foreman had told him that if he took the day off, he would lose his job. We didn't know this, of course. So after we cleared customs, we just stood there a long time. The one thing I remember very distinctly was a person who came over to us. He was black. I had never seen a black person before. He was trying to talk to us, but of course, we couldn't understand him.

Finally, my Uncle Ignatz from Baltimore showed up—my father had arranged with him to meet us—and we went to Baltimore by train. After a few weeks, we left Baltimore. My father, a carpenter with the George A. Fuller Construction Company, was so pleased to have his family reunited with him that he couldn't do enough for us.

We arrived in Washington from Russia in 1912 when I was eight years of age. I learned English quickly. That was the way my father wanted it. I spoke Russian but my father admonished us to forget Russian as quickly as possible. He just hated Russia with the most intense hatred you could imagine. He wanted to knock Russia out of us, and he succeeded.

At 14, I wanted a job as a Western Union messenger boy, but my mother wouldn't hear of it because I had to wear a uniform, and that made me look like a soldier. My mother didn't want to have anything to do with anything that looked like a soldier because of the old country, the compulsory military service. So I got a job as a messenger in the Interior Department of the government, a temporary summertime job.*

*Leon Shinberg was a lawyer and in 1977 was elected president of Adas Israel. During their first years in Washington his family lived in a six-room row house at 137 N Street N.W., a dwelling without heat or running water. In 1924, Shinberg's father bought a Jewish book store from Bernard Danzansky, who had decided to open a funeral home. Shinberg's reflections here are excerpted from his oral history interview in *Jewish Historical Society of Greater Washington Record* 11, no. 1 (July 1982): 14–16.

~ *Leo Bernstein* *Reflections*

My grandfather, Hyman, in Latvia, wanted nothing to do with the compulsory military service required by the Czars, which was always especially harsh and lengthy for Jewish conscripts; they were required to serve more years than others. The sole exception to compulsory conscription were only sons. So Jewish families with more than one male child would apprentice all but one of their sons to relatives with no male children.

My grandfather was one of those apprenticed "only sons." He attended yeshiva and spoke five languages by the time he came to Washington about 1885. He set up a kosher butcher shop at 816 4 1/2 Street, Southwest, and was an active member of Adas Israel Congregation.*

~ *Rose Hornstein* *Reflections*

Mrs. Simon Oppenheimer was president of the women's auxiliary. Their business, for the most part, was conducted in Yiddish. Once, when I stopped in at a meeting to meet my mother after cheder, I heard a resolution had just been passed to donate $5 to some worthy cause. The treasurer, wife of one of our affluent members, but not known for generosity, refused to issue or sign the check because she opposed giving the money. The women at the meeting each pitched in to raise the $5.00.[10]

~ *Stanley Rabinowitz* *Reflections*

After becoming the rabbi of Adas Israel, in 1960, I often wondered why so many of the descendants of the congregation's founders were no longer members, but were affiliated with either the Wash-

*Leo Bernstein is a prominent Washington banker and real estate broker.

ington Hebrew Congregation or Temple Sinai—both Reform. One day, returning from the funeral of an elderly Adas Israel member, riding from the cemetery with the president of the congregation, Joseph Blumenthal (his attendance mandated by constitutional requirement), I observed that I had recognized no Adas Israel members at the funeral, and said, in jest and somewhat crudely, "The only Adas Israel members at the funeral were you, me and the corpse. Where were our members?" Blumenthal responded with a shrug.

The answer was provided by Dr. Moshe Davis, who, in his *The Emergence of Conservative Judaism,* described the impact of the Russian Jewish influx on the Orthodox Beth Shalom Congregation in Richmond, Virginia. Once Russian immigrants began joining Beth Shalom in force, the congregation's Orthodox German members began transferring to the Reform temple. For the German Orthodox Jews, association with other German Jews of the same social class, even though Reform, was more important than remaining in an Orthodox congregation whose membership included lower-status Russian immigrant Jews. Ethnic identity overcame religious preference.

This same tendency repeated itself in Washington. A sizeable defection of German Jewish founding families of Adas Israel followed the affiliation of Russian Jews; the "needs of our children" was the rationalization.

With the end of World War II, time and generational distance from the "old country", and new wealth, which bestowed its status upon its possessors without regard to synagogue affiliation or ethnic origin, reduced the distance between the two groups and diminished the social gap that separated the congregations. The social cleavage persisted through the second generation. Thereafter, marriage between the two groups advanced the levelling process.

In retrospect, it was fortunate that Adas Israel was established as a traditional congregation in 1869, for when the great influx of Russian Jews came to the United States, and eventually to Washington, a traditional synagogue was available to them; a Reform congregation could not have met their needs. The separation of Adas Israel from the original congregation thus turned out to be in the best interests of the Jewish community. Diversity is as important to the health of a community as is unity. People require alternative choices especially in religion.

# 16

## TOWARD CONSERVATIVE JUDAISM

### The Seminary

The rabbis who founded the Jewish Theological Seminary had prevailed on their congregations to join them in supporting the new institution. The congregations, however, acquiesced more out of loyalty to their rabbis than from a sense of identity with the seminary. With the exception of the one year when Jacob Voorsanger served as its Hazzan, 1886, Adas Israel was without a Rabbi or any leader who could lead them into affiliation with any movement.

At the turn of the century, after the rabbi who had led them into affiliation with the seminary had passed away, almost all of the congregations transferred their affiliation to other movements. Of the twelve rabbis and congregations present at the formation of the seminary in 1886, only one among the eight liberal congregations, B'nai Jeshurun in New York, remained committed to the seminary; the others reverted to Reform. Among the four traditional congregations, only two, Chizuk Amunah in Baltimore and Mikveh Israel in Philadelphia, remained affiliated; the other two, both in New York, turned to the Orthodox movement. Baltimore's Chizuk Amunah's commitment to the seminary was due largely to the influence of Rabbi Schneeberger and the Friedenwald family. Philadelphia's Mikveh Israel, Sephardic and traditional, first served by Leeser and then by Morais, remained committed to the seminary because of the influence of Cyrus Adler.

The path that led from Orthodoxy to Conservative Judaism was strewn with obstacles, difficult to overcome, both at the seminary and in Adas Israel. The rabbis serving Adas Israel who were determined enough to lead the way in negotiating the tortuous course would pay the price in personal frustration and professional failure. A complicating factor was the lack of agreement in the seminary movement itself. Its leaders were positioned along a broad philosophical spectrum so diverse that it was difficult for them to agree on a name for the movement much less a unifying ideology. To affirm the term "Conservative" Judaism, would take the movement longer than it did Adas Israel.

**Name and Philosophy**

While the *American Hebrew* had applied the name "Conservative" to the Seminary movement in 1885, the term was rarely used when the seminary was founded in 1886. Alexander Kohut had used the term in his address at the Seminary's opening exercises in 1887; Sabato Morais had used it only as an adjective, with a small "c". Schechter, in the hope of creating an American Judaism that would transcend its diverse strands, resisted using the term lest he be accused of divisiveness.

Cyrus Adler had published an open letter in the *American Hebrew* rejecting the Pittsburgh Platform and calling for the establishment of a "Conservative College."[1] Nonetheless, Adler insisted that the seminary remain primarily an institution of learning rather than the proponent of a new viewpoint in Judaism. In his writings, he refered to a "conservative tendency," never a Conservative Movement. This position enabled him to retain the support of backers who were not Conservative Jews; it also represented his personal conviction.

It was the critics of the movement who fixed on it the name "Conservative Judaism." J. D. Eisenstein, the Orthodox scholar, writing in the New York *Yidishe Zeitung* in 1886, observed, "In my opinion, the objective of Conservatism and the law of the Radicals lead to the same path, the path of change, though at differing rates of speed."[2]

When Schecter realized that the seminary was not the vehicle that could unify the diverse approaches to Jewish life, he sought to organize a union of seminary congregations which was to become the United Synagogue of America. It was to be a broad-spectrum organization open to all congregations that required head-covering for males at worship and that did not use the Reform Prayer Book.

Agreement on a constitution for the United Synagogue, founded in 1913, followed a struggle between the left and right segments of the movement which resulted in a compromise that omitted the term "Conservative Judaism" in favor of a preamble that affirmed the maintenance of "the traditional character of the liturgy," and the fostering of "Jewish religious life in the home as expressed in traditional observances." At the same time, the statement took pains to distance itself from Orthodoxy by including a defining premise which read, "It shall be the aim of the United Synagogue of America, while not endorsing the innovations introduced by any of its constituent bodies, to embrace all elements essentially loyal to traditional Judaism."

The handful of early seminary graduates would be responsible for introducing new approaches to worship and religious practice and to propose reinterpretation of halachic procedures. It was left to the Rabbinical Assembly to spearhead the recognition of the Conservative Movement for what it was, a separate movement, but even in that body, the move was halting.

The first formulation of the Rabbinical Assembly constitution in 1928 defined the objective of the organization as "to promote traditional Judaism." Reworked in 1940, moving slowly and still resisting the acceptance of the tell-tale name, the constitution redefined the objective as one that would "conserve and promote traditional Judaism." Finally, in 1962, a revised constitution affirmed with overdue clarity: "the object of this organization shall be to promote Conservative Judaism."[3]

The conservative rabbis were challenged to resolve the conflict between their loyalty to their professors (and their orthodox parents,) with the demands of their congregations. Many were torn by guilt for abandoning past authority: all were forced to mediate between tradition and change. Leaning toward change, the Rabbinical Assembly, in 1945, published a new Sabbath and Festival Prayer Book and, in 1950, issued responsa allowing driving an automobile to the Synagogue and the use of electricity on Sabbath. Leaning toward tradition, the Assembly struggled with the question of the *agunah,* the abandoned wife, and, while differing with the seminary faculty, ultimately yielded to them the traditional authority to decide questions of marriage and divorce.

For many years, the movement continued to experience difficulty in accepting the implications of its creation. It had "a long history of dodging and denying the importance of ideology," stated the current Chancellor of the Seminary, Dr.Ismar Schorsch.

~ *Ismar Schorsch* *Reflections*

In seeking to define the Conservative Movement, the Seminary has not played a very constructive role. Dr. Schechter came to bridge differences. He came to unite American Judaism. Consequently, he was adverse to the idea of forming another denomination. . . . Dr.

Finkelstein's vision of the institution was to make American Judaism respectable in the land of immigrants—and he succeeded mightily. Eventually, he came to be regarded as the spokesman for American Judaism. . . . But one who seeks to make all of Judaism respectable to American society is not going to be preoccupied with the creation of a powerful religious movement.

That orientation began to change under my predecessor, Dr. Gerson Cohen.*

**Yiddish and English**

The quest for definition was rendered more difficult in the early years because of the gap between the intellectual elite on the seminary faculty and the great masses of immigrant Jews they wanted to serve. They didn't speak the same language, literally and figuratively. The Jewish immigrants from Eastern Europe, whom the seminary leaders desired and needed as a constituency, knew little of the German dialect, *jüdische Wissenschaft*, the scientific study of Judaism, or the Historical Judaism of the Seminary founders. They looked askance at the European manners of the Seminary officials. They spoke little English and understood no German; they understood Yiddish.

Schechter refused to cater to proponents of Yiddish because he saw no future for Yiddish in America and looked upon those Jews who wanted it to be the language of instruction and preaching as romantics given to nostalgia for the "old country." For him, Hebrew was essential for worship and English was essential to the sermon. "To banish the English sermon from the Synagogue means to condemn our youth to the ignorance of the teachings of Judaism," he asserted.[4]

*Address delivered by Dr. Schorsch to the West Coast Leadership of the Conservative Movement at the University of Judaism, June 6, 1988. Dr. Gerson Cohen was chancellor of the Seminary from 1972 to 1986. He passed away in 1991.

The synagogues dominated by East European immigrants had more in common with Yeshivath Etz Chaim, the forerunner of the Orthodox Yitzchak Elchanan Yeshiva, than with the seminary. Because of its antipathy to Yiddish and its West European image, the seminary became more and more isolated from the masses of Russian immigrants, and because it was Orthodox, it could not place its graduates in those congregations inclined to Reform.

**At Adas Israel**

In its early years, Adas Israel, like the seminary, stressed its Orthodox identity. The Adas Israel constitution stipulated that the congregation would follow the "German Orthodox Minhag Ashkenaz" in ritual and worship, and required that its officers and clergy adhere to orthodox practices.

Solomon Schechter stamped his philosophy on the Rabbinical students who came under his influence. At least two of them, among others, tried their best to implement a Schechter-type program and ideology in their congregations. One was Mordecai M. Kaplan, who became the modern rabbi of the most prominent Orthodox Congregation in New York, Kehillat Yeshurun. The other was Louis Egelson, who was elected Rabbi of Adas Israel.

Both were determined to bring to their respective congregations what they felt to be an exciting modernized form of tradition. Both were to fail. They shared the fate of Seminary trained Rabbis who ventured into moderately Orthodox congregations. Their efforts would result in disputes which led both Rabbis to leave their congregations in bitter resignation. That they received little support from the Seminary in facing their challengers added to their frustrations. Nonetheless, both paved the way for the emergence of Conservative Judaism in name and philosophy.

It would be a transforming experience for both men, one that would lead to changes in the direction in their careers. "I found myself beyond the point where I could consistently serve my Orthodox congregation and retain my inward peace," wrote Kaplan.[5] Subsequently, in 1909, Kaplan was invited by Solomon Schechter to head the Seminary's Teachers' Institute; later. he became the founder and Rabbi of the first Jewish Center. Louis Egelson would be no more successful at Adas Israel.

### Rabbi Louis Egelson

With the dedication of the new synagogue, Adas Israel eagerly awaited the arrival of its new rabbi, Louis Egelson, who had been recommended to them by Schechter himself. Adas Israel was to be his first pulpit. He arrived in 1908.

Louis Isaac Egelson was born in Rochester, New York, on August 29, 1885. He earned degrees from New York's City College (B.A. 1904) and Columbia University (M.A.,1907,) and was ordained by the Seminary in 1908. Rabbi Charles Hoffman, the president of the Seminary Alumni Association, recognizing Egelson's ability as an organizer, later appointed him to the committee charged with organizing the United Synagogue.

Fresh from his ordination, imbued with the enthusiasm of youth and energized by Schechter, Egelson was determined to bring the seminary's approach to the congregation. He took charge of school and pulpit, invigorated committees and, together with the new cantor, brought a welcome freshness to the worship service. As an experiment, the cantor was allowed to "import" a choir from Baltimore for the team's first High Holy Day service at an expenditure limited to $300. Their Sabbath services met with widespread if not unanimous approval.

When Egelson's first one-year contract came up for renewal, however, it became apparent that his innovations had disturbed some of the members. Following a motion by Simon Atlas to renew the contract, a bitter debate erupted. While approving applause followed the motion to ratify new contracts for both rabbi and cantor, a minority, in opposition, agreed to retain the two only on condition that they receive no salary increase. The motion to renew the contracts at their current levels eventually carried.

In April 1909, Egelson was given a three-month leave of absence to enable him to travel to Egypt. The cantor received a six-week leave in June. Salaries were paid to both during their leaves. Upon his return, Egelson presented a gift to the congregation of "a beautiful Olive wood Box for keeping of the *Essrogim*." One may conclude that he had visited Palestine as well as Egypt, though the minutes make no mention of a pilgrimage to the Holy Land.

### The Classroom

In 1910, Egelson involved Adas Israel with two other Orthodox synagogues, Ohev Shalom and Talmud Torah, then located at 4 1/2 Street S.W., in an attempt to establish a citywide Talmud Torah. The proponents of the school consolidation stressed the several advantages of a unified Talmud Torah: it would make for more effective teaching, it would be more economical and it would be insulated from the frictions of congregational life. The new school would charge no tuition, so that parents who could not afford to pay would be able to send their children. The board reluctantly and tentatively agreed to participate.

Rabbi George Silverstone, who had been engaged in 1907 to serve as rabbi for the Washington Jewish community at large, together with lay leaders headed by Barnett Cohen, president of the Hebrew Free School, raised sufficient funds to open the communal school in June 1910. A remodeled private home at 1003 K Street provided classrooms, an office, and a meeting room, for which the school board paid $50 per month in rent. Sixty children were enrolled, and there were three teachers. A branch school was opened to serve children in Southwest Washington, meeting on the premises of Congregation Talmud Torah.

The curriculum and achievements of the school were impressive, and it met with considerable success during its first summer of operation. With the onset of the fall, however, it became more difficult to maintain the demanding schedule. A precipitous drop in registration caused a financial crisis. Pledges to maintain the school were difficult to collect; debts accumulated.

In an attempt to reduce expenses, Adas Israel was asked to house the unified school. The board declined, feeling that it could operate its own school with greater effectiveness and economy, and that the presence of another school on its premises would interfere with the congregational school. As a result, the communal school was forced to close.

### Conflict

Though he was reelected in 1910, all was not tranquil with Rabbi Egelson.

> Mr. L. Cohn complained of some remarks having been uttered by the Rev. Dr. Egelson to which he takes exception and insisted that the Rev. Gentleman be summoned to explain. Quite an argument was had on this account but good council prevailed and finally Mr. Cohn withdrew his complaint.[6]

We have no way of determining the nature of Cohn's "complaint," but other complaints came up with increasing frequency after Egelson introduced English readings into the Friday evening service. The older members of the congregation registered what a report in the *American Hebrew* termed "a mild protest."[7]

The opposition to Egelson solidified after the High Holy Days in 1910, when he delivered a sermon entitled "Some Weeds of Orthodox Judaism," challenging certain Jewish folk practices which he described as "little more than the superstitious baggage of an outmoded past." After hearing his sermon, a number of the more traditional members of the congregation threatened to resign unless he was dismissed.

Later, adding force to the demands for his resignation, Egelson was accused of seeking to impose the Reform *Union Prayer Book* on the congregation. Adding fuel to the fire was the charge that he had been seen dating the daughter of a member of the Reform Washington Hebrew Congregation; Egelson was young and single.

A special meeting was called to consider Egelson's status. Those who opposed renewing his contract prevailed by a majority of two votes, but not without bitter debate. After the results were announced, Egelson's supporters challenged the decision and threatened to resign unless it was reversed. Two trustees rose to announce their resignations to take effect immediately; others threatened to follow.

Egelson's supporters announced that they would initiate a campaign to conduct a new vote. They admired the rabbi and felt he had brought fresh vigor to the congregation. The more Orthodox members, on the other hand, were elated over the young upstart's defeat and did their utmost to prevent another ballot.

News of the dispute spread quickly. The seminary had held out great hopes for the promising young Egelson. His conflict with the congregation was worrisome in seminary circles and embarrassing to Adas Israel because word of it had reached the Jewish press in New York. The *American Hebrew* headlined its article "Rabbi

Egelson Not Re-Elected," with the subtitle, "Washington Congregation, by Close Vote, Rejects Its Rabbi's Plans for Reform."

Simon Oppenheimer, distressed by the furor, tried to dampen the dispute by saying, "I want to smooth the matter over if possible. It is most unfortunate that this trouble should have broken out, and more unfortunate that the general public should have gotten hold of it. Rabbi Egelson does not finish his present term until March. Before that time I hope to see the matter finally settled. The rabbi is a young and successful man, and will have no difficulty in obtaining another synagogue, if it is decided not to keep him here."

One of Egelson's opponents, L. Cohen, who represented an Orthodox faction in the congregation, declared that the controversy over Egelson was over and the next order of business would be to select his successor. The majority of the members, he added, were pleased with the vote and would be content to see the last of Egelson.

Even though he did not consider the vote a fair reflection of the wishes of the congregation, Egelson recognized that he had no alternative but to abide by its results; he would be guided by the wishes of his supporters before challenging the ballot. He stated that he had done his best to help the members of the Congregation learn to read and understand the Hebrew prayers and had tried to give them a contemporary understanding of Judaism. He denied the charge that he had neglected the Congregation, asserting that the opposite was true, but that despite his best efforts, he had found it difficult to arouse any enthusiasm in the membership, many of whom he had found apathetic and unresponsive.

The following week Egelson visited the seminary to take counsel with his teachers and colleagues. In New York, a writer for the *American Hebrew* interviewed him "to ascertain the true reason for the rupture" at Adas Israel.

Egelson denied that he had intended to introduce the *Union Prayer Book*. "All that I suggested," he explained, "was that a certain number of the Hebrew prayers could be also repeated in English on the High Holidays, so that the younger members of the Congregation, who, unfortunately, do not know Hebrew, might be able to follow some of the service instead of attending listlessly at the synagogue, as they do at present."

The rumor that he himself was turning to Reform was "absurd," he said. Unlike Reform, he had instituted Friday night and Sabbath morning services "all in Hebrew; the chief change I suggested was the translation of a few of the prayers." Furthermore, he insisted, he favored the retention of Hebrew in worship and was strongly opposed to Reform as inconsistent with the teachings of the Jewish Theological Seminary, whose professors were also strongly opposed to Reform.

"Then how did the notion get about that you were not Conservative?" asked the reporter.

"That I cannot say," responded Egelson, "except, possibly, because I lectured on the last High Holidays on what I called 'Weeds of Orthodoxy' in which I referred chiefly to the undesirable habit still kept up in my congregation of selling the mitzvoth on the High Holidays in the synagogue itself. I need scarcely say that this is not an essential point of Orthodoxy, though I would have no objection if the auction took place provided it was not in the Synagogue during the service."

"But is not the use of English in the service against notions rabbinic?" the reporter persisted.

"Not at all," was Egelson's response. "Certain portions of the *Tefillah* are to this day in Aramaic and the rabbis say that even the *Shema* may be said in the vernacular if Hebrew is not understood."

The dialogue reflected some of the philosophical conflicts inherent in the Conservative approach to Jewish tradition. The interview continued with the reporter asking,

"What are your intentions for the future, Rabbi Egelson?"

"I cannot say, as it is by no means certain that the recent vote asking for my resignation will be carried into effect, as the many members of the congregation who agree with my views are to attempt to have the matter reconsidered. They were only defeated by two votes on the former occasion, though several of them were absent and proxies were not allowed."

"One word more, Rabbi Egelson. Considering the objection of some of your congregants to the use of English, could not you obtain the same result by teaching the younger members Hebrew more energetically?"

"I should, of course, prefer that, but the members of our congregation are scattered over the city, and it is therefore very difficult to get their children to come to a Talmud Torah to learn Hebrew an hour every day. Many of them would have to spend half an hour coming and half an hour going, and it would be cruel to demand this after their day's work in school. Of course we teach Hebrew in our Sunday School, but you know how little can be taught in this way."

The dialogue has a contemporary ring.

Egelson concluded the interview by denying the rumor that he intended to leave the rabbinate to study law. His experience with his congregation, as difficult as it had been, had only "firmly endeared him to the life of a Jewish clergyman."

Like his classmate, Mordecai Kaplan, Egelson struggled with disillusionment following his experience in his first congregation. Despite his hopes, he discovered that Adas Israel was not prepared to embrace Conservative Judaism. He experimented in the pulpit once more in another congregation: Temple Emanuel in Greensboro, N.C., a congregation of more liberal leanings as might be deduced from the incorporation of the word "Temple" in its name. Egelson served Temple Emanuel from 1911 to 1914, a term equal to the three years, 1908 to 1911, that he had served Adas Israel.

Egelson was a dedicated young rabbi who had been influenced by Schechter. He was searching for a more liberal approach to Judaism than he could find in the Conservative Movement of his day. Despite his previous protestations, ultimately he turned to the Reform Movement, though not to its pulpits.

He became the assistant director of the Department of Synagogue and School Extension of the Union of American Hebrew Congregations, a position he held until his death on April 10, 1957. At the Reform headquarters, he supervised rabbinic placement, chaplaincy procurement, and tract publication. The Hebrew Union College awarded Egelson the degree of Doctor of Divinity, Honoris Causa. He served as Chaplain with the 91st Division of the U.S. Army during the first World War. Married to Gussie Cronheim, they had one son, Louis I. Jr.

Eulogizing Egelson, Maurice N. Eisendrath, the chief executive of the Union, described him as "merciful and gracious... kindly and sympathetic ... understanding and forgiving of the frailties of his fellow creatures."

> Although not a fellow alumnus of most of us who are the sons of the Hebrew Union College-Jewish Institute of Religion, none served more loyally in our Reform Jewish cause than he who adopted our alma mater as his own and served with faithfulness and never swerving fidelity the liberal faith which he adopted in sincerity and truth.

Egelson was the second Rabbi of Adas Israel to turn to the Reform movement; the first had been Jacob Voorsanger. There would be others from other congregations who would follow the same path. In 1913, Dr. Solomon Shechter, as head of both the Jewish Theological Seminary and the United Synagogue, pondered the causes which prompted some Seminary-trained Rabbis to turn to Reform congregations.

*~ Solomon Schechter* *Reflections*

That some students, trained in the Seminary, have accepted Reform positions is to be regretted. . . . But let no man who knows the conditions of most of our strictly Orthodox synagogues, the poverty prevailing there, the starvation wages which they grant to their Rabbis, the constant strife within the congregation itself, the first victim of which is the Rabbi, the ungenerous treatment of the young men on the part of those who consider themselves the pillars of the congregation—no man who knows these conditions will judge uncharitably those men who have not proved themselves strong enough to become martyrs of the cause. It is with the Orthodox they broke, not with Orthodoxy. I do not justify them. I only contend that if they sinned, there were also sinned against. The majority have remained loyal at a sacrifice impossible to be appreciated by those whose lives have fallen on more pleasant places, and are constantly proclaiming and admiring their own virtues.[8]

*~ Rose Hornstein* *Reflections*

My father often interviewed prospective rabbis. He was particularly pleased with one, Louis Egelson, a bachelor. Everyone was pleased with him, but, in a short while, the controversies started, particularly when he began calling on a lady of the Washington Hebrew Congregation. There was an uproar, with people saying that he was too reformed for our congregation. The last I heard of him he was affiliated with the Reform movement in Cincinnati. The lady in question was shipped off to Europe so she could forget the Orthodox rabbi.[9]

# 17

## OPPENHEIMER AND THE RABBINIC PARADE

Between 1900 and the beginning of World War I, the lines on the graph of Washington's economy projected the silhouette of an Alpine landscape with the valleys deeper and broader than the occasional peaks. Adas Israel, ever vulnerable to recessions, found it difficult to pay salaries or to meet mortgage payments. The energies of the board members were consumed with finding ways to meet operating expenses.

Simon Oppenheimer, elected president in 1888, was well suited to cope with these difficulties; he understood the "bottom line" and knew how to meet its demands. While he ruled with an iron hand and not to everyone's satisfaction, few dared challenge him.

Oppenheimer's authoritarian manner came to the fore soon after his election in a dispute over the pricing of seats. The constitution assigned to the board the responsibility for setting the prices for seat-rentals for the High Holidays. While two rows were to be set aside for the indigent, other seats were to be rented at the rate of $3 for one person and $5 for a couple. Oppenheimer took it upon himself to negotiate exceptions to the established schedule.

At its meeting in August 1891, the board moved to "enjoin the president from violating" the right of the board to set seat prices." It was to no avail; Oppenheimer could not be restrained. The following month, Secretary Baumgarten "complained that the president had taken out of his hands the rental of seats and that he feels aggrieved at this action." He appealed to the membership for support. No action was taken. Morris Notes ran for president in opposition to Oppenheimer in 1901. Notes was defeated.

Between his election in 1888 and 1911, Oppenheimer presided over the employment, dismissal, or resignation of three hazzanim, Heiman, Rosenzweig, and Samuels (twice), and three rabbis, Morris Mandel, Julius Loeb, and Louis Egelson. Others were yet to come. His control of the clergy and of the members left the hapless hazzan or rabbi with little recourse.

Cantor L. J. Gargunsky had been elected in 1908 together with Egelson. Soon after his arrival, a real estate broker complained that the cantor had not paid his rent. "The Secretary was requested to touch the subject as delicately as possible."[1] At the expiration of the year, Gargunsky failed to win re-election, but only after a "lively discussion" which ended in granting him three months salary as severance. Until a successor could be found, the board turned to the old faithful standby, Hazzan Isadore Samuels, on a month-to-month basis.

A new cantor appeared on the scene in 1910 shortly before the holidays. Rev. Samuel. Glushak, a recent immigrant from Scotland, was elected for one year but not without the familiar bargaining process focusing on both salary and duration of contract: What salary could they afford? Should the contract be for twelve months from the date of hiring or fifteen months to the end of the fiscal period, December 31, 1911? Proponents of the twelve-month period prevailed, electing Glushak to serve as "Chazan, Teacher and Bal Koreh." Rose Hornstein would remember Glushak as "venerable and white-haired."

In the precipitous departure of Rabbi Egelson in 1911, the congregation saw an opportunity to effect some necessary economies. At Oppenheimer's behest, it decided not to engage a successor and to maintain its services with Cantor Glushak alone, who in addition to other responsibilities, was asked to supervise the school for his annual $1,500, a salary so frequently in arrears that he was finally forced to write a letter to the board demanding payment. The board did not take kindly to the letter's tone.[2]

There was seldom enough money in the treasury to meet the monthly expenses. Herman Blumenthal, the treasurer, particularly generous, frequently advanced his own funds to pay Glushak's wages. In 1911, the board considered a proposal to sell shares of stock in the congregation as if it were a corporation. When the plan failed to gain acceptance, members were asked to sign notes for bank loans with interest at 6 percent.

When interest payments on the notes reached $700 each month while income was seldom more than $400 monthly, Falk Harmel, the finanical secretary, could not contain his indignation. "The ultimate outcome of such a sad state of affairs can only lead to failure," he warned in dire conclusion to his annual report in 1912.

In this context, Glushak's lot was not a happy one. His request for an allocation of "about $400" to engage a choir for the High Holy Days was indignantly rejected. His request for an advance of $200 to enable him to bring over his family from Scotland was postponed.

In 1913, Glushak felt impelled to turn to the board with a new complaint. Ten dollars had been deducted from his wages. In a letter to the board, he referred to the "universal custom that no Chazan officiates on the Sabbath before Rosh Hashanah." However, he continued, when he told Oppenheimer that he would not be present to chant the services on the Sabbath preceding Rosh Hashanah, the president had threatened to deduct $10 from his salary.

"As it happened," Glushak wrote, "I suffered that week from an abscess of the gum and could not attend services." Nonetheless, Oppenheimer had made good on his threat, deducting $10 from the cantor's salary. "Where in the face of all the world is such an act of injustice exercised on a minister of a Synagogue, a family man whose humble wages are very limited?" Glushak pleaded. "I appeal for your discretion and hope that your decision on the matter may be one more consistent with common sense than that of your president who has been too hasty in effecting evil." Moreover, Glushak complained, he had not been paid for a month, his daughter was ill, and the treasurer could no longer help him.[3]

Many on the board were appalled at Oppenheimer's treatment of the cantor and demanded that his wages be paid forthwith and without any deduction. In the heat of debate, "in a rather boisterous manner, Mr. I. Small called Oppenheimer 'a czar and a crook.'" The president's defenders leveled charges against Small; he was expelled from the congregation.

Oppenheimer was not accustomed to being challenged, especially by a cantor; he did not forget the affront to his authority. In March, he reported to the board that Glushak had failed to attend "Roginski's funeral without giving any reason and had left the District without the permission of the president."[4]

In June, claiming it was in order to effect necessary economies, Oppenheimer recommended that the cantor should be dismissed. There had been complaints that Glushak "had been uncivil to the children," he said. Though the board overruled the president, Glushak's annual salary was reduced to $900. Even those wages were usually in arrears, angering board members who felt that Glushak was being mistreated by a vindictive president.

The next month, Oppenheimer called a special meeting to report that Glushak had requested a three-week leave to visit his family in Scotland. When the request had been refused, Glushak had responded that "he would go to Europe without leave."[5] Oppenheimer seized upon the cantor's response as an implied resignation. Glushak surrendered. Weary of the conflict, he agreed to resign if he were paid the $270 due him for wages in arrears. The money was borrowed and paid, whereupon Glushak resigned as of July 15, 1914.

After a search requiring several tryouts, the congregation engaged Cantor Adler Shefferman of Baltimore to succeed Glushak at an annual salary of $900. The new appointment, while welcome, failed to ease the underlying tensions in the congregation. At Oppenheimer's instigation, the board suspended several members for their "hostile attitude" and for "holding rebellious meetings." The "rebellious" members were demanding that the congregation engage a rabbi, perhaps in the hope of providing some alternative leadership to that of Oppenheimer.

To meet the deadline for payment of the mortgage, Oppenheimer solicited loans from several members of the congregation and pledged $1,000 himself. The lenders failed to appear at the meeting called for assembling the loans. When challenged to offer his own check, Oppenheimer refused on the grounds that "he was not treated right . . . he wouldn't pay 10 cents more; he had paid enough." Baumgarten concluded his minutes with the comment, "Confusion arose and the meeting adjourned."[6]

Pressure for engaging a rabbi intensified. While Oppenheimer continued to insist that a rabbi would be a needless expenditure, he agreed to write to Solomon Schechter for recommendations. In response, Schechter recommended Harry Davidowitz, a recent seminary graduate. The motion to invite Davidowitz for a trial sermon was amended to read that "whenever the congregation finds it expedient to try to elect a new rabbi, not more than $900. salary should be paid."[7] As a result, nothing came of the proposal to invite Davidowitz.

Throughout the year, suspensions were heaped upon resignations; quorums were wanting. A group threatening resignation conveyed the message that "for the sake of harmony," they wanted the congregation to engage a rabbi and again suggested, "the one Dr. Schechter had recommended a year ago."[8] When a group of suspended members suddenly appeared at a special meeting, one of them, challenged by Oppenheimer, responded, "If we are suspended why do we receive a notice and an invitation to appear at this meeting?" It was a mistake, Oppenheimer answered. "After a few more remarks, Mr. Cohen, Mr. Harmel and Mr. John Wolf said goodbye and withdrew."[9] Eventually, the suspended members, including I. Small, found their way back into the congregation.

The ill-wind that blew from the European battlefields in 1914 could not help but stimulate Washington's economy and, consequently, the fortunes of Adas Israel, leading to an increase in membership and requiring the employment of an enlarged staff. Ever on guard, Falk Harmel, the cautious treasurer, again warned the congregation against continuing its "hand to mouth existence."

The war attracted both capital and population to Washington; financial pressures eased. Oppenheimer viewed the improvement with amazement. "God seems to have looked with favor upon us," he noted in his annual message, "and brought us to the shore of prosperity which we had strived to attain."

The congregation, strengthened by the affiliation of newcomers and realizing that the sanctuary alone no longer sufficed to serve its membership on the High Holidays, decided to utilize the vestry rooms for an auxiliary service. Of necessity, it would be limited to male worshippers. Should a "lady apply for admission in the vestry, she should be assigned a seat upstairs, in the sanctuary, not in the vestry room.[10]"

Finally realizing that the congregation could not satisfy the needs of the members without engaging a rabbi, Oppenheimer yielded to the board's demands and wrote to "Professor Schechter in N.Y. if he knows of a young Rabbi who possesses the ability to influence the younger element and also teach the children and lecture occasionally."[11] Schechter responded by recommending Rabbi Benjamin L. Grossman, who, once interviewed, was promptly engaged.

### Rabbi Benjamin L. Grossman

Benjamin Grossman, who came to Adas Israel in 1914, succeeded in invigorating the congregation and its school. Oppenheimer praised him in his annual report.

> The innovations of our Rabbi Grossman in conducting services at eight o'clock on Friday nights has proved a splendid success.... The prayers read by Rabbi Grossman, in English, as well as in Hebrew, his usual good sermons, and the beautiful music rendered by Rev. Shefferman and his well trained choir, provide a service which surely inspires every one. Attendance is most gratifying.[12]

English readings could now be included in the service without negative reactions; it was a new generation, though not yet Conservative.

Grossman trained the students of the Hebrew school to lead the Sabbath afternoon Mincha services. Oppenheimer recognized that "Rabbi Grossman is an energetic and arduous worker and is always planning something of interest for the good and welfare of the congregation."[13]

The school boasted 112 students enrolled for daily three-hour sessions with a special class for advanced students meeting with Grossman for an extra hour each week. The school had suffered under Glushak's supervision; he had lost rapport with the children. In addition to the Hebrew instruction, 213 children were registered in seven classes taught "by an efficient teacher who receives a remuneration." The congregation's two schools, daily and Sunday, were "conducted in accordance with all the latest approved methods, rules and regulations of public school instructions . . . and were the best regulated Hebrew School ever established in this city."

With the founding of the United Synagogue in 1913, Grossman urged Adas Israel to "join in the national Movement to join all Orthodox congregations." Adas Israel rejected the suggestion because "the necessary funds were lacking."

The United Synagogue suffered from being born at the wrong time, the depression period prior to America's entry into the first World War. More compelling issues challenged the Jewish community during and after the War: relief to the suffering Jewish communities of Eastern Europe, fulfilling the promise of the Balfour Declaration through the Zionist Movement and planning for the post-war world.

World War I broke out in August 1914. It was not lost upon Jews that the war had begun on the historically tragic day of the Ninth of Ab. Predictably, Jews in Eastern Europe were singularly brutalized especially by the Ukrainians. Jews in the United States were divided in their sympathies. Largely an immigrant community with pogroms and expulsions still fresh in their minds, many found it difficult to identify with an alliance that included Tsarist Russia. America was officially neutral.

Once the United States entered the war in April 1917, the Jewish community no longer hesitated and mobilized to support President Wilson's war aims. In Washington, 300 young men entered the armed forces.* Except for the regular worship schedule, other synagogue activities were suspended. Minutes of meetings are

*Nationally, 250,000 Jews served in the armed forces. Jews were 3.27 percent of the population and 5.73 percent of the armed forces. See J. George Fredman and Lewish A. Falk, *Jews in American Wars* (Hoboken: Terminal Publishing Co.: 1942).

silent. Synagogues offered their facilities to war dictated needs as the membership concentrated on essential projects. Under the supices of the Red Cross, women knitted gloves and socks and rolled bandages for shipment overseas. The YMHA on 11th and Pennsylvania Avenue sponsored dances and entertainment and offered servicemen billiards, desks, writing materials, and dormitory facilities at twenty-five cents per night.

The community conducted massive fundraising campaigns to feed the starving multitudes of Russian Jews. Rabbi Grossman threw himself into the fundraising efforts for Russian Jewish War Relief and the recently organized Joint Distribution Committee. Jews along with others bought Liberty bonds in great numbers. The Armistice on November 11, 1918 was greeted with relief.

Rabbi Grossman enjoyed the broader vistas which Washington afforded him. He wrote to his fiancée, who lived in Boston, that he had attended a meeting at the Daughters of the American Revolution Hall where Secretary of the Navy Josephus Daniels had presided. The speaker, Henry Morgenthau, had been the U.S. ambassador to Turkey, and he told of the Turkish atrocities against the Armenians and of the suffering of the Jews in Poland, where thirty Jews had been executed in Pinsk.

"He also thanked Daniels for the ship he sent for the relief of Jews in Palestine," Grossman continued. "I appreciated the Jewish note. I did not think our former ambassador to Turkey would be so thoughtful. I felt that he was now beginning to redeem himself toward his 'co-religionists.' At any rate, I was more charitably disposed to him than ever before."[14]

In another letter, Grossman reported to his fiancée, whom he would marry six months later, that he had met with several Senators and the Secretary of State to persuade them to grant a visa to a distressed Russian Jewish family.[15] In a later letter, he told of attending a Jackson Day dinner where William Jennings Bryan had "electrified the audience of worldly men of power and ambition."[16]

Though Grossman was a positive force in the congregation, he was not without his detractors. I. Small, who had been temporarily expelled from the congregation for insulting Oppenheimer, became one of Grossman's defenders, pressing charges against Mr. Robbin for having insulted the rabbi in the presence of children, and against Mr. I. Glazer for calling him "a liar 5 times and other words not fit to use to a Rabbi."[17]

Despite the tensions, Oppenheimer himself proposed that Grossman's contract be extended year after year and, in 1920, that his salary be increased from $2,000 to $3,000. At the same meeting he recommended increasing Cantor Shefferman's salary to $1,500.

Board meetings became increasingly rancorous and the president grew more irritable, frequently absenting himself from attendance. Relations between the congregation and Grossman eventually deteriorated. In August 1920, the first item on the agenda was the election of a new rabbi.

Grossman left Washington for Boston, where he became the rabbi at Roxbury's Beth Hemedrash Hagadol, known popularly as the Crawford Street *Shul*, succeeding his friend Rabbi Louis Epstein. When the neighborhood gave way, Grossman became chaplain at the City Hospital. He was a friend of Boston's famed Cardinal Cushing, who delivered one of the eulogies at Grossman's funeral, at which Rabbi Israel Kazis officiated, in 1964.

With Grossman's departure after a six-year tenure, the rabbinic parade resumed.

**Rabbi Nathan Colish**

Grossman was succeeded by Rabbi Nathan Colish in 1920. Born in Lithuania, Colish had been brought to the United States in 1899 when his parents joined the great wave of East European migration. His father was a traditional scholar while his mother managed both the family of ten children and the New Jersey farm on which they lived.

Colish, who retained a lifelong love for the land, left the farm in order to enter the university and prepare for the rabbinate. Graduating in 1916, he was ordained at the Jewish Theological Seminary in 1920. Adas Israel was his first pulpit,

His tenure was not a tranquil one. He was charged with failure to attend daily services and neglect of duties. Cantor Shefferman too did not escape reprimand. The cantor was repeatedly notified that he was "expected to attend services every day," and was rebuked both for sending bills to the families of the boys he tutored for Bar Mitzvah and for selling wine "presumably for sacramental purposes for his own profit."

During the Prohibition years, when the possession and sale of alcoholic beverages was outlawed, clergymen were granted an exemption which allowed them to possess and distribute wine for sacramental purposes, but the idea of rabbis and cantors selling wine was troubling, and allegations of abuse were commonplace.[18] When Shefferman asked permission to apply for a wine permit, the board refused. Mr. S. Feldman, a liquor store operator, suggested that the congregation endorse his application to sell sacramental wine, promising to share his profits with the congregation. The board first agreed to the arrangement on condition that sales be limited to members of the congregation, but at the following meeting, it restricted the agreement still further by insisting that it apply to "only that wine now owned by Mr. Feldman."[19]

Little more than a year after his arrival, Rabbi Colish was informed that because of "the lack of harmony existing between him and the congregation, that it was not considered conducive to the best interests and welfare of the Congregation to retain him as Rabbi beyond his present term of office."[20]

After leaving Adas Israel, Colish served a congregation in New York. Ambivalent about the rabbinate, he entered law school, graduating in 1926 and passing the New York bar one year later. Later he accepted a pulpit in Houston, Texas where his three children were born and where he served during the difficult years of the depression and the rise of Nazism in Europe.

Colish, an ardent Zionist, was one of the founders of the American Zionist student organization. At the age of 67, in 1962, he moved to Israel, where he served as a volunteer to the Or Hadash Congregation and the Leo Baeck School in Haifa, both associated with the Reform movement. His association with the Reform institutions did not reflect a change of ideology so much as his love of learning. Combining his love of Israel with his love of the land, he tended the school's garden.

Colish lived in Haifa for 20 years. At age 87, on Yom Kippur, 1982, he walked from his home to the synagogue, fasted the day, and even chanted the Maftir. Two months later, he died following a stroke. His eulogy was delivered in Haifa by Rabbi Robert L. Samuels of the Leo Baeck School, who said of him, that he loved family, Judaism, books, and Eretz Yisrael.

In June, 1921, the board advertised for a Cantor to succeed Cantor Shefferman, whom they wanted to retire, and for a Rabbi who would act as principal of the Hebrew school. In addition, the board moved to remove the cuspidors from the Synagogue.

Several applicants responded to the ads; three rabbis and two cantors were invited for trial visits on successive Sabbaths. The rabbis were E. Hurwitz of Charleston, H. A. Liebowitz of New Haven, and Salo Stein of Middletown, Ohio. The two cantors were Morris Schrager and Louis Novick of Baltimore. Novick was elected cantor, but none of the rabbinic applicants were accepted.

**Rabbi Theodore Shabshelowitz**

Finally. in 1921, the Congregation elected Theodore Shabshelowitz as Rabbi. Born in Godingen, Russia, in 1886, he had attended the yeshiva in Telz, Russia, where he absorbed the Talmudic learning for which Telz was renowned. To earn a livelihood he had mastered the art of *shechita*, (ritual slaughter).

Shabshelowitz entered the seminary in 1917 after graduating from a New York high school and City College. At the seminary, thanks to his previous training, he was considered the student body's most knowledgeable Talmud student, so much so that his friends called him, affectionately, "Reb Tuvieh." In addition, his voice earned him the position of hazzan at the seminary's synagogue, where he read the Torah and led the services. He was a serious student whose scholarship was praised by his professors. It was this praise that had commended him to Adas Israel.

His success as a seminary student was not matched by a successful pulpit career. Shabshelowitz was a gentle, modest, retiring person, hardly the kind who could or would stand firm against the demands of lay leaders, and certainly not against Oppenheimer. Less than a year after his arrival, Shabshelowitz received the now familiar letter, "advising him that his services as Rabbi are no longer satisfactory and that he has permission to leave the congregation at any time prior to the expiration of his contract."[21]

Neither Adas Israel nor the communities he served afterward appreciated Shabshelowitz's learning and piety. With his wife and children, he wandered from place to place, year after year, seeking not success, but a measure of security which continually eluded him.

Shabshelowitz was an illustration of the gap between the seminary's definition of the rabbinic role and the expectations held by congregations. He passed away after a lengthy illness in 1968. "He had much to give, but there were no takers," said Rabbi Max J.

Routtenberg, the friend and colleague who officiated at his funeral; "The emerging American Synagogue moved in a direction and at a pace which left him out of the running."[22]

The epitaph on his tombstone reads:

A Gentle Soul
A Dedicated Rabbi—A True Scholar
A Man of Integrity

**Finale**

In 1922 Adas Israel selected Benjamin Grossberg as its sexton, a wise choice, for Grossberg was to serve effectively for many years. The rabbinic post remained vacant for over a year.

During that year, the congregation negotiated with several candidates: Rabbi Samuel Benjamin of Cleveland,* Rabbi Steinback of Norfolk, Virginia, and Rabbi Pinchas (Phineas) Israeli of Woonsocket, Rhode Island.‡

The president of the seminary, Dr. Cyrus Adler, wrote to the congregation recommending Rabbi Morris Teller of Tulsa, Oklahoma.‡‡ After a single interview, in November, 1923, Teller was elected for one year at a salary of $6,000.

The congregation was relieved that a new rabbi would finally arrive. Their elation was short lived, however, for in the following month, Teller informed Adas Israel that his congregation in Tulsa refused to accept his resignation.

*Ordained in 1919; he later moved to Tel Aviv.

‡Ordained in 1902, Israeli served in Roxbury, Massachusetts, Des Moines, Iowa, and Allentown, Pennsylvania, where he succeeded Morris Mandel, Adas Israel's first ordained rabbi.

‡‡Ordained by the Seminary in 1916 he served in Tulsa from 1916 to 1926 and in Chicago from 1926 to 1965. He died in 1967.

The search began anew. Two candidates were invited for trial visits, a Rabbi Schwartz and Rabbi Louis Schwefel. The congregation elected Schwefel, for one year, beginning September 1, 1924, at an annual salary of $6,000.

In the meantime, all had not proceeded smoothly with the presidency. At the annual meeting the previous January, 1924, Oppenheimer had been elected for the thirty-seventh time. Following the election, the board asked him to reestablish the custom of reciting the hymn Anim Zmirot at the end of Sabbath morning services. Oppenheimer refused "on the ground that such custom created a disturbance."[23] * When the discussion became heated, Oppenheimer angrily shouted "I resign," and stalked out of the meeting room. Instead of being shocked, the board was delighted to accept the resignation of the increasingly petulant president and immediately elevated the vice-president, Louis Rosenberg, to the presidency.

Simon Oppenheimer was the last of Adas Israel's German leaders. His repudiation in favor of Louis Rosenberg, as much as anything else, reflected the wishes of the emerging majority of East European members, now in a position to name a leader of their preference.

It had been Oppenheimer's role to lead the congregation with a strong hand for thirty-six years, from 1888 to 1924. Without his leadership, however heavy-handed it may have been, the move to the second synagogue on 6th and I Streets would probably not have succeeded.

*Anim Zmirot (the *Shir HaKavod*, the Hymn of Glory), recited at the very conclusion of services, did not always command every worshipper's attention; some would begin removing their prayer shawls, and many would engage in conversation with each other. Oppenheimer demanded decorum.

Despite their repudiation of their-long tenured president, the board respected his dignity and honored him for his years of service. They presented him with an inscribed resolution of appreciation and ordered flowers to be sent to him on his illness as well as on major festivals.[24]

The new rabbi would serve with a new president.

~ *Joseph Blumenthal* *Reflections*

Arguments at a board meeting once became so heated that Mr. Oppenheimer simply declared the meeting closed, and when the board members objected, he simply called the janitor to turn out the lights, ordered him to close the doors, and he went home.[25]

~ *Leon S. Oppenheimer* *Reflections*

My grandfather, Manassas Oppenheimer, was one of the original members who failed to desert the Orthodox group to join the Reform movement. He came to this country in 1847 and was a devoted member of Adas Israel from the first.

My father, Simon Oppenheimer, was a staunch supporter of Adas Israel and served as president for many years. He was the moving spirit in the building of the new synagogue at 6th and Eye Streets, N.W.

My mother, Carrie Oppenheimer, and my aunt, Julia Oppenheimer, were the moving spirits in establishing the Ladies' Auxiliary, now the Sisterhood. Both served as officers of the organization and devoted much time and effort to its development.

I have been a member of Adas Israel since birth and have remained a member going on 75 years. Although many of my friends in the synagogue transferred their membership to the Washington Hebrew Congregation, I remain one of the few who have remained loyal.*

*Letter from Leon S. Oppenheimer, Miami Beach, Fla., to Stanley Rabinowitz, December 31, 1969. In an earlier letter to Shefferman in 1959, Oppenheimer declared, with underlined indignation, that his grandfather's name was not Manasseh but Manassas.

# 18

## ROSENBERG AND SCHWEFEL

Rosenberg's election to the presidency had been as much a repudiation of the founding German generation as of Oppenheimer's heavy-handed rule. Rosenberg, however, proved to be no more democratic than his predecessor, with the result that tranquility was as elusive as ever; turmoil continued to disrupt successive board meetings.

A sturdier breed of rabbi was needed to meet the challenge of serving Adas Israel. Louis Judah Schwefel, who came to the congregation in 1924, was forceful enough to withstand the president and the board, and sufficiently engaging to win the support and affection of the members. Schwefel had the advantage of beginning his tenure with a new administration at the helm, which enabled him to initiate his innovations without having to contend with Oppenheimer's restraining control. As a result, he brought the congregation closer to Conservative Judaism than any of his predecessors.

Louis Schwefel, who in 1918 was one of the founders of Young Judea, loved the Hebrew language and was an active Zionist. He was also a follower of Mordecai M. Kaplan, an association which hardly endeared him to the elders of Adas Israel. Suspicion of Kaplan and Reconstructionism would continue to be expressed in opposition to rabbinic candidates as late as 1960.

Schwefel quickly assumed an active role in the community and especially in Zionist circles. His participation in communal affairs enhanced his recognition in the community and brought prestige to the congregation. On several occasions, he was called upon to open sessions of the United States Congress with an invocation. During the administration of Calvin Coolidge he was invited to receptions at the White House.

An able writer, Schwefel wrote numerous articles for publication in the *Washington Jewish Ledger*, alternating between two pseudonyms, Hillel Isaiah and Mordecai Israel, the names of his two sons. The articles addressed controversial Jewish issues.

The first evidence of Schwefel's assertiveness was his insistence on attending meetings of the board of managers. When the board informed him that his presence at its meetings "was not thought to be a wise procedure," Schwefel responded that "as head of the Congregation it was his duty to give counsel." He prevailed.

Having established his authority, Schwefel turned his attention to attracting new members to the congregation. Despite the many newcomers who had arrived in Washington, the membership of Adas Israel had not grown beyond 200 families. In March 1925, seven months after his arrival, he announced that 141 new members had responded to his recruitment efforts, bringing the roster to a record total of 341; the following year it leaped to 420. Schwefel attracted new members with his preaching ability and his several innovations in worship and in education.

Loyal to the seminary, Schwefel endeavored to make the congregation more responsive to its need for support. Due to a chronic lack of funds, the congregation had declined to affiliate with the United Synagogue in 1913 when it was founded and again in 1920, even though Samuel Cohen, its executive director, had urged the board to affiliate. In 1924, when the United Synagogue asked the congregation to help organize its national convention, which it intended to hold in Washington, the board replied that it was unhappy with the plan because Washington lacked the necessary kosher facilities to service the delegates. The United Synagogue decided to hold its convention in Atlantic City instead. The following year, however, finally recognizing its obligation to support its national movement, Adas Israel responded to the seminary's appeal for maintenance funds by pledging $3,000 to be paid over three years.[1] But it still resisted formal affiliation with the United Synagogue.

In the mid-1920s, for the first time in its history, Adas Israel attracted some important political figures. Representative Sol Bloom of New York, the most influential Jew in Congress, announced that he was planning to affiliate with the congregation when he addressed its annual meeting in January 1926. Later in the year, two other congressmen joined, Ben Golder and Samuel Dickstein. Bloom frequently attended Sabbath morning services, but in retrospect, his questionable role during World War II in protecting Franklin D. Roosevelt against the pressures of Jewish concern about the Nazi treatment of the Jews diminishes the significance of his affiliation.[2]

In 1926 Schwefel was toastmaster at a colorful banquet marking the fiftieth anniversary of Adas Israel's first synagogue structure. The roster of speakers included Major Ulysses S. Grant III, director of the Office of Public Building and Parks, Representative Sol Bloom, and Rabbi Samuel Cohen, director of the United Synagogue. Vice President Charles Dawes, Secretary of Commerce Herbert Hoover, and other members of the administration sent congratulatory messages.*

*Attorney General John W. Sargent, Postmaster General Harry S. New, Secretary of State Frank E. Kellogg, Secretary of the Interior Hubert Work, and Secretary of Labor James J. Davis, who wrote a two-page letter. It is noteworthy that the messages were addressed to Schwefel and not to the president of the congregation.

Cantor Novick and the choir offered a musical program. Rabbi Judah Loeb, the former rabbi of the congregation, and Rabbi Abraham Simon of the Washington Hebrew Congregation offered the appropriate prayers. Simon Oppenheimer, the longtime president, was given an ovation. Blessings were extended to the current president, Louis Rosenberg, on his approaching voyage to Europe and Palestine. The *Washington Star* recounted the history of the congregation in a lengthy article.[3]

Schwefel was determined to revitalize the Hebrew school. When Paul Himmelfarb, a member of the congregation, offered to build a branch school in the suburbs, he urged the board to accept, insisting that a branch school "would have a beneficial effect on the welfare of the congregation . . . and . . . if the Adas Israel does not take measures to do so, some other congregation will step in ahead of us."

The board did not accept Himmelfarb's generous offer.* Nonetheless, Adas Israel's educational program prospered. Sixty students were enrolled in the daily school and 340 in the Sunday school. There were four daily school teachers and seventeen Sunday school teachers, with an annual budget of $4,000.

In an effort to make the Sabbath morning worship services more decorous, Schwefel began to reduce the number of times the congregation was asked to stand for the recitation of certain prayers. Each suggested change in customary practice met with bitter opposition.

Another bone of contention was the public auctioning of honors during services on the High Holy Days. Every year, prior to the Holy Days, the board would heatedly debate whether the auction should take place. Every year, financial concerns rather than aesthetic

*Schwefel's prediction proved to be accurate. B'nai Israel, another Conservative congregation, accepted the endowment offered by Himmelfarb and built the school.

considerations governed the decision. Schwefel, opposed to the public auction, suggested a compromise: the auction could be conducted before the services began. Eliminated in 1927, the auction was reinstated the following year. The troublesome procedure was not permanently eliminated until the congregation moved uptown to Connecticut Avenue.

The synagogue was filled to overflowing on the High Holy Days. To accommodate the crowds, the District commissioners agreed to block off the corner streets during the hours of Holiday worship. The Board thanked Commissioner Proctor Dougherty for issuing the order.

Schwefel guarded the dignity of his position. A traditionally ordained European rabbi, Rabbi Barishansky, had come to Washington in the mid-1920s to serve the Orthodox community as the *stadt rav* familiar to East-European Jewry. His duties included resolving ritual questions and supervising kosher facilities in the community.

Arriving at services one Sabbath morning, Schwefel was shocked to discover Rabbi Barishansky seated on the pulpit; Rosenberg, the president, had invited him. Following services, Schwefel protested vigorously, arguing that he should have been consulted or at least told that another rabbi would be seated on the pulpit. Challenged, Rosenberg called a special meeting of the board to discuss the situation. After bitter debate, the Board upheld the the president's action, but by a vote of 14 to 11. The close decision was a harbinger of decisions to come.

Schwefel related well to the students in the school. Realizing that many girls felt unfairly treated by their exclusion from synagogue ceremonials, Schwefel proposed instituting confirmation for girls. The proposal was bitterly resisted by the board but Schwefel persisted and eventually prevailed.

Once instituted, the presidents took pride in addressing the annual confirmation service though in a manner that would hardly serve to inspire the confirmands. According to the testimony of one of Schwefel's students, both Rosenberg and later Wilner, would begin their addresses to the confirmands with an identical preamble, "We know we won't see you any more."

Financial problems continued to plague the congregation. In 1926, dues were raised to a minimum of fifty dollars per year, a sum which many members found excessive and difficult to pay. Adding to the financial burden, was the need to renovate the aging synagogue structure. Between the need to repair the roof, the boiler, the bath rooms or the windows, renovation was a constant item on the agenda. Fred Gichner, the chairman of the building committee was forced to draw upon his personal funds and the resources of his iron works company to repair the building.

In light of Adas Israel's ongoing financial difficulties, some members regarded Schwefel's annual salary of $7,000 and Cantor Novick's $4,000 as burdens the congregation could ill afford. They felt they could manage well enough with only one clergyman. The generalized unhappiness about costs expressed itself in resolutions of reprimand. On one occasion the board notified "the rabbi, both chazonim and the Shammes that no official should leave the city without previously notifying the President."[4] Novick was retained in 1926 despite the fact that the board had recommended his dismissal.

In a now familiar pattern, Schwefel and Novick were criticized for their failure to attend the daily morning minyan with sufficient regularity. Both were ordered to be present at every morning service, and either one or the other had to attend each evening service. If they failed to do so they would be considered in breach of contract. "Their salaries would be stopped as of that day."[5]

Unlike his predecessors, who had passively accepted similar admonitions on attending daily services, Schwefel was outraged. He and Novick submitted a jointly written letter to the board, outlining their own grievances, their extensive responsibilities, the endless demands upon their energies, and objecting to the board's action as unfair and inconsiderate. Though unaccustomed to being challenged, the board, a few days later, rescinded its motion and extended to both clergymen a unanimous vote of confidence. Though Schwefel succeeded in resisting hostile resolutions, their cumulative effect could not be denied.

Despite opposition, Schwefel continued to press innovative ideas and new programs. He was successfull in reintroducing late Friday night services together with a discussion at an Oneg Shabbat gathering. On one particularly stormy Friday night, unable or unwilling to walk in the rain, he rode the street car to the Synagogue, an act that came to the attention of the fiery president, Louis Rosenberg. While the two were standing on the pulpit in front of the open Ark, the president angrily declared Schwefel to be summarily dismissed. The dismissal was not upheld by the Board, who may have been more interested in repudiating Rosenberg than in upholding Schwefel.

Unhappiness with Rosenberg's rule produced another rebellion which unseated him to replace him with a caretaker administration headed by Fred Gichner, a popular and influential member, who was less interested in serving as president than he was in unseating Rosenberg. Elected in 1928, Gichner resigned his office after serving only six months.

Fred Gichner, born in Bielitz (now Bielsko), Poland, had been apprenticed to a locksmith and eventually became a blacksmith, although as a youth he had really wanted to be a sculptor. He migrated to the United States in 1890, lived briefly in Baltimore and in 1899, now married, moved to Washington, where he resided on Seventh Street, the Jewish street.

Drawing upon what he had learned in Europe, he launched an ironworks business with little more than a few tools and a wheelbarrow, investing his profits in buildings and land. His wife, Tina, was actively involved in the synagogue and its ladies auxiliary. The Gichner children continued their parents' active involvement in Adas Israel.

Gichner, after his brief term in office, yielded the presidency in 1929 to another strong willed and long tenured president, Joseph Wilner, who would remain in office for 24 years.

Louis Rosenberg, the repudiated president opened the annual meeting which elected Wilner with a prayer in which "he prayed for the peace and good will of the members of the congregation and for the success of this meeting." He also offered a prayer "for the peace of the souls of the late Simon Oppenheimer, Simon Atlas and Mrs. Carrie Oppenheimer," All had passed away the previous year. The aspiration for peace and good will would continue to elude the congregation.

Because he was an iconoclast whose statements and behavior were sometimes considered irreverent, Schwefel's tenure became increasingly stormy. His fierce independence and confident manner incurred the anger of many board members. In response to their increasing agitation, Wilner, soon after his election to the presidency, appointed a committee of five "to devise ways and means to bring about harmony."

Several thorny issues had embittered the board against the rabbi, and in June 1929, the committee concluded that for the sake of harmony, and in the best interests of the congregation, Schwefel should be asked to resign. A committee of three, Fred Gichner, Leo Freudberg, and Irving Wilner, were to offer him a severance of two months salary in exchange for his immediate resignation. Schwefel angrily rejected the offer. Even if they were to offer him his full salary, he said, he would refuse to resign before the expiration of his contract.[6]

There was no way to avert the decree. In November, weary with the endless struggle to retain his position, Schwefel accepted the terms. A check for two months salary was placed in his hands.[7]

After leaving Washington, Schwefel moved to New Rochelle, New York, where he served the Beth El Synagogue. In 1936, undoubtedly affected by his Adas Israel experience, he left the rabbinate to become a full-time worker for the Zionist movement. In 1950 he and his wife settled in Israel. Hebraizing his name to Judah L. Shuval, he became a consultant to the Ministry of Education, and in this capacity introduced the now widely used ulpan system for teaching Hebrew. In addition, he was the director of the B'nai B'rith Hillel Foundation at the Hebrew University, serving until his death in 1960.

*~ Toba S. Herzenberg* *Reflections*

I remember Louis Schwefel. He was clean-shaven except for a mustache, handsome, tall, well built, and I think American born. He must have been very different from those who preceded him in the pulpit.

Rabbi Schwefel met opposition for his newer ways, but, with the help of his devoted followers, he prevailed. I stayed away from the synagogue for at least two years because of anger over how supposedly religious people could behave in synagogue toward a "man of God."[8]

*~ Hillel Shuval* *Reflections*

I remember my father's bitter disappointment with the Congregation leaders of his time who were ultra conservative and who rejected his proposals for modernization of the service, My father was a student and follower of Rabbi Mordecai Kaplan.*

*Hillel Shuval to Stanley Rabinowitz, June 29, 1988. Hillel Shuval, professor of environmental science at the Hebrew University and an authority on water conservation, was born in Washington during his father's tenure at Adas Israel. He and his brother Mordecai fought in Israel's war of independence.

# 19

## THE WILNER YEARS

Joseph Wilner, who was elected president after Fred Gichner's brief term, led the congregation through the turmoil precipitated by the departure of Rabbi Schwefel and during the bitter depression years that followed the stock market crash of October 1929. In his twenty-four-years in office, he presided over the move from 6th and I Streets to Connecticut Avenue and the selection of two rabbis, Solomon Metz and David Panitz, and one cantor, Jacob Barkin.

At the time of Wilner's election, the professional staff of Adas Israel had expanded to include Rabbi Louis Schwefel, Cantor Louis Novick, Assistant Cantor Adler Shefferman, sexton Benjamin Grossberg, and a part-time salaried secretary, Abe Shefferman, the son of Cantor Shefferman.

With Schwefel's departure, the burden of conducting the worship services fell to Novick and the aging Shefferman. The latter, who had served since 1914, had been named to the newly created post of assistant cantor in 1925, with responsibility for the daily services.

Beyond providing the kindly Cantor Shefferman with a position and income, the congregation hoped that the new post would once and for all solve the problem of providing leadership for daily worship. The newly created post eventually developed an identity of its own and remained thereafter an essential position in the congregation's roster. After Shefferman's death in December 1926, the post was filled by a series of rabbis. The first assistant cantor after Shefferman was the *stadt rav*, Raphael Barishansky, who was engaged in January 1930 at an annual salary of $1,000 to perform "such services as the Board may direct."

To mark its fortieth anniversary in 1930, the congregation placed a marble tablet in the lobby entrance listing the names of those who had rendered significant service to Adas Israel: Simon Oppenheimer, the president from 1888 to 1924, Simon Atlas and Isaac Levy, vice-presidents, Julius Baumgarten, president in 1880 and secretary in 1881, Louis Cohen, treasurer, Adler Shefferman, cantor from 1914 to 1925, and Isadore W. Samuels, the repetitive hazzan, who served in 1879, 1894, and 1907 to 1908.* The tablet, which was transferred to the Connecticut Avenue Synagogue, remains inexplicable both in its omissions and its inclusions.

### Joseph Wilner

Joseph Wilner, born in Orlowa, Poland, in 1879, the son of Rabbi Baruch and Bessie (Halpern) Wilner, studied in the yeshivot of Slonim and Lomza in Lithuania-Poland in preparation for the rabbinate. While he gave up his plans to become a rabbi when he migrated to the United States in 1896, he retained his Jewish commitment and his respect for tradition. He valued the synagogue as a means of transmitting Jewish knowledge and strengthening Jewish identity.

In the United States, Wilner joined his older brothers in Baltimore, mastering the skills of tailoring to earn a living while pursuing his education. With his talent for management, Wilner moved to Washington where he hired a staff of tailors to open several work-

*The inscription on his tombstone in the Adas Israel Cemetery reads, "Rabbi Isadore W., age 72, b. Russia, 8 July 1918."

shop-stores to produce and sell tailor-made clothing. His headquarters firm, Jos. A. Wilner and Co., which still bears his name, was founded in 1897.

Wilner married Ida Berkow of Baltimore in 1903. They had four sons, Bernard, Morton, Paul, and Jack. Tragedy entered their lives when two of their sons, Captain John Wilner and Major Bernard Wilner, lost their lives in World War II.

While actively managing his extensive tailoring enterprise, Wilner matriculated in the Georgetown Law School, located across the street from his place of business, to receive his law degree in 1917. Although he was admitted to the District of Columbia bar in 1919 and maintained an office in the Ouray Building, he did not actively practice the profession.

A competent businessman, Wilner's success and personality projected him into positions of civic leadership. His reputation for personal service brought him many prominent clients, including General Dwight Eisenhower, for whom he helped design the garment that came to be known as the Eisenhower jacket. Among his other customers were General Douglas MacArthur, Associate Justice Hugo Black, and numerous senators and representatives.

Aside from his active role in Adas Israel, Wilner pursued broad community interests. Among his several elected offices, he was president of the local Zionist Organization in 1924 and of District B'nai B'rith in 1925. He presided over the transition of the YMHA to the Jewish Community Center in the 1920s and the construction of the Jewish Social Service Agency building on Spring Road. He was elected to represent Washington as its delegate to the American Jewish Conference, which convened at the Hotel Biltmore in New York in May 1943 to consider postwar Jewish interests. The Jewish Theological Seminary honored him with a Citation for Distinguished Service in 1949.

Wilner's civic activities earned him several honors and citations. He served on the D.C. Draft Board during the war and was one of a three-men trial board charged with hearing complaints against the Fire Chief and the Chief-of-Police. When, in 1945, General Patton was accused of anti-Semitism, the General addressed a letter to Wilner defending himself and denying the charges. His interest in athletics gained him the friendship of prominent sports figures. Wilner prided himself on his knowledge of the fine points of baseball.

While Wilner was part of the revolution that had unseated the dictatorial Louis Rosenberg, in his management of the congregation, he replicated the style of his predecessors. Wilner passed away during his presidency, on March 30, 1953; his wife, Ida, on May 22, 1960.

**The Depression**

As the result of the stock market's collapse in October 1929, the United States was plunged into one of the worst and longest economic depressions in its history. In 1931, the unemployment rate hovered at 16 percent; by 1933 it had reached 25 percent. Men and women tramped the streets in search of work, stood in bread lines for food, and looked to charitable societies for shelter. Dr. Nicholas Murray Butler, president of Columbia University, evaluated the country's plight in ominous terms: "The period through which we are passing . . . is a period like the fall of the Roman Empire. . . . it holds more of the world in its grip."[1]

The sharp downturn in the nation's economy forced the congregation to retrench. Rabbi Schwefel's departure provided the congregation with the opportunity to evaluate the changes that Schwefel had introduced during his tenure with the result that it retreated to settle on a less costly level of activities.

The nation's somber mood began to lift after President Franklin D. Roosevelt installed his New Deal administration which included a package of hitherto unheard of economic and social programs; it transformed Washington's culture. A presidential "Brain Trust," consisting of numerous experts and advisors, together with a selected staff to administer new alphabetically titled government agencies, streamed into Washington, propelled by the conviction that they could heal the economic ills of the country and replace its widespread despair with optimistic hope. Many of the bright young men who came to Washington during the Roosevelt years were Jewish. A survey of Washington's Jewish community in the mid 1950s revealed that over half of Washington's Jewish residents had settled in the capital area after Roosevelt's election in 1932.

The history of Adas Israel during the decade of the thirties reflects both the despair of the depression and the enthusiasm engendered by Washington's population growth. During the dark days of the depression, synagogue membership was a luxury which many could ill afford. Longtime members fell into arrears for as much as two and three years. Activities declined to a minimum. The congregation could not afford to sustain its Hebrew school, choosing instead to send its children to a newly organized communal school under the aegis of the Washington Jewish Education Association, a project which would itself succumb to the depression after only one year of operation.

As the economy improved, in the later 1930s, the fortunes of Adas Israel improved along with it. With the outbreak of the war in Europe in 1939, the congregation emerged into a period of comparative prosperity as a result of a growth in membership and, consequently, income. With activities and programs increasing, it was time to take inventory of the congregation's strengths and to plan for the future. Changes in the professional staff would be necessary.

### Benjamin Grossberg

The long-serving sexton, Benjamin Grossberg, engaged in 1922, was a remarkable person who made a significant contribution to the growth of Adas Israel. He attracted an extensive following by virtue of the warmth of his personality.

Benjamin Grossberg taught Talmud to the worshippers at the daily evening service. A faithful group, who attended regularly, eventually completed the entire Talmud, a monumental undertaking. They celebrated their achievement with a traditional banquet, a *siyum hashass*. When the class finally disbanded, it was not for lack of interest; it succumbed to the participants' mortality. Grossberg outlived his students.

During the depression years, Grossberg volunteered to chant the morning service on the High Holidays and read the Torah on Sabbaths without additional compensation. He continued teaching and chanting the Torah until 1947, when, at age eighty-five, his eyesight failing, he retired on a modest pension. Warmly regarded by the congregation, he had been an important link to the Old World origins of many of its members. The congregation officially recognized that Grossberg had been "just and untiring in his duties." He lived to age 104.

### Cantor Louis Novick

Shefferman's predecessor, Cantor Samuel Glushak, who had served as the Adas Israel cantor from 1910 to 1914, passed away in October 1939. His son David served as secretary of the congregation for many years. David Glushak formed a partnership for the practice of accounting with Louis Grossberg, the son of Benjamin Grossberg, the sexton. Louis Grossberg has remained active in the congregation throughout his life.

The congregation had engaged Louis Novick to replace the aging

Cantor Shefferman in 1923. In Novick, the congregation found a new kind of cantor, one who was formally trained, erudite, knowledgeable in classical music, and able to address issues beyond the cantorial pulpit.

Novick, who came to Washington from Baltimore, had studied in the music schools of Odessa and Vienna and was trained for the cantorate by two distinguished cantors, Meyer Pisak in Berditchev and David Moshe Steinberg in Odessa.[2] He introduced the compositions of the classical cantors to the congregation and wrote a regular column in the newly instituted *Adas Israel Chronicle*, addressing Jewish communal issues as well as musical subjects. He also contributed articles to the locally published *Jewish Ledger* and the London-published *Jewish Review and Observer*.

An active Zionist, Novick organized and led the Hebrew-speaking Chavrutha Organization and Washington's Jewish National Fund Council, which he headed as president for eight years. President of the local Mizrachi organization, he became its national vice-president and in 1935 was its delegate to both the World Mizrachi Convention in Cracow, Poland, and the Nineteenth World Zionist Congress, which met in Lucerne, Switzerland.

Among the Washington figures with whom Novick was acquainted was Vice President Henry Wallace. In January 1945, after leaving office, Wallace accepted Novick's invitation to visit the synagogue and expressed his fascination with the symbolism in the sanctuary. Wallace revealed to Novick his interest in Chassidism and its founder, the Baal Shem Tov. He invited the cantor to accompany him on a tour of the Capitol.

Novick served Adas Israel until his retirement in 1946. A factor contributing to his retirement was his refusal to accept the ritual committee's decision asking him to chant while facing the congregation rather than facing the ark as had been the custom.[3]

In 1950 Cantor Novick and his wife moved to Jerusalem, where Novick became literary secretary to Rabbi Yehuda Leb Maimon, the Minister of Religious Affairs in David Ben-Gurion's cabinet. The Novicks eventually moved to Natanya, where they helped organize a Conservative synagogue which Novick served as volunteer cantor. He passed away in Netanya in 1974. His wife, Sarah, died in Jerusalem in December 1989. Of their four children, three remained in the United States. Their son, Rabbi Ezra Novick, became head of Yeshivat Hasharon in Herzliya, Israel, and later in B'nai Brak.

**Abe Shefferman**

With the easing of the depression in the latter half of the 1930s, Falk Harmel, the financial secretary, announced that Adas Israel had grown in both membership and income. In fact, Harmel observed in his 1936 annual report, the membership of 424 was "the highest mark on record in the history of the congregation." He added, characteristically, "Of course, there is always a possibility for improvement."[4]

With the increase in membership and activities, many members felt that it was time to engage a professional administrator rather than continue depending upon volunteers. An amendment to the constitution in 1934 provided for the employment of an executive secretary who would be responsible for the management of the synagogue and the cemetery, but its implementation was resisted because many members feared both the increased cost and the depersonalization of the administrative office. By 1937, three years after its authorization, the need for full-time management could no longer be denied, whereupon Abe Shefferman was engaged as the full-time executive secretary. He was assigned a part-time secretary to assist him and was promised part of the vestry room for his office.

Abe Shefferman was born in Baltimore in 1891. He had come to Washington in 1910 to work for the Census Bureau and had become a permanent resident when his father became cantor of Adas Israel in 1914. He served in France with the Army in World War I, remaining there after the Armistice to help the Jewish Welfare Board resettle displaced persons. In Paris, in 1919, he and Edward Rosenbloom, another Adas Israel member, conducted one of the largest Passover *Sedorim* on record for the 4,000 Jewish troops stationed in Europe.

A graduate of Georgetown University Law School, Shefferman opened a law practice on his return to Washington. In addition, he served as secretary of the Jewish Community Center, which he had helped establish as the Young Men's Hebrew Association, and was active in the B'nai B'rith, heading its East Coast District Five.

Abe and his five brothers and sisters, all blessed with fine voices, formed a cantorial choir to assist their father. Later, Abe sang baritone with the Washington Opera Company. His wife, Belle, became actively involved in Adas Israel, first as a volunteer and later as the salaried office manager.

Shefferman's administrative ability and creative mind transformed the image of the congregation. As one of his first innovations, he initiated the regular publication of a monthly house organ, the *Adas Israel Chronicle*, which disseminated information of interest to the congregants and encouraged attendance at services and meetings. Its publication of the milestones of births, marriages, and deaths and its listing of contributions strengthened the fellowship of the expanding membership.

Abe Shefferman soon became the dominant figure on the professional staff. It was he who rendered the "state of the union" reports at the congregation's annual meetings. In his first report, in 1938, one year after he took office, he pointed to the successful Friday night services, with their weekly attendance of 300 to 400, to the forums following the services which he arranged and conducted, and to the choir which he had helped form. He also called attention to his introduction of organizationally sponsored services as an innovative method for stimulating attendance.

In 1940, Abe reported that the congregation had reached its capacity; there was no need to solicit new members. He credited the sisterhood for its support of the school and called for increasing its representation on the school board. He suggested that Rabbi Metz (who had been engaged in 1930) would be wise to visit the Hebrew school more frequently.[5] Abe attended all synagogue activities and meetings as well as meetings of other organizations taking place in the synagogue. He was easily the central professional figure in the congregation as well as a recognized leader in the community.

Shefferman's reports, which dominated every annual meeting during his tenure, covered all areas of the synagogue program; the rabbis remained silent. His annual reports soon became more and more didactic and sermonic in tone, and before very long, repetitive, using identical language in their tributes and reports of activities, changing only the year and the statistics.

Abe invariably praised the president, Joseph Wilner, with whom, he said, "he consult[ed] fully and frequently." In consecutive years he would repeat, "The high standing which our congregation holds in this community and elsewhere and its continuous progress forward, financially and in all other respects, are due to his [Wilner's] understanding and leadership."

In ritualized annual repetition, he would pay tribute to the rabbi's "scholarly sermons and the beauty of the services." While lauding the consistently high attendance at services, he would invariably castigate the members for their failure to attend.

Throughout the war years, Shefferman concluded his reports with the repeated hope that "when this mad era of destruction is ended and the forces of good prevail over the forces of evil, we shall be ready to meet the needs of a better world, the demands of a more wholesome and lasting peace, for the good of Israel and humanity in general."[6]

Shefferman's annual reports were reprinted in the *Chronicle* along with a statement that the rabbi "extended greetings and brief remarks."[7] At each board meeting and at men's club breakfasts, Shefferman offered a review of events in the Jewish world. Well read, proficient in writing and speaking, and skilled in the art of public relations, he encouraged the congregation's commitment to Zionism and the community. With an appreciation for history, he carefully preserved the congregation's important papers in bound volumes.

As the executive secretary who attended all board and committee meetings, Abe Shefferman was in the center of the decision-making process; the rabbi and cantor were not. Rabbi Metz, ever passive and gentle, surrendered policy decisions to Shefferman, and, of necessity, so did Metz's successor, the more assertive Rabbi Panitz, who was engaged in 1951. Shefferman guided the congregation over the transitions from Metz to Panitz to Rabinowitz (1960), from cantor to cantor, and from president to president. He subtly influenced major decisions in the congregation.*

Shefferman and his wife, Belle, who served as office manager, retired in 1961. He yielded his office by prearrangement to the sitting president, Stanley Wiener. In retirement, the Sheffermans lived in the Quebec House, an apartment building adjacent to the synagogue. He continued to volunteer his service in various capacities until his illness and death at age eighty-five, in December 1976.

*With Metz's impending retirement in 1950 drawing near, Shefferman phoned me in New Haven, Connecticut, where I was serving as the rabbi, and politely suggested that I take the initiative in applying for the soon-to-be-vacated Adas Israel pulpit. I no less politely declined the suggestion; I felt that I was too young.

A tribute to him in the *Adas Israel Chronicle* read, "He was as skilled in the choir loft as in the classroom, in the Cantor's pulpit as in the Rabbi's podium." He passed away during Chanukah. In eulogizing him, I stated, "Abe was like the Shammash candle of the Menorah; he kindled the light that brightened the community. He felt the pain of his people; he ached for the indignities inflicted upon them; he lived their history." It was also true that he "knew how to drop hints in the right places and to make the kind of suggestions to the appropriate committees that would make certain that decisions would be made in the best interests of the congregation."

Belle Shefferman passed away on October 24, 1980.

### Jacob Barkin

With the departure of Cantor Novick after twenty-three years of service, the congregation engaged Cantor Jacob Barkin, who began his distinguished though ultimately stormy tenure at Adas Israel with the High Holy Day services of 1946.

Born in the Ukraine in 1912 and brought to this country at age fourteen, he was the son of a traditional cantor, Abraham Barkin, who had served a congregation in Toronto for many years. Barkin's cantorial training came from his father, and his formal musical education from the Eastman School of Music in Rochester. Before coming to Adas Israel, he had served the Community Synagogue in Atlantic City and Beth El Congregation in San Francisco. He and his wife, Mildred, had two children when they came to Adas Israel.

Blessed with a rich and vibrant tenor voice, Barkin soon distinguished himself on the concert stage and the radio as well as on the pulpit. He was a frequent guest soloist with the National Symphony Orchestra at concerts conducted by Howard Mitchell at Constitution Hall and at summer concerts on the shell alongside the Potomac River. "Cantor Barkin's Symphony Debut an Unqualified

Success," was the headline in the *Washington News*'s review of one of his concerts.[8]

Barkin brought impressive musical events to the congregation and infused the worship services with classical cantorial renditions. He dominated the pulpit, imposing his personality on the mood of the services. In 1956 the congregation proudly recognized his tenth anniversary at Adas Israel with a testimonial service. He was easily the most popular cantor in the Washington area; in fact, he became one of its Jewish tourist attractions. He was also one of the founders of the Cantors' Assembly, the national association of Conservative cantors.

Barkin endeared himself to the members not only by his musical talent but by his outgoing personality. He could relate to the leaders in ways that neither Rabbi Metz nor his successor, Rabbi Panitz, could. Barkin was warm and earthy, while Metz appeared distant and intellectual. Barkin socialized and golfed with the congregation's business leaders; Metz and Panitz could do neither.

The congregation's affection for Barkin became strained as he absented himself more and more from the Sabbath pulpit in order to fill concert engagements. His tenure came to a conclusion in 1958 amidst growing dissatisfaction fueled by complaints that he neglected the congregation for the sake of his concert tours and was more interested in the operatic stage than in the pulpit. Amidst charges of inappropriate behavior, he resigned to accept a post with Congregation Beth Shalom in Pittsburgh, later moving to Toronto. "It is with genuine regret and a feeling of personal loss that I am forced to accept your resignation," wrote Julius Wolpe, the president, to Barkin.[9] Later efforts to return him to Adas Israel failed. After serving in one of Canada's leading Reform congregations, he and his wife retired in Florida.

### Samuel Weiss

With Barkin's encouragement, Rabbi Samuel Weiss was engaged as assistant cantor to chant the Shacharit services on the High Holidays, conduct the daily services, read the Torah, and instruct Bar Mitzvah students. Born in Czechoslovakia in 1910, Weiss arrived in the United States in 1937. Traditionally ordained, he had served as rabbi in Braddock and Donora, Pennsylvania.

Trained as a mohel, Weiss provided an essential service to Adas Israel and the Washington community. Although he did not possess a trained voice, he was a patient teacher and a friendly person. After a few years, he began to feel that he was not sufficiently appreciated. On the verge of leaving several times, he invariably yielded to those who persuaded him to remain.

Rabbi Stanley Rabinowitz, upon his arrival, sensing Weiss's unhappiness and his usefulness to the congregation, made a point of referring to him as rabbi rather than assistant cantor, much to the consternation of the congregation's leaders. In 1960, the title of assistant cantor was replaced by that of "rabbi of the chapel" and then simply rabbi. Weiss remained in that capacity until his voluntary retirement in 1969.

### Ritual and Classroom

The constant struggle to reconcile the sincere desire to uphold religious traditions with the equally sincere attempt to render the services attractive to the congregants continued to be a source of tension throughout Wilner's administration. The most contentious issues were the school curriculum, the repetition of prayers, the amount of English in the services, men and women sitting together, the role of women in the services, and, later, the installation of an organ.

Prior to each High Holy Day period the board heatedly debated whether the public auction for the right to honors should take place during the services, as had been the custom for many years, prior to services, or even not at all. Except for the few years when the congregation felt sufficiently secure to abandon the procedure, financial needs determined the decision. Rabbi Schwefel had opposed the public auction. Rabbi Metz did not enter into the debate. By the time Rabbi Panitz arrived, in the Connecticut Avenue synagogue, the procedure had been abandoned.

Under the guidance of Leopold Freudberg, who in 1922 became "supervising principal," the school board administered a school with 400 children, 60 in the daily afternoon school and 340 in the Sunday school, an annual budget of $4,000 and a teaching staff of four in the daily school and seventeen for the Sunday school. Classes met both in the vestry rooms and at the nearby Jewish Community Center. In 1928, for the first time, the school board chartered busses to bring the children to afternoon school and, in a move toward professionalism, hired an educator, Mrs. Bertha Hollander, to supervise the Sunday school at an annual salary of $300. Sunday teachers were paid $10 per month.

The driving force in implementing improvements in the school was Julius Wolpe, chairman of the school board and a future president. Under his initiative, Bar Mitzvah candidates were instructed in classroom groups with Cantor Novick as the instructor. A daily kindergarten, an innovation in those years, was established in 1931 under the direction of Mrs. Jacob M. Schaffer.

The school board, with Wolpe as chairman and Judith Harmel as secretary, struggled to protect the school from the budget cuts necessitated by the depression of 1929. Economic conditions and philosophical considerations lay behind an attempt to open a communal school to which participating congregations contributed a monthly sum. Because of deficits, the attempt failed after operating two years, 1931 and 1932. In 1933, the twenty Sunday school teachers agreed to waive their salaries so that the school could remain open.

With the death of Mrs. Hollander in 1934, Maxwell Ostrow took over the supervision of the school. Unable to overcome the deficit, he recommended that Adas Israel abolish its school and contract with the Washington Hebrew Congregation to educate its children. The recommendation was rejected.

Ostrow set out to collect the many delinquencies in tuition payments. He proudly announced in 1936 that he had collected $200 in delinquent tuition and that the school was now able to pay its rent to the Jewish Center without requiring any subsidy from the congregation or the sisterhood.

Distressed by the cost of maintaining the school, the congregation debated its purpose. To the traditional element in the membership, the school's goal was to impart sufficient mastery of Hebrew for students to know the Bible, be able to follow the worship service, and, if possible, understand the prayers; to others, it was of greater importance to transmit knowledge of Jewish history and an understanding of Jewish values. Still others wanted to introduce music, art, and dramatics into the curriculum. After each academic year, curricula, textbooks, and goals were subjected to searching analysis and review; there was no agreement.

Rabbi Metz, who arrived in 1930, shocked the congregation by suggesting that the limited school hours made it impossible to achieve the traditional goals of teaching the Hebrew language and prayers, Jewish literature and history. In 1939, in an attempt to reach more students and to improve the curriculum, the congregation decided to operate three Hebrew school branches, one at the Jewish

Community Center, one in Southwest, and another at the Devitt School on Connecticut Avenue. Eighty children enrolled for a weekday curriculum stressing Hebrew and Bible, while the Sunday curriculum focused on Jewish history, customs, and current events.

Cantor Novick led periodic assemblies to teach hymns and prayers. To elevate standards, the board enacted a requirement that boys preparing for Bar Mitzvah and girls desiring to be confirmed attend the daily Hebrew school for at least three years. The requirement proved difficult to enforce. More than ten years would elapse before it was possible to overcome the opposition to the imposition of any requirements for Bar Mitzvah and confirmation.

The summer of 1944 brought with it an unusually severe polio epidemic in Washington. Parents were afraid to allow their children to participate in group activities. On the advice of Isabel Gichner, junior congregation services for the High Holy Days were canceled; parents were advised to keep their children at home.

By 1948, 100 elementary school children were attending classes two and three afternoons each week, over 80 junior and senior high school students were attending on Saturdays and Sundays, while only the youngest attended on Sunday alone. Extracurricular activities, including a school newspaper, a choir, a debating club, and a post–Bar Mitzvah "Minyannaire" group meeting on Sunday mornings for worship, breakfast, and discussion enriched the curriculum.

With Israel Mendelson as chairman of the school board and Irving Wilner, and later Shalom Pomeranze, as principal, the school population grew impressively. Its three branch operations would continue until Adas Israel moved into its new facilities on Connecticut Avenue. The relatively high enrollment prompted several attempts to liquidate the one-day Sunday school in favor of requiring three-session-per-week attendance. The ensuing controversy, reflecting the diversity as well as the ambivalence within the congregation, invariably compelled the school board to rethink proposals for its elimination.

*~ Morton Wilner* *Reflections*

My father opened his first store on Sixth Street between E and F, North West. His first Washington residence was on 104 Massachusetts Avenue, one block from the Union station and near the site of the first Adas Israel structure. There was one other family in the neighborhood, that of Edward Cooper, who had a grocery store nearby. He later went into the hardware business which would eventually be operated by his son-in-law, Stanley Weiner, who would become the president of Adas Israel.

Our family moved uptown to the corner of Connecticut Avenue and Calvert Street in 1917. At Adas Israel we had Hebrew school classes in the basement. Rabbi Colish, our teacher, introduced sports to the boys. That took my fancy and that of everybody else. We had a baseball team. I remember playing against the boys' team from the Washington Hebrew Congregation.[10]

*~ Louis Grossberg* *Reflections*

I sang with Cantor Glushak's choir. The cantor was a tough taskmaster and became very annoyed whenever there was any cutting-up by the boys in the choir during rehearsals. One evening, after services, my father asked Cantor Glushak how his son, Louis, was getting along in the choir. "Ah, he is a bum like all the other bums in the choir," was his answer. We were all alike to Cantor Glushak.

When my father came home that evening, he was so incensed that he slapped my face. "You shamed me before the cantor and all the other people who heard the conversation," he said. This was the only time my father ever laid a hand on me.

Simon Oppenheimer was a despotic boss. He hired and fired personnel and appointed officers at will. I became corresponding secretary by his invitation without the benefit of an election. With all his faults, as we would view them today, he was an excellent president for Adas Israel in those days.

In the depression years, Adas Israel was in dire financial straits. Salaries were paid ten days after the month's end for lack of funds.

In some respects Joe Wilner followed in the footsteps of Simon Oppenheimer. He was much more the boss or dictator type of president than were any of the presidents who followed him. At a board meeting, when a matter Joe Wilner proposed was defeated by a vote of seventeen to sixteen, Joe declared, "One vote is not enough of a majority to defeat this motion. The motion is carried." And that was that.[11]

# 20

## THE METZ PULPIT

With Schwefel's departure in November 1929, many members of the board, frightened by the stock market's crash and convinced of impending financial difficulties, advised postponing the selection of a new rabbi until the crisis had passed.[1] Joseph Wilner did not agree. He insisted that a rabbi be engaged as soon as possible. On his own initiative, he turned to Cyrus Adler, the president of the Jewish Theological Seminary, asking him to recommend a successor to Schwefel; one was soon forthcoming.

The recommendation in hand, Wilner called for a special meeting of the membership in May 1930. Surrendering to his persuasion despite their apprehensions, the members agreed to engage Adler's nominee, Rabbi Solomon Metz, at an annual salary of $6,000 as of August 1, 1930, and "to continue indefinitely." For the first time in its history, the congregation had not imposed the onerous one-year limitation on a rabbi's engagement; it would make a significant difference in rabbinic tenure and stature. For the approaching Passover of 1930, Wilner arranged for a seminary student to officiate.

### Solomon Metz

Born in Kul, Lithuania, on October 10, 1890, Solomon Metz was recognized by the well-known European yeshivot of Telz and Slobodka in Vilna as one of their outstanding students. Coming to this country as a young man, in 1907, he entered the Orthodox

Yitzchak Elchanan Yeshiva in New York, now part of Yeshiva University, where he soon rose to the top of the student body. When he applied to the Jewish Theological Seminary, his reputation as a keen student of the Talmud gained him immediate admission as well as a place on its tutorial staff. He was ordained by the seminary in 1918 with a citation of distinction in recognition of his scholastic brilliance.

While still a seminary student, Metz was employed as assistant principal by Rabbi Herbert Goldstein at the West Side Institutional Synagogue in New York City. After ordination, unable to find a position to his liking, he left the rabbinate to join his family's clothing-manufacturing firm in Pittsburgh. He returned to the pulpit in 1929 to serve as rabbi of Manhattan's Washington Heights Congregation. One year later, he came to Adas Israel.

Solomon Metz married Gertrude Krieger in 1917 during his last year at the seminary. Mrs. Metz did not participate actively in congregational activities. Years later, reviewing her life, she expressed regret that she had not been more helpful to her husband's career.*

With his formal installation on December 21, 1930, Metz began an impressive twenty-one-year tenure whose duration exceeded that of any of his predecessors; it spanned war and peace and the two most significant events in Jewish history since the destruction of the Temple in Jerusalem, the Holocaust and the birth of the State of Israel. Metz addressed these important themes with eloquence, feeling, and conviction.

Metz was admirably suited for the congregation at that point in its history. After Schwefel, a more tranquil personality was welcome. Metz was modest and unassuming, and, unlike his predeces-

*Together with their four children, Haskell Mordecai, Rayanna Ruth, Ezra David, and Emmanuel Wolpert, they resided at 36 Channing Street N.W., a short distance from the synagogue.

sor, he respected the inclinations of the board of managers to follow a less innovative path. Metz sought to avoid confrontation with the congregation's leaders even on issues of ritual, where he had the right to press his point of view. Though his sympathies were with the traditionalists, he preferred to allow the congregation to chart its own direction.

His gentle nature was an important factor in healing the divisiveness which had plagued Adas Israel since the repudiation of the longtime president, Simon Oppenheimer, a cleavage which had been sharpened by Louis Rosenberg's defeat by Fred Gichner, and accentuated further by Louis Schwefel's forced resignation. Each confrontation had left an unhappy dissident minority.

Although Metz was highly respected by the members, he did not succeed in changing the leaders' appraisal of the rabbinic role. His status in the congregation may be deduced from the fact that while ample space was assigned to the administrative office, he found neither office nor secretary assigned to him. A month after his arrival, his request for a study was discussed by the board, but "no definite action was taken." His request for a secretary was left to the discretion of the president. Metz prepared his sermons at his home.

### Depression Years

The effects of the depression, which had begun to be felt even before Metz arrived in Washington, pervaded the early years of his tenure. Concern for covering the budget and paying salaries dominated the board meetings for several years. The board estimated a deficit of $1,400 for 1932. Its recourse was to reduce the salaries of the religious staff by 10 percent. The next year, with budgetary problems worsening, the board sought to repeat the same formula; it ordered an additional reduction of 10 percent in the salaries of rabbi, cantor, and sexton.

Benjamin Grossberg, the sexton, humbly accepted what he could not change; the rabbi and cantor objected. Metz, who had not claimed the right to attend board meetings, asked to appear at the February 1933 meeting, where he explained that in view of his family responsibilities, he could not see his way clear to accept a further reduction. If the congregation could not continue to pay his salary, he stated, he was prepared to announce his six months' notice prior to "change of status."

In April, Metz concluded that, rather than resign, it would be best for him to accept a reduction of $400 per year; Cantor Novick agreed to accept a reduction of $200. There were few alternatives available to either of them. Their salaries as of April 1933 were $5,000 for Metz and $3,850 for Novick, and would remain at that level during all of 1934. The Sunday school teachers agreed to serve without salary for the remaining three months of the school year.

The reductions in salary enabled Falk Harmel, the financial secretary, to report in 1933 that the deficit had been held to $373. To meet its needs, Adas Israel relied more and more on borrowed funds; even the cemetery income was insufficient to sustain the congregation. In fact, the needs of the cemetery exceeded the income from sale of graves. Though more and more members were in delinquent status, no one was dropped for being in arrears.

With the approach of 1935, the board voted to retain the lower salaries, but to repay the rabbi, cantor, and sexton for their voluntary cuts of the previous year. It was not until 1937 that salaries were raised to $6,000 for the rabbi and $4,000 for the cantor, reflecting the improved economic climate under the Roosevelt New Deal. For 1939, a suggested increase of $500 for rabbi and cantor was compromised at $250 for each.

### His Sermons

Metz preached in the classical rabbinic tradition, applying an appropriate passage from the Torah portion of the Sabbath or festival, together with its rabbinic commentaries, to a current situation. He drew upon an impressive vocabulary. His sermons stressed the eternal verities: truth, integrity, faithfulness, love, charity. Their titles revealed conventional themes: "Torah and Commandments," "Sukkah and Civilization," "Shofar and Jubilee," "Science and Religion," "Ritual and Faith," and "Life Eternal," all typical examples.

His most passionate feelings were expressed in addressing the need for Jewish dignity, defense of Zionism, and concern for the fate of European Jewry, whose precarious condition affected him deeply and emotionally. In all likelihood, some of his sermons were beyond the reach of many in the pews, as when he spoke on the Spinoza Tercentenary: "Jewry judged Spinoza by his acts and found him a deserter," he concluded, "and with grief in their hearts, they read him out and martyred him as one dead."[2]

On the lecture platform, he analyzed contemporary issues, such as "A Plan for Solving Post-War Employment Problems." His carefully crafted radio addresses reached a broad audience, as, for example, when he discussed "The Legacy of Lincoln."[3]

Metz's sermons were well organized and fully written. He either committed them to memory or knew the contents well enough to deliver them without appearing to be fixed to his manuscript. He wrote in flowery metaphor and spoke with oratorical flourish. His High Holy Day sermon for 1931, contrasting the prosperity of the city with its slums, offers an example of his vivid style.

> I watched the labyrinthine, hydra-headed metropolis, prostrate in the heavy sultriness of a mid-summer night. Cloud-piercing sky-scrapers, mute and unconcerned, flanked the wide, light-flooded avenue. An interminable crawling train of automobiles, glistening like black beetles, purred across the asphalted traffic lanes. From the barrack-like buildings of steel and brick, and from the alleys and narrow streets, an endless, gaudily arrayed swarm of humanity, drawn, like maggots, by the glamour of the White Way, poured into the avenue in a continuous stream. Against the sky and over the multi-colored cinema temples, where life is flattened to one dimension, electric signs weaved their spell, gliding like the fabled flaming serpents of primitive folklore. Abutting this fairy-land of fanfare, there stretched the slums of the city, the empire of squalor and poverty, where undernourished, forgotten men muttered their muffled outcries of impotent rage, and envy hissed its futile protestations.

The sermon described metropolitan civilization as spiritually bankrupt. "We have built gigantic palaces and we are homeless. We have conquered the earth and we are rootless. Instead of power we have vehemence." More denunciatory than comforting, more flowery than realistic, the sermon concluded with his prescription for solution: "Return, O Israel, unto the Lord thy God; For thou hast stumbled in thine iniquity." Repentance was the cure for social ills.

Metz was skilled in expounding Talmud and Midrash; it must have been painful for him to be forced to write speeches for children to deliver at their Bar Mitzvah services.

The September 1931 issue of the *National Jewish Ledger*, which carried a reprint of Metz's holiday sermon, printed a message from Adas Israel's president, Joseph Wilner, who noted,

> The financial catastrophe that has shaken the world about two and a half years ago, the decline in investments, the fall of securities,

> and the diminished incomes that followed in its wake left a great many of our co-religionists who were formerly wealthy or at least comfortably situated in a chaotic condition, facing deprivation, compelled to abandon their former standard of living and in certain instances undergoing suffering.

Wilner's message concluded that only those who were dedicated to causes beyond the self could rise above the financial catastrophe that had followed the market crash of 1929.

### The Community Pulpit

While Metz attracted a popular following in the community, his relationship to the congregation's leaders was not always harmonious. Since almost everyone in the congregation was beset with financial concerns, he could obtain little understanding from those who themselves were hard pressed to make ends meet. Even the wealthy members could find little surplus to support the synagogue budget.

Metz refrained from involving himself in the congregation's management; he did not attend board meetings unless invited. With his passive nature, he recoiled from confrontation and was unable to withstand either Wilner's dominance or Shefferman's influence. He was content to deliver sermons, teach classes, and faithfully visit the sick and the bereaved. If he could not find fulfillment in the synagogue, he would find it outside, in the Jewish and civic community, where his participation and leadership were welcomed and appreciated.

Warmly regarded in the community beyond Adas Israel, Metz organized and taught adult education classes once each week at the Jewish Community Center. In a two-month period, he addressed such diverse groups as the young people of the Mormon Church, the

Rock Creek Episcopalians, and the Quakers, speaking on the "Principles of Judaism." He was an active participant in the program of the National Conference of Christians and Jews and led services at the Naval Academy in Annapolis; he shared the pulpit at the Washington Hebrew Congregation.

The *Chronicle* reflected the approbation of both the congregation and the community. "Our Rabbi spreads good-will and understanding," it proclaimed, reprinting a letter from a member of the Foundry Methodist Church, who wrote,

> It was enlightening to learn that, when fundamentals are stressed, different faiths are in so much more agreement than is commonly realized when only differences are stressed. . . . I wish to express my appreciation for your sincere presentation.

When community representatives decided in 1938 that it was time to form a Jewish Community Council, they asked Metz to serve as temporary chairman of the planning committee. After a year of intensive planning, the thirty-nine participating organizations elected him the council's first president. The purpose of the council was defined in the preamble:

> to help preserve and maintain the dignity and integrity of the Jewish people; to defend and protect its rights, wherever such rights are in jeopardy; to advance and promote the cultural, social, economic, and philanthropic interests and national and spiritual aspirations of the Jewish people.

With Jacob Kammen as executive director, the Jewish Community Council played an important role in countering the influence of such notorious anti-Semites as Gerald L. K. Smith and Congressman J. E. Rankin of Mississippi, the latter persisting in spewing vitriolic anti-Semitic statements on the floor of the House of Representatives.

Under Metz's presidency, the council attempted to elevate the standards of Jewish education in Washington by establishing a committee on education. Israel Mendelson, a member of Adas Israel, was designated to head the newly formed committee in 1944. Metz served as president of the council from its founding in 1938 to 1943. He was succeeded, in sequence, by four Adas Israel members, Hymen Goldman, 1943–1949, Isadore Turover, 1949–1953, Aaron Goldman, 1953–1957, and Louis Grossberg, 1965–1969.[4]

When the Hebrew Academy, Washington's day school, moved into the building that had formerly belonged to the Curtis School, at 3235 O Street N.W., in 1944, Metz, delivering the dedicatory address, called for a change from education's traditional three Rs to what he called the four Rs: "reading, 'riting, 'rithmetic and religion."

Because of his scholarly interests, and his skills as teacher, lecturer, and interpreter of Judaism, Metz was in great demand as a guest speaker. He thus helped broaden the congregation's horizons and its identification with the larger community.

### Patterns of Religious Observance

Members of Adas Israel had long been disturbed by the lack of decorum at services and made several attempts to "standardize" the responses to the prayers, especially for the High Holy Days. The chief cause for the dissonance in the High Holy Day service was the diversity of prayer books. The worshippers brought their own books to services. Some had contemporary editions with English translations, others, the old family *machzor*. The random collection of prayer books differed in pagination, sequence of liturgy, and instructions for standing, depending upon the whims of the respective publishers. Many members felt that it was time for the congregation to impose a uniform prayer book at least for the High Holy Days.

Several attempts to introduce a uniform prayer book failed to receive popular acceptance because the congregants were expected to purchase them for their own use. Different editions remained in use until the children of Samuel and Mary Livingston resolved the issue in 1939 by donating 850 copies of the *machzor* edited by Chief Rabbi Herman Adler of the British Empire and published in the United States by Bloch Publishing Company. A furor erupted when it was discovered that the edition lacked the prayer *Hinneni.** Later editions corrected the omission.

A survey of ritual practices in Conservative congregations undertaken by Rabbi Morris Silverman in 1933 revealed that 70 percent conducted daily services and 95 percent conducted late Friday evening services. The Friday night services were usually abbreviated and incorporated English readings not based on the traditional liturgy. Saturday morning services conformed to tradition. While 20 percent of the congregations had organs, only half of these allowed them to be played on the Sabbath or holidays. Bat Mitzvah was nonexistent. Finally, prayer books were not uniform. Seven different siddurim and machzorim were in use in the congregations polled. A small number, including Adas Israel, used the *United Synagogue Festival Prayer Book*, published in 1927.[5] The latter was limited to the three pilgrim festivals of Sukkot, Passover, and Shavuot.

For its Friday night services, Adas Israel used the *Sabbath Prayer Book* edited and published by Rabbi Morris Silverman, until it was replaced by the *Sabbath and Festival Prayer Book* published by the Rabbinical Assembly and the United Synagogue, copyrighted in 1946, but introduced for the first time at a joint convention of the Rabbinical Assembly and the United Synagogue in Chicago, on the day that the State of Israel declared its independence, Friday, May 14, 1948. Unable to anticipate the unexpected, the book used the

*Recited by the cantor on the High Holy Days.

term "Palestine" in place of "Israel," rendering the volume outdated even before its distribution. The publication of this official prayer book, the product of the Prayer Book Commission of the Rabbinical Assembly, symbolized that Conservative Judaism had at last become a unified if not a uniform movement. "A Congregation which adopted our Prayer Book," said Rabbi Aaron Blumenthal, president of the Rabbinical Assembly, "is by that very act putting a distinctive stamp upon itself and forging ties of unity and cooperation with the movement as a whole."[6]

Metz worked assiduously at encouraging religious observance. In his preaching and teaching he stressed observance of the dietary laws and the Sabbath and upholding halachic standards in marriage and divorce. While the congregation's ritual committee moved to approve a mixed choir of male and female voices, its recommendation was rejected by the congregation. The members also insisted that the choir be restricted to Jewish singers.[7]

In an effort to shorten the length of the Sabbath morning service, the congregation, in 1948, decided to reduce the time allocated to the Torah reading. Since it could not elicit guidance from the United Synagogue when it sought a ruling, it undertook to survey the practices of other Conservative synagogues of similar size. On the basis of personal opinions expressed in letters from Rabbi Mortimer Cohen in Philadelphia and Rabbis Albert Gordon and Max Routtenberg of New York, and the example of Rabbi Solomon Goldman, it give up the traditional practice of reading all of the fifty-four Torah portions in their entirety and instead adopted a modified triennal cycle, reading only one third of the assigned portion each week.*

*"The Committee on Jewish Law [of the Rabbinical Assembly] has never discussed the problem of introducing the Triennial Cycle. . . . Several members . . . are opposed." Albert I. Gordon, United Synagogue executive director, to Abe Shefferman, February 4, 1948.

Relations with the United Synagogue, which the congregation had finally joined, were not always smooth. Disputes usually centered around the annual dues, which were based on a per capita charge on synagogue membership. In calculating its liability, Adas Israel did not include non-dues-paying members or those who paid partial dues, much to the displeasure of the national office. Sometimes the dispute became more complicated, as when the United Synagogue applied a current year's payment to an allegedly unpaid balance from previous years.

In 1930, claiming that a large unpaid balance had been accrued, the United Synagogue threatened to file suit against Adas Israel and even retained an attorney to press its case. The board rejected the claim, insisting that it had paid all past indebtedness, and threatened to withdraw from the United Synagogue if an apology was not immediately forthcoming. A separation followed until a compromise brought about renewed affiliation.

### Anniversaries

The congregation celebrated its sixty-fifth anniversary with a program at the synagogue on Wednesday night, March 7, 1934. Rabbi Elias Margolis of Mount Vernon, the president of the Rabbinical Assembly, was the principal speaker. The former Adas Israel rabbi, Judah T. Loeb, delivered the invocation, and Rabbi Metz, the benediction. Colonel Ulysses S. Grant III extended greetings. Cyrus Adler, president of the seminary, conveyed a congratulatory message. Despite the involvement of officials from the Conservative Movement, the local Jewish paper headlined its news item, "Largest Orthodox Congregation in Washington to Mark Anniversary."

The anniversary celebrations became more elaborate with each observance. For the seventieth anniversary, in March 1939, Rabbi Simon Greenberg, of Philadelphia, opened a three-day celebration with a sermon on Friday night. Rabbi Julius Loeb offered remarks. Rabbi Edward L. Israel, of the Reform Har Sinai Temple in Baltimore, addressed a banquet on Sunday night.

For the eightieth anniversary, celebrated in November 1948, Rabbi Irving Lehrman, of the Miami Beach Jewish Center, was the principal speaker at a dinner at the Mayflower Hotel. Six hundred people attended the banquet, where a model of a projected new synagogue was exhibited and the formal fund-raising campaign for its construction initiated.

~ *Cyrus Adler* *Reflections*

It awakens old memories in me to know that the Congregation Adas Israel will be celebrating its sixty-fifth anniversary on March 7. Indeed, I would like to be there, but I cannot come. Some of the older members may recall that I was once a seat-holder in that Congregation, and unless I am mistaken, I was present at the dedication of the new building, although I have been present at so many dedications that I cannot be sure. [He was not present.]

During the greater part of my stay in Washington, I lived at Kalaroma Heights and it was quite a distance to walk from there to Sixth and Eye Streets. Still, I had friendly relations with many of your members. If any elders are left, please give them my warmest regards and tell the newer and younger people that there is a great opportunity and duty resting upon their congregation in the Capital of our Nation. The religious life of this great political center to which representatives of all the States and of all foreign governments come, ought to reflect the very highest and best that the Jewish people can afford.

I wish the Congregation and yourself [Rabbi Metz] much usefulness in the future and express the confident hope that you will bear aloft in Washington the highest standards of our traditional Judaism.[8]

~ *Flora Atkin** *Reflections*

Every Rosh Hashanah and Yom Kippur my family and I moved in with my grandparents at their home above their 7th Street store because we didn't ride on those holidays. Nearly everybody walked; my grandparents would look askance if they heard of anyone who didn't. People rented hotel rooms or, if they drove, they got out of the cab or parked their cars blocks and blocks away.

I can remember walking to the synagogue with my grandmother on Yom Kippur. She would carry my lunch in a paper bag because I wouldn't be seen carrying lunch, but I couldn't go all day without eating. The custodian kept the lunch bags.

At the synagogue, to free one from carrying money, tables were arranged for arrivals to empty their pockets of coins or bills as a charity offering. Father and grandfather were both treasurers. We were always amazed that for someone who used to fall asleep at services in the third row, my father, once elected to office, could sit restrained and dignified in his high hat and cutaway suit, wide awake, on the pulpit.

The oldest members sat in a section reserved for them. They wore the same dress clothes every year. Those on the other side were the newer members. They wore the latest styles with such outlandish hats that it caused comment among the elder members who, secure in their status, didn't bother changing garb to keep up with changing styles.

I can remember the odors of smelling salts and perspiration masked by strong perfume and, late in the day on Yom Kippur, the

*Flora Atkin is the daughter of Anna and Joseph Blumenthal. Her father was president of Adas Israel from 1961 to 1964.

women cooling themselves with their paper fans. When I started squirming, my grandmother would say, "Just wait a little longer." She would show me how many more pages were left of the service.

Teenagers, along with other young people from Ohev Shalom, would walk in a small triangular park where we would eat from our luncheon bags. We didn't see many young people from the Washington Hebrew Congregation on Yom Kippur because their service had already ended.

In fact, there were more people outside the synagogue than inside. It was terribly hot in those buildings. Many people came dressed in their new fall clothes, velvets and velours, and wore uncomfortable new shoes.

On Yom Kippur, the men stayed at services until the last prayer. After the Shofar, they could ride home on streetcars. We left early so we had to walk. My grandmother and mother would accompany my sister and me home early. While the women helped prepare dinner, my sister and I would sit at the bay window and watch the streetcars, looking out for the one bringing my father and grandfather. When the men finally arrived, we would eat right away because everyone was so hungry.*

I ate nonkosher food for the first time at my Jewish sorority in college. Even those whose families were less observant observed the High Holy Days and especially Passover, their favorite holiday.

*~ Leon Shinberg* *Reflections*

Not every family was pious. My father took pride in his "socialist atheism." He was a cultural Jew. When I was ten years old, my father did not want to continue my Hebrew education. He sent me

*An early rabbinic comment suggests that one reason for sounding the shofar at the conclusion of Yom Kippur was to signal the women at home to begin preparing the evening repast. B. Yeushzon, *Otsrenu Hayashan* (Tel Aviv, n.d.), p. 53.

to Mr. Taishoff, a *melamed*, and told him, "I want you to teach my son to read, write and speak Yiddish, but not Hebrew." Mr. Taishoff did teach me Yiddish. But apparently I showed an interest in Hebrew, too. When I became thirteen years old, I did a *maftir*, but it was not a Bar Mitzvah.*

~ *Henry Gichner* *Reflections*

On Yom Tov, my parents would stay at a downtown hotel and my brothers and I would join them. There was no objection to our riding, but we liked the idea of walking and making it feel more of a holiday. We would go to each of the three main synagogues (all in the same neighborhood) and see all of our friends. At that time, most of us knew nearly every Jewish person in Washington or had some connection with them. Although my father wasn't particularly religious, my mother was, and my father followed in her footsteps because he thought we children should learn about our faith. Of course, there were many things that my mother allowed. When our chauffeur took her to Friday night service at the temple, he would drop me off at the Episcopal Church for my Boy Scout meetings. On Saturdays, we would attend services at Adas Israel. Sometime we walked there. From our home [in Cleveland Park] to Adas Israel [at 6th and I Streets] was a long walk, but we enjoyed it. Adas Israel had no Friday night service, so father also joined the Washington Hebrew Congregation, and we enjoyed the sociability of both congregations.

*The lack of a formal Bar Mitzvah service bothered Shinberg for many years, especially after he became president of the congregation in 1977. So, at the age of seventy-three, determined to experience the formal ceremony, he studied diligently in order to be able to chant the appropriate portion of the Torah and in the presence of his children and grandchildren celebrated his Bar Mitzvah. Reversing the usual procedure, his son, Milton, presented his father with a tallit.

Hebrew school, for me, wasn't a very good place. I wasn't a good Hebrew scholar and didn't do particularly well there. I was thinking more of baseball.

My parents were the first practicing and religiously observant Jews to move to Cleveland Park, near where the future Adas Israel would be built.[9]

# 21

## ZION, WAR, AND HOLOCAUST

In the year the United States became independent, 1776, the Jews of Palestine numbered 4,000 souls and were concentrated in four cities: Hebron, Jerusalem, Safed, and Tiberias. The Holy Land was no longer a land of milk and honey. To sustain its impoverished residents, agents were sent out to Jewish communities in other parts of the world to solicit financial support. These agents reached the United States as early as 1759; eventually some came to Washington.

The fund-raising agents were known as shedarim, an acronym for *Shelichey de-rabbanan* (messengers of the rabbis). While Moses Malki, an early "messenger," had travelled to the United States in 1759 and Haim Isaac Carigal in 1771, the first "messenger" to come to Washington was Nasan Noteh Notkin who visited the city in 1868, one year prior to the formation of Adas Israel.

His meticulous records reveal that the congregation, as yet undivided, allocated $3.00 from its treasury to aid his cause. In addition eighteen individuals gave him gifts ranging from 50 cents to $3.00. Among the donors listed were at least three founders of Adas Israel: Bendiza Behrend, Nathan Gotthelf, and A. S. Solomons. The largest single gift from the city, $10.00, came from the Elijah Lodge No. 50 of the B'nai B'rith.[1]

Almost two decades passed before a "messenger" formally approached Adas Israel on behalf of Palestinian Jewry.

> Mr. Mendelsohn, a traveling gentleman, whose aim and mission is to erect a hospital in the holyland presented credentials and numerously signed recommendations from various congregations, [attesting] that he was trustworthy to collect funds for his undertaking, [and] asked the support of his undertaking. The president replied that owing to the delicate state of the finances of this Congregation he regretted that he could not do anything for him.[2]

While individuals may have been more forthcoming, the first recorded congregational gift to a Holy Land installation was $10 appropriated to aid a Jewish hospital in Hebron in 1890. More generous responses would await later generations and events.*

With the development of political Zionism after the Zionist Congress at Basle, Switzerland, in 1897, the question of aid to Palestine took on a new dimension. Funds and backing were now being solicited for broad-ranging secular purposes and not only to help pious individuals and charitable institutions.

Adas Israel's hazzan, Jacob Voorsanger, who attacked the Zionist Congress when it convened, was an outspoken opponent of Zionism throughout his carreer. Judah Loeb, on the other hand, was the first Adas Israel rabbi and among the first in Washington to affirm Herzl's political Zionism. If the congregation's response was less than enthusiastic, it paralleled the attitude of the mother institution. Neither Sabato Morais nor Cyrus Adler were sympathetic to early Zionist efforts because they perceived it as a threat to religion and Jewish status. If Zionism were successful, Adler felt, the anti-Semites would be able to say to the Jews, "Get out to your own homeland."[3] ‡

*Later fundraisers for Yeshivot in Palestine were called *meshullachim* (agents).

‡It was Solomon Schechter who made Zionism an integral part of Conservative Judaism.

Loeb, with no particular loyalty to either Morais or Adler, and motivated to support Zionism from his personal recollections of Jewish life in Europe, took the leadership in organizing Zionist activities in Washington. Louis Egelson travelled to the Middle East in 1909 and no doubt reached the Holy Land since he brought back with him one of its tourist products: an olive wood box for Etrogim. Nathan Colish, Louis Schwefel, and Cantor Louis Novick, all three ardent Zionists, spent their last years in Israel.

On July 19, 1914, to mark the tenth anniversary of Theodor Herzl's death, Nachman Syrkin, an important Zionist leader, addressed a memorial meeting in Washington.* Zionist activities in the city intensified after the British government issued the Balfour Declaration in November 1917, recognizing the right of the Jews to a national home in Palestine. Shortly thereafter, on December 9,the first day of Chanukah, a victorious General Allenby marched his troops through Jerusalem's Jaffa Gate. Both events were hailed at a stirring mass meeting at a theater on Lafayette Square on the morning of December 25. Among the participants was Adas Israel's Rabbi Benjamin Grossman.

~ *Rebecca Safer* *Reflections*

In the winter of 1916, a Council of Jewish Women meeting addressed by Henrietta Szold became the nucleus of a new Hadassah chapter in Washington that would meet regularly to sew little garments which they sent to Hadassah nurses in Jerusalem.

It was the following month that the Allies were successful in the Middle East, and Allenby entered Jerusalem on the first day of Chanukah, December 9, 1917, ending the Turkish suzerainty after

*At Flynn's Hall, 8th and K Streets N.W. Admission fee, 10 cents. A Yiddish broadside announced the event.

four hundred years. We, in Washington, celebrated the event with a stirring and solemn meeting on Christmas morning at the old Belasco Theater on Lafayette Square. The place was filled to the rafters. Many educators and clergymen spoke.

The sewing circle held a meeting at the Lafayette Hotel, through the courtesy of Emil Berliner, with Mrs. Rose Jacobs as guest speaker. A large number of garments were made and sent to Jerusalem where, by this time, the Rothschild-Hadassah Hospital had been established in an old building on the outskirts of the Old City.[4]

~ *Isadore Samuel Turover* *Reflections*

One day in 1926. Louis Grossberg, my accountant, and Hymen Goldman, my friend, came into my little shanty office in the lumberyard. They found me sitting in a small room behind a great big second-hand desk, and began telling me about the work of the Jewish National Fund in Palestine. I took out my checkbook and wrote a check for the largest amount they had collected in their door-to-door campaign. Instead of the usual one or two dollars, I made out a check for $25.00, an unheard of donation.

Later I was invited to Paul Himmelfarb's house to meet the famous Zionist leader, Usshisken. He had come to town to talk about the need for funds to buy land for more Jewish settlers. I developed a great respect for him. He renewed my unterest in the ZIonist movement because I remembered the terrible misery of the East European Jews from my childhood in Poland.*

*Isador Turover, born near Warsaw in 1892, migrated to the United States in 1907, leaving his family behind in Antwerp where they had fled. Arriving in New York, he worked at a variety of menial jobs. His chief asset was a remarkable skill in chess.

His chess playing ability brought him to the attention of prominent chess players in New York and Washington. A leading member of the Washington

Throughout the 1920s and 1930s, Adas Israel members took the lead in local Zionist activities. In 1926, a 5 percent surcharge was added to each holiday seat to support the Jewish National Fund, and before long membership dues in the Zionist Organization of America were added to the dues bill of each congregant. Isadore Turover, president of the Brandeis Zionist District, the local ZOA chapter, was the proponent of the dues surcharge.

The announcement of the British White Paper of 1939 closing the doors of Palestine to Jewish migration and restricting Jewish land purchase prompted a congregational decision in 1940 to place both the United States and the Zionist flag on the pulpit at all times. When the community became aware of the world's abandonment of European Jewry and British refusal to open the gates of Palestine for their refuge, the congregation joined in the community protest meetings and fundraising efforts.

The views of all of Washington's Zionist groups were represented in the Adas Israel pulpit. One month's calendar of Friday evening services in 1941 included speakers from the Zionist Organization of America, the Labor League for Zionism, Young Judea, and the Orthodox Mizrachi Organization.

Rabbi Metz took the lead in conveying protests to the State Department and the British government for their denying Jewish refugees entrance to Palestine. In 1940, refugees arriving by sea from Rumania, were apprehended by the British and packed aboard another vessel for deportation. The refugee-laden ship, the *Patria,* sank in Haifa harbor with a loss of 250 lives. Two years later, in 1942, another refugee vessel, the *Struma,* whose passengers were turned

Chess Club, eager to bolster his team's strength, provided Turover with a job in his father's lumber company to enable him to live in Washington. His employer later provided backing when Turover opened his own lumber company where he prospered even as he achieved greater fame in chess playing circles. Turover became a chess grandmaster.

back at Haifa harbor, sank in the Marmora Sea with the loss of all but one of the 769 passengers aboard. Rabbi Metz organized and conducted memorial services for the unfortunate victims.

Stunned by the deportations and the loss of lives, leaders in the Jewish community proposed calling a city-wide mass meeting to protest British policy, but others were opposed, feeling that, while a memorial meeting was in order, any public criticism of the British, who were our allies in the bitter struggle still raging against the Nazi, was ill-advised and would be regarded as reflecting divisiveness in the democratic alliance.

Rabbi Metz chaired an emergency meeting of the Jewish Community Council in March, 1942 called to resolve the issue. Cantor Novick of Adas Israel and president of Mizrachi, advocated calling a mass meeting and openly announcing it as a protest against British policy. Rabbi Norman Gerstenfeld of the Washington Hebrew Congregation spoke against the proposal, feeling that this was not the time to attack the British. Washington Jews were trapped in the dilemma which all American Jews faced: whether to mount a protest against a wartime ally, or whether to lament quietly for those who had perished, but without formal public protest. In the end, the proposal for a protest meeting was defeated.

As an alternative, Rabbi Isadore Breslau, a Zionist leader, proposed that the council frame a resolution that would express the community's anguish and indignation and its hope that there would be no sinkings of refugee ships in the future. The motion passed, but with the nine members of the Washington Hebrew delegation recorded in the negative, to the surprise of the majority, who had expected unanimous consent.*

*Hymen Goldman was the president of the Jewish Community Council at the time, and Aaron Goldman, his son, was its secretary. For a full account of the meeting, see Aaron Goldman's retrospective article in *Washington Jewish Week*, February 27, 1992, p. 19.

So wide was the growing rift between Zionists and anti-Zionists that the Washington Hebrew Congregation, in 1944, resigned from the Jewish Community Council, to return only in 1949, after the establishment of the State of Israel.

When, after the war, it became evident that Britain would persist in refusing to admit the Jewish displaced survivors to Palestine, many Jews determined to assist in breaching the blockade. Several members of the congregation quietly and secretly joined with others to raise funds to purchase a vessel that would run the blockade to carry Jewish refugees from the displaced person's camps to Palestine's shores. Fund raising efforts were conducted in parlor meetings in key cities of the United States. In Washington the gatherings took place at members' homes and in the vestry room of the synagogue. As a result of the combined efforts, Jewish authorities, in 1946, were able to purchase a Chesapeake Bay ship, the *President Warfield*, a flat bottomed four decked ferry named after the president of the Old Bay lines, an uncle of Wallis Warfield Simpson. Renamed the *Exodus*, the ship, with 4,554 passengers from displaced person's camps aboard, embarked on a two month odyssey in July, 1947 that would take them to Haifa harbor where, intercepted by the British, they were consigned to barbed wire enclosures in Cyprus where they were to remain until they were liberated after Israel's independence.

Wealthy members of the Congregation made major contributions for the purchase of weapons, uniforms, and other essential equipment, that were secretly smuggled to Palestine to help the Haganah in its struggle to defend the soon to be created state against Arab attack.

On Friday morning, May 14, 1948, Washington area Jews rejoiced at the announcement of Israel's declaration of independence. Rush hour traffic slowed to a crawl along Massachusetts Avenue as motorists paused to watch the flag with the blue and white star of

David hoisted above the office of the Jewish Agency's Washington headquarters at 2210 Massachusetts Avenue. Oren Zinder, an eight-year-old Alexandria child born in Palestine, raised the flag. Many in the crowd, which included Congressman Jacob Javits of New York and other government officials, were in tears.

The new state was hailed at a community meeting on Sunday, May 16, at the Shoreham Hotel. Speakers included Javits, Congressman Chet Holifield of California, and Eliahu Epstein, the director of the Jewish Agency's Washington office. A capacity congregation filled the Adas Israel sanctuary the following Friday night at a service of thanksgiving.

Hailing the emergence of Israel, Rabbi Metz wrote,

> The astounding emergence of the republic of Israel, out of the ashes of the satanic conflagration that destroyed one-third of the our people, is divine proof of the indissoluble bond between God and Israel. No nation has ever survived two thousand years of homelessness and persecution.[6]

When the first exciting hours of independence gave way to Arab attack, Washington Jewry responded generously, raising tens of millions of dollars for the newly created state, whose needs they would support with increasing generosity each year.

The representatives of the State of Israel found a far more receptive Adas Israel than did the first "messenger" who had knocked on its doors in 1886. The congregation responded not only with generous gifts but with investments. The harsh economic realities of state building and immigrant absorption had prompted Israel's Prime Minister, David Ben-Gurion, to float a bond issue to provide investment capital for Israel's economic development.

Heretofore, it was noted, Jews could be divided into two groups, those who gave charity and those forced to accept charity. Now, there would be a new category in Jewish history: Jews who lent money to other Jews. There was no historic precedent on which to base the prospects of a successful venture.

Ben-Gurion invited fifty American Jewish leaders to meet with him in Jerusalem's King David Hotel in September 1950, to plan an Israel Bond campaign. Abe Kay of Adas Israel was among them. Soon thereafter, Ben-Gurion himself inaugurated Washington's Bond campaign at the Woodmont Country Club. Adas Israel members predominated among those who assumed leadership roles.*

The first year's campaign, under the leadership of Leopold Freudberg, realized almost $970,000. At the insistence of the leadership group, pledges to purchase Israel Bonds were made part of the Rosh Hashanah services. Prior to each High Holy Day season, Rebecca Safer would host a parlor meeting at her apartment where advance commitments were solicited from those able to make large purchases, a practice she would continue as long as she lived. The lessons of helplessness which characterized the Jewish condition in the prewar years would not be forgotten.

### World War II

The ominous reverberations from the European field of battle which erupted with the German invasion of Poland in September 1939 resounded in the American Jewish community long before the Japanese attack on Pearl Harbor on December 7, 1941. For the Jewish community, the war had begun in 1933 with Hitler's accession to power. After Kristallnacht, November 9–10, 1938, when synagogues were burned and Jewish stores looted throughout Germany, Jews mobilized to facilitate the emigration of German Jews trying to escape the Nazi peril.

*Among them were Dr. Seymour Alpert, Jack Bender, Hyman S. Bernstein, Leopold Freudberg, Ceil and Louis Grossberg, Sylvia and Alex Hassan, Rosa and Jack Kraft, Meyer Mazor, Rebecca Safer, Isador Turover, and, of course, Abe Kay.

Adas Israel joined the countrywide effort to rescue German Jewish scholars, an effort which resulted in bringing hundreds of distinguished writers and thinkers to the United States, among them Abraham Joshua Heschel, the distinguished theologian, who joined the faculty of the Hebrew Union College and later the Jewish Theological Seminary.

Proof of employment was a prerequisite for obtaining the precious visa essential for entry to the United States. In December 1938, at a special meeting called for the purpose, the Adas Israel board elected Rabbi Gerhard Frank of Ichenhausen, Germany, as associate rabbi at a salary of $1,400. Rabbi Metz had urged issuing him a contract as a means of saving a precious life while filling the need for rabbinic assistance. The following month, Rabbi Klavan, the leading Orthodox rabbi in Washington, called upon the congregation to underwrite the support of a German Jewish refugee student to enable him to attend the Ner Israel Yeshiva in Baltimore. Joseph Wilner appointed a committee to solicit the necessary funds.*

In April 1940, the congregation received a letter from Mr. Eisenstein, a cousin of Frank's, inquiring whether the position was still open. The congregation responded that the post would remain open until October 1940. Even with a visa, Rabbi Frank was unable to leave Germany.

Adas Israel joined the Washington Hebrew Congregation and Temple Beth El in Alexandria, Virginia, in extending an employment contract and thus the means for obtaining a visa to Rabbi and Mrs. Hugo B. Schiff who had been serving a beleagured congregation in Karlsruhe, Germany. The couple arrived safely in 1939 and Rabbi Schiff was immediately engaged by the Virginia congregation. Washington Hebrew Congregation named him assistant rabbi

*The committee members were Charles Pilzer, J. B. Spund, Herman Robbin, Dr. Charles Basseches, Herman Berman, Joseph Blumenthal, Joseph Mendelson, Israel Mendelson, Meyer Sawyer, Harry Haber, David Hornstein, and Leo Schlossberg.

in 1948. He lectured in the community and served Adas Israel in various capacities. As a token of appreciation for the kindnesses extended to them, Schiff presented Adas Israel with a *Megillah* scroll (i.e., a handwritten copy of the Book of Esther, used in the service for Purim) which had been rescued from the Nazis by a Christian family in Holland and given to him for safekeeping.

When the United Jewish Appeal, in 1939, allocated a gift of $250,000 to be divided between the Catholic Church and the Federal Council of Churches for war refugee relief, Jewish reactions were mixed. Rabbi Metz spoke in favor of the allocation, and the *Chronicle* reprinted a letter from President Roosevelt, dated January 8, 1940, praising UJA for its nonsectarian generosity.

Metz's somber Rosh Hashanah message for 1940 reflected the prevailing mood in the Jewish community. "Civilization has become a wilderness, the habitation of the jackal," he wrote. Nonetheless, he concluded on a note of hope: "Let us be strong in our faith. Surely the dominion of arrogance will dissipate like smoke, making way for the emergent 'new heaven and new earth.'" Little did he know.

In December 1940, a recent immigrant, Rabbi Vitzik of Baltimore, asked the congregation to bring his father to the United States and employ him as assistant rabbi. The board responded, "Since we had employed another assistant Rabbi who was unable to come to this country, the matter was referred to Mr. Wilner. . . . we could not engage an assistant Rabbi at this time."[7]

In February 1941 Metz circulated a letter to the congregation headed "Extraordinary Appeal to Rescue Torah Students," seeking to raise $15,000 to save fifty students from Europe.

After Pearl Harbor, December 7, 1941, the congregation mobilized its members in support of the war effort. The vestry rooms were given over to Red Cross projects, sewing, knitting, and first aid courses. The civil defense committee used the synagogue for its neighborhood gatherings. The *Chronicle* ran wartime slogans such as "Drive the Ax in the Axis—Buy Defense Bonds and Stamps," and carried a regular column entitled "Adas Israel and the War."

One of Adas Israel's Torah scrolls was loaned to the Army Chapel in Arlington, Virginia. The *Chronicle* carried a regularly updated Honor Roll listing members and children of members serving in the armed forces. Before very long it displayed thirteen gold stars for those who had lost their lives in combat.*

Routine congregational activities gave way to war-centered gatherings. Issues of war aims, peace plans, and Zionism dominated the Friday night pulpit. Chaplains, political personalities, and Zionist leaders were frequent guest speakers. Among them were Marquis Childs and Pierre Van Paasen, authors and journalists; Arnold Margolin, the Russian Jewish lawyer who had defended Mendel Beilis at his blood-libel trial; Rabbi Isadore Breslau, a local Zionist leader, who chose the topic "This Is Worth Fighting For"; Chief of Chaplains Aryeh Lev; Carl Alpert, editor of the *New Palestine* magazine; and Stanley Rabinowitz, then a seminary student, who, in 1940, spoke at an AZA-sponsored Sabbath.

"Victory Donor Teas" replaced the annual Sisterhood Donor Luncheon. Mrs. Walter Lippmann, director of the Volunteer Nurses Aid Corps of the Red Cross and wife of the columnist, addressed the Sisterhood Donor Luncheon in 1941.

The congregation took pride when Fred Gichner received the prestigious Army-Navy "E" Award. Servicemen on leave were

*Sergeant Albert Sidney Altman, Commander Morris I. Bierman, Ensign Herbert Sheldon Cohn, Sergeant John Ferber, Captain Isadore Hurowitz, Captain Sidney Harold Katzoff, Private First Class Lloyd M. Keller, Lieutenant Matthew Jerome Levy, Captain Paul Pascal, Lieutenant Colonel Jerome Gerald Sacks, Lieutenant Louis Oscar Sherman, Major Bernard Wilner, and Captain John Wilner.

welcomed at worship services; semimonthly dances and buffet suppers were sponsored by the newly created Adas Israel Servicemen's Fund.

Rabbi Metz spoke at a fund-raising benefit to support Russian War Relief. He devoted considerable time to conducting services in military hospitals in the Washington area and served as civilian chaplain in nearby Fort Myer, where he conducted regular services and programs.

Occasional air raid drills disrupted both services and activities, prompting school principal Irving Wilner to implore, "Let us not permit the occasional wail of the air raid siren to silence the voice of Torah in our midst." Routine synagogue activities were subordinated to more urgent needs; energies were required elsewhere. Young men were in short supply; the men's club and young adult groups floundered and reorganized, only to flounder again. The school suffered from the rapid turnover in faculty.

When the government proclaimed "war-time," which translated into a double-hour advance of the clock during the summer and one hour in the winter, the congregation turned to the United Synagogue for advice on scheduling Sabbath and festival services. The United Synagogue replied that it was permissible to usher in Sabbaths and festivals before sunset and advised starting Yom Kippur services later or extending the afternoon recess to adjust to the later hour of sundown.

Not until December 1942 did American Jews became completely aware of the full extent of the devastating Nazi slaughter of European Jewry. It was time to mourn. Adas Israel was the site of a community memorial meeting on December 13.

In 1943, Rabbi Metz delivered an impassioned denunciation of the world's silence.

> When the fury of Teutonic bestiality broke upon hapless Israel in 1933, the world stood by and did nothing. When the Nazis began their cold blooded, Mephistophelian degradation of the Jewish people in demoniacal jubilant defiance of all the sacred ideals of the West, the conscience of the world went into a state of coma. When the swine-eyed blond beasts started their avowed campaign of extermination of the Jew, the mighty custodians of our modern civilization went about expending their moral militancy in appeasing the forces of evil, went about unimpressed and undisturbed by the frantic cry of trapped Jewry. Now, when the nations are locked in bloody combat with the demented hordes of totalitarianism, high diplomacy is evidently impervious to the muffled groans of the millions of tortured and starved in the ghettos of Europe.
>
> Demagogues have ridden into power on the crest of waves of anti-Semitism. So long as Jews could be slaughtered in cold blood, the Christian conscience carries a heavy burden of guilt.

Metz called for an annual day of remembrance. At the war's end, the congregation, with prayerful expressions of gratitude for the hard-won victory, joined in the prevailing mood of thanksgiving. At its annual meeting in January 1946, Rabbi Roland Gittelsohn, who had been a chaplain at Iwo Jima, repeated the famous address he had prepared for delivery at the memorial services on Iwo Jima but had been unable to deliver because the Christian chaplains had objected to the participation of a rabbi.

Later, in conjunction with the Alex D. Goode Post of the Jewish War Veterans, the congregation instituted annual services of tribute to the memory of the four chaplains who lost their lives in the sinking of the U.S.S. *Dorchester* after having surrendered their lifejackets to others. The post was named after the Jewish member of the group, Chaplain Alex D. Goode.

Appalled at the destruction of European Jewry, the congregation mobilized support for resettling the wretched survivors languishing in the Displaced Persons Camps of Europe. The sisterhood pledged funds to Youth Aliyah "for the relief of two children who will be taken from Arabian oppression in Yemen to Zionist protection in Palestine."

To honor Rabbi Metz on the fifteenth anniversary of his tenure, a testimonial banquet had been planned for April 8, 1946. Though grateful for this expression of affection, Metz asked that the banquet be canceled to save food for the hungry. "I feel that any food that might be consumed at that dinner would better serve humanity," he wrote to Wilner. Metz and Rabbi Gerstenfeld of the Washington Hebrew Congregation were appointed to the Washington Food Committee.

The outbreak of the war had frustrated Metz's hope to develop a more intensive adult education program. Once the war was over, he resumed his efforts to create an adult learning facility. In 1948 he organized a local college of Jewish studies and served as its dean. He had hoped it would develop into a recognized four-year college which would award the degree of *Chaver* (Fellow) to its graduates. Although the college did not attain the goals that Metz had set for it, those who studied with him recall his ability to stimulate their interest and credit him with influencing them to deepen their commitment to Jewish learning.

### The Holocaust

The monstrous juggernaut that was Hitler's Germany rolled over Europe with heartless brutality, taking the lives of fully one-third of world Jewry while obliterating centuries-old centers of Jewish life. The famed Yeshiva Etz Chayim in Volozhin, which had been founded in 1803 and where more than one of Adas Israel's rabbis had studied, was turned into a restaurant and bar. The Jews of the community were brutally slaughtered. Other communities in Germany, Poland, and the rest of Nazi-occupied Europe met similar fates.

The Holocaust could not help but affect families in a congregation whose members traced their origins to Germany and Eastern Europe. Over eighty near relatives of members of Adas Israel were killed in the Nazi death camps. Their names are recorded in a Memorial Booklet prepared for Yom Kippur and recalled in annual commemoration.

In many instances, there were multiple deaths in the same family. The Berlins and the Herzenbergs each lost twelve of their kin, the Margolis family, seven, and the family of Julius Wolpe, a president of the congregation, eleven members. Several refugees from Hitler's Germany joined the congregation.

Among the most poignant of the Holocaust experiences involving people connected with Adas Israel, is the tragic saga of Rebecca Gotthelf, born in Washington, who at the age of five returned to Germany together with her sister Sarah and her parents, Julie and Nathan Gotthelf, the congregation's second president who, it will be recalled, had concluded, in a tragic misreading of history, that Germany offered a more promising opportunity for living a traditional Jewish life than did Washington.

On an earlier visit to his native Germany in 1869, Nathan Gotthelf had met Emil Berliner, a neighbor's son who displayed remarkable scientific proficiency. Impressed with the young man's talent, Gotthelf had urged Berliner to come to the United States to further his inventive talents. Gotthelf had promised to employ Berliner in the dry goods store which he and Bendiza Behrend owned. Berliner was to achieve widespread recognition for his invention of the basic principles underlying the modern microphone. When Berliner came to the United States, he lived with the Gotthelf family and worked for the Gotthelf and Behrend partnership until he was able to capitalize on his invention.[8] Berliner remained a lifelong friend of the Gotthelf family.

In 1881, six years after his return to his native land, the family was left fatherhless and Julie Gotthelf a widow when Nathan lost his life in the tragic accident caused by his rearing horse. Sarah, the elder Gotthelf daughter, married Adolf Wolff; they bore four sons Egon, Norbert, Ernest, and Herbert. Rebecca, the younger daughter, did not marry. With the menace of anti-Semitism growing more ominous, Sarah became convinced that her sons should leave Germany to find a more promising future in the United States. Though she herself was a citizen of the United States by birth, her children were citizens of Germany; visas for them to immigrate to the United States were not readily obtainable.

By a stroke of good fortune, Sarah read in a newspaper that Emil Berliner, whom she remembered from her childhood in Washington, was about to visit Hanover because the town fathers wanted to honor their native son in recognition of his remarkable achievements in eloctronic communication. She resolved to enlist his help to obtain the documentation necessary for her sons' entry to the United States. She reached Berliner when he arrived in Hanover; he assured Sarah that he would do whatever he could to help his old friends who had done so much for him when he had needed assistance.

Berliner found the way to fulfill his promise to Sarah by drawing upon his acquaintance with the U. S. Consul in Stuttgart who had been a classmate of his son, Henry. He lost little time in communicating with the consul and prevailed upon him to process the necessary certificates that eventually enabled Sarah's children to secure their life-saving visas.

When Sarah Wolff died in Germany in 1930, she was confident that her children would find their way to the land her father had left so many years earlier. One by one, each son came to the United States. Ernest was first and then, in sequence, Egon, Norbert, and

Herbert in 1935; they came to Washington. Ernest, an economist, became the first Jew to be employed by the Riggs National Bank, and that, too, had been with the intercession of Emil Berliner.

The four brothers renewed the family's affiliation with Adas Israel. Their children, the great-grandchildren of the synagogue's second president, celebrated their Bar Mitzvah, confirmation, and marriage within its sanctuary.

Rebecca, the younger Gotthelf daughter, remained in Germany. Unmarried and in poor health, she lived with caring relatives in various provincial towns. As the Nazi menace became more threatening, Rebecca realized that the time had come to claim her right of citizenship and to return to her birthplace in the United States.

Rebecca applied to the U. S. Consul in Germany for a visa in 1935. As required, she submitted her birth certificate showing she had been born in Washington, her father's U. S. citizenship papers proving that he had been naturalized in 1856, and his passport, establishing that he had not renounced his American citizenship nor had he become a German citizen.

Rebecca Wolff had satisfied all the legal requirements for securing a visa; there should have been no question about her right of return to her native country. In the 1930s, however, immigration policy was dominated by an unfriendly State Department headed by Cordell Hull and administered by the notoriously anti-Semitic Breckenridge Long, Under Secretary of State, whose opposition to Jewish immigration to the United States was an open scandal. Acting in accordance with clearly defined policy, the American Consul in Hamburg, John James Meily, first delayed and then withheld the response to Rebecca's petition for a visa.

Rebecca resubmitted her petition over and over again, but it was to no avail. Soon thereafter, once the United States severed relations with Nazi Germany, there was no longer any escape. Though a U.

S. citizen by birth, she was declared "stateless" by Nazi authorities. She was sent to the concentration camp in Theresienstadt on March 24, 1943. Three weeks later, while much of the world slept, she became one of the six million victims of Nazi bestiality.

Another poignant recollection is that of Richard Schifter, who served as Under Secretary of State for Human Rights in the administrations of Presidents Ronald Reagan and George Bush. Schifter was born and raised in Vienna, but in December 1938, when he was fifteen, his parents sent him to the United States via Rotterdam. He was able to obtain a visa even though they could not because he had been born in Austria, and therefore was counted on the relatively generous Austrian immigration quota, whereas they were from Poland, and the Polish quota was already overdrawn.

Upon taking leave of his parents, Schifter recalled,

> My father gave me last-minute advice and instructions. My mother, normally a proud and strong woman, wept quietly. Finally, the stationmaster's whistle blew and the train began to move. I waved from the open train window as we pulled away. My parents waved back.

Schifter never saw his parents again. Stripped of their citizenship by the Nazis, they managed to "escape" by crossing the border into Poland, traveling on foot through one of the wooded areas along the border, only to discover that they had also been stripped of their Polish citizenship. Along with many other Jews, they were trapped between two countries that did not want them; they were stateless and homeless.

Schifter, in the United States, was able to correspond with his parents until the end of 1941, when the United States declared war against Germany, after which correspondence was intermittent. Suddenly the State Department informed him that his parents had finally reached their "turn" on the quota list. He immediately made arrangements for their departure only to discover that they had been denied permission to leave Europe. Once again, they were trapped.

He received only one further message, dated July 1942, transmitted through the International Red Cross. It came from Lublin, a city in Poland designated for Jewish resettlement. On the return address there was a new designation, Maidan Tatarski. As the months passed without further word, Schifter came to the painful realization that Hitler's threat to destroy all the Jews he could reach was more than a figure of speech and that his parents were probably among the victims.

Upon the Soviet army's entry in the Lublin area, Schifter addressed a letter to his parents' last known address. His letter was returned with the notation "addressee unknown."

Upon enlistment in the army, Schifter was posted as an intelligence officer first to England and then, in 1944, to Germany. The allied offensive, which began in early 1945 and which would break Nazi resistance, ultimately led to the occupation of a number of major German cities. After Germany's surrender, Schifter remained in Germany to assist in the de-nazification program and where he reviewed documents collected from German archives.

While passing through one of the U. S. military installations in Frankfort, he came across a group of civilians on a clean-up detail. They were speaking Yiddish! He quickly asked, in Yiddish, whether anyone of them had been to Maidanek, for by then he had learned that this was the name of the extermination center near Lublin.

One of the group volunteered that he been a prisoner in both Maidanek and Auschwitz. "I gave him my parents' names," said Schifter, "and he told me he remembered my mother, adding softly, '*Keiner hot iberlebt in Maidanek*' [No one survived in Maidanek]."

Later in his career, as Secretary for Human Rights in the State Department, Schifter would be responsible for protecting the rights of Jews and others who were vitimized by authoritarian and totalitarian regimes. He was to be especially helpful in securing visas for Jews seeking to leave the Soviet Union. Schifter resigned his post in April, 1992.

Other Adas Israel members who escaped from Germany include:

Eva Rehfeld, born in Berlin, reached the United States in 1948 after a brief sojourn in Sweden. She lost twenty-three members of her family.

Simon J. Nathan, born in Schildberg, his wife Gertrude Schlesinger born in Hanover, and their son Michael, were fortunate enough to come directly to Washington in the worst year of Nazi depredation, 1941. Their parents were lost. Simon gave his partially burned talit to the Synagogue as a memorial. He had rescued it from his burning Synagogue.

Simon and Rosa Kilsheimer Laupheimer were able to escape prior to the outbreak of war, reaching Washington in 1938. The remaining members of their family were lost.

Alfred Jospe, born in Berlin, his wife, Eva Scheyer Jospe, born in Oppeln, Upper Silesia, and their daughter Susanne, barely escaped the war to arrive in the United States in June, 1939. Alfred Jospe headed the B'nai B'rith Hillel Foundation for many years while Eva Jospe became a recognized authority on Martin Buber, publishing a book on his life and writings. The 12 other members of their family did not survive the early years of the war.

Having lost many relatives in Germany, Julius Wolpe, the president of Adas Israel, felt it important for the congregation to somehow memorialize the victims of the Holocaust. He persuaded a Dallas business leader and philanthropist, Paul Lewis, to underwrite a memorial wall in their memory.

Lewis, a Polish-born building contractor, was driven by a compulsion to endow Holocaust memorials throughout the country as "a stern warning against silence in the face of tyranny." The Adas Israel memorial, dedicated as the Hall of Memories on April 22, 1963, was the first of several Holocaust memorials to be established in Washington.

Participating in the dedication ceremonies, in addition to Lewis and the synagogue officials, were Myer Feldman, representing President John F. Kennedy, whom he served as special counsel; Senator Thomas Dodd of Connecticut, who had been chief prosecutor at the Nuremberg trials; Associate Justice Arthur Goldberg; Avraham Harman, the Israeli ambassador; Ralph M. Paiewonsky, the governor of the Virgin Islands; and Mrs. Sol Frederich, of Silver Spring, Maryland, who had lived through the horrors of the Nazi period and had lost her four-year-old child and husband in the camps. The presence of Mrs. Frederich, whose maiden name was Luba Tryszynski, elicited profound emotions in several spectators. They knew her as "The Angel of Belsen," a title bestowed upon her by the King of Sweden for her role in shepherding ninety-four children from Nazi control to safety in Sweden.

The memorial included a heroic-sized six-candle menorah, crafted by Emanuel Milstein for the Jewish Museum in New York, fixed alongside a large, appropriately inscribed marble tablet. A small glass-covered crypt at the base of the tablet contained religious objects found in pillaged German synagogues, a crushed Kiddush cup, Torah ornaments, a broken Chanukah menorah, a Torah pointer, a spice box, and Simon Nathan's tallit. A collection of watercolors depicting concentration camp scenes by Mykolo Schramchenko, a Christian survivor of Treblinka, presented to the congregation by Norman Bernstein and Joseph Borkin, completed the setting. Stephen Keyser, director of the Jewish Museum, designed the memorial.

~ *Richard Schifter* *Reflections*

People who reflect on the Holocaust keep asking why the Jews walked to their death and why they did not resist. On the basis of my own childhood experience, as I think back to a whole day which I spent with a group of Jews standing in front of a jail in which my parents and many other Jews of Vienna had been temporarily imprisoned, I think I can understand what happened.

Over a period of eighteen centuries we had been conditioned to accept the idea that all the might is on the other side, that resistance was hopeless, and that it is best to bend.

My parents and others in our family were victims of their conventional belief in human decency; they could not believe that mass killings would be allowed in the modern world. They waited for the rescue that would never come.*

*From an address given by Schifter at Adas Israel, Friday, May 5, 1978.

# 22

## POSTWAR: TRANSITIONS

During the Roosevelt years, government service replaced agriculture as Washington's primary economic base. The number of federal employees spiraled from 70,000 in 1933 to more than 275,000 by V-E day in 1945. The newcomers, Jews among them, "Jewish New Dealers," as Joseph L. Ruah Jr., a Roosevelt appointee who came to the capital in 1935, called them, did not readily relate to the local Jewish populace. In turn, the Washington Jews, more conservative in outlook, regarded the newcomers as "intruders or changers."[1]

Many of those who had come to Washington during the Roosevelt years remained in the area after the war. Time and common interests gradually bridged the gap between natives and new arrivals. While they created a few new synagogues, most of the newcomers, like the immigrants of earlier generations, turned to the established congregations which could offer them educational and social facilities. With demobilization, synagogue membership, which had plummeted during the depression in the 1930s, rose to new heights. Adas Israel, like synagogues throughout the country, experienced a resurgence of membership and activity.

The postwar period accentuated the tendency toward suburbanization that began before the war. As more families left the downtown area, moving northward to Cleveland Park and further to Chevy Chase on the District of Columbia's border with Maryland, the congregation realized that it had no alternative but to follow its members uptown. The downtown location had long since had lost its usefulness as a school site. Adults, too, found the downtown site inconvenient. Attendance at Friday night services was so poor that it was proposed to abandon them.[2]

### The Proposal

The suggestion to move the synagogue uptown was first made at the annual meeting in January 1941. Though no proposal could be initiated during the war years, it was not too soon to begin planning for the future.

A year later, in 1942, the congregation authorized Abe Kay, the prominent builder, to head a committee to survey available sites for a new structure. A membership survey had revealed that 85 percent of the members lived above U Street and between 16th Street and Wisconsin Avenue. Several locations were considered before the committee proposed the purchase of a site on the southeastern corner of Connecticut Avenue and Ellicot Street. There were objections to the selection: many felt that the site was too small, and some thought it too far from the central area of residence. Louis Rosenberg, the stalwart past president, opposed any move that "might effect religious practice," which meant one that would require members to drive to the synagogue.

Rejecting the objections, Abe Kay urged the acquisition of the Ellicot Avenue site. He recommended that the purchase be made in his name, since he had been advised by realtors that the seller would not sell to a synagogue. To reassure the board, Kay promised that should the members reject the purchase after they were given an opportunity to consider it, he would retain the site for himself as an investment. With the board's approval, Kay purchased the site in November 1943 for $58,780.

At a meeting the following month, an enthusiastic burst of applause accompanied the members' unanimous endorsement of the acquisition. Fred Kogod, a movie theater owner, builder, and future president, David Hornstein, an attorney, and Leo Freudberg, an insurance underwriter, were appointed to head a finance committee to raise funds. A parlor meeting at Kogod's home raised $50,000. The remainder of the purchase price was borrowed from the cemetery's perpetual maintenance fund. With the war still raging in Europe, no further action could be taken.

At the war's end, the federal government instituted a policy to encourage builders to construct new homes and small apartments to accommodate the numerous singles and newly married couples whose numbers had increased Washington's population. Encouraged by the federal program, a group of congregational leaders formed a private partnership to buy eleven acres of land on a triangular site bounded by Quebec Street, Porter Street, and Connecticut Avenue, where they planned to construct two large apartment houses. Since the site contained more land than they needed, they suggested a trade: they would exchange three acres of the Connecticut-Porter-Quebec Street triangle for the Ellicot Street site owned by the congregation.

Abe Kay, chairman of building-site committee, stated that, in his opinion, the Connecticut-Porter-Quebec Street site was preferable to the one he had originally favored. He pointed out that while both sites carried an equal valuation per front foot, the Quebec Street site was larger and therefore more valuable. The two interlocking parties agreed to an even exchange, which they concluded in 1945.[3]

### Cleveland Park

Many of the more fashionable areas of Washington west of Rock Creek Park, including Forrest Hills and Spring Valley, and Shepherd Park, east of Rock Creek Park, were closed by restrictive covenants to "Negroes, Armenians, Jews, Hebrews, Persians, and Syrians." Only in 1948 were the covenants rendered unenforceable by a Supreme Court decision. Despite the restrictive covenants, many Adas Israel members lived in the area even before they were invalidated. According to a 1964 estimate, Shepherd Park had become about 80 percent Jewish.[4]

In the 1960s, North Portal Estates, east of the Park, on the northeastern corner of Northwest Washington, was developed by Jewish builders and investors who had responded to the opportunities that had opened up after the 1948 Supreme Court decision invalidating racial covenants. Many of the builders and even more of the residents were members of Adas Israel. The 220 houses that were built in North Portal were even more impressive than those in the previous upper-class Jewish neighborhood in Shepherd Park.

Jews tended to move in communities together with their synagogues and their domestic suppliers: kosher delicatessens, butcher shops, and bakeries. From 1947 to the late 1950s, four kosher meat markets, a Jewish bakery, and Posin's, the first Jewish "supermarket," opened on Georgia Avenue, north of Shepherd Park. Hoffberg's, a popular delicatessen and center for Jewish "dining," opened near the corner of Georgia and Eastern Avenues. Several Orthodox and two Conservative synagogues, B'nai Israel and Tifereth Israel, were built on 16th Street, east of the Park. Unlike these, Adas Israel saw its future as being west of Rock Creek Park.

Cleveland Park, the area on Connecticut Avenue which Adas Israel selected for its future home, projected a small village atmosphere which included the Uptown Theater, built in 1936, and a small shopping area, "Park and Shop," a forerunner of today's mammoth shopping centers, all located between an undeveloped wooded area and the grandly impressive Broadmoor Apartments across the street from the future Adas Israel.

When the District of Columbia was established in 1791, the future Cleveland Park was rolling farmland, part of a large land grant acquired by George Beall in 1723. What is now Wisconsin Avenue, its western border, was originally an old Indian trail leading from the port of Georgetown to Frederick Town, and was used most frequently by tobacco farmers to take their produce to Georgetown. In 1790, part of this land was purchased by General Uriah Forrest, who gave his name to the uptown section called Forrest Hills. A former mayor of Georgetown, a successful tobacco merchant, and a land speculator, Forrest was the first documented inhabitant of Cleveland Park. He named his estate and his home, still standing, Rosedale. Cleveland Park took its name from the summer White House of President Grover Cleveland and his bride. Their home, built in 1885 at 36th Street and Newark Avenue, was known as Oak View. Electric streetcars on tracks reached the area in 1892.

### The New Structure

Joseph Wilner proposed asking the United Synagogue to designate the projected building as the "National Synagogue." He, together with Abe Kay and Fred Kogod, approached Congressmen Sol Bloom of New York and Herman Koppelman of Connecticut for their official endorsement. The two representatives gave their endorsement and promised to try to gain the support of a number of their wealthy constituents. Nothing came of the proposal or the promise of assistance.

Bids were solicited from two architectural firms, Courland & Sons and Frank Grad & Sons. Both submitted preliminary sketches. The building committee selected Frank Grad, a firm best noted for designing theaters.[5] The postwar boom had inflated building costs; an initial estimate of $350,000 soon escalated to $1,300,000. Countless parlor meetings, luncheons, dinners, and projects would be required to gather the pledges and collect the necessary funds; not everyone was wealthy. Instead of free seating for the High Holy Days, it was found necessary to sell reserved-seating rights in order to raise funds.

An architect selected, building plans took tenuous shape only to be reviewed, rejected, and reconsidered before being finally confirmed. While the building committee felt the structure ought to be monumental, in keeping with the character of the nation's capital city, it could not decide whether the design should be Moorish or Byzantine, the favored patterns of many synagogue builders of the day, or whether it should be contemporary in style. The downtown building "looked like a synagogue"; they wanted a design that would give the new structure a recognizable "synagogue look."

Finally, after seemingly endless discussions and with the involvement of the architect, the committee approved a plan for a building to be built along contemporary lines. An appropriate insignia would be incised on the majestic front facing Connecticut Avenue to give the structure its "Jewish look." Abe Kay displayed a plaster cast of the proposed frontal facade: in bold relief, Moses holding the tablets of the commandments aloft. The proposed design met with considerable disapproval both on aesthetic and ideological grounds.[6]

Abe Shefferman was instructed to write to Rabbi Albert Gordon, executive director of the United Synagogue, to seek the guidance of its Architectural Commission on the propriety of the design. Gordon, sensing that the question touched more on Jewish law than on aesthetics, submitted the question to the Joint Commission on Jewish Law and Standards for an advisory ruling.

The ruling of the Law Commission, issued by its chairman, Rabbi Ben Zion Bokser, informed the congregation that the proposed facade was improper. "There is the danger of people giving undue reverence to the figure of Moses," Bokser wrote. "In Judaism, there has always been a reticence to allow the man to be central. It is the idea, not the man, that is central in our tradition." There would be no objection to placing a painting of the same scene in another part of the synagogue for decorative purposes, Bokser concluded.[7]

At the same time, Rabbi Michael Higger, secretary to the Law Commission, conveyed to the congregation its rulings on synagogue structures, which included subjects that the congregation was loath to consider but could not avoid.

1. The cantor should face the ark during worship. If the cantor faces the congregation, he should turn to face the ark at Borchu, the silent Amidah, and Aleinu.

2. A menorah in the synagogue cannot be made with seven branches.

3. It is not advisable to use electric lights instead of oil for the *ner tamid* (perpetual light).

4. A visible choir without an organ is preferable to a hidden choir with organ accompaniment—it being understood that the choir is not a mixed one.

Each ruling would be debated in due course.

His initial proposal rejected, the architect returned with the design of a large Magen David for the front of the structure. This design, too, was rejected as "pedestrian." Not that it was too Jewish, went the objection, but it was too common, and not even an authentic Jewish symbol at that.* Louis Firestone, an artist-member of the congregation, submitted a design for a heroic-sized menorah which, as he said, was more aesthetic, more appropriate, and

*The six-pointed star is common to India and Nepal, where it denotes a school.

unmistakably authentic. The menorah design would replace the six-pointed star in construction, though not in the blueprints.

With plans finally confirmed, the contract for construction was awarded to the M. Cladny Construction Company for $30,000. Morris Cladny, the builder, was a member of the congregation. Ground consecration ceremonies took place on September 18, 1949, with excavation beginning the following month. Dr. Louis Finkelstein, chancellor of the Jewish Theological Seminary, delivered the address at a cornerstone-laying celebration on May 7, 1950.

Joseph Blumenthal, chairman of the event, recalled that his father had "gloriously mounted the platform at 6th and I Streets to take part in the cornerstone ceremony of a new synagogue building. . . . Little did I dream that even as my father before me, I, too, would live to see the day that history would repeat itself."

This would be Adas Israel's third synagogue, Blumenthal noted, concluding, "A congregation continues in existence through the children, and I am happy to have with us today children of the second and even third generation of our Adas Israel members." Kinship and community were important factors in the growth of Adas Israel.

The structure, expressing the tri-fold functions of the classic synagogue as a place of prayer, study, and assembly, incorporated a sanctuary, school, and social hall. The sanctuary with its balcony would accommodate 1,500 worshippers. Five pairs of heavy bronze doors leading to a red marble lobby dominated the entrance. The Torah ark, at the eastern wall, was framed in Moroccan onyx and Levantine marble, a hidden choir loft above it. The sanctuary, with the exception of the ark, was free of ornamentation.

The school building, with fourteen classrooms, included a 300-seat chapel for daily worship and a social auditorium that would later be named for Abraham Kay, whose extraordinary efforts had initiated and successfully concluded the building program. The building included two modestly sized kitchens. Kay did not want the synagogue to be a place for large banquets. He felt that the aroma of cooking was objectionable in a sanctuary building; banquets belong in hotels and clubs, he said. The small-sized kitchens turned out to be a defect which later construction would seek to rectify. The total cost of the building came to $1,281,194.48.

The dedication ceremonies took place on September 21 to 23, 1951. A new rabbi, David Panitz, had been engaged to succeed Solomon Metz, who was named rabbi emeritus. Morris Gewirz, the principal owner of the apartments on Quebec Street at the rear of the synagogue and co-chairman of the building committee, affirmed, "This great edifice stands like a mighty colossus of spiritual strength."

The location had a serious deficiency. Its most convenient entrance and its parking lot, on Quebec Street, had no outlet. The dead-end created monumental traffic jams on Sabbaths and festivals, since most members no longer hesitated to drive on these days. Joseph Blumenthal attempted to persuade the District government to give Quebec Street an outlet to Porter Street. Extending Quebec Street, he argued, would relieve "intolerable conditions" and would meet the complaints of residents in the surrounding apartments. "Another year will soon pass, and still no relief," he wrote to the Highway Department.[8] Despite the complaints and the pleas, the District, ever short of funds, refused to grant Blumenthal's request.*

The members were proud of their new building and especially pleased that their congregation had not only erected the first synagogue in Washington but the first synagogue outside of the downtown area. The new house of worship had been built by an immigrant generation that had risen from poverty to achieve a measure

*The dead-end was not relieved until the building program of 1990 provided an outlet from the parking lot to Porter Street.

of success they could not have envisioned when they had first come to Washington. The building had met their specifications. It was impressive in appearance; it was contemporary in style; it projected a dignified Jewish image; it would serve their needs as American Jews. Of equal significance, the new structure would reflect their success and status.

### The Organ

Before the completion of the building, the congregation was forced to face what was then one of the most divisive issues in Conservative Judaism, the question of playing the organ at services. Mixed male and female seating was another.

Reform Judaism had introduced the organ into the American synagogue. Traditionalists in the Conservative Movement had vigorously opposed its use, feeling that it was not only un-Jewish but would stifle participation in prayer. Nonetheless, three leading members of the Historical School, Szold, Jastrow, and Hochheimer, two of them in Baltimore and one in Philadelphia, had permitted the use of the organ in their synagogues.

At Adas Israel, advocates of modernizing the ritual won a major victory when the congregation approved the installation of an organ in the new building, but once it was installed, further debate was necessary before it was allowed to be used on Sabbaths and holidays. Cantor Barkin had proposed the installation of an organ in 1950, but the building committee had felt unqualified to approve the suggestion. Abe Kay, who favored an organ, asked Barkin to solicit bids, which Kay promised to submit to the board.

Kay's recommendation was heatedly debated at a board meeting and finally approved in a resolution to accept a bid from the Lewis-Hitchcock Company to install an organ in the new building at a cost of $14,000, with the vague understanding that it would be played only at weddings and concerts.

Neither Rabbi Panitz nor the cantor was prepared to authorize its use for Sabbath services; each expected the other to issue the authorizing statement. Even without a clarifying policy, the organ began to be used at Friday night services. Playing it on Sabbath mornings, festivals, and the High Holidays would come later.

### The Builders

Building the new structure required the generous cooperation of the mass membership; each member was urged to make a contribution according to his or her ability. A small group of members took the lead. Among the leaders were:

Samuel Cohen, European-born, arrived in the United States as a child, and was reared in a Washington home for orphan children together with his brothers and sisters. He became a successful real estate developer and builder of office buildings and apartments and contributed generously to several Washington institutions. Together with Julius Wolpe, he endowed one of the auditoriums in the new synagogue structure.

Leo Freudberg came to Washington from Riga, Latvia, in 1906, at the age of twelve. He lived with an older brother and worked his way through high school and the Washington College of Law as a door-to-door salesman, peddling collar buttons, shoelaces, and candy. After graduating and passing the bar, he opened a law office and was admitted to the Supreme Court bar. He joined the faculty of American University as a part-time teacher. Later, he joined Young & Simon, an insurance firm, to become one of their leading underwriters. Their building on Connecticut Avenue bore Freudberg's name.

A respected Jewish communal leader, Freudberg made the synagogue his primary interest. His granddaughter, Jennifer Berlowe, became Adas Israel's first Bat Mitzvah. He is memorialized at the

Woodmont Country Club in gratitude for his perspicacity and generosity in acquiring a huge tract of land in Rockville and turning it over to the club without profit to himself after the club had declined to acquire a new site in the face of the threatened condemnation of its property by the federal government.

Morris Gewirz, a communal leader and philanthropist, who would give his name to one of the auditoriums that was later added to the synagogue, endowed the Hillel Foundation at George Washington University, the Monsky Foundation of the B'nai B'rith, and the Touro Synagogue in Newport, Rhode Island. Gewirz, who acquired the Quebec House Apartments after the exchange of land with the synagogue, was recognized as one of the District's leading real estate investors.

Fred Gichner, discussed previously, was president for a brief period. His firm designed the ornate iron gates of athe White House and for a private residence on 2315 Massachusetts Avenue in 1913. The building would later become the Embassy of Pakistan.

Abraham S. Kay, never a president or even an officer, was nonetheless, in his lifetime, the most influential member of the synagogue. His approval was essential to the success of any significant project. Fortunately, he was man of breadth. He understood the importance of the seminary and the Conservative Movement and was responsible for garnering support for their fund-raising drives. He was equally committed to Zionist causes.

Abe Kay had come to the United States from Vilna in 1909. His astute investments in real estate enabled him to grow from a small grocery-store owner to become a leading Washington investor and philanthropist. In addition to supporting Jewish causes, he gave generously to local universities. Kay explained that he was motivated to express his gratitude for "all that America has done for those who seek freedom." He died in July 1963. His children, in his memory, endowed the Kay Spiritual Life Center at American University on October 31, 1965. The State of Israel sent the family a handsome calligrapher's copy of the responsive reading read at Kay's funeral service signed by Israel's leaders, Kay's friends: David Ben Gurion, Levi Eshkol, Moshe Sharett, Teddy Kollek, and Avraham Harman. It was to hang in the Kay Auditorium.

Fred Kogod, finance committee chairman for the building campaign, was born in the Ukraine and came to Washington in the early 1900s at the age of fourteen, with a single dollar in his pocket and an identification tag round his neck directing him to the care of a near relative. He worked in a grocery store while attending night school. Opening a grocery store of his own, he helped organize an association of grocery store owners that was able to compete with the larger chain stores. His purchase of a market building that housed a theater put him in the movie business in partnership with his brother-in-law, Max Burka. Before long, the single movie theater became a chain of theaters, and Kogod, one of Washington's leading exhibitors.

Kogod received an honorary doctorate from the Union Theological Seminary in New York and played an active role in several Jewish and civic organizations. He died in December 1956 at age fifty-seven in the first year of his presidency of Adas Israel.

Julius Wolpe was propelled into the presidency by the sudden death of Fred Kogod. While he freely admitted his lack of organizational experience, he had a richer classical background than most of his predecessors. He was well grounded in Jewish learning and sensitive to his lineal relationship to the Gaon of Vilna and Professor Louis Ginzberg.* Wolpe, a jeweler and watchmaker, taught Sunday

*Wolpe's father's great-great-grandfather was Rabbi Reuben of Kaidan, whose brother, Elijah Ashkenazi, was the grandfather of the Gaon of Vilna. Professor Ginzberg was similarly related. Wolpe was also a descendant of Rabbi Yehuda Chassid, the founder of the Hurvah Synagogue in Jerusalem.

school at Adas Israel and headed the school committee for many years.

He migrated to the United States in 1905, at age fifteen, at the urging of his mother who feared the Tsar's conscription. He never saw his family again and shared with Rabbi Metz the pain and terror of the approaching Holocaust.

All three Adas Israel synagogues were built under the leadership of people who had arrived on these shores as penniless immigrants. Except for Morris Gewirz, who was born in Washington to immigrant parents, all of the leaders responsible for the new building had come to Washington from Eastern Europe. The new Adas Israel structure attested to the fulfillment and success they had found in America's promise.

### Rabbinic Transition

The implications of the projected new synagogue were not lost upon Rabbi Metz. He had heard rumors that some officers had suggested that it was time to engage a younger rabbi on the premise that a new synagogue deserved a new spiritual leader. Although he recognized the added burden he would be forced to carry when the congregation moved uptown, he felt that, with assistance, he would be able to continue in active service.

Testing the waters in the summer of 1949, Metz met with Joe Wilner to request a six-month sabbatical leave, telling him that he needed to rest. According to friends of Metz, Wilner's response was unexpected. The president suggested that it would be best if Metz retired, and if he would agree, Wilner would propose that he be named rabbi emeritus with an appropriate pension for life. Though taken aback, Metz was in no position to reject the proposal outright. He would be sixty years of age in 1951, when the new synagogue was ready for occupancy, and he was not in good health; he suffered from high blood pressure.

Metz gave no outward indication that he would agree to Wilner's proposal. Although he declined to address the annual meeting scheduled for October 1949, he informed Wilner that he would be willing to discuss his situation with a small group but, pending any decision, he expected his salary to be increased along with the increases granted to others on the religious staff.

A series of meetings was needed before Wilner could implement his proposal; there were constitutional obstacles to naming a rabbi emeritus for life, and Metz emphatically rejected any proposal that would require annual review of his status. After discussing Metz's reaction with several leaders, Wilner reported to the board on September 8, 1949, that the rabbi had asked for a sabbatical leave and would consider becoming an emeritus thereafter.

Under pressure to frame a response, Metz discussed his situation at a meeting of the officers, which Wilner had called at his request. Speaking with unusual candor, Metz told the group that "he had been under the constant care of a physician for the past two years and that he was burdened with many problems. His physician advised him to take a long extended vacation. He had been suffering from terrible headaches . . . and an erratic blood pressure."[9]

After reviewing his years of service to the congregation, he stated that "some influential members had told him that they would approve a sabbatical leave but he felt that he was entitled to security thereafter." He had heard that "there was quite a bit of opinion in favor of getting a young man when we go into the new synagogue building." If the members wanted a new rabbi, he "would be satisfied to return as the Rabbi Emeritus."

In response to several questions, Metz denied the rumor that he had been offered a post at a local university. He wanted to remain in Washington, he said, and further, "What congregation would take an old rabbi?" As emeritus, he suggested, he should be paid half of his present salary but would leave the matter of compensation to the judgment of the congregation. Metz then left the meeting.

Following a lengthy discussion, the officers adopted a resolution recommending to the board that Metz be given a leave of absence with full pay from June 1 to September 30, 1950, after which he would be named rabbi emeritus at an annual compensation of $5,000.

At its meeting in March, the board expanded the officers' resolution by extending the dates of Metz's leave with full salary to run from June 1 to December 31, 1950. The resolution was now submitted to the members for their approval.[10] The membership meeting in April approved the resolution but, over Wilner's objections, insisted that steps be taken to change the constitution to permit a lifetime appointment for Metz without requiring his annual reelection. A constitutional amendment, not on the agenda of the current meeting, would require still another membership meeting.[11]

Wilner reported to the board in June that, working on the assumption that Metz would become emeritus on January 1, 1951, he had felt at liberty to take steps to seek a new rabbi. He had invited Rabbi Max Routtenberg, chairman of the Joint Placement Commission of the Rabbinical Assembly, to visit Washington to discuss the procedure for selecting a successor and had appointed a search committee that had already interviewed one candidate; three others had been recommended.

When called upon to speak to the board, Metz revealed that he was hesitant about leaving on a sabbatical without the assurance of security for himself and his wife. He could not rely on annual election to assure his status. Asked whether he would be willing to remain in active service as senior rabbi with an assistant, he responded, "Yes, if I can get a contract for three or five years." He indicated, in response to another question, that he would accept the emeritus status only if the constitution was changed to permit lifetime tenure.[12]

Although Wilner argued that Metz's demand for a constitutional amendment to assure him a lifetime appointment reflected lack of trust in the congregation, the meeting insisted that the constitution be amended to provide the assurance Metz had requested and that Mrs. Metz be guaranteed one half of the rabbi's pension after his death.

Metz was invited to address the special meeting called shortly thereafter to consider the proposed amendment. After repeating his previous statements, he insisted that it was he who had initiated the proposal to become rabbi emeritus. He stated further that "the greatest goal in his mind was to have the building completed as early a possible and, with God's help, when he returns, he wanted to be helpful in the work of the congregation." One may conclude that Metz's supporters felt that their rabbi had been forced to retire against his will and, if so, were prepared to challenge the decision.

Having been reassured that Metz was agreeable to the retirement proposal, the members approved an amendment which affirmed that a rabbi of the congregation could be elected rabbi emeritus for life on condition that he had served as rabbi of the congregation for not less than twenty years.

The amendment did not meet with the unanimous approval of Metz's supporters. Despite his reassurances, some still felt that he had been forced to retire against his will; others objected to the precipitous and unauthorized steps taken to secure a successor, which they felt had been initiated without the congregation's knowledge or authorization. Despite the parliamentary efforts to table the amendment, Metz's lifetime status and the assurance of a pension for Mrs. Metz after his death were approved.[13] The meeting adjourned at 11:30 p.m. Interviews with candidates could now proceed openly and officially.

Metz's retirement closed a pivotal era in Adas Israel's history. The congregation had grown and was about to move from its downtown location to a new structure uptown. Metz was the first rabbi to have enjoyed an extended tenure. He remained a respected figure in the community.

The congregation honored Rabbi Metz with a festive testimonial dinner at the Mayflower Hotel on January 11, 1951. He now endeavored to define a role for himself in a position that was new to him and to the congregation. His emeritus period would not be a happy one for either. Beyond conducting the overflow services in the new Kay Auditorium in the Connecticut Avenue building, his skills were not utilized. His attempts to revive the community Adult Education Institute were futile; he turned inward.

In his later years he suffered from deteriorating health and failing eyesight. He passed away in 1959. His eulogist at the Rabbinical Assembly convention described him as "learned in Jewish tradition and Jewish law, but likewise erudite in matters outside of Judaism; a fine leader, who made possible very important educational projects in the community in which he last served, an inspiration to his colleagues in the community because to them he was the true rabbi."[14] The eulogy was an honest appraisal of Metz's influence in Washington and Adas Israel.

Rabbi Stanley Rabinowitz officiated at the unveiling of Metz's tombstone in the Adas Israel Cemetery; Metz was the second ordained rabbi serving Adas Israel to be buried there.* Loeb was the first.

### The Search

The Rabbinical Assembly submitted four recommendations for the congregation's consideration: Rabbis Irving Lehrman of Miami

*Gertrude (Mrs. Solomon) Metz passed away in November 1992 and was buried alongside her husband.

Beach, Israel Kazis of Boston, and Abba Abrams and Morris Kertzer, both of New York City. The search committee proceeded to arrange for interviews and exploratory visits.

The first candidate interviewed, Rabbi Abba Abrams, stipulated a salary of $15,000 and a five-year contract. The salary requirement disturbed the pulpit committee less than the commitment for five years. The stated reasons for not giving further consideration to Abrams were his age, his Orthodox leanings, and his obvious rigidity.

Subcommittees were appointed to visit Rabbi Israel Kazis in Boston and Rabbi Morris Kertzer in New York. So impressed were some of the subcommittee members with the intellectual level of Kazis's sermons that they favored engaging him forthwith even to granting his salary request of $20,000. Others, however, felt that Kazis seemed cold and aloof, an unwarranted conclusion. In any event, the board strongly opposed engaging an unmarried rabbi. Neither Kazis nor Kertzer was married at the time.

It was Rabbi Irving Lehrman of Miami Beach who captured the enthusiastic support of a majority of the search committee. Members of the congregation who attended services at his synagogue while wintering in Florida were impressed by his sermonic ability as well as by the huge attendance he attracted each week. If Irving Lehrman were brought to Washington, they reasoned, he would surely attract a similar following. Their enthusiasm influenced the committee to invite Lehrman for a Sabbath visit. He came and, as anticipated, he conquered.

The board authorized a negotiating committee to offer Lehrman an annual salary of $17,500, plus the free use of a home and the assurance of a pension. Lehrman was agreeable; he was ready to come to Adas Israel in June.[15]

The board members congratulated the negotiating committee on its success and themselves on their good fortune; they made arrangements for public announcement of the new appointment. Their elation, however, was short-lived. Instead of the formal agreement that Wilner had been led to expect, he received an apologetic letter from Lehrman saying that he could not bring himself to leave his present congregation.[16]

The board felt that Lehrman had misled them. Rabbi Routtenberg, invited to address a board meeting and embarrassed by the outcome of the negotiations with Lehrman, urged the consideration of another candidate whose abilities he lauded: Rabbi Isaac Klein of Springfield, Massachusetts. Invited to preach at Sabbath services over the weekend of May 4, Klein made a positive impression on the committee and on the congregation. He was delightfully warm and able to convey profound ideas by illustrative and readily understandable parables. He was well versed in Talmud and midrashic literature.

Klein would have received the board's unanimous endorsement had he not responded negatively when asked about the use of the organ at services, a subject which still troubled the congregation. To the question about installing an organ, Klein responded, "If you install an organ, you will want to use it. I cannot stop you from using it because I am not your Rabbi. But, were I to officiate at services when the organ played, I would go home, put on a tallit, and recite my Sabbath prayers." Although the answer appealed to some, it destroyed the base of Klein's support.

The congregation had considered ten candidates. While each had attracted a following, none, except for Lehrman, had been able to garner a majority. After assessing the results of their search, Joseph Wilner submitted the name of still another candidate, who had been recommended not by the Rabbinical Assembly, but by

Wilner's friend, Israel Goldstein, the rabbi of New York's Congregation B'nai Jeshurun and president of the Zionist Organization. The candidate was Goldstein's assistant, a young rabbi named David Panitz who had been ordained in 1943.[17]

In recommending Panitz to Adas Israel, Goldstein had written, "He and his wife, Esther, brought impressive dimensions of Hebraic and general culture to B'nai Jeshurun." Panitz had assumed full responsibility in the distinguished New York congregation during Goldstein's two-year absence in 1948–50. "We have remained good friends and colleagues across the years," Goldstein recalled in his autobiography.[18]

Panitz made modest demands for salary and tenure: he was willing to accept a one-year agreement. Nor did he object to the organ, since one was in use at all services in his present synagogue. The congregation was ready to accept Wilner's recommendation; they had enough of the search process.

Rabbi David Panitz was formally elected on June 6, 1951; the congregation agreed to lend him the funds for a down payment on a house.

# 23

## THE PANITZ YEARS

Rabbi David Panitz participated in the Sabbath service at which the new synagogue building was dedicated in September 1951. He was installed one year later, on November 4, 1952. Participating in the installation ceremonies were Rabbis Norman Gerstenfeld of the Washington Hebrew Congregation, Henry Segal of the B'nai Israel Congregation, Herman J. Waldman of the Orthodox community, and representatives of the Washington Federation of Churches and the Catholic Diocese. The installation address was delivered by Panitz's sponsor, Rabbi Israel Goldstein.

David Panitz was born in Baltimore and educated at Johns Hopkins University and Baltimore Hebrew College. Ordained by the Jewish Theological Seminary, he occupied pulpits in Syracuse, New York and, briefly, Jacksonville, Florida, before becoming the assistant to Rabbi Israel Goldstein at Congregation B'nai Jeshurun in New York City in 1946.

### A Golden Era

The decade beginning in 1950 held the promise of being a golden era for Adas Israel; it began with a new synagogue and a new rabbi. The congregation's programs were probably the most popular in the Washington Jewish community; no classroom remained unused for long. Indeed, the school's activities soon outgrew the available space.

In his interview with the board, Rabbi Panitz had promised to give priority to the daily and Sabbath services. In fulfillment of his commitment, he encouraged community participation in the Friday night services by inviting the sponsorship of communal organizations and thereby the presence of their members. He chose simulating sermon topics such as "Are We Closing the Doors to Immigration?", "Where Can We Find Peace of Mind?", and "What Is Godliness?"

To maintain the daily chapel service, Panitz devised a rotation procedure that would assure ten volunteers at each morning and evening service. He reorganized the junior congregation and instituted an hour of study preceding the service. The post–Bar Mitzvah "Minyanaires" were asked to meet for one weekday session in addition to their regular Sunday morning service, breakfast, and discussion.

Panitz organized an Institute of Adult Jewish Studies in which he, Esther (Mrs. David) Panitz, Henry Margolis, and Irving Wilner taught courses in Basic Judaism, as well as periodic forums which offered lectures delivered by prominent guests. Lecturers included Abraham S. Halkin, who spoke on "The Debt of Islam to Judaism," William F. Albright, on "Recent Discoveries in Bible Lands," and Mordecai M. Kaplan, on "A Program for Jewish Life." Maurice Samuel spoke on "Toynbee and the Jews," Morris Kertzer, on "The Future of Religion in Soviet Lands," Gershom Scholem, on "Cultural Factors on the Israeli Scene," and Yochanan Merog, the First Secretary of the Israeli Embassy, on "The Arab Population in Israel." At last, it seemed, Adas Israel could compete with the popular endowed-lecture series sponsored by the Washington Hebrew Congregation.

A highlight of the year was the presentation of the Handel oratorio *Samson*, featuring Cantor Jacob Barkin, as soloist, with the

Washington Hellenic Choral Society and members of the National Symphony Orchestra. The *Washington Post* profiled Rabbi Panitz favorably in a feature article.[1]

With its enlarged facilities, its more accessible location, and fed by the postwar "baby boom," school enrollment reached new highs. It became necessary to employ additional supervisory staff. Henry Margolis had been engaged in 1951 as full-time director of education and youth activities; he was later succeeded by Isadore E. Krakower. Rabbi Bernard Mussman, a personable 1952 graduate of the Jewish Theological Seminary, and a former chaplain at Fort Benning, Georgia, was named to the education post in 1955.

Disagreements over curriculum were resolved by accepting the standards of the Joint Commission on Jewish Education of the United Synagogue and Rabbinical Assembly, which deemphasized the stress on Hebrew instruction in favor of a value-centered history curriculum. A high school program attracted older students.

Extracurricular activities expanded to include photography, painting, social dancing, and even a school orchestra. An adjunct athletic program offered basketball, volleyball, bowling, and ping-pong. A weekly junior congregation Sabbath service, adjusted to three grade levels, each followed by its own socializing Kiddush, attracted a hitherto-unreached teenage population. A newly organized parent-teachers association provided both a forum for curriculum planning and sponsorship for a milk-and-cookie program for children in the afternoon school. Picnics attracted over 600 families.

Rabbi Panitz introduced the seminary-sponsored Leaders Training Fellowship for teenagers who were receptive to more intensive Jewish studies. Its first achievement was a *siyum hasefer* gathering (a celebration on completing the study of a book of the Bible) at which Sander Mendelson, Howard Bleich, and Goldie Weiss commented on biblical teachings. The fellowship, later under the direction of Kopel Weinstein, attracted many young people, some of whom fulfilled their early promise by becoming leaders in the congregation and community.

A less exacting and broader-based teenage group, the United Synagogue Youth (USY), founded in 1953, with its age-graded subdivisions, dominated the social life of the young people in the congregation for several decades. The influence of a popular and charismatic youth director, Obadiah Cohen, whom most people called "Vadie," attracted almost 100 young people to his programs, which now included a well-trained choir and a monthly "Dinner with the Rabbi."

Other youth groups came within the orbit of Adas Israel. A Boy Scout troop met under the leadership of Helmut Winterfeldt. Its success served as a model for synagogue-sponsored Girl Scout and Cub Scout troops. In addition, there were three Young Judea–sponsored Israeli dance clubs. Athletic teams competed in neighborhood and synagogue leagues.

A Young People's League and a Young People's Club, both for singles aged eighteen to twenty-five, organized in 1952, sponsored discussion groups and social dancing. By the time Rabbi Mussman resigned in 1959 to become the assistant to Irving Lehrman in Miami Beach, school enrollment had reached 600 students.

Stanley Wiener, chairman of the house committee, and a future president and executive director, told the 1952 annual meeting,

> Almost every night will find every facility of this building being used in some manner. . . . The College of Jewish Studies will again use our classrooms. In addition to this there will be our own Adult Education Institute and a resumption of the Supper Club.
>
> We will be host to the national convention of the United Synagogue Youth when there will be over 700 young people for all over the U.S. making Adas Israel their convention headquarters.

In view of the extensive program, there was little opposition to the decision made in 1956 to build an annex to the synagogue expressly for school and youth activities. It would be named for Joseph Wilner, who had passed away in 1953.

The Wilner building was dedicated in 1959, under the chairmanship of Samuel P. Cohen. Its rooms relieved the space limitations of the synagogue and encouraged an expansion of youth and cultural activities. Samuel Cohen and Julius Wolpe joined together to endow one of the large rooms in the new annex, to be known as the Cohen-Wolpe Auditorium, while Morris Gewirz underwrote the cost of another room, to be called the Gewirz Auditorium. Fred Kogod had endowed the chapel in the synagogue. The camaraderie among the leaders stimulated fund-raising for the building and motivated them to vie with one another in expressions of generosity to the congregation.

Panitz instituted an early and late service on Rosh Hashanah eve and invited the scholar Abraham Halkin, Esther Panitz's cousin, to officiate at the overflow services in the Kay Auditorium. Abba Eban, Israel's ambassador, was pleased to accept an invitation to worship with the congregation at its High Holy Day service.

The new generation that had come of age simultaneously with the move uptown demanded more decorum at religious services. To influence the congregation's conduct, instructions suggesting appropriate behavior at services were affixed to the inside front covers of the prayer books. In addition, Panitz initiated a campaign for greater Sabbath observance.

In his sermons, Panitz stressed identification with the seminary as the "fountainhead" of the Conservative Movement. A "Seminary Corner" reprinting news releases from the seminary and featuring addresses from seminary professors became a regular feature of the *Adas Israel Chronicle*. Reprints from the bulletins of the United

Synagogue and the seminary defined the Conservative position on ritual observance.

Panitz and Shefferman planned elaborate celebrations to mark significant anniversaries. A Sabbath eve service in April 1954 marked the congregation's eighty-fifth anniversary with Rabbi Ira Eisenstein, president of the Rabbinical Assembly, delivering the sermon. A dinner dance at the Mayflower Hotel on Sunday night concluded the weekend celebration.

The ninetieth anniversary of the congregation, in May 1959, celebrated more elaborately than previous anniversaries, included the dedication of the Wilner building. Dore Schary, the playwright and motion picture producer, delivered the Friday night sermon. Rabbi Harry Halpern, past-president of the Rabbinical Assembly and chairman of the seminary's Rabbinic Cabinet, preached on Sabbath morning, and Colonel Shoshana Gershoni, commander of the Women's Corps of the Israeli Army, spoke at the afternoon Oneg Shabbat. There was a teenage dance in the evening, and on Sunday night, a dinner dance at the Indian Spring Country Club. Dr. Lawrence G. Gerthick, U.S. Commissioner of Education, dedicated the Wilner building on Sunday morning. Shefferman prepared an impressive anniversary booklet to mark the occasion.

In 1957 Adas Israel and the Washington Hebrew Congregation were recognized as the two leading congregations in the Washington area in an issue of the Russian-language publication *America*, published by the U.S. Information Agency for distribution to Eastern bloc countries. The special issue, devoted to religion in the United States, included a photograph of the new Adas Israel synagogue. The Voice of America recorded activities at Adas Israel to illustrate examples of religious freedom and interfaith unity in a program broadcast to sixty-five countries.

The congregation, in 1956, replaced the old Adler High Holiday prayer books with the edition presently in use, edited by Rabbi Morris Silverman. Subsidized by memorial gifts, the prayer books were provided to members without charge.

With Cantor Barkin's resignation in 1958, the congregation engaged Burton Lowell Kaplan only to discover a new problem: Kaplan was a Kohen. According to traditional Jewish law he could not set foot in a cemetery or enter a funeral home. While Panitz was instructed to seek the guidance of the Rabbinical Assembly's Law Committee. Julius Wolpe, the president, sought the private opinion of Rabbi Mortimer Cohen of Philadelphia.

Responding for the Law Committee, Rabbi Ben Zion Bokser stated that while the committee could not suspend traditional practice, the participation at a funeral of a rabbi or cantor who was a Kohen was permitted if deemed vital by the bereaved family and if a clergyman who was not a Kohen was not available. However, a Kohen who regularly officiated at funerals would have to forfeit his priestly prerogatives; he would no longer be entitled to officiate at the redemption-of-the-firstborn ceremony (*pidyon ha-ben*) and could not be the first person called to the Torah.[2]

Mortimer Cohen informed Wolpe that he followed the permissive opinion of Professor Louis Ginzberg, who had ruled that the halachic requirements would be satisfied if the coffin were closed before the Kohen entered the place where the funeral service was being held. Besides, wrote Cohen, in his opinion it was high time that the categories of Kohen and Levi were ignored.[3]

### Fault-Line

Despite the outward image of a successful synagogue and the appearance of enthusiastic approval for Rabbi Panitz's innovative leadership, an underlying fault-line threatened to disrupt the tranquility of the congregation and frustrate Panitz's fondest hopes. From the day of his election, Panitz was determined to bring the procedures he had learned at B'nai Jeshurun to his new position. He approached his new challenges with optimism and firm resolve. First, he had to assert his authority as the rabbi; there were obstacles. Panitz soon discovered that Adas Israel was dominated by its officers and the executive director; his predecessor had not exercised strong leadership. Not since the ill-fated Schwefel had a rabbi been allowed to attend board meetings as a matter of right. Panitz demanded the right to attend; his request was granted.

Next, there was a rabbi emeritus who retained a faithful, though not extensive, following among the congregants. More disturbing to Panitz was the custom for the president of the congregation or his designee to welcome the worshippers, make announcements, and deliver a message of his own at the end of Sabbath services. On Yom Kippur, the president delivered a lengthy report on the "state of the Congregation." Panitz felt it would be necessary for him to confront each of these obstacles in turn.

Rabbi Metz came first. Studying a segment of Mishnah at the *seudah shlishith*, the repast following the Mincha service, had been a long-standing and pleasant aspect of Sabbath afternoons at the synagogue. Rabbi Metz had led the sessions at 6th and I Streets and continued the custom in the new building. On the first Sabbath after his arrival, following Mincha, Panitz entered the room where the "students" were gathered around a table with Metz at its head, and stated, "I'm the rabbi here now. If you don't mind, I will lead the class." Metz stood up, nodded to those assembled, and, taking his coat, quietly, surely crestfallen, left the room, never to return to that setting. The act left a deep impression, not a positive one, on many members.

To Cantor Barkin and Rabbi Weiss, Panitz revealed his reservations about the appropriateness of the president's delivering a postservice "announcement" speech each week. They advised him to discuss the matter with the president himself rather than take unilateral action. The custom was a long-standing one and not unique to Adas Israel; other congregations in the community followed a similar practice. Heeding their counsel, Panitz invited Wilner to attend a staff meeting at which Panitz commented on the need to establish order on the pulpit and to define a protocol on the right to address the congregation. He recommended that only those who had been invited by the rabbi should have the right to address the congregation. Wilner voiced no objection, thinking that Panitz wanted to protect the pulpit from uninvited organizational representatives who were sometimes injected into organizationally sponsored services without anyone's prior knowledge.

On the following Sabbath morning, at the conclusion of the mourner's Kaddish, and prior to the benediction, Wilner began to rise from his seat on the bimah to approach the podium, as was his custom. He was still in the process of rising when Panitz grasped his shoulders and pushed him back into his seat. Panitz then made the announcements, acting in accordance with the protocol which Wilner himself had previously approved. Thereinafter, the rabbi made the concluding announcements.

The lesson and the affront made a lasting impression upon Wilner. That summer, 1951, while Panitz was out of the city on vacation, he told the board that he had regretfully come to the conclusion that Panitz "was not the man for this congregation." Wilner urged the board not to renew Panitz's contract after its first year.

There was an uproar in the boardroom. Panitz had been Wilner's candidate in the first place and had hardly been at Adas Israel long enough to have a real opportunity to serve the congregation. In his brief tenure, he had been an effective and innovative leader and had made many friendships. The board members refused to repudiate Panitz or to initiate another painful search process.

Wilner had to accept his defeat and the rabbi's ascendancy. Panitz had achieved the status he desired. He had asserted his authority, but without the security that should have come with it, for he continued to serve under one-year contracts. Each year, Wilner opposed Panitz's retention. Eventually others came to agree with him.

Wilner passed away in 1953 during his twenty-fourth year in office. He was succeeded by Isaac Jacobson, who, suddenly and unexpectedly propelled into office, felt an obligation to conclude the late president's unfinished agenda. The rabbi's contract was a part of that agenda.

In May 1955, Jacobson called a special board meeting to discuss Panitz's tenure. Jacobson stated that problems had begun as far back as 1951, shortly after Panitz's installation. Wilner, he revealed, had called the officers together in the spring of 1952 to discuss "certain short-comings" of the rabbi; Wilner had concluded that it was necessary to "change Rabbis,"[4] but the matter had been deferred.

Jacobson, now speaking for himself, charged that Panitz lacked the qualities necessary to lead the congregation; moreover, he had failed in his responsibilities to the school and the youth department. As evidence, Jacobson pointed to the poor attendance at Sabbath services, especially on Friday nights, and to the deterioration of the junior congregation. There had also been complaints that Panitz was neglecting the confirmation class.

Jacobson stated that he had already revealed his feelings to the officers of the congregation at a private meeting and that they, too, had concluded that Rabbi Panitz was not suited to the congregation.

At their initiative, the officers had met with Panitz a few days previously and had advised him that they would not recommend his retention to the annual meeting later that month. The rabbi had responded that he would like some time to think through his situation. It had been agreed that their discussion would be kept confidential until the rabbi had time to frame his response.

Instead, said Jacobson, immediately after their meeting, Panitz alerted a number of his friends in the congregation telling them that he had been summarily dismissed. The rabbi was himself responsible for creating an uproar in the congregation, said Jacobson. The heated reverberations in the congregation forced Jacobson to call a special board meeting since the issue now had been made public.

Jacobson added that Panitz, while attending the recent Rabbinical Assembly convention in Chicago, had discussed his situation with Dr. Max Arzt, the vice-chancellor of the Jewish Theological Seminary. Upon his return to Washington he had asked to meet with Jacobson privately. Jacobson had insisted that Stanley Wiener, the vice-president, be present. At the meeting, Panitz had asked for a one-year renewal of his contract and would agree to resign at its conclusion. He agreed to submit a letter of resignation to take effect one year hence, May 1956.

Jacobson had reported this account to the congregational officers at a lunch meeting earlier in the day. They had drawn up a letter confirming the private negotiations and had submitted it to Panitz, who, after consulting Arzt, had countered with a letter containing slightly different provisions.

The officers' proposal allowed Panitz to remain in the post for one year, until May 1956, but gave the congregation the right to begin interviewing rabbinic candidates immediately. Panitz's counterversion denied the congregation the right to interview candidates or to make his resignation public until March 1, 1956, but reserved for himself the right to accept another position prior to that date. Both versions were now submitted for the board's consideration.

Fred Kogod, the future president, spoke against Panitz's proposal, indicating that he had informed Panitz long ago of his opposition to his reelection. Isador Turover, in sympathy with the rabbi, deplored the fact that the board had not been brought into consultation at the outset of the dispute. While regretting the turn of events, he urged the acceptance of the rabbi's formulation. Isidore Alk and Hymen Goldman agreed with Turover. The latter three represented the traditional stratum in the congregation; Goldman and Turover had yeshiva backgrounds and were predisposed to show respect for the rabbinate. For the sake of avoiding further controversy, the board agreed to accept Panitz's formulation of the terms of his resignation.

As agreed, Panitz tendered his resignation to take effect fifteen months hence on August 31, 1956, asking that no successor be interviewed prior to March 1956, and concluding,

> My association, and that of my family, with the congregation has been pleasant and fruitful, and we cherish the friendships that we have formed here. I will serve the congregation and community devotedly and zealously until the very last hour of my affiliation with Adas Israel. I pray for the continued well-being and advancement of the congregation in the service of our faith, people and country.

Jacobson, in exchange, confirmed the congregation's acceptance of Panitz's terms, concluding

> Your association with the congregation has created a feeling of respect among the officers and members for your earnest endeavors on their behalf, and we wish you the utmost of success.

Both letters were dated May 9, 1955. The negotiations had taken place in the five days between May 1 and May 5, 1955.

At the annual meeting on May 24, 1955, Panitz was reelected for one year through August 31, 1956. Although it was widely known that this would be his last year in the Adas Israel pulpit, there was no mention of resignation in the proceedings. In addressing the meeting, Panitz spoke as though there were no problems. He called for home-study groups and greater participation in services. He pointed out that errors in inscriptions on tombstones could be avoided by consultations prior to installation.[5]

As though it were the scenario for a novel, the denouement of the encounter between rabbi and congregation took an unexpected turn.

Rabbis, like other professionals who meet privately with clients or patients behind closed doors, are sometimes targets of allegations of sexual impropriety. Familiarity, frequent meetings, the process of transference, the needs and frustrations of the client and, sometimes, of the professional, make the clergy, psychiatrists, politicians and other professionals, particularly vulnerable to accusations of improper behavior.

No more exempt from this professional hazard than anyone else, Panitz was accused of an improper relationship with a member of the congregation. Members heatedly took sides. The charges, vigorously denied by the rabbi and the accused woman, could not be verified and were widely rejected.

Panitz was not the first rabbi of Adas Israel to be accused of questionable conduct with a person of the opposite gender, nor would he be the last professional on the staff to be so charged. Twenty-six years earlier, in 1929, similar allegations had clouded the departure of Rabbi Louis Schwefel and surely contributed to it. In the past, even the rumor of sexual misconduct was enough to disqualify a clergyman; congregants acted on the principle that where there's smoke, there must be fire. In more recent days, congregations, more sophisticated, have weighed such charges with more caution and understanding before acting upon them.

The board faced a painful dilemma. The majority of its members were convinced that the charges were groundless, even outrageous. To allow Panitz to resign at this point, though in accordance with the prior agreement, would be to mark him guilty of the allegations and would doom his career for all time. No one wanted to harm Panitz, his family, or his career. At the November board meeting, Isadore Turover, ever sensitive and compassionate, moved that "Rabbi Panitz's letter of resignation be returned to him." The motion passed unanimously.[6]

Panitz continued serving Adas Israel until 1959, when he accepted the invitation to become the Rabbi of Temple Emanuel in Paterson, New Jersey, where he served until his retirement in June 1988. He died in Paterson on January 25, 1991.

### The End of the Parade

David Panitz was the seventeenth clergyman to serve Adas Israel in the 87 years since the appointment of its first Hazzan in 1872, Panitz was the end of a rabbinic parade. During that same period, the congregation was lead by twelve presidents.

Except for Voorsanger, each rabbinic tenure was terminated by the congregation. Except for Metz, who served for twenty-one years, each tenure was relatively brief. This was understandable when the congregation was served by poorly qualified hazzanim whose training scarcely exceeded that of a traditionally trained layman. Once the congregation engaged university-educated and seminary-ordained rabbis, however, it becomes more difficult to explain the brevity of each tenure and the rapidity of turnover. The reasons bear analysis.

Much of the history of Adas Israel may be portrayed as a study of the relationships between strong-willed presidents and powerless rabbis. The rabbi was regarded as an employee; he served at the pleasure, not of the congregation nor even of the board, but of the president. More than one rabbi was dismissed by presidential fiat. Paradoxically, there were favored rabbis for whom the president sought more generous treatment than the board was willing to allow. Rabbis were largely dependent on the goodwill first of the president and then of the board. The membership's wishes carried less weight.

In every confrontation between president and rabbi, the president had the advantage of the support of his friends and his badge of authority, while the rabbi, however self-assured he may have been, without tenure or pension, and completely dependent upon the board's willingness to renew his one-year contract, was forced to chose between compromise and resignation. Alternatives for the rabbi were few; it was an uneven struggle. So the scorecard tallied a continual parade of brief-tenured rabbis alongside long-tenured presidents.

The reasons for the tensions between rabbi and congregation were not unique to Adas Israel. In most congregations, there was a divergence between congregational expectations of the rabbi and the rabbi's perception of his role. Adas Israel members judged the rabbi by his projected religious persona, his personal observances, his manner of conducting worship, and his response to their personal needs. The rabbi judged the congregation by the extent of the members' religious observance, their attendance at worship services, their response to the goals and programs he outlined for them, and, inevitably, the salary they paid him. More than one rabbinic tenure ran afoul of an alleged breach of halachic behavior. Similarly, more than one rabbi had reason to complain about the level of religious commitment in the congregation, as reflected by the statements made in the interviews with Rabbis Morris Mandel in 1901 and Louis Egelson in 1911.

A constant source of friction in Adas Israel, as in many congregations, was the task of maintaining a minyan for daily services, especially when members ceased residing in the neighborhood of the synagogue. The usual solution was to demand more frequent participation by the rabbi and the cantor, and to charge them with devising ways of rotating the responsibility for providing the necessary quorum of ten. The suggested remedies seldom worked for long, for clergy and board each expected the other to compensate for their own failures. Not one of the rabbis of Adas Israel, however religiously observant, succeeded in escaping the complaint that he did not attend daily services with sufficient regularity.

Another factor which contributed to the instability of the professional positions at Adas Israel, and is frequently a cause of staff turnover in many congregations today, was the antagonistic relationships between rabbi, cantor, and executive director. At Adas Israel, Cantor Barkin was far more popular than either Rabbi Metz or Rabbi Panitz; neither could compete with his outgoing personality, his love of sports, and his familiarity with the golf course and the social circuit, all of which contributed to a close relationship with the decision-makers on the board. While Metz did not approve of Barkin's many solo renditions of the prayers, he refrained from objecting to the cantorial domination of the service. Panitz, seeking to diminish the number of musical renditions and to subordinate choral arias in favor of congregational recitation, challenged Barkin. The conflict between them was evident for all to see, both in the pulpit and outside of it. Each had partisan supporters in the congregation.

Similarly, Abe Shefferman, the able executive director, felt that his responsibilities for the synagogue's efficient operation included the supervision of the rabbi and cantor. He did not hesitate to criticize either of them, both publicly and privately, thus contributing to the tensions in the congregation. As an example, at an annual meeting, he chided Metz for not visiting the classrooms often enough, which resulted in a board resolution advising Metz to give more attention to the school. When parents or members voiced a complaint against the rabbi for failing to visit a sick person or being inattentive to the needs of a child, instead of discussing the matter with the rabbi privately, Shefferman would transmit the complaint to the president of the Congregation.[7] This procedure could not help but disrupt relationships among the professional staff and contributed to increasing the discord within the congregation.

Another reason for rabbinic "turnover" was the differing definitions of the rabbinic role as enunciated by the congregation and as defined by the Seminary. Adas Israel wanted a rabbinic functionary who would teach, guide, inspire, visit the sick, console the bereaved, and serve the members at life cycle events. In other words, the congregation, as many congregations, wanted a rabbi who would function as a priest rather than a prophet, a role which the rabbi frequently arrogated to himself. The congregation, like many congregations, also wanted its rabbi to be a pastor; the Seminary trained him to be a scholar. The seminary was more successful in giving its students an understanding of the history of the prayer book than in answering the quandry over the effectiveness of the prayers. The Seminary trained its graduates in mastery of the traditional texts; congregations were far more interested in other areas which, if pursued, would leave little time for scholarly pursuits, much less for the preparation of sermons. Always working under pressure, the rabbi had to steal time in order to study.

Schooled in the exposition of midrashic, biblical, and talmudic commentaries and texts, the seminary graduate had little training in what was called practical theology. He had to learn from experience or from the guidance of practicing rabbis when called to officiate at marriages or funerals or to counsel the troubled. More than one rabbinic career was undermined by blunders due to inexperience.

Cyrus Adler felt that the years a rabbi spent at the seminary were far too few and precious to waste time learning about such "simple" matters as conducting a marriage ceremony, blessing a Bar Mitzvah, or consoling a bereaved family, at the cost of the more important goal of mastering the sacred texts. For both Schechter and Adler, the synagogue was primarily a place for scholars to earn a living so that they could pursue their real purpose: scholarship.

Until recently, it was the seminary president rather than the Rabbinical Assembly placement commission that selected rabbis for specific congregations. Schechter had recommended Louis Egelson to Adas Israel; he was one of his prize students. Cyrus Adler had recommended Solomon Metz in 1930; he respected his scholarship. The most generous evaluation that Adler could offer a congregation was that the candidate was a fine scholar. The rabbi's ability as a pastor or counsellor, or even as a speaker. counted for less. The differing evaluations led to tragic encounters between a rabbi's performance and the congregation's expectations.

Then, as now, rabbi and congregation differ in their definitions of rabbinic responsibilities. Congregations do not feel they have an obligation to enable their rabbi to spend a great deal of time ministering to causes beyond the congregation. Their own needs are primary; they pay his salary. Congregation Mikveh Israel in Philadelphia in the 1860s resented Isaac Leeser's preoccupation with national concerns. A century later, many congregants are annoyed when their rabbi is not readily available to them when they need him. A congregational leader who signs the rabbi's salary check may be disturbed when the rabbi he "employs" is beyond immediate reach of the telephone.

Finances were another frequent source of tension. Seminary graduates were unprepared for the realities of congregational life. They frequently assumed that the laymen would raise the funds for maintaining the synagogue while the rabbi pursued his primary duties: preparing sermons and lectures, and ministering to the needs of the members. They soon discovered that many congregations expected them to help meet the budget, at least to raise the funds to cover their salaries.

At Adas Israel, not to be ignored in any analysis of the causes for rabbinic discontent, was the low standard of compensation in comparison to other congregations. In 1873, Benjamin Szold's Baltimore congregation paid him $4,500, and in 1876, Chizuk Amunah, also in Baltimore, paid Henry Schneeberger $1,200, raised to $1,400 in 1882. During the same period, Adas Israel paid its clergy $600 to $900. The salaries of Schwefel, Metz, and Panitz, though more substantial, were intermittently frozen or even reduced due to economic recession. Rabbis and cantors discovered that one way to secure a salary increase was to seek another post, when other positions were available, since a new rabbi, at the outset, could usually command a higher salary than his predecessor.

In most instances, however, due to depressed economic conditions and the lack of available pulpits, the incumbent had little leverage. Morris Mandel, in 1901, quickly changed his mind about leaving Adas Israel once he perceived the lack of alternatives; it proved to be of no avail. Rabbi Metz decided not to resign when his salary was reduced; he had no other place to go. In some instances, the departing rabbi left the pulpit for other pursuits; some turned to Reform congregations, where salaries were higher. Schechter alluded to this tendency in his address to the United Synagogue in 1913.

Nor did it help the rabbi's self-esteem that some members of the seminary faculty expressed contempt for the congregational pulpit because they felt that its demands interfered with the rabbi's primary obligation to study and write. To the distinguished professor of Talmud, Louis Ginzberg, rabbis were wasting their time delivering invocations and preaching to "pants pressers." He was unhappy when prized students deserted the academy in favor of the pulpit.

Under the best of circumstances, conflict in expectations is inevitable in the rabbi-congregation relationship; rabbinic duties and responsibilities, unless defined, are too vast and too extensive to provide satisfaction to either congregation or rabbi. Every rabbi needs to reconcile his finite hours and energy with the seemingly infinite needs and demands of the congregation, community, friends, family, and his personal life. A young rabbi, in an initial burst of enthusiasm, may be tempted to accept the premise that he can reconcile all of these expectations. When it becomes apparent that filling the role is beyond his capacity, the rabbi, initially idealized as the spiritual leader who will fulfill his promise, soon finds himself abandoned by those who once held high hopes for his success. In failing to meet their expectations of him, the rabbi arouses both disappointment and hostility, driving congregants to seek another spiritual leader who will not disappoint them, but in the attempt to meet their expectations, the successor falls into the same trap as his predecessor. In seeking alternatives, the congregation succeeds only in repeating the process.

There is another key to understanding, if not the turnover of rabbis, their variety. While every rabbi, even as every human being, possesses areas of strength and of weakness, each rabbi can excel only in limited areas. No rabbi can be totally effective in every area of the congregation's expectations. In reviewing the abilities of a departing rabbi a congregation tends to emphasize those areas in which the incumbent or departing rabbi was deficient. In seeking a successor, it looks for someone who lacks the deficiencies perceived in the predecessor, forgetting that the successor, along with his areas of strength, will bring with him his own inadequacies, which will be perceived only later. Thus the congregation succeeds in trading a rabbi with certain deficiencies for another with others. In the exchange, the effective strengths of each rabbi frequently are ignored.

With each departing rabbi, Adas Israel demanded of the seminary that it send them an "inspiring and innovative rabbi" who would attract more members and enable the congregation to maintain its prestige in the community and in the movement. And with each departing rabbi, it became more and more difficult for the congregation to find a candidate to its liking.

Over the years, with maturing leadership, successive rabbinic tenures lengthened as changing conditions and the change of generations contributed to improving the rabbi-congregation relationship.

*~ Cyrus Adler* *Reflections*

The years that they spend in this Institution should be devoted almost exclusively to Jewish studies, and to fitting themselves for active duties and scholarly work. In fact, the educational course which we have in mind for a student of the Seminary is that he should be a man of sound general education when he enters, and that whilst here, he should devote himself to building upon this foundation a structure of Jewish scholarship, which in the end, will be translated into Jewish work in the pulpit, in the school room, the general community, and occasionally, let us hope, in the enrichment of Jewish learning.[8]

# 24

## MALE AND FEMALE

### Far Above Rubies

In premodern times, men and women were assigned different roles in nearly every area of life, and, as a consequence, they were segregated at public gatherings; religion followed the conventional social pattern. Scholars debate whether gender-based separation was the cause or the effect of women's lesser status in the premodern era.

According to some, the separation of the sexes in Jewish history was not due to a feeling that women were secondary or inferior, but a reflection of concern for their welfare. Thus, women were exempt from prayers and ritual obligations that had to be performed at specific times, because time-bound observances would add a burden to their responsibilities toward home and family. But exemption was not prohibition; women were not precluded from voluntarily observing the prayer regimen. Some prayers were as obligatory for them as for men.

Similarly, women and men were separated at worship in order to help both sexes to concentrate on the prayers without social distractions. Women were not called to the Torah because they were not obligated to hear the public reading of the Torah.* Another explanation for their separation from men was that women were

*Except on Shabbat Zachor, the Sabbath before Purim, when the portion of Amalek (Deuteronomy 25:17–19) is read.

deemed to be periodically unclean due to their menstrual cycles. Women were exempt from giving charity because they owned no property in their own name.

While separation by gender was a product of the times, the traditional explanations only reinforce the conclusion that women occupied a secondary, or inferior, status to men. Whatever justifications may have existed in the past, neither the disabilities nor the lesser status can be sustained in the modern world.

At Adas Israel, the quest for women's equality met with intense resistance, sometimes on the part of women as well as men. Although men may have praised their wives as the valorous woman who "looketh well to the needs of her household,"* the male worshipper continued to bless God for not having created him a woman. The blessing, however interpreted or justified, was recited at every morning service until it was eliminated by a new rendition in the Rabbinical Assembly–United Synagogue daily prayer book, which Adas Israel immediately adopted after its publication in 1985.

Adas Israel, like all traditional congregations in the nineteenth century, was a patriarchate. Women were respected but lacked the power to vote. It would take many decades before the influence of women was recognized in the chambers of management. At first, only husbands or single males were registered as members. Widows were granted life "membership" for a onetime payment of a $100 fee and were assigned seats in the balcony. Alternatively, a widow could remain a "contributory member" upon payment of $1 per month, which gave her a reserved seat in the balcony and cemetery privileges.[1] Mrs. Carry was retained in that category in 1891, but a year later, Mrs. Rasher was rejected. No explanation.

*From Proverbs 31:10–31, "The Woman of Valor," recited by husbands to their wives every Sabbath eve in traditional households.

Women expressed their commitment to the congregation by making generous gifts: a parochet for the ark, a mantle for the Torah, a reading desk, a house in the cemetery, the embellishment of the sanctuary, and even a set of spittoons, but most of all, women gave generously to sustain the religious school.

While a ladies' auxiliary, the forerunner of today's sisterhood, was not formally organized until 1897, a group of women formed a club to aid the congregation in 1878, promising to "contribute their mite monthly," offering $40 as their initial gift.[2] Their primary goal was to maintain the religious school which could not have functioned without their support.

President Simon Oppenheimer, in his 1901 report to the congregation stated:

> Another important factor of our well being . . . is the Ladies' Auxiliary Association, Through their efforts the members have been aroused to greater interest in the affairs of the congregation. The several social entertainments which it has given from time to time have been the pleasant means of bringing about a close acquaintanceship of our members. From its limited treasury it has donated the sum of $100.00 toward the improvement of our Vestry room. For their kindness . . . they are entitled to our highest appreciation and our heartfelt gratitude.[3]

The Ladies' Auxiliary, like the board of managers, conducted its business meetings in German. By 1900, Yiddish was spoken.[4] The Ladies' Auxiliary eventually became the Sisterhood of Adas Israel. While the date of its affiliation with the National Women's League, founded by Mathilda Schechter in 1915, is unclear, the local group played a significant role in the national program, with some of its members achieving national recognition. Mrs. Samuel Speigel, president of the National Women's League, addressed the sisterhood's first Chanukah Gift Donor Luncheon, held at the Jewish Community Center, on December 7, 1932. The admission of $5 provided funds for the religious school.

In addition to supporting the school, the sisterhood provided funds to equip the kitchen and, when Friday night services were instituted, for the Oneg Shabbat. In 1930, the sisterhood reinforced the motion to adopt uniform texts for the festivals by giving the congregation 100 United Synagogue festival prayer books.[5] In 1934, Mrs. Falk Harmel was asked to be the "Orthodox representative" to the Hadassah convention held in Washington.[6]

In 1940, the sisterhood offered to buy an electric refrigerator for the congregation if sufficient electric current could be provided. Shefferman's annual report in the same year acknowledged the sisterhood's contribution in attracting large numbers of enlisted men to attend wartime Friday evening services.

Despite the absence of equal recognition, women did not raise any objection to their secondary status until the late 1920s. The contentious issues which were yet to be faced included their right to representation on the board, the right to vote, the right to sit alongside men, and the right to participate in services. Each step provoked sincere opposition from the traditionalists, whose number included some women as well as many men.

### Voting Rights

Weary of being excluded from the decision-making process, the sisterhood, in 1927, requested representation on the board of managers. Recognizing the justice of the request, the board acquiesced. From that day onward, women played a more important role in shaping policy. The first women to serve on the board were appointed to represent the sisterhood.[7]

Achieving representation on the board as sisterhood appointees did not satisfy the women; they wanted to be represented as members in their own right, and they wanted to vote. A motion was submitted in 1954 giving members' wives the right to vote and to speak at regular meetings but without other benefits of membership. The motion was defeated.[8]

Later, the by-laws were broadened to state that "the wife of a member shall be entitled to vote in place of her husband at any meeting at which her husband was absent." Male centrality remained.

Sympathetic to the equality issue, Julius Wolpe invited Isabelle Gichner to attend a board meeting in 1957. She urged the board to amend the constitution to allow women to vote and to serve on committees. Under the existing regulations, only board members could serve on committees, but women could not be elected to the board; they could be board members only by appointment. Since only a few women could be appointed by the sisterhood or the PTA, "the Congregation is thus deprived of the services of many who might make a real contribution to the life of the Synagogue through its committees," Isabelle Gichner contended. After considerable discussion, the motion was tabled for "future consideration."[9]

Subsequently, Isabelle Gichner pointed to an anomaly in the constitution which held that "*any* person of the Hebrew faith and of good moral character shall be eligible to membership in this congregation."[10] The provision was only partially true, she argued, the privilege was limited to male Hebrews.

It was another eight years (1965) before the voting clause read, "the term 'right to vote' is defined as one vote for each individual," thus assuring equal rights for all members, including spouses. Hereinafter, women could be elected or appointed to the board and to congregational office. The first female elected officer was at the starting rung: assistant recording secretary.

### Separate Seating

Few practices were more rigidly fixed in Orthodox congregations than separate seating for men and women. In the early decades at Adas Israel women were relegated to the balcony just as they were originally at the Washington Hebrew Congregation.

Isaac Mayer Wise was the first to introduce family pews, during his tenure at Congregation Anshe Emeth in Albany, New York in 1850. Temple Emanu-El in New York City followed in 1854. The practice soon became the touchstone of the distinction between Reform and traditional congregations.

Within the Conservative Movement disputes over family pews often splintered congregations. Proponents demanded mixed seating as a test of Judaism's ability to meet modernity's challenge; opponents defended separate seating as a test of Judaism's ability to parry modernity's threat.

Rev. Samuel M. Isaacs of New York's Congregation Shaarey Tefilah declared, in 1875, that "the promiscuous seating of sexes during divine worship" violated German-Polish practice.[11] Orthodox authorities today insist that one can pray halachically only in synagogues that separate men from women either by a balcony or a *mechitza* (partition).

The removal of the traditional dividing partition to allow mixed seating symbolized a congregation's turning from Orthodoxy to Conservative Judaism; the issue was subject to bitter disputes and even legal action within the Conservative Movement. When called to testify on the subject as an authority on Jewish law, the seminary's professor of Talmud, Louis Ginzberg, stated that while the women's gallery was no older than the medieval period and was not essential to Judaism, the practice could not be lightly abandoned because people were accustomed to it. Ginzberg told a congregation in Baltimore in 1947 that if "continued separation of family units during services presents a great danger to its spiritual welfare, the minority ought to yield to the spiritual need of the majority." While admitting privately that separating women from men had become obsolete, he refused to issue a definitive ruling.[12] The United Synagogue, to which the congregations turned for advice, could not provide guidance, and Ginzberg would not.

At Adas Israel, separate seating remained a visible demarcation between it and the Washington Hebrew Congregation. Only in 1921 were there rumblings of discontent. "Mrs. Levy moved that arrangement be made for the ladies of the Congregation to sit together with the gentlemen, and that the seats be changed into family pews." The board moved to look into the advisability of recommending the change.[13] Because of intense objections by a sizable majority, the congregation rejected the resolution.

Slowly, and by 1927 more obviously, although without official sanction, a few women began to join their husbands on the ground floor of the sanctuary. Their audacity prompted a petition, signed by forty-eight members who objected "to this breach in the Orthodox traditions of our religion."[14] This was a move whose time had not yet come, but the desire to achieve it would not be stilled.

In his annual message for 1936, President Joseph Wilner, more far-sighted than most, urged the congregation to permit family seating. "There is a great agitation in our midst," he began. "The younger group of our membership advocate the doctrine of husbands and wives sitting side by side." To achieve family pews, he recommended doing away with reserved seats on the High Holy Days so that worshippers could take any available seat. "Men and women would thus be seated not only on the main floor but on the balcony as well."

> We are a Conservative congregation. Wherein do we differ from our other sister [Orthodox] congregations? We huddle the women up in the balcony with insufficient seating capacity. We are unfair to our members.[15]

Wilner's recommendation, heatedly debated, was assigned to a committee for "further study." The motion to adopt his recommendation was technically defeated. Again, the time was not ripe. Moreover, the issue was intermingled with another emotional issue: doing away with reserved seats.

Agitation favoring mixed or family seating could not be readily silenced. In 1939, Meyer Sawyer and Israel Mendelson again raised the issue, suggesting that the congregation appoint a committee of five to "consider the advisability of changing the seating arrangement in the Synagogue so that men and women may sit together on all occasions."[16]

The committee failed to render a completed report. A majority of the board stubbornly refused to consider the question. Only in the last years at 6th and I, a few more venturesome women, ignoring the glares of other worshippers, persisted in sitting with their husbands, first at Friday night services, anyway considered non-halachic by many, and later at Sabbath morning services, but never on the holidays. The question remained divisive, but there were other problems to face: World War II.

The decision to do away with separate seating would await the decision to relocate to Connecticut Avenue. As with other congregations, once the members decided to build a new house of worship, they were forced to consider questions of design: whether or not to have a separate women's gallery and whether or not an organ should be installed. Design usually follows function. In the new synagogue on Connecticut Avenue, while a balcony would be installed, it would not necessarily be a women's gallery.

At the dedication of the new building in 1951 and thereafter, men and women sat alongside each other; no objections were raised; neither was it officially authorized. A 1955 survey revealed that most Conservative congregations practiced mixed seating even though no rabbinic ruling had validated the family pew. "The tacit surrender of the segregation of the sexes in the synagogue was an example of *minhag* (custom) triumphing over accepted law. This was Minhag America," wrote Robert Gordis, faculty member at the seminary and past-president of the Rabbinical Assembly.[17]

**At Worship**

In 1939, the ritual committee proposed a mixed choir of male and female voices for the High Holy Day services only to have its recommendation overturned at a congregational meeting. In the Connecticut Avenue structure, the blended voices of the mixed choir of men and women were heard only on Friday nights; the choristers were hidden from view, protected by the walled-in choir loft. Girls were confirmed; boys became Bar Mitzvah. Women were assigned one aliya each year, a group aliya on Simchat Torah. They could not and did not ask to carry the Torah scroll in the festive procession.

Samuel Lebowitz reported that many members were disturbed by the presence of girls on the pulpit during the 1958 Passover services. Young people, including females, had been invited to be seated on the pulpit during the Torah service and Musaf. The board heatedly discussed the propriety of the practice but took no action. The discussion was a catharsis for the opponents of egalitarian treatment, who contented themselves with demanding that women attending services be required to wear a head covering.[18]

A proposal to permit girls to become Bat Mitzvah had been submitted by Israel Mendelson as early as 1940 only to be rejected as too radical. Not until 1962 would the congregation be ready to accept this innovation. It was not yet time to remove the invidious distinctions between male and female worshippers. Several more years went by before women could successfully challenge the sanctity of the remaining male bastions: the right to be called to the Torah, the right to be counted as a member of the minyan, and the right to lead the congregation in worship.[19]

Their lesser, secondary, or inferior, status did not prevent the women of the sisterhood from contributing handsomely to the welfare of the congregation and the success of its programs. They supported the school and the social activities, and played those roles which women traditionally assumed in the home. Their annual campaign for the Torah Fund provided scholarships to the seminary. They also attended services in greater proportions than their menfolk. Many sisterhood members held important leadership posts in the national and regional organizations of the Women's League, the association of Conservative sisterhoods.

~ *Rose Hornstein* *Reflections*

In the synagogue, the women sat apart from the men, in the gallery. Those in the front rows could look down and motion to their husbands. For those seated in the back rows, one of the children would have to go up or down the stairs with messages. Our family was friendly with Mr. and Mrs. Fred Gichner, leaders in the congregation. As a bride, Mrs. Gichner, or "Aunt Tina" as many referred to her, sat in a section of the women's gallery which gave her a clear view of the synagogue. Years later, she told me that my mother was kept busy at services on the holidays finding the places in the prayer book for the women around her.[20]

### The Men

In 1930, the board urged the president to appoint a committee to organize a brotherhood. The committee included Edward Rosenblum, Abe Shefferman, Joseph Blumenthal, Joseph Mendelson, and Oliver Atlas.[21] At its organizational meeting, on April 21, 1930 Joseph Stein was elected president. The group remained ineffectual; the congregation's other needs consumed the energies of the members.

As the membership of Adas Israel grew, the leaders, realizing that many new members remained uninvolved in synagogue activities, decided to try once again to activate a men's auxiliary. Joseph Mendelson was appointed to head the effort. At a meeting at his home on February 13, 1941, Irving Goldstein was elected president, and Hyman Berman, vice-president. Jerome Fischgrund, Joseph Mendelson, and Barney Krucoff were named members of the executive committee. All male members of the congregation and their sons above the age of twenty-one were urged to affiliate. Membership was at first restricted to members of the congregation but later opened to the community.

The first meeting of the group, on March 18, 1941, enrolled seventy-five men. "A long felt need in our Congregation was the organization of our men into a group which would interest itself in promoting and developing educational, religious, and welfare activities in our Synagogue," reported Abe Shefferman in his annual message of October 12, 1941.

The brotherhood accepted the obligation to raise funds for the seminary, raising $600 in 1942 and $1,100 in 1943. It offered a varied program of cultural and social activities. Distinguished personalities were invited to address its meetings, including Dr. Louis Finkelstein, the seminary's president, Rabbi Max D. Klein of Philadelphia, Carl Alpert, managing editor of the *New Palestine*, and Dr. Max Arzt of the seminary faculty. With the outbreak of the war the members undertook to sell war bonds.

David Hornstein succeeded Goldstein as the brotherhood's president in 1942. Despite the group's energetic efforts, it could not surmount the obstacle which claimed most of its potential membership: the draft. Two hundred and forty men from the congregation served in the armed forces during World War II. The brotherhood became dormant after Pearl Harbor and ceased to exist in 1944; there were not enough men available for a meeting.

Efforts to revive the group after the war were initiated by Joseph Mendelson in 1947.[22] The group that came into being at the home of Edward Ostrow changed its name to the Adas Israel Men's Club and elected Samuel Lebowitz president. Hobart Rowen, economics writer for the *Washington Post*, was named secretary. This time, the group would not yield. At a social meeting held at the Indian Springs Country Club in January 1948, 125 men became charter members of the revived group.

Affiliation with the United Synagogue–sponsored National Federation of Jewish Men's Clubs added national stature to the local group. The federation cited the Adas Israel group in successive years for its imaginative programs.

The members conducted Sabbath services annually, the first, on January 22, 1948. They sponsored a post–Yom Kippur dance in 1948 and, under Joseph Mendelson's leadership, initiated the Jewish Laymen's Institute in 1949, a weekend retreat at Camp Wohelo, in cooperation with Congregations Beth El and Chizuk Amunah of Baltimore. The institute invited prominent Jewish thinkers as speakers, among them Drs. Abraham Joshua Heschel, Mordecai Kaplan, Robert Gordis, and Harry Orlinsky. In 1954, the men's club introduced a scholarship program subsidizing the enrollment of religious-school students in Camp Ramah.

With Rabbi Metz and Cantor Barkin, the group conducted a model Passover Seder to instruct the uninitiated. Social meetings featured prominent sports figures and attracted many members. By the time the campaign to build the new synagogue began, the men's club had grown to a membership of 600.

The men's club became the politically active arm of the congregation, sponsoring a reception and dinner dance at the Mayflower Hotel on January 18, 1950, to honor the Jewish members of Congress, with Senator Herbert H. Lehman as the principal speaker. The event was repeated in 1953 with the roster of speakers including Vice President Richard Nixon, Speaker of the House Joseph W. Martin, Jr., President Pro Tempore of the Senate Styles H. Bridges, and Senator Herbert H. Lehman and Representative Emanuel Celler, both of New York.* Political figures were frequent speakers at men's club events. They included Congressman Daniel J. Flood, Senator Wayne Morse, and Jack Anderson, columnist.

With the move to Connecticut Avenue, the men's club members assumed responsibility for ushering at Sabbath and festival services, wearing striped trousers and morning coats at the morning service and tuxedos in the evening. Men's club volunteers also assisted in the annual UJA and Israel Bond campaigns.

The men's club soon became the dominant group in the Sea Board Region of the National Federation of Jewish Men's Clubs and later acquired considerable influence on the national organization's policies. Joseph Mendelson was elected national secretary of the federation in 1949. Three of the local presidents were elected national president: Philip Goldstein in 1961, Max Goldberg in 1957, and Jacob Lish in 1959.

Joseph Mendelson, who played an important role in the organization of the men's club, and his brother Israel, who was the first

*The members of Congress in attendance included Earl Chudoff of Pennsylvania, Samuel N. Friedel of Maryland, Sidney R. Yates of Illinois, and Isidore Dollinger, Sidney A. Fine, Louis B. Heller, Lester Holtzman, Jacob K. Javits, Arthur G. Klein, and Abraham J. Multer of New York. Yates, who for many years lived in the Quebec House adjacent to the synagogue, is today the dean of Jewish congressmen.

to propose allowing girls to become Bat Mitzvah, were born in Georgetown in the District. They graduated from George Washington University and received their legal training at Georgetown Law School. Israel's primary interest was education; he headed the school committee for many years. Joseph, who was elected president of the congregation in 1969, pioneered in the establishment of the Solomon Schechter Day School, which later became the Charles E. Smith Day School. He was actively involved in the Jewish Publication Society and the Jewish Theological Seminary, which recognized his leadership by awarding him its Community Service Award in 1966.

A cooperative relationship existed between the sisterhood and the men's club; they were not competitors. They sponsored joint meetings and joint projects. The auxiliary organizations, both of men and of women, provided an opportunity for social interchange on a more intimate level than could be provided by the congregation as a whole. They also could appeal to the unaffiliated and even to those who were affiliated with other congregations. Both groups provided a leadership pool for the congregation.

The sisterhood served the generations of nonworking women who were to be found at home. Its meetings, therefore, could take place at lunch or during the afternoons. The men's group met either in the evening or on Sunday mornings. As women began to enter the workplace, it became more difficult to attract them to monthly noon meetings. Sisterhood and men's club took to the co-sponsorship of Sunday morning meetings. The older generation of women together with the younger home-bound women continued to press for the separate meetings at the noon hour which they enjoyed as a social and intellectual experience.

# 25

## TRANSITIONS: THE PULPIT

Isaac Jacobson, who became president after the death of Joseph Wilner in 1953, was succeeded in 1956 by Fred Kogod, who also died in office after serving less than a year. He was succeeded by Julius Wolpe. Unlike many of his predecessors, he ruled and related to rabbis with gentleness and understanding; he presided over the tenures of Rabbis David Panitz, Bernard Mandelbaum, Morris Gordon, and, for one festival, Stanley Rabinowitz.

Wolpe's administration was the last to retain the custom of requiring officers to wear white tie and top hat on Kol Nidre eve. Formal morning attire, striped trousers and cutaway coat, remained the style for officers at festival and Sabbath morning services.*

Abe Shefferman's annual review of 1960 recognized that it had been a "very unusual and trying year."[1] Adas Israel entered the new decade with key positions vacant or deficient; Rabbi Panitz had left for Paterson in the summer of 1959; Rabbi Bernard Mussman, the director of education, had resigned earlier in the spring, and there was unhappiness with Cantor Burton Lowell Kaplan.

Rabbis who were members of the congregation were called upon to fill the pulpit, but no one was available to supervise the school. After a hurried search and a superficial inquiry, Dr. Irving Ashrey was engaged to succeed Mussman as director of education.

*The formal mode of dress was abolished during the presidency of Wolpe's son, Donald, in 1973; from then on dark suits would suffice.

In his report to the congregation, Shefferman expressed his gratitude to Rabbis Morris Gordon, Simon Noveck, and Bernard Mandelbaum for the "unstinted service rendered to the congregation" in the absence of a permanent rabbi; to the rabbinic search committee, whose members had "traveled long distances" in their quest for a successor; and to the president and the officers, "with whom I have consulted for advice and counsel."[2] In the absence of a resident rabbi, Abe Shefferman took charge of the congregation.

Although the year 1959–60 may have been administratively difficult, it was not wanting in effectiveness in other areas. Despite the turmoil in the pulpit, other departments, youth activities, the school, and the junior congregation thrived. The synagogue's young people were unaware of deficits and mortgages, and little concerned with the absence of a rabbi. The momentum of previous years continued to propel an enthusiastic youth program which produced a choral society, a dance group, an orchestra, a dramatics club, and a newspaper. Each Sabbath, 125 children attended junior congregation services, and there were more than 750 participants in the young people's High Holiday services. Obadiah Cohen, the charismatic youth leader, was the key to the success of a youth program so remarkable that it achieved national recognition.

The Wilner building, with its several classrooms and two auditoriums, had been completed in time to serve the growing needs of an expanded synagogue program and a membership which now reached 1,131 families. It also left the congregation with a mortgaged debt of $240,000.

With the pulpit vacant, the congregation drew upon local talent to conduct adult education classes, member rabbis to conduct services, and nationally recognized scholars to deliver sermons. The guest lecturers and preachers included Maurice Samuel and Rabbis Simon Greenberg, Israel Kazis, Abraham Joshua Heschel, Louis

Levitsky, and Bernard Mandelbaum. Philip Goldstein and Ida Hellman, active members, coordinated the lecture series and the adult education program.

At the end of his presidency, Julius Wolpe defined his unfinished agenda: to build a parking garage, to air-condition the sanctuary, to arrange transportation for children residing in Maryland, to begin an endowment fund, and to set up a retirement fund for the office staff.

**The Rabbinic Search**

Soon after Rabbi Panitz's departure, a pulpit committee consisting of Stanley Wiener, Leopold Freudberg, and Louis Grossberg, under the chairmanship of Abe Kay, began the search for a successor. The Rabbinical Assembly submitted the names of several rabbis whom the committee proceeded to interview. Each one was rejected; none could satisfy the committee members. As in a previous search, the congregation threatened to reject the Rabbinical Assembly's recommendations and make its own selection. Kay warned Wolfe Kelman, executive director of the Rabbinical Assembly, that "if the Seminary could not meet our needs . . . we may have to look for a rabbi elsewhere."[3]

Kay had a likely candidate in mind who had already been introduced to the congregation, Rabbi Bernard Mandelbaum, who served as assistant to Dr. Louis Finkelstein, the seminary's chancellor. Of all the guest lecturers who had occupied the vacant pulpit during the past year, Mandelbaum was the most popular. As chairman of the seminary campaign, Kay was often in contact with Mandelbaum and had worked with him in promoting seminary interests.

Kay urged the search committee to recommend Mandelbaum as Panitz's successor. The committee members agreed; they invited him to conduct services for the approaching High Holy Days, but specified that they would not propose his election to the congregation until after the holiday period. Mandelbaum, aware of their strategy, agreed to the proposal. "It would take some doing," he later admitted, "because it meant breaking a previous commitment I had in Toronto."[4] In preparation for what he had been assured would be his inevitable election, Mandelbaum agreed to request a release from his seminary post.

As planned, Mandelbaum officiated at the High Holy Day services of 1959 and later delivered a public lecture. The congregation was enthralled with his friendly manner and his distinctive approach to preaching: hasidic, midrashic, and rich in striking parables. His election to the pulpit was a foregone conclusion; it was all but official. At Mandelbaum's request, the board agreed to do away with the use of the organ once he became the rabbi.[5]

Neither Mandelbaum nor the congregation had considered two significant forces: Judith Mandelbaum, his wife, and Finkelstein, his superior at the seminary. In the midst of negotiations, Mandelbaum regretfully concluded that he could not accept the offer to come to Adas Israel. In retrospect, he insisted that the primary influence on his decision was his wife, Judith, who refused to consider "a situation which would require her to ride on the Sabbath."[6] Moreover, she hesitated to leave the religious atmosphere of Far Rockaway, Long Island.

Although Mandelbaum denies that Finkelstein influenced his decision, knowledgeable authorities attest that the chancellor did not want to lose his young associate. The seminary board, too, wanted to retain him because of his effectiveness as a fund-raiser. Finkelstein, it is said, convinced Mandelbaum that he was needed at the Seminary and that his talents would best be expressed in scholarship; other rabbis could be found to fill a synagogue's pulpit.

It is also alleged that Finkelstein promised, if Mandelbaum were to remain at the Seminary, he would recommend him as his successor when he retired and would immediately elevate him to the post of provost.

Whatever the circumstances, Mandelbaum found himself in a painful quandary. He could not bring himself to turn his back on his revered teacher and mentor, yet it would be no less difficult to withdraw his commitment to Abe Kay. At Finkelstein's behest, he met with Kay to assure him that Finkelstein himself would find a replacement for the Adas Israel pulpit.

Abe Kay's anger was not easily assuaged, but ultimately his sense of proportion prevailed over his disappointment. He joined Mandelbaum in placating the members of the search committee. The board suddenly discovered or was made to realize that, after all, Mandelbaum was "too Orthodox" for the congregation. Without Mandelbaum, they could still use the organ.

Soon thereafter, Abe Kay and others traveled to New York to meet with Finkelstein, to whom they expressed their distress at their inability to secure the rabbi of their choice. Whether justified or not, they held the seminary responsible for Mandelbaum's withdrawal. They extracted a promise from Finkelstein that he would help them find a suitable rabbi to fill the vacant pulpit. They would rely on his judgment.

~ *Stanley Rabinowitz* *Reflections*

It was a cold blustering day in March 1960, when Rabbi Bernard and Leah Raskas, Anita, my wife, and I drove to Rochester, Minnesota, to visit its art galleries. Rabbi Raskas served at the Temple of Aaron in St. Paul, and I at Congregation Adath Jeshurun in Minneapolis. I had no sooner opened the door of our hotel room when the phone rang. I was pleasantly surprised to hear the voice of Dr. Louis Finkelstein and stunned to learn the reason for his call. Even now, after over thirty-two years, I can recall the conversation virtually verbatim.

"How would you like to move to Washington, D.C.?" he began. I responded, "The thought of leaving Minneapolis has not occurred to me." He continued, "Adas Israel in Washington is looking for a rabbi; there is an opportunity for you there. I think you would do very well in Washington, but I am not asking you to go there if you want to remain in Minneapolis, where you are evidently quite content. I think you should give this opportunity serious thought before rejecting it. This congregation has been badly treated by rabbis they have interviewed. It's an important congregation. I must ask this of you. Should you respond to their invitation to visit Washington, and should they make you a reasonable proposal, you must accept it. Otherwise, if you are fixed in your resolve to remain in Minneapolis, please do not accept their invitation. Don't play around with them."

I told Dr. Finkelstein that I would discuss the proposal with my wife and would call him the following day when I returned to Minneapolis. I knew in my heart that I would accept the invitation. As contented as we were in Minneapolis, and no other congregation in any other city could have tempted us, working in the nation's capital was precisely the kind of rabbinate that I had wanted.

Though she was content in Minneapolis, Anita was not averse to pursuing the invitation. I phoned Dr. Finkelstein the following day, indicating to him that Anita and I would be receptive to an invitation to visit Washington. Within a few hours, Julius Wolpe, the president of the congregation, called to tell me that Dr. Finkelstein had recommended me as a candidate to fill their vacant pulpit and invited me to meet with their board in Washington on March 21. I agreed.

A few days later, I received a letter from Rabbi Albert I. Gordon of Newton, Massachusetts, the former executive head of the United Synagogue, who previously had been the rabbi of the congregation I was serving in Minneapolis. He wrote:

"I have received word that you have been or will be asked to consider Washington, D.C. Without invitation, I venture to offer a few comments:

"I know the place.

"To date, the leadership has been 'right wing'— difficult to get along with—a long tradition of this kind—also a longtime executive director who is 'in charge.'

"I understand that there is no study in the building for the rabbi. If this is true, does it not say something?

"Washington is terrific for national standing, and you would certainly do a good job as a spokesman but—there are sacrifices to be made."[7]

When I arrived in Washington, snowdrifts were slowly melting. First came the pulpit committee: Abe Kay, Leopold Freudberg, Louis Grossberg, and Stanley Wiener, who, as he told me, would succeed Wolpe as president. They raised the appropriate questions: Why did I want to leave Minneapolis? What was my philosophy of Judaism? What was my attitude on rituals and observances? They asked me to recap my career. All went well. After dinner at the home of Mr. and Mrs. Philip Goldstein, who were active in men's club, sisterhood, and adult education, I was brought to the synagogue, introduced to the board, and queried with a repetition of the previous questions and several new ones.

Two are fixed in my mind. One person wanted to know the role my wife would play in the congregation. The questioner was Dr. Benjamin Manchester. In response, I asked Manchester, "Doctor, does your wife write prescriptions?" The laughter that followed relieved the tension of the dialogue. I responded that my wife would participate in synagogue activities, but would encourage other women to take leadership roles.

The second question was one of philosophy. I was asked, "Rabbi, we have learned that you are a follower of Professor Mordecai Kaplan and his Reconstructionist teachings. In the opinion of many of us, these teachings have no place in our congregation. How can you reconcile your philosophy with our traditions?"

I conceded that I was indeed a "follower" of Dr. Kaplan, and a Reconstructionist, and stated further that it was the writings of Dr. Kaplan that had attracted me to the seminary. "As the rabbi of the congregation," I responded, "I would not think of imposing my will on any congregational practice; I would respect the traditions of the congregation. If there should be some practice that I believed needed adjustment or some procedure that I would like to introduce to the service, I would first submit it to your ritual committee, who, if it approved, would then seek the approval of the board. Therefore, the traditions of the congregation would be safeguarded; I would institute no departure from established procedure without the approval of this body."

This response may not have pleased everyone, so deep was the inexplicable antipathy to Dr. Kaplan in some quarters of the congregation, but it was not enough to disqualify me. The evening ended on pleasant note.

They were eager to hear me preach a sermon. I informed them that I would rather not deliver a "trial" sermon in Washington at this point, because a public lecture would embarrass me in Minneapolis. Instead, I invited them to send a delegation to Minneapolis on any Sabbath of their choice. After the meeting, Abe Kay took me aside to say, "You're my boy." On the following day, the president informed me that their delegation would attend services in Minneapolis on the Sabbath of April 1.

Unable to reach Dr. Finkelstein on my return to Minneapolis, I conveyed an account of my progress to Dr. Max Arzt, vice-chancellor of the seminary and my former employer in my first position after ordination. Dr. Arzt was torn between his concern for the seminary and his friendship with me. He balanced his considerations by writing to me:

"You seem to be fed up with the peace and tranquility [*menucha v'hanahala*] which is yours in Minneapolis. If you are willing to live dangerously and to redeem a congregation which has not learned to treat the rabbinate with the respect due to it—you should go.

"During its entire 90 years, the congregation in question had fine but timid souls in the pulpit. The absence of a rabbi's office is symbolic evidence of the abdication of authority. . . .

"Your announced platform of radical changes in the traditional policy of the congregation is an honest way of stating your position. Unfortunately, your liberalism attracts those who want Judaism to be anemic and who do not desire intensity in education or religious awareness. The rank and file membership of modest means already fear lest you convert the synagogue into a second rate reform Temple.

"Because I have such high regard for you and your sincerity, I believe your accepting the position will be a benefaction to the congregation. Whether they will be a benediction to you remains to be seen."[8]

Dr. Arzt had been privy to the anguish suffered by both Rabbi Metz and Rabbi Panitz; the latter's experience was still fresh in his mind.

Three "agents" appeared at Sabbath eve services in Minneapolis on Friday, April 1, 1960. Leo Freudberg, Louis Grossberg, and Stanley Wiener took seats in the rear of the sanctuary. While I could hardly introduce the visitors to our Minneapolis congregants, we spoke briefly at the Oneg Shabbat following the services and continued the conversation at our home. They would attend the Sabbath morning services as well.

A Bar Mitzvah had been scheduled for Sabbath morning. Congregants assumed the three strangers were guests of the Bar Mitzvah family, while the host family assumed they were native worshippers they did not recognize.

While the three expressed approval of my preaching, they were enthusiastic about the extent of the worshippers' responses to the cantor's chanting. The congregation chanted much of the service along with the cantor. If I could guarantee to transport this participation in worship to Adas Israel, my election to that pulpit would be assured, they said. I politely indicated that I was not yet sure that I wanted to be elected to their pulpit. Despite my promise to Dr. Finkelstein, the letters from Dr. Arzt and Rabbi Gordon had given me reason for pause. Nonetheless, I agreed to come to Washington again to deliver a sermon in their synagogue and this time to come with my wife.

On Monday, Julius Wolpe notified me by mail, "Our *meraglim* ['spies,' written in Hebrew] brought back glowing news.' He invited Anita and me to come to Washington for the two closing days of Passover, April 18 and 19, *al daat ha-kahal* ['with the approval of the congregation'] and scheduled a reception for the day of our arrival, April 17. We stayed at the home of Ceil and Louis Grossberg; we walked to the synagogue.

Seated on the pulpit alongside the president, Julius Wolpe, I found the experience a pleasant one and the service dignified but restrained. Congregational participation consisted of little more than the perfunctory "Amen."

With Passover's conclusion on April 19, we dined with the "spies" at the Indian Springs Country Club. While Anita joined the wives of the three, I retired with them to a private office to begin serious negotiations. It was a foregone conclusion that they were empowered to invite me to fill the open position, and I was mindful of my commitment to Dr. Finkelstein.

They invited me to become their rabbi and asked me to state my terms. I responded that their invitation honored me, and that I was inclined to accept it if they would meet several conditions: a five-year contract, a private study in the synagogue, the right to attend board meetings, their assistance in providing me with a home, and a salary commensurate with Washington's cost of living. With these conditions, I felt, I could offset the warning cautions of my friends.

Louis Grossberg responded that the conditions were acceptable to him except for my request for a five-year contract. He felt that a one-year agreement would be more appropriate as a beginning, but that he would be willing to recommend a three-year agreement, which, after evaluation, could be extended. I indicated that it would be irresponsible for me to leave a congregation where my tenure was unlimited for another where my security would be weighed in the balance each year. "What's the matter, Rabbi," asked Grossberg, "have you no confidence in yourself?" I, amazed at my own temerity but recalling Dr. Arzt's letter, responded. "I have confidence in myself. I have no confidence in your congregation." Leo Freudberg actually applauded. "The rabbi is right," he interjected. "We have no right to bring him here from a secure pulpit unless we can assure his security. Five years would be the minimum. I am confident that his tenure will be extended." Stanley Wiener agreed.

Before leaving Washington I consulted further with my friends, Rabbi Morris Gordon, who had been my immediate predecessor in Minneapolis, and Dr. Max Baer, director of the B'nai B'rith Youth Organization, whom I knew from my early days as an officer of the Aleph Zadik Aleph. Both extended encouraging guidance.

We returned to Minneapolis the following day. The three agents lost no time in making their recommendations to a special board meeting held that same night, Monday, April 20. The president notified me by phone that the board had unanimously elected me to be their "spiritual leader" for a period of five years at an annual compensation of $25,000. My other conditions were understood; I had been faithful to my commitment to Dr. Finkelstein. I prepared to face the painful ordeal of informing our Minneapolis congregation that I would be leaving as of July 31, 1960.

Anita and I returned to Washington on May 22 and 23 to look for a home and to address the annual meeting of the congregation. I met with the synagogue staff and was not displeased to learn that Cantor Burton Lowell Kaplan would be leaving; I looked forward to working with a cantor of my choice.

Rabbi Samuel Weiss, the "assistant cantor," was unhappy and threatened to leave. Weiss filled an important role in the congregation. He conducted daily services, taught Bar Mitzvah students, read the Torah, and chanted Shacharit on Sabbaths and holidays. He would be difficult to replace. I urged him to remain and promised to recommend that he be named assistant rabbi rather than assistant cantor. He seemed pleased.

During my visit, Mrs. Joseph Wilner, widow of the longtime president, passed away. I had an opportunity to attend the funeral and to meet her family.

At a regular meeting of the board following my election, and prior to my arrival, Stanley Wiener, by now the president, delicately raised the question of permitting me to attend their meetings. There was opposition to this departure from procedure. Max Baer and others who were aware that I had requested this right indicated that in their opinion there were "advantages in having the rabbi at all of our Board meetings."[9] Wiener stated that he would implement the practice without putting the issue to a vote. My request that Rabbi Weiss be named assistant rabbi rather than assistant cantor was debated but tabled. The change in title would be implemented without board action or approval.

Having selected a rabbi, the board lost no time in searching for a new cantor to replace Burton Lowell Kaplan. I had looked forward to the prospect of selecting a cantor who would share my approach to congregational worship and with whom I could enjoy a congenial relationship. Accordingly, I was deeply distressed to learn from Stanley Wiener, who had phoned me before my final departure from Minneapolis to tell me that the congregation had elected a cantor, Jacob Koenigsberg. Wiener was elated with the news he conveyed while I could barely conceal my disappointment; there was little that I could do except to ask for Koenigsberg's address.

Koenigsberg had been invited to conduct Sabbath services at Adas Israel in mid-June, and the eighteen board members who were present were enthusiastic about his voice and manner; he chanted in the traditional European style so beloved by them. Koenigsberg, who had been on the concert circuit for the previous two years, had told the committee that he was ready to return to the pulpit. He had received offers from congregations in Pittsburgh and Montreal. The board offered him a one-year contract for $15,000. He was to begin his tenure after the High Holy Days.

For the High Holy Days of 1960, Louis Shub was engaged as the guest cantor. The distinguished scholar Dr. Abraham Halkin would continue as preacher for the overflow services in the Kay Auditorium.

# 26

## THE SIXTIES

When I arrived in Washington, on August 1, 1960, I was relieved to learn that Koenigsberg, with his Adas Israel contract in hand, had accepted an offer from another congregation. Well aware that my definition of the ideal cantor differed from the preferences of the cantorial search committee headed by Louis Grossberg, I determined to take the initiative in finding a cantor lest the board make another selection without consulting me.

I called my colleague Rabbi Bernard Mandelbaum, who had already been helpful in persuading me to come to Adas Israel and in guiding me through the political shoals, for advice. "If you had accepted the post at Adas Israel," I asked, "whom would you have chosen as your cantor?" Without hesitation he named Raphael Edgar, one of the first graduates of the seminary's Cantorial School.

I was delighted with Mandelbaum's preference. Edgar's father had been the cantor in the Conservative synagogue in Des Moines, my hometown. I knew his parents well. Moreover, Edgar was the cantor in Brooklyn's Temple Shaarey Zedek, a Reform temple served by my uncle, Rabbi Max Schenk, and I had heard him officiate. Edgar possessed a glorious, rich baritone voice and a perfect sense of pitch; he was knowledgable in traditional *chazanut* as well as contemporary music. He was the perfect cantor, the image of what the contemporary cantor should be. He possessed a warm personality, was sensitive to the needs of children whom he delighted to train, and was an honorable person. His voice was trained; he chanted in a modern mode, without the false falsettos, extravagant trilling, and repetitive flights through the upper registers, the style so beloved by traditional European cantors and the members of Adas Israel's cantorial search committee.

To approach Edgar, I had to consider not only the preferences of the search committee but the feelings of my uncle, to whom I revealed my intentions. He observed that Edgar was wasting his talents in a Reform congregation whose members had little appreciation or even need for his skills, and felt he would find greater fulfillment in a more traditional setting. Without my prompting, my uncle told Edgar about my inquiry. Soon thereafter, on September 8, I received the following telegram from Edgar:

> Heard tonight that you inquired after my availability. My contract at Shaarey Zedek runs out in January and I am not planning on renewing it which means that I am looking around. Please contact me as to any further steps I should take in this matter.

I arranged for Edgar to come to Washington to officiate at a trial Sabbath service on October 21, after having secured the approval of the Cantorial Assembly, which for reasons best known to them had not included him among their recommendations. I was impressed by Edgar's chanting, and so were many others. Not everyone, however, shared my enthusiasm for him, least of all the cantorial search committee and its chairman, Louis Grossberg.

The search committee was determined to hear and interview other candidates. The committee was "looking for a big name with a glorious voice who will make the rafters quake,"[1] while I was seeking a cantor who could elicit the participation of the worshippers and would involve himself with me in the congregation's daily program. The difference of opinion represented a difference in approach to worship. I made my feelings known to the search committee but was not allowed to enter into their deliberations. While I was kept in the dark, they interviewed five candidates and were ready to announce their decision at the board meeting scheduled for January 9, 1961.

Shortly before the meeting, Edgar phoned to ascertain the progress of his candidacy. While he was eager to come to Washington, he said, he could not ignore the fact that other desirable congregations were pressing him for a response to their offers; he was not bluffing. After considering the situation and feeling that my goals were at risk, I called Edgar the following day to offer him the post on his terms: a one-year open-ended agreement with a first-year salary of $12,000 plus retirement benefits. It was a hazardous and irresponsible step for me to take; I realized that the board would regard my act as insolence, which it was, and that I might be jeopardizing not only my career but Edgar's. It was an impulsive act born of desperation.

On the fateful night of the board meeting, Louis Grossberg rose to deliver his report. He informed the board that after considering all of the candidates he was pleased to recommend the election of Cantor Louis Danto. Applause. I asked for the floor.

I told the board that it was common knowledge that there had been a lack of harmony between the rabbi and the cantor, and that on occasion the congregation had witnessed the open hostility between the two during and after Sabbath worship. This conflict, an embarrassment to the worshippers, flowed from legitimate differences in philosophies of worship, I explained. Danto and I represented divergent approaches to worship which would be difficult to bridge.

It was time that harmony prevailed in the Sabbath pulpit, I continued. "If the congregation wants to engage Cantor Danto, then, for the good of the congregation, I would submit my resignation to take effect at the end of the year. You will then be free to select a rabbi who will share Cantor Danto's style of worship. On the other hand, if you want to retain me as your Rabbi, you must allow me to select a cantor with whom I share the same approach to worship, an approach which places the emphasis in religious services in the pew rather than on the pulpit."

A dead silence came over the room; the shock of the unexpected paralyzed everyone. The board members were not accustomed to a rabbi's presence at their meetings, much less to his publicly challenging their leaders' decisions. After a moment's pause, Grossberg rose to respond. He solemnly declared, "We once had a president who was a dictator and now we have a rabbi who is a dictator."* Disdainfully ignoring my comments as though they deserved no response, he moved the election of Cantor Danto. His motion was loudly seconded. My heart sank; I felt that all was lost.

At that point Abe Kay asked for the floor. (May God preserve his memory.) "After much difficulty we have finally found a rabbi," he began. "I think he has made his first mistake, in which case he will suffer. While I disagree with him on this point, I feel that it is time we listened to our rabbi. We should give him a chance." Few people had the temerity to disagree with Abe Kay. I could have kissed him; I contented myself with thanking him. I lost no time in sending a confirming telegram to Edgar.

### The Next Crisis

Norman Gerstenfeld, the rabbi of the Washington Hebrew Congregation, proved helpful and hospitable to me and my wife. He introduced me to various civic and communal activities and their leaders. In addition, he suggested that our congregation join in the

*He was alluding, of course, to Simon Oppenheimer, who had served for thirty-six years, including the period when Grossberg's father had been sexton and he had been secretary.

United Thanksgiving Service sponsored by the churches formerly or presently located in the downtown area. The group included the oldest churches in Washington and was an association which had existed for many years.

The Washington Hebrew Congregation was the only synagogue among the participants, and Gerstenfeld felt, properly I thought, that Adas Israel belonged in the group. The locale of the service and the preacher rotated year by year. The service for 1960 would be held at the National City Christian Church on Thomas Circle. I eagerly accepted the invitation to participate in behalf of the congregation.

When I informed Stanley Wiener, now the president, of my decision, he exploded in anger. It was the same reaction that had followed my expression of preference for Cantor Edgar. "How dare you make such a commitment without the approval of the board?" he stormed. The congregation had previously conducted its own services on Thanksgiving morning, but they were poorly attended. I was crushed, but was forced to admit that Wiener's objections were justified. I was gradually learning my place in the scheme of things.

I realized that I had no choice but to withdraw my acceptance but hesitated to call Gerstenfeld. I revealed my disappointment and unhappiness to Isaac Franck, the director of the Jewish Community Council. Wiener, I said, was exercising a tight rein over my decisions. He expected me to submit my sermon subjects and even my nonliturgical responsive readings for his approval prior to each Sabbath. He also wanted an advance copy of the texts of my eulogies for the few funerals at which I had officiated.

Franck had been the executive director of the Jewish Community Council since 1948 and had turned it into an assertive, influential body. He also played an active role in Adas Israel. Knowledgeable in Hebrew, Bible, Talmud, and contemporary philosophy, he could easily bridge the philosophical gap between rabbi and lay leader.

Annoyed by Wiener's reaction to the Thanksgiving invitation as much he was shocked by his close supervision over me, Franck advised me to do nothing more until he had spoken to Wiener. Within a few days, Wiener entered my office in an expansively warm manner, with a broad smile on his face, to say that after thinking about the matter, he could see nothing wrong in our joining the downtown Thanksgiving group. And so it was. Edgar and I both participated in the Thanksgiving service, as did an exceptionally large contingent of our members. We wore skullcaps in the church, as did most of the Jewish worshippers.

**Presidential Succession**

One bright morning after that Thanksgiving Day, Wiener came into my study to inform me that Abe Shefferman, the longtime executive director, was retiring. That was not all. Shefferman's successor would be Wiener. The good wishes which I reflexively extended were mumbled. My fears for my future intensified. Wiener had ruled the congregation and me with the heavy-handed pattern established by his predecessors. I feared his control would be even heavier now that he was to be the resident executive director and in daily contact with me. There was little that I could do. The exchange of offices had been previously agreed upon in private discussion and was ratified by the board without opposition on December 8, 1960.

Shefferman had served the congregation in his executive capacity for twenty-four years; his wife, Belle, had been office manager for twenty-one years. Both received an appropriate pension upon their retirement, which would take effect February 1, 1961.

The vice-president, Joseph Blumenthal, was now the president. Blumenthal, whose father had been the longtime treasurer, was as genial as he was stalwart. I confided my fears to him; I feared Wiener's heavy-handed supervision. Blumenthal reassured me that once he was in control, he would attend all staff meetings and was prepared to address any disagreements to make sure the staff worked harmoniously. I suggested that I would prepare a "position analysis" to define the areas of responsibility for each person on the staff, and he agreed. The formal analysis, once distributed, brought about a transformation of relationships.

The exchange of offices proved to be fortunate. Blumenthal turned out to be an effective president. His memory embraced the earliest days of the congregation's first synagogue on 6th and G Streets, where he had been Bar Mitzvah. He respected the congregation's traditions but at the same time accepted the need to grapple with the challenge of the present.

Wiener proved to be far easier to work with as executive director than as president. In the presidency he had followed the strong-handed example set by Simon Oppenheimer and his tight control of the rabbi. As executive director, he was willing to share control of the congregational program with me. My concern that he would confuse the roles of executive director and president were soon eased. A warm personal friendship developed between us which prevailed throughout his career and his retirement. Until his death, we remained good friends.

### Advice and Consent

The services and the educational system invited corrective attention. High Holy Day prayers were interrupted by two fund-raising appeals, with pledges openly announced, one on the second day of Rosh Hashanah for the purchase of Israel bonds, and another on Kol Nidre eve, for the benefit of the synagogue. In addition, a lengthy recitation of the names of the deceased disrupted the Yizkor service on Yom Kippur day. As a result, services were protracted. On Yom Kippur, an exodus began following Yizkor; a sparse congregation remained for the end of the service. Except for Kol Nidre, many of the sanctuary worshippers were strangers. I learned that many members gave their reserved tickets to friends and employees, while they themselves retired to mountain resorts or their summer homes.

Despite the impressive enrollment statistics, chaos prevailed in the school. Children were sometimes confirmed at age twelve. Confirmation took place on the Sunday following Shavuot. One child, in 1960, observed his Bar Mitzvah on Saturday and his confirmation on the following Sunday.

Attendance at Friday night services consisted largely of mourners and those reciting the Kaddish in observance of Yahrzeit. Attendance on Saturday mornings was mostly made up of Bar Mitzvah families; there were usually two and sometimes three. Most of the Bar Mitzvah boys were the privately trained children of nonmembers; they displayed minimal skills. Except for the participation of the elders, few responded to the prayers. There were endless aliyot to the Torah, especially when multiple families laid claim to honors. Services ended as late as 1:00 p.m. with a shrinking congregation remaining for the benediction.

The congregation used the edition of the Bible edited by Alexander Harkavy and published by the venerable Hebrew Publishing Company. Its pagination was random; only the initiated could find the page for the assigned text even when it was publicly announced. Its use, or lack of it, made the Torah-reading period seem interminable. One Sabbath morning, exasperated by my inability to announce the pages for the multiple Torah readings with any clarity, I publicly urged the introduction of a more suitable edition of the Bible, the one edited by Chief Rabbi Joseph Hertz and published by the Soncino Press in London. Before the end of the day, without further prompting, several generous worshippers committed themselves to donating sufficient funds for the immediate purchase of a suitable number of Bibles.

At the next board meeting, a member challenged my right to have done away with the familiar Harkavy Bible without seeking prior permission. "What other innovations do you intend to introduce?" he challenged. Apologetically, I again promised that I would follow all established procedures and introduce no changes in ritual or procedure without the prior approval of the appropriate committee and its ratification by the board. To further reassure the board members, I told them of my intention to conduct a series of meetings to canvass the opinions of the entire membership and, if possible, elicit their evaluation of the congregation's programs and suggestions for possible improvements. The board gave the proposal its endorsement.

A series of gatherings were conducted to which fifty couples were invited each week. With a distributed questionnaire, the participants were invited to appraise the congregation's programs. If a couple failed to respond to an invitation, they were pressed to attend the following week. By this means, the survey reached virtually every member of the congregation over a six-month period. I become acquainted with the members and learned their names; I heard their views and, what was also important, they learned mine.

Over 1,500 people attended the weekly meetings out of a membership of 1,100 families. The questionnaire asked each participant to indicate the extent of his or her religious observance and to evaluate the congregation's programs. Those who failed to attend were canvassed by mail.

The survey, tabulated, revealed that two-thirds of the responding members observed the dietary laws in their homes, a larger number blessed the Sabbath eve candles, a lesser number recited the Kiddush. An overwhelming majority observed the regulations of Passover, and almost everyone kindled and blessed the Chanukah candles. Few recited the grace after meals, and only a small minority put on tefillin daily.

As for synagogue attendance, 18 percent stated that they attended the Friday night service regularly, 10 percent never, 42 percent once in a while, and 30 percent often; 14 percent attended the earlier sundown service from time to time. A larger number, 22 percent, stated that they never attended Sabbath morning services, 38 percent attended once in a while, and 12 percent attended regularly. The membership was divided in equal thirds between those who could follow the Hebrew service readily, fairly well, and not at all, but 88 percent felt that the amounts of English and Hebrew in the services were just right. Most respondents, 96 percent, found the prayers meaningful.

Almost everyone drove to the synagogue on Sabbaths. A small minority refrained from driving on the High Holy Days. Few used the synagogue library; most felt that the dues were "just about right," and 34 percent felt they were too high. On the equality issue, 40 percent opposed calling women to the Torah, 22 percent were in favor, while 38 percent abstained. Doing away with reserved seats on the Holy Days was opposed by 51 percent, while 30 percent favored their abolition. A majority opposed conducting High Holy Day services in a hall that could accommodate the entire membership in one place. A majority favored air-conditioning the sanctuary. A large majority felt that "there was not enough congregational singing."

Conflicting trends were indicated in preferences for sermon topics and in how much importance was assigned to diverse rabbinic duties. To the question "How many hours per week [should the rabbi spend] in listed areas?" the responses exceeded the number of hours in a week.

The tabulations were reported to the congregation at a meeting in November 1962. On the basis of the responses I was able to offer several proposals including those I had intended to suggest all along.

Several proposals were subsequently implemented; others would remain for the future. Together they were:

1. To air-condition the sanctuary.

2. To refurbish the sanctuary.

3. To construct a parking garage.

4. To acquire a new cemetery site.

5. To acquire or rent a summer camp for retreats and summer encampments to supplement the Hebrew school.

6. To establish a branch school in Maryland.

7. To form home and downtown study groups.

8. To offer scholarships for postconfirmation pilgrimages to Israel.

9. To place an information rack in the foyer for the free distribution of educational materials.

10. To prepare manuals for life-cycle events: birth and naming, marriage, Bar Mitzvah, death.

11. To prepare a booklet to explain our services to visitors and especially to non-Jews.

12. To publish a hymnal to encourage participation in services.

13. To shift the Israel Bond appeal from Rosh Hashanah morning to Kol Nidre eve.

14. To publish the names of the deceased in a memorial booklet rather than read them at Yizkor on Yom Kippur.

15. To allow the use of the organ on Rosh Hashanah and Yom Kippur.

16. To allow girls to be Bat Mitzvah on Saturday mornings.

**Implementation**

As a result of the discussions at these meetings it was easier to obtain approval for several innovations. In the school, Confirmation would be limited to high school tenth-graders and would take place on the first day of Shavuot. Minimum requirements would be established for Bar Mitzvah; there would be no more recitations of the Haftarah by transliteration. Nonmember, privately trained Bar Mitzvahs would be restricted and eventually eliminated. We would encourage Camp Ramah attendance by an extensive scholarship program.

The number of aliyot on Sabbaths would be limited to seven. To facilitate attendance at daily evening services, it was agreed to schedule them for 5:30 p.m. summer and winter, except for Saturday nights, when the time of services would be governed by the setting sun. In the summer, a selected psalm would be recited in place of the nighttime Maariv; in the winter, a selected psalm would substitute for the afternoon Mincha. It was felt that dependability of hour and brevity of service would attract a stable attendance.[2] Tape-recording of services and sermons would be permitted.

For the High Holy Days of 1961, the board agreed to move the appeal for the purchase of bonds for the State of Israel from Rosh Hashanah to Kol Nidre eve, and readily accepted the substitution of a printed booklet containing the Yizkor service for Yom Kippur and a list of the congregation's deceased, rather than reading the names aloud, as had been the practice for many years. The board also agreed to replace the prayer book's Eleh Ezkerah, describing the murder of ten sages during the Roman persecutions in the year 135, with contemporary readings reflecting the Nazi Holocaust.

At the same time, it was agreed to print a Sabbath "Order of Service" to eliminate both page announcements and the lengthy reading of the names of the deceased on their Yahrzeits. In recognition of the diversity in the congregation, it was decided to conduct two services on Purim. One would be the traditional service, and the other, in a contemporary style. This pattern of dual services was later applied to other festivals as well, including Rosh Hashanah.[3] When an alternative adapted service for the second day of Rosh Hashanah, prepared by Cantor Martin Robbins with instrumental accompaniment arranged by Cantor Edgar, was introduced, both the sanctuary and the auxiliary service attracted capacity congregations. In prior years, attendance had diminished drastically on the second day.

Opposition to expanding the role of women at services yielded slowly, with resistance challenging every step. There were those who felt duty-bound to uphold the tradition which forbade the participation of women in the Torah service. The ritual committee had been willing to permit Bat Mitzvah for girls if the ceremony were on Friday night. Somehow, the late Friday night services were regarded as nonhalachic; the congregation became more Orthodox during the daytime. Abe Kay was instrumental in persuading the board that girls should be allowed to be Bat Mitzvah on the same basis as boys (he was concerned for his granddaughters). The authorization to permit Bat Mitzvah on Saturday morning passed despite opposition.[4]

Jennifer Berlowe, daughter of Grace and Ralph Berlowe, and granddaughter of Rose and Leo Freudberg, was the first girl to be called to the Torah as a Bat Mitzvah, in February 1962. Jennifer, now married and a mother, lives in Israel, where her mother also resides. Permitting Bat Mitzvah gave way to corollary questions which led to further disputes: Could a girl who had been Bat Mitzvah in another congregation be given an aliyah in our congregation? Further, could Jennifer Berlowe be permitted an aliyah on any subsequent Sabbath? The ritual committee insisted that allowing Bat Mitzvah for Jennifer set no precedent for routine aliyot for girls or women. It would take many more meetings over several more years to resolve these questions. Some considered it sufficient to grant women the right to receive a single group aliyah on Simchat Torah. Only in 1965 did the board agree that "girls who have been Bat Mitzvah in Adas Israel be permitted an aliyah to the Torah on any sabbath."[5]

Then came the question of whether to allow the mother of a Bar Mitzvah or Bat Mitzvah or of a child being named, or a bride prior to her marriage, or a wife celebrating an anniversary to ascend the pulpit for a blessing. Samuel Lebowitz, who to his credit later became a champion of women's rights, opposed allowing a female on the pulpit under any circumstances. "If we eliminate segregated seating are we obligated to eliminate other aspects of the way of life in a synagogue," he asked. After much and sometimes bitter discussion, it was agreed that women should be allowed on the pulpit on appropriate occasions.[6]

Eventually the congregation would agree to broaden women's rights, to remove all limitations, and even to include women in the count for a minyan.

Another source of controversy was the treatment of Christians who attended Sabbath services either as guests or as grandparents of a Bar or Bat Mitzvah. The ushers persisted in pressing skullcaps and talliot on them, which led to occasional embarrassment. I turned to the Law Committee of the Rabbinical Assembly for guidance. Unfortunately, Rabbi Isaac Klein, who had been asked to write a responsum on the question, had taken ill, so that I was left to my own devices. I found a statement by a sixteenth-century authority, Rabbi Solomon Luria, in an article by Rabbi Theodore Friedman, the president of the Rabbinical Assembly, which included the lenient opinion that there is no halachic basis for requiring head-coverings during prayer. Luria concluded, "But what can

I do if the people consider it prohibited [to be with uncovered head]? I am not permitted to be lenient in this matter."

Writing my own halachic responsum, I suggested that we should not impose our pattern on others. "There is no justification for asking a Christian to don a tallit. The principle "when in Rome do as as the Romans do" does not apply to religious practices. A skullcap may be offered to every worshipper, but should not be imposed on him if the guest declines," I concluded. The subject was laid to rest only temporarily. It would come up again whenever we conducted joint services with the Washington Hebrew Congregation or with Christian churches.[7]

Even more contentious because it was so sensitive was the pattern of not allowing funerals in the synagogue except for "important persons." The established pattern was to grant a request for a funeral service in the sanctuary only after it had been approved by a majority of the board of managers. The board's approval had to be solicited by phone, and the bereaved family had to wait for the results of the vote before they could make funeral arrangements. For years, families had hesitated to request this honor for their deceased because they did not want to suffer the pain of rejection or delay. Rejection would inevitably be followed by resentment. It was a cruel procedure to which I bitterly objected.

I discovered that a death in a family belonging the "inner circle" usually merited an honorable sanctuary funeral without any prefuneral ballot, while a death beyond the ruling group required the painful polling; the decision was in the hands of the executive director. In one case, with scarcely a nod to the voting procedure, the "authorities" had allowed a sanctuary funeral for someone who was married to a non-Jew without her conversion and who was only superficially involved in the congregation but was a social friend of the leaders. I resolved to put an end to this practice.

Shortly thereafter, the teenage daughter of members was killed in an auto accident. Her parents, understandably, were disconsolate. I knew the child well and felt their pain. Without thinking of the prevailing dispute, I told the parents, "Your daughter was an innocent child. She deserves to have her funeral in the sanctuary." Somehow, the parents were comforted by the suggestion. And so it was. The explosive outrage of the officers could be expected. I had robbed them of their authority. It took a special meeting of the board for me to state my position; I was upheld, but only in this case. No precedent was to be assumed.

Eventually, we were to allow sanctuary funerals for all deceased members without distinction or ballot, to combat the excesses practiced by the funeral directors. Bereaved families were pressed to outdo one another in the selection of expensive mahogany caskets which were promoted as "kosher" because they were made without nails, jointed by dowels and glue, and decorated with a Magen David on the cover.

I first established that halacha did not prohibit a coffin with nails and then persuaded the board to accept a trade-off. Funerals would be allowed in the sanctuary for all bereaved member families who accepted our selection of a standard simple coffin and would follow traditional mourning procedures. The dispute was an opportunity for education in the Jewish customs of mourning. I prepared a pamphlet entitled *A Time to Mourn* to be given to each bereaved family. The dispute ended on a positive note.[8]

An art committee was formed to supervise the artistic embellishment of the synagogue, arrange for art exhibits, and organize art appreciation classes for adults. Anita Rabinowitz accepted its chairmanship and sponsored several exciting art exhibits. With profits from the sale of paintings, the committee purchased a valuable Chagall lithograph "Joseph and his Brothers." The art instructor, Mykolo Schramchenko, a Hungarian Christian Holocaust survivor, faithfully conducted courses for several years until his death.

### The Pulpit

With Cantor Edgar's arrival, we lost little time in striving to put some life into the Sabbath service, which we both considered dull and lifeless. The congregation had been stifled; they had grown accustomed to listening to the rendition of the service rather than to participating in it.

After the board heard a recording of the Sabbath morning service of my former Minneapolis congregation led by Cantor Morris Amsel, there was no resistance to introducing the *Hoche Kedusha*, i.e., to eliminating the cantor's repetition of the Amidah and arranging the cantorial portion of its rendition for congregational recitation.[9]

Edgar transcribed the musical responses for the Sabbath Musaf service and the congregational hymns, drawing upon the compositions of Israel Goldfarb, Emanuel Barkin, and traditional sources to publish a congregational hymnal. Month after month, he taught and rehearsed the responses at sisterhood and men's club meetings. Before long, members of the auxiliaries became so familiar with the Sabbath worship responses that they constituted a veritable massed choir. Their participation transformed the spirit of the Sabbath service.

The first edition of the hymnal, endowed by Dianne and Norman Bernstein, was published in 1962. A revised and expanded edition was printed in 1966. A third and expanded edition would come later. The mode of worship with its emphasis on spirited congregational participation remains the pattern today.

Edgar suffered his disappointments. He needed a tenor to round out his choir. When he could not find a Jewish tenor, he asked for permission to employ a non-Jewish singer. The board rejected his request.[10] Eventually, the addition of non-Jews to the choir was allowed. Halachic sources stated that it was permissible to include non-Jews in a synagogue choir because the choir served only to embellish the services and was not a substitute for the required *ba'al tefillah,* the leader of the prayers.

While my Sabbath morning sermons drew upon the weekly biblical texts and the midrashim that flowed from them, my sermons on Friday night stressed current political issues, Jewish sociology, and concerns about Israel. Not everyone was pleased with this allocation of subjects. Some complained that there were enough problems in the outside world; they came to the synagogue to get away from them. They wanted repose and spiritual inspiration when they attended services, not more agitation about contemporary problems. Nonetheless, the outpouring of attendance for Friday services when the sermon addressed current issues and the discussion of the topic at the Oneg Shabbat outweighed the occasional expressions of disapproval.*

Guest speakers invited to lecture in the early sixties included prominent thinkers such as Abraham Joshua Heschel, Everett Gendler, Cecil Roth, Harry Orlinksky, Drew Pearson, Ira Eisenstein, Secretary of Health and Urban Affairs Wilber Cohen, Archbishop Philip H. Hannan of the Washington archdiocese, and historian Howard Sachar. Mordecai M. Kaplan delivered a brilliant series of six weekly lectures which attracted community-wide audiences. Kaplan in the flesh overcame the suspicion of Kaplan in the abstract. It was not I but the men's club that prompted the selection of Kaplan for this series. I remembered my first encounter with the board.

*A High Holy Day–sized congregation attended my Friday night presentation and discussion of Roth's *Portnoy's Complaint*.

Another innovation in the pulpit, one which drew widespread approval despite initial doubts about its appropriateness, was the enactment of significant dramas at Friday night services. The first presentation, in 1963, was Archibald MacLeish's *J.B.*, which was followed by several sermons on the challenge of the existence of evil. The widespread acceptance of this approach prompted presentations of other dramas whose themes lent themselves to sermons and discussions. Dramas were selected because they addressed ethical issues; among them were *Death of a Salesman* by Arthur Miller, *The Deputy* by Rolf Hochhuth, which raised objections from those who felt that it unfairly targeted papal complicity in the Holocaust, and *The Visit* by Frederick Durenmatt, which suggested that most people will abandon their conscience for a price. Its presentation, one month following the Yom Kippur War in 1973, had chilling implications.

A series of lectures which attracted widespread interest, presented as part of the adult education program, was based on James Michener's *The Source*, with each stage of the novel's progression through Jewish history forming the basis for a lecture by an expert on the specific era. In a subsequent year, George Washington University joined the synagogue in sponsoring classes offering college credit.

Early in 1967, a press photographer appeared at the Sabbath morning service, with my permission, to photograph a Bar Mitzvah service, posting himself in the balcony, out of sight of the worshippers. His photo essay appeared in the *Sunday Star* under the heading, "A Jewish Boy Comes of Age." I justified granting permission to the photographer on the grounds that the article would enhance the image of the Jew and our synagogue; it had not been requested by the Bar Mitzvah family, nor was it designed to serve their ego. My position was not widely accepted.[11] The congregation was not willing to allow a photographer at Sabbath services.

I made an attempt to bring college students closer to the synagogue by writing monthly letters to members' children on campus. They were given subscriptions to the *Jewish Week* and guest subscriptions to the Jewish Publication Society underwritten by Mr. and Mrs. Joseph Mendelson. Reunions, dances, and a college homecoming service and discussions were held during the winter break.

It is difficult to evaluate the success of a program targeted at college students away from home. In 1965, I reported that "over 1200 of our college young men and women are on our mailing list. In many cases, the initial antagonism to any attempt to communicate with them, the expression of the desire to be independent of home influences, has given way to a more congenial acceptance."

### The Shem Tov Award

With the death of Abe Kay in 1963, the board appointed a committee to suggest an appropriate memorial for one who had been a leader in the community and the congregation, and in supporting Israel and the seminary. The committee proposed an award which would portray Kay as a role model for others to emulate. The Shem Tov Award, as it was named, was to be given annually to the member of the congregation whose communal and civic activities reflected honor upon the congregation. The first year's presentation would be to Abe Kay posthumously.

As vehicle for the awards, Dianne and Norman Bernstein endowed a sculptured menorah, the work of Milton Hebald of Rome, which was to be placed in the entrance lobby of the synagogue. The name of each year's recipient was to be affixed to the pedestal of the menorah. A small-scale replica would be awarded to each recipient.[12]

In succeeding years, the award recognized Isador S. Turover in 1966, Joseph Andelman in 1967, Leopold V. Freudberg in 1968, and

Mrs. Fred Gichner in 1969. Each of the recipients had indeed played significant roles in the community, the synagogue, and the Conservative Movement.*

The basis for designations became a source of dispute between those who wanted the award to recognize members who made distinguished contributions to the civic and broader Jewish community and those who felt it should be based on service to the congregation itself. Differences of opinion about the basis of the award reflected differing attitudes on the place of the synagogue in the community.

### John F. Kennedy

The Thanksgiving services which rotated among the former downtown congregations were held in Adas Israel in 1961. It was the first joint interfaith service held in the synagogue. The ark doors remained closed, and the ritual committee agreed that wearing skullcaps would be optional, as was the protocol when services were held in a church or a Reform temple. The sermon was delivered by the Catholic archbishop, Cardinal O'Boyle, another first not only for Adas Israel but for the joint service. In 1962, the services were held in the Calvary Baptist Church, with Dr. George Davis of the National City Christian Church delivering the sermon. In 1963, services were scheduled for the Mount Vernon Methodist Church; I was to deliver the sermon. Mindful of the significance of the occasion, I carefully prepared my sermon well in advance of the day.

Friday, November 22, 1963, remains a day fixed in memory. Each person then alive will recall forever when he or she heard the news of the assassination of President John F. Kennedy. Time has not dimmed the traumatic shock of the announcement of his death.

* A complete listing will be found in the appendix.

Anita and I were landing at Milwaukee's airport when the captain of the airliner announced the news over the loudspeaker. We had flown to Milwaukee because I was slated to address the annual meeting of the board of the Aleph Zadik Aleph of B'nai B'rith. I was also to deliver the sermon at Sabbath services that night. In the aftermath of the assassination, the AZA board meeting was canceled. Joseph Blumenthal phoned, urging me to return immediately to Washington for memorial services scheduled for Sunday. This proved to be impossible because poor weather conditions in Milwaukee had closed down the airport.

I adjusted my sermon that night to fit the mood and the occasion, and returned to Washington on Sunday too late to participate in the memorial service. It was a week of mourning over the tragic death of the young President. It was also the week of Thanksgiving.

Late Wednesday night, the evening before the Thanksgiving service, Rabbi Norman Gerstenfeld called me at home to tell me that the newly inaugurated President, Lyndon Johnson, and his family would be attending the morning Thanksgiving service. I shall remain forever grateful for his warning. I spent much of the night preparing a new sermon which I felt would be more appropriate for the new situation.

The sermon, entitled "Out of Evil," expressed the idea that evil can be redeemed, that every evil situation contains within it the opportunity to extract from it a blessing.* The thought was based on the observation of Rabbi Akiba, "We should thank God for the evil in life just as we express gratitude for its good."[13]

*The sermon was included in a commemorative volume, *That Day with God: The Religious Expression of All Faiths Following the Death of President Kennedy*, edited by William M. Fine (New York: McGraw-Hill, 1965).

The President and his family were indeed present. When I returned home following the services, Stanley Wiener phoned to tell me that Lady Bird Johnson had called Adas Israel and he had encouraged her to call me at home. Had he not warned me, I would have surely felt that the female caller, with her striking southern accent, was a mimic playing a joke on me. Mrs. Johnson, after commending me on my sermon, stated that she would like to have a copy. Flattered, I responded that I would be very happy to deliver it to her. "When?" she asked. "Tomorrow," I responded. She seemed disappointed.

When I heard the President's Thanksgiving address televised that night I realized that he was using a theme similar to my sermon that morning. I felt that I understood the reason for the President's wanting my text. Yet the written text did not appear to be all that important; he had paraphrased the ideas with clarity.

As promised, the following morning I delivered my sermon text, retyped on clean vellum, to the Johnson residence. Linda Baines Johnson, the elder daughter, politely received me at the door.

The following month I received a letter from Assistant Secretary of State Harlan Cleveland, which read in part,

> On Thanksgiving Day, I happened to be working in the office and got an urgent call from one of President Johnson's assistants. The President was at his home, not yet having moved into the White House, and wanted the context of the quotation you used in your Thanksgiving sermon that morning.
>
> I am flattered that you thought some words of mine were worth repeating at all, let alone in a sermon to the President of the United States.[14]

I had quoted from an article in which Cleveland had said that he received a good deal of mail from people who could be reasonably polite at cocktail parties but thought nothing of writing vilifying letters, the implication being that we kill with words. The quotation hardly seemed to justify an inquiry from the President.

Over a month later, I received a letter from Abe Sirkin, a member of the congregation who was posted to the U.S. Agency for International Development in Madras, India. He enclosed a press release dated December 31, 1963 containing the text of an address which President Johnson had delivered at the dedication of the Agudas Achim Synagogue in Austin, Texas. It began as follows:

> On Thanksgiving Day, Mrs. Johnson and I attended a worship service in Washington. The sermon then was delivered by Rabbi Stanley Rabinowitz. The Rabbi told this story, which I have remembered so vividly ever since Thanksgiving Day. He said that once in the past, birds had no wings. They could not fly. They walked in the dust, earthbound. Then one day God threw wings at their feet and commanded them to carry the wings. At first this seemed very difficult. The burden was heavy. But in obedience to God's will, they held the wings closely to their sides and the wings soon grew to their bodies. At last, what they once thought were hampering weights lifted them unto the heights, and enabled them to soar on to the very gates of heaven. Out of evil . . . blessings can come.

The "story" can be found in the writings of Gustave Schiller, a German-Jewish writer. The President wanted to use it in his Thanksgiving address but couldn't bring himself to ask me for it.

President Johnson easily won reelection in November 1968. He arranged for an interfaith service to take place at his church, the National City Christian Church, the morning of his inauguration on January 20, 1969. His minister, George Davis, conducted the services. Johnson invited me to deliver one of the prayers.

### The Facilities

Since the sanctuary was not air-conditioned, summer and fall heat made holiday worship at Adas Israel uncomfortable. When the new structure was being planned, the building committee had felt that it was hardly worthwhile to expend funds for air-conditioning "which would be needed only on 2 or 3 days a year." Julius Wolpe, unhappy with the decision, continued to press for its installation, but to no avail. Air-conditioning was finally installed in 1963 thanks to the instigation and leadership of Robert Rothstein.

By 1965, the peak year of the congregation's membership and activity, many felt that the synagogue's facilities had become inadequate. When an offer was received to purchase the synagogue and its grounds for $45 per square foot, contingent upon a zoning change to permit building a high-rise apartment, it was pointed out that the proceeds of the $3 million plus sale would suffice for relocation and a new building.

The board, seizing the opportunity, applied for rezoning on October 7, 1965 and appointed a committee to recommend new sites. Two were considered: Ambassador Davies's mansion on Klingle Road (the setting of the movie *Advise and Consent*) and a site named Bonnie Brae on Oregon Avenue, the outer fringe of the District. The Soviet Union had held an option to purchase the Bonnie Brae locale for its embassy, but objecting neighbors had blocked the sale.

An ad-hoc group agreed to lend the congregation funds for a thirty-day option to acquire Bonnie Brae. A membership meeting was called to consider the purchase. It produced an overflow attendance. The members angrily refused to consider any plan to relocate the synagogue. The fifteen-year-old Connecticut Avenue structure, though no longer adequate, was too new to be destroyed. Most of the members had an emotional commitment to the present location.

A long-range planning committee headed by Norman Bernstein in 1965 projected goals to be achieved in the congregation's second century: to build a branch school in the suburbs, to find facilities to serve the total congregation in one place for the High Holy Days, to renovate the existing synagogue structure in its present site, to build a parking garage, to acquire a new cemetery site, to upgrade the dues structure, and to establish an endowment fund. Only the proposal to renovate the sanctuary and Kay Auditorium was implemented.

The survey of membership, conducted by Bernstein's committee, revealed that of the 1,132 family members in 1965, 781 lived in the District, 321 in Maryland, and 30 in Virginia. The school enrolled 478 children from 254 families with 117 of the children living in the District, 134 in Maryland and 3 in Virginia. The survey revealed that 87% respondents found the present synagogue location adequate to excellent; 13% found it inconvenient.

In retrospect, the members were wise in preferring to remain in the present location. It is better for an urban congregation to be centrally, though inconveniently, located for many, rather than conveniently located only for some. The riots which would sweep Washington three years later would have rendered Bonnie Brae, without access to public transportation, beyond convenient reach for most of the members.

### Civil Rights

Despite Supreme Court rulings nullifying restrictive covenants, Washington was a segregated city in 1961; apartment managers excluded blacks. One morning, the headmaster of the Episcopalian St. Alban's School phoned to tell me that one of his black students had been invited to a classmate's apartment only to be denied entrance by the doorman. The owner of the apartment building was a member of Adas Israel. The headmaster felt I should be informed of the owner's policy.

Embarrassed, I called the building's owner, who explained to me that although he regretted the situation, he had no alternative but to respect the expressed wishes of his tenants. To do otherwise would be to court disaster. And thus was I introduced to the realities of the real estate world. With Joseph Blumenthal's endorsement I invited every real estate developer and apartment-house owner in the congregation to lunch at a downtown hotel. The group listened respectfully but silently to my statement that it was unworthy for a Jew to practice discrimination and that the group should take the initiative in announcing a nondiscriminatory open-housing policy in their buildings.

One of the participants, Jack Kay, the son of Abe, indicated that he would be very happy to adopt an open-housing policy in sales and rentals if his competitors would do the same. The largest real estate developer and apartment-house owner in the District, a non-Jew, was known to discriminate against blacks and Jews and did not suffer from his practices. "We are not big enough to make any difference," said Kay, and others agreed.

Norman Bernstein suggested that we try to persuade Morris Cafritz, the largest Jewish real estate developer in the city, to set an example by taking the first step. Norman announced that he would be willing to announce an open-housing policy in all of his rentals, but that the impact would be a modest one. A committee did indeed call upon Cafritz, and soon thereafter the press announced that all Cafritz apartments would now practice equal opportunity and open housing in rentals and sales. Others soon followed suit.

While Morris Cafritz was a recognized leader in the Jewish community, his wife, Gwendolyn, "sometimes took pains to tell friends that she herself was not Jewish."[15] According to a newspaper account, Gwendolyn Cafritz was the "daughter of a Hungarian immunologist who had a role in devising the early Wassermann test to detect syphilis." Gore Vidal included a character modeled after Gwendolyn in his novel *Washington, D.C.* At a time when upper-class Washington was considered anti-Semitic, dinner parties and receptions at the Cafritz home on fashionable Foxhall Road rivaled those of Cafritz's chief rival, Perle Mesta.[16]

Morris and Gwendolyn Cafritz had been affiliated with Adas Israel at a time when the congregation would not have accepted the membership of an intermarried couple. The *Chronicle* had congratulated the couple on the birth of their youngest son, Conrad Barry Cafritz.[17]

### The Classroom

In the early sixties, synagogues throughout the country experienced a remarkable increase in membership and school registrations. At Adas Israel, the school population rose to record highs. The principal, Rachel Frank, who had succeeded Dr. Irving Ashrey, was herself succeeded by an inspired educational director, Joseph Bruckenstein. Formerly a teacher in St. Thomas, Virgin Islands, where he was also the private tutor for the children of Mr. and Mrs. Herman Wouk, Bruckenstein, together with Reuben Yalon as youth director, presided over an exciting educational system and youth program. For Adas Israel, the first half of the decade was another golden period.

While segregation in public schools was outlawed by the Supreme Court's epic 1954 decision in *Brown v. Board of Education of Topeka*, the district school's multiple-track system separated students on the basis of academic qualifications and thus effectively perpetuated separate racial groupings in the classrooms; the system remained a source of contention. Jewish children were to be found overwhelmingly in the Honors track, especially at nearby Alice Deal Junior High and Woodrow Wilson High School, the two schools which most Adas Israel children attended.

Class divisions based on scholastic aptitude were declared illegal only in 1967. Many in the congregation opposed the elimination of the track system and the bussing in of children from other areas of the city. Responding to letters protesting bussing and boundary shifts in the public school system, John Sessions, the superintendent of schools, wrote, "Parents objecting to boundary changes frequently, as an ultimate threat, warn the Board of Education that if the boundaries change, they will then withdraw their children from the public schools and enroll them in a private school. This, of course, always involves pupils changing from one school to another and it usually involves greater travel than would have been necessitated by the boundary change. I am, therefore, not very much impressed by their arguments."[18]

The changes in the public school system, the elimination of the track system, the introduction of bussing of students from other parts of the city to achieve a greater measure of racial integration, along with the riots of 1968, precipitated a migration to the suburbs. School registration at Adas Israel plunged, and membership soon followed as families with children abandoned the District. The departing families felt that the District schools could no longer properly educate their children.

The population of the Adas Israel school dropped from 492 in 1960 to 390 in 1968 and continued to decline thereafter. Bar Mitzvahs dropped from forty-five in 1960 to twenty-one in1968–69. Some members concluded that the mandatory requirement of three-day-per-week attendance was driving children away from the school. The distance between Adas Israel and suburban addresses made it difficult for parents to transport their children, especially during the afternoon traffic rush-hours.

Departing families joined suburban synagogues and schools, either Congregation Beth El in nearby Bethesda or Congregation Har Shalom in more distant Potomac, both Conservative synagogues; others joined Reform congregations. Suburban affiliation was very often a revolving door. Families affiliated when their children reached Bar/Bat Mitzvah or confirmation age only to withdraw following the ceremony. In many instances, departing families returned to Adas Israel when their children's Jewish education was no longer a consideration.

With the flight to the suburbs, Adas Israel was faced with the problem of maintaining an aging congregation with a shrinking school population. To increase the school population, the children of nonmembers were admitted to the classroom. In some age groups the number of children of nonmembers equaled or exceeded those of affiliated families. Since the school was subsidized, the school committee ruled that the nonmember children in any class should not exceed 20 percent of the class total.

Bruckenstein struggled valiantly to meet the challenge of a demographic situation he could not control. The congregation opened a branch school at the suburban Jewish Community Center despite the active opposition of the Conservative congregations in the area, which resented the potential competition.

Following the Six-Day War in 1967, Bruckenstein felt impelled to go on aliyah to Israel. He and his family returned briefly after the Yom Kippur War in 1973 and later resumed permanent residence in Israel. Bruckenstein was succeeded as educational director by Rabbi Herman Cohen.

### The National Scene

Our location in Washington projected us into several situations with implications beyond our walls.* To pressure the Soviet Union to ease its restrictions on Jewish migration and civil rights, members of the congregation with the participation of other synagogues, in 1965, launched a daily vigil across the street from the Soviet Embassy (abiding by legal restrictions against picketing within 500 feet of a foreign embassy.) The vigil included the noon recitation of the Mincha service. Soviet personnel objected to the resulting adverse publicity.

Frequent anti-Zionist and anti-Semitic diatribes emanating from the various Arab embassies distressed the Jewish community. Reacting to the charge of anti-Semitism, one Arab ambassador asserted that Arabs could hardly be called anti-Semitic since they themselves were Semites. Moreover, he stated, he had nothing against the Jews; it was Zionism that he opposed. The argument became a familiar ploy.

One day, David Brody, the director of the Anti-Defamation League of the B'nai B'rith, called me to propose that we give the Arabs an opportunity to prove that they were not anti-Semitic by inviting their ambassadors together with ambassadors from other countries to a synagogue service. It would also be an opportunity to see how many Third World African embassies would respond to our invitation. In retrospect, I now realize that the Israeli embassy, headed by Ambassador Avraham Harman, was behind the project.

Sheldon Cohen, the director of the Internal Revenue Service, obtained the agreement of Vice President Hubert Humphrey to deliver the address at the service, which was designated Human

*In the aftermath of the Cuban Missile Crisis in 1962 the Federal Government designated Adas Israel as a civil defense air raid shelter and stored massive drums of sterile water and biscuits in its underground vaulted sub-basement.

Rights Sabbath, on December 10, 1966, the anniversary of the United Nations Declaration of Human Rights. Every ambassador in Washington was invited. The dean of the diplomatic corps, Ambassador Sevilla Sacassa of Nicaragua, attended. The Voice of America transmitted the service to the Soviet bloc countries with simultaneous translation into several languages including Yiddish. In his address, Humphrey challenged the Senate to ratify the Genocide Convention, which it had not yet approved.

It was an impressive worship service which was followed by a buffet luncheon Kiddush. The content of the service was not compromised. Attendance at the Kiddush-luncheon had to be restricted due to requirements of security and limitation of space. Those worshippers who were excluded from the Kiddush were not mollified by later explanations and apologies.[19]

While there had been no mention of Zionism or of Israel in the service, beyond the latter words' place in the prayers and in the name of the congregation, only countries which maintained relations with Israel responded to the invitation. These included many African embassies but not a single Arab one. The press took note of the fallacy in the argument that Arabs were not anti-Jewish but only anti-Zionist.

In 1967, the Jewish Theological Seminary asked the congregation to represent it at a reception at the Polish embassy to celebrate the forty-ninth year of Polish "independence." The Israeli embassy strongly objected, feeling that Jews should boycott the reception on the grounds that "the Polish government is preparing a public trial at which trumped up anti-Semitic charges will be made against Jews,"[20] and that any approach to Poland by Jews should be through the Israeli embassy. Numerous agencies including the United Synagogue called to urge the congregation not to send a delegation.

The seminary felt obligated to participate because of the generosity of the Polish Information Service, which had released vivid and hitherto-unseen German films of the destruction of the Warsaw Ghetto to the seminary for inclusion in an *Eternal Light* telecast on the Holocaust. The United States had refused to release its own war footage, nor would the German authorities cooperate. Poland, alone, had been forthcoming. The cold war had turned former allies into adversaries and, conversely, former enemies into allies. Russia wanted to embarrass Germany, America's ally in the cold war, while the United States sought to protect Germany. The seminary felt an obligation to reciprocate to Poland.

We were caught in a conflict between the Israeli embassy and the seminary. I tried to justify my intention to attend the reception, stating that protest is best expressed in face-to-face contact. Refusal to speak to one's opponent will not resolve any problem, I wrote to the congregation.[21] I attended the reception; many did not. In presenting the video reel of the controversial program to the Polish ambassador, which was my assignment, I voiced my protest against the treatment of the Jews in Poland and expressed the hope that their rights would be respected.

### The Community

The District of Columbia, more than a city and less than a state, remains a unique area in the United States not only because more than half of its citizens live outside of its boundaries, but because of its population mix, the Jewish as well as the general population.

Surveys and Jewish Federation statistics indicated that 35% of the District's Jewish population are affiliated with Conservative Congregations and 38% with Reform; 3% are Orthodox and 61% profess no affiliation.[22] The area has the lowest over 65 population than any other major city in the United States and the highest proportion of singles.* (The government employs a large number of young people, especially female.) Adas Israel pioneered in sponsoring services for Jewish singles and attracted thousands from this group to its services and activities, establishing a pattern that would come to be emulated by other congregations.

The area contains the most highly educated Jewish population in the country, 48% with advanced degrees, with a heavy concentration in the professions. It includes the lowest proportion of foreign born than any other major metropolitan area, 8% compared to a national figure of 23%.‡ Only 36% of the population were born in the area. The city with the lowest proportion of native born Jews is Miami.

The statistics reveal that D.C.-area Jews attend religious services less frequently than those who live in other cities. Slightly less than 30% of the Conservative Jews purchase kosher meat; 68% for the Orthodox and 3% for the Reform.

There remained a lingering gap between the "newcomers" to Washington and the native born. It would take time for the new arrivals to feel at home or to commit themselves to a long term residence in the new area. Some were "sitting on their suit cases" for extended periods and therefore were loathe to fund capital building campaigns for local synagogues and institutions.

While the native born, for the most part, tended to disregard the implications of living in the nation's capital city, regarding the White House as little more than an address on Pennsylvania Avenue, the newcomers, having been drawn to Washington because of its unique features, tended to be more politically sensitive, sometimes exhibiting a "capital city complex," a pretension which made

*Over-sixty-five Jewish population: D.C. and Los Angeles, 8.1 percent; Cleveland and Chicago, 14 percent; San Diego, 16 percent. Singles population: D.C., 25 percent; New York, 15 percent. Divorced: D.C., 7 percent; Los Angeles, 14 percent.

‡Jewish foreign-born: D.C., 8 percent; Los Angeles, 24 percent; nationally, 23 percent.

them look upon themselves as spokesman or representatives of the country as a whole, turning even a local event into a national situation.

The differences in outlook were felt in formulating synagogue policies. Some were of the opinion that the synagogue should place a greater emphasis on broad issues: political action, Soviet Jewry, Israel and Zionism, inner city development, inter-faith activities. Others felt that the Congregation should limit its expenditures and energies to the benefit of the Congregation and its related institutions. The annual debate on selecting a recipient of the Shem Tov Award was a reflection of the two differing emphases.

Three fourths of the Jews in Washington had moved to the area since the second world war, mainly as professionals, to work in the government or related services. Because these new comers came from diverse backgrounds, some Orthodox and some Reform, they demanded recognition of their diversity. With the influx of new members, Adas Israel was no longer an homogenous institution. The native element in the congregation would eventually yield leadership to the newer arrivals.

To serve this diversity it would be necessary to offer not only overflow services but different kinds of services, not only on Rosh Hashanah and Yom Kippur but on Festivals and even on Sabbaths; no longer would one type of service satisfy the entire congregation. The Congregation needed to see itself as a cathedral synagogue incorporating smaller worship groupings. The sanctuary High Holiday service on the second day of Rosh Hashanna was conducted with instrumental music, the others were traditional, without musical accompaniment. On Sabbaths, there were separate services for singles, for families, for beginners or "learners" ,for the traditional, and for the "innovative." A havurah, offering a free flowing neo-hassidic type of family service would eventually come into being.

The havurah, by virtue of the intensity of the commitment of its membership, soon excercized an influence over congregational policy and its ritual far beyond its numbers. The group, meeting separately every other week, tended to reject the rabbi/cantor-centered formal service and much of the institutional social activity which it considered ephemeral to the religious spirit. Insular, the group did not identify with many of the Jewish activities in the community. Its members stressed services that encouraged personal involvement and self-expression, and they "exhibited an intensified respect for the requirements of halacha."[23]

Time and changing fortune contributed to levelling the social distance between Adas Israel and the Washington Hebrew Congregation. Among Washington's one hundred wealthiest citizens, *Regardies*, a Washington monthly business magazine, included 54 Jewish families, of whom twenty-two were affiliated with Adas Israel and an equal number with the Washington Hebrew Congregation; the others were distributed amongst suburban congregations, including some Orthodox. The same pattern prevailed in the year of Adas Israel's centennial, 1969.[24]

Among the influential Washingtonians identified in the survey who were affiliated with Adas Israel was the family of Charles E. Smith. His building and management firm, the Charles E. Smith Company, which he had founded and now managed with the assistance of his son, Robert Smith, and his son-in-law Robert Kogod, was one of the leading corporations in the area.

Charles Smith became one of the District's most influential citizens endowing civic and Jewish institutions alike. Several buildings at George Washington University bear the Smith name. He also endowed its Jewish Studies program. He was instrumental in building a complex of Jewish communal buildings in the suburbs which included the Jewish Community Center, the Home for the

Aged, and the Day School, whose name was changed from the Solomon Schechter Day School to the Charles E. Smith Jewish Day School. Smith was recognized by the Jewish Theological Seminary for his generous support of the institution and by Adas Israel with the Shem Tov Award in 1970.*

Smith made educational institutions central to his philanthropy. Anguished at the pain of Jewish suffering and stirred by the establishing of the State of Israel he contributed handsomely to its institutions and especially to the Hebrew University in Jerusalem.

Smith's life was another Horatio Alger story. Born on a tenant farm in Russia in 1901, he recalls being raised in a dirt floor house. His parents and their children migrated to the United States in 1911; his father changed the family name from Schmidoff to Smith. They lived in Brooklyn where he attended public schools. Smith became a carpenter and builder of homes.

Invited to Washington by a real estate broker in 1942, he launched his building career at a time when there was a need for low cost housing. Successes prevailed over the occasional downturns.

His autobiography,[25] reveals a sensitive and creative person, deeply religious in his outlook and grateful for his good fortune, who felt that he owed it to his faith and to his community to make them the beneficiaries of his success.

### Crisis in the Middle East

In the spring of 1967, war clouds again engulfed the Middle East. Prompted by Russia, Syria accused Israel of planning an attack. Israel's Independence Day celebration in May was muted when it

*In gratitude for his generous endowment gift, the Adas Israel sanctuary was named the Charles E. Smith Sanctuary in 1991.

appeared that the Arab states were mobilizing under a unified joint command. An attack on Israel appeared imminent.

The Rabbinical Assembly had convened its annual national convention in Washington in May 1967. The famed Israeli author Shai Agnon and Ambassador Avraham Harman delivered memorable addresses at the convention's banquet. The final session, converted to a public mass meeting to mobilize concern for Israel's safety, was addressed by Rabbi Ralph Simon of Chicago and Senator Eugene McCarthy.

Egypt's Nasser concentrated his forces along the border with Israel and ordered the U.N. troops that were supposed to police the area to leave. On May 23 he announced the blockade of the Straits of Tiran, cutting off all shipping to Israel's southern port of Eilat. Television screens portrayed frenzied masses in Cairo screaming for Jihad, a holy war against Israel. When Jordan and Iraq joined the Egyptian-Syrian command, war became inevitable.

A huge crowd flocked to the sanctuary on Friday night, May 26, sensing that it was the place to be at a time of crisis; most people were terrified at the prospect of what they feared would be another Holocaust. I put aside my scheduled sermon to address the implications of the crisis and to call for contributions to the United Jewish Appeal and for the purchase of bonds. Publicly announced pledges were recorded by tape-recorder. An intensive campaign for financial support for Israel followed. The congregation responded more generously than ever before.

On Monday morning June 5, the Israeli air force surged into the skies and her armies flung themselves into the Sinai, driven by the apocolyptic vision of the oblivion that awaited her people should her soldiers fail. Six days later came the incredible realization of deliverance; it was a Sabbath of peace. The televised spectacle of Cairo's hysterical street mobs shrieking for jihad was replaced by scenes of thousands of Israelis making their first Shavuot pilgrimage to the Western Wall that most of them had never seen before.

Adas Israel found its Zionist soul during the crisis. It had not been lacking in commitment prior to that year, but after 1967, Israel and Zionism played an even more important role in its concerns, activities, and curriculum.

Adas Israel philanthropists made generous endowment gifts to Israel to establish a military convalescent home in Nahariya and several educational institutions. Notable among the supporters of Israel was Nehemiah M. Cohen, founder of the Giant Food supermarket chain. Cohen was born in the old city of pre-World War I Jerusalem, then under Turkish control. Yeshiva educated, he was ordained as a rabbi but was attracted to farming and construction, which led him to seek further training in England, reaching there shortly before the outbreak of War in 1914. With his Turkish passport he was an enemy alien in England. Unable to return home and prevented from bringing over his wife and two infant sons, he decided to travel to the United States, where he earned his living as a teacher and shochet.

After the war, reunited with his family, he became the owner of a small meat market, which he expanded to become one of the foremost and extensive chain of supermarkets on the east coast. Cohen endowed several trade schools in Israel because he felt that Israel needs good plumbers and carpenters as well as scientists and philosophers.

Bond purchases soared. Synagogue teams assisted UJA in its annual campaign. More scholarship funds were raised to send a greater number of children to summer programs with Camp Ramah in Israel. A summer in Israel became a postconfirmation activity.

A close relationship was forged between Adas Israel and the Israeli embassy in the nearby international area off Connecticut

Avenue. On the death of Itzhak ben Zvi, Israel's former President, the embassy had turned to Adas Israel to conduct memorial services in May 1963, with the memorial address delivered by Ambassador Avraham Harman. Memorial services for David Ben-Gurion and Golda Meir were similarly held at Adas Israel as were services memorializing Israel's first president, Chaim Weizmann.

Children of embassy personnel turned to Adas Israel to celebrate their becoming B'nai Mitzvah and for their marriage ceremonies. Among those who became Bar Mitzvah were Yuval Rabin, the son of Ambassador and Mrs. Yitzchak Rabin, and Michael Dinitz, the son of Ambassador and Mrs. Simcha Dinitz; the marriages included Naomi Harman,* the daughter of the Harmans, who was wed to Barry Chazen. Like Abba Eban before them, the later Israeli ambassadors worshipped at Adas Israel as honorary members.

### I Have a Dream

The roaring twenties, the depression-ridden thirties, the war-ravaged forties had yielded to the passive fifties. All were overtaken by the rebellious sixties, a decade of confrontation and clashing encounter. Fueled by divergent opinions on our military involvement in Vietnam, the streets and the campus erupted in demonstration and riot. On the streets, the issues focused on poverty, racism, and inequality; on the campus, the issues were diffuse.

The decade began with sit-ins in Greensboro, North Carolina, where four black college students refused to move from a Woolworth's lunch counter where they had been denied service. In 1962, James Meredith became the first black student to enter the University of Mississippi, but only after 3,000 troops had been called in to put down the riots.

*Elected to the Israeli Kenesset in 1992.

All of these issues polarized Adas Israel. The activities of its social action committee under Leonard Rodberg led to confrontations with the "law and order" element among the members. A series of sermons on "What Ails America?" followed by discussions, provided a forum for expressing divergent opinions. Despite the unhappiness of many members with the tactics of the congregation's activist group, there was no attempt to stifle contrary opinions.

Eventually, the activist group, led by Rodberg, resigned from the congregation to affiliate with the Tifereth Israel Congregation, whose members were more sympathetic to their approach than was Adas Israel.

The Rev. Martin Luther King Jr., champion of the struggle for racial equality and head of the Southern Christian Leadership Conference, addressed a citywide meeting at Adas Israel in 1963. Later that year, in August, he delivered his dramatic address at the Lincoln Memorial, where over 200,000 people heard his stirring words, "I have a dream that this nation will rise up and live out the true meaning of its creed," which envisioned the promise of a more peaceful and equitable era. A large delegation of students and adults from Adas Israel marched in the demonstration. Hundreds of students from other parts of the country, bringing their sleeping bags with them, turned the synagogue into a hostel. Auditorium and parking lot served as a rallying site. Sisterhood and men's club provided breakfast and later refreshments.

After months of civil rights demonstrations led by King, racists bombed the Sixteenth Street Baptist Church in Birmingham, Alabama, and killed four young girls. The dreadful attack took place shortly before the High Holy Days of 1963. Prompted by Norman Bernstein, an appeal for funds was launched at the service to assist the bereaved families and the bombed church. The funds were conveyed to Drew Pearson's America's Conscience Fund and to the church in Birmingham.

Unfortunately the sixties were also the decade of assassination: President Kennedy in 1962, his brother Robert in 1968, and in the same year, Martin Luther King Jr., whose murder had serious and long-lasting effects on the District and on the congregation.

Barely one hour after the news of King's assassination reached Washington, a brick crashed through a window of the People's Drug Store at 14th and U Streets, the heart of the black neighborhood; it was a signal for the riots to begin. Three days of fire-bombing and rioting left thirteen persons dead and more than a thousand injured. The riots destroyed the black business strip centered on 14th Street and H Street, the old downtown, which was once the area of Jewish residence and was still an area of significant Jewish business operation.

A board meeting at the synagogue on the night of King's assassination was quickly adjourned by Milton Baldinger, the president, in observance of a hastily imposed curfew. Fire and smoke from burning buildings were clearly visible from the synagogue's parking lot. President Johnson called in federal troops who set up machine guns around the Capitol, the White House, and other important government buildings. The curfew, which compelled cancellation of synagogue meetings and late Friday night services, was lifted on Friday, April 12, as peace was restored in the riot-torn area, but too late to make a difference for that evening's service.

An exceptionally large proportion of Jews owned businesses in the riot-torn neighborhoods. Several Adas Israel members, who for decades had operated stores or owned rental property in the area, found themselves the targets of looting and arson. Some businesses and buildings belonged to children of the immigrant generation; it was, after all, the area of first Jewish residence. In some instances, a single night of rioting destroyed a lifetime business.

Audrey Freedman, a government statistician in the Department of Labor and the wife of George Washington University professor of law Monroe Freedman, organized a committee to urge and assist Jews who were operating businesses in the riot zone to sell their business to blacks on lenient terms. She was mildly successful.

Despite the anger among Jews, many of whom felt themselves unfairly targeted for blame for the prevailing conditions, synagogue members and the organized Jewish community remained involved in efforts to rehabilitate the destroyed area. The riots brought the congregation face to face with the problems of the inner city. Its urban affairs committee solicited contributions of food, clothing, and funds for the benefit of families whose homes and apartments had been destroyed. Fortunately, the families of the custodial staff of the synagogue, a loyal and long-tenured group, who were brought together in an expression of concern, did not suffer any loss.

The following year, Mayor Washington appointed Joseph Danzansky, a member of Adas Israel and president of the Giant Food Company, to head a committee to secure donations of food to sustain the Poor People's Campaign and Resurrection City, the tent settlement encamped on Washington's mall, led by King's successor in the Southern Christian Leadership Conference, the Rev. Ralph Abernathy.

Sermons, discussions at meetings of youth and adults focused on urban problems, race relations, and the implications of "law and order," a favorite theme of Vice President Spiro Agnew.

The synagogue's presence on Connecticut Avenue was an expression of faith in the future of the District and served as a stabilizing influence on its neighborhood. A move to Bonnie Brae or elsewhere in the District or suburbs would have been regarded as an irresponsible escape from the challenge of the city.

**The Centennial**

Elaborate plans for a year-long celebration of the congregation's centennial year, 1969, had been carefully planned to include a cantorial concert, a tour to Israel, an art exhibit, the writing of the congregation's history, launching an endowment fund, and a major anniversary service to be followed by a Friday night lecture series. Unfortunately, the centennial year was overtaken by the continuing social unrest in Washington and the tensions in the Middle East; the enthusiasm which had accompanied the planning for the year-long celebration evaporated in a mood of despondency. The carefully laid blueprint for launching the endowment fund was shelved and the reams of elaborately designed promotional and solicitation material consigned to storage bins.

The embers from the 1968 riots had yet to cool; broken glass from numerous demonstrations protesting the war in Vietnam still littered some streets. Many Jewish families, along with others, were leaving the District. Relations between Jews and blacks had deteriorated after a Black Caucus in Gary, Indiana,[26] had expressed deep-seated antagonism toward the Jews for making Israel rather than the black ghettos their primary concern. In New York, a disastrous teachers' strike and a struggle over school decentralization, which threatened the jobs of white and especially Jewish teachers, acerbated the hostility between the black and Jewish communities.

The Rabbinical Assembly joined the American Jewish Committee and the Synagogue Council in a cooperative effort to meet the needs of the poor in Washington's inner city; the effort was only mildly successful. The congregation was concerned with demonstrating its solidarity with the Jews of Russia, who were suffering from increased discrimination while being denied exit visas.

Unrest in the Middle East continued unabated as Israel administered the areas overrun in the 1967 Six-Day War. Israel had responded to a series of Arab hijackings with a surgically executed raid on the Beirut airport. Worst of all was the War of Attrition along the Suez. Israeli casualties mounted almost daily.

Responding to the prevailing mood in the community, my sermons addressed the conflicts in the streets and on the campus, charges of police brutality, and relations between blacks and Jews. I also postponed plans for taking a six-month sabbatical leave. In August, Rabbi Jacob Garfinkel joined the rabbinical staff, replacing Stanley Dreifuss.

Reflecting the prevailing mood, the centennial-year observance was far less elaborate than the celebrations accompanying prior key anniversaries. Over the objections of President Milton Baldinger, who advocated adhering to the earlier more ambitious plans, observances were kept low-key. Baldinger, who had served only one two-year term, announced that he would not accept reelection. His successor was Joseph Mendelson.

A restrained celebration of the centennial year began with the High Holy Days in September. Clarice Smith prepared an impressive photographic exhibit of important events in the congregation's history. Cantor Edgar's centennial concert in April featured a one-act opera presented by the Music-Drama Theater of New York under the direction of Cantor Raymond Smolover, with Edgar singing a major role, in addition to a concert of Jewish folk melodies and a rock-folk presentation by the confirmation class.

The "centennial sermon" was delivered by Rabbi Simon Greenberg, vice-chancellor of the Jewish Theological Seminary, on Shabbat Bereshith, 1969. Subsequent speakers included Senator Harold E. Hughes of Iowa, Mrs. Avraham Harman, director of Israel's Demographic Center and wife of the former ambassador,*

*General Yitzchak Rabin, who was to be Israel's Prime Minister from 1974 to 1977 and again in 1992, had succeeded Harman as ambassador to the United States in 1967.

and Cleveland Amory, a prominent author and defender of wild life, who spoke on the subject, "A Proper Bostonian Discovers Israel." Rabbi Joshua Haberman of the Washington Hebrew Congregation delivered the sermon at the annual combined service with the two nearby Reform temples, which finally concluded the centennial year on Sabbath Eve, January 2, 1970.

Earlier there was an unexpected burst of excitement in the congregation when the Prime Minister of Israel, Golda Meir, attended services on the Sabbath of Sukkot to join the congregation in marking the Bar Mitzvah of Gideon Argov, the son of Minister and Mrs. Shlomo Argov of the Israeli embassy.* The Prime Minister had come to Washington for an official meeting with President Richard Nixon. She consented to address the congregation. Throwing caution to the winds but mindful of the historical significance of her visit, I arranged for the presence of a photographer. Negative reaction, if any, was muted.

At the annual meeting in November, the three members with the longest links to the congregation, Rose Hornstein, Joseph Blumenthal, and Louis Grossberg, reached back to the days of their childhood to recount their earliest recollections of Adas Israel. And so ended the first hundred years.

*~ Golda Meir* *Reflections*

*Kavod harav, Gidon, Shlomo, v'Chava, b'rachot m'omek lev.* [My heartfelt blessings.]

Dear Friends,

Over and over again, we listen to the same services in the synagogue, and each time there is something new, something more

*Shlomo Argov was wounded and permanently incapacitated in an assassination attempt by terrorists in London in June 1982.

relevant, something more meaningful. As the rabbi has said, there is nothing in the Torah that has no meaning for our days. It occurs to me, as it always has, that the fact that we are here today, the fact that the Jewish people is still here, the fact that we have been privileged to live in the generation in which Israel has been reborn, independent and sovereign, is due to one thing, something which many in the non-Jewish world have never understood and do not understand now. We are *am k'shey-oref* [a stiff-necked people]. We are a people of whose number millions have been led to gas chambers by tyrants who destroyed their bodies but never their spirits. This people went to the gas chambers with a song on their lips, Ani maamin b'viat ha-Mashiach [I believe that the Messiah will come.]

We have always believed, we have always had faith. They could destroy us physically, yet the spirit lived and the faith remained. They never succeeded in uprooting the faith that we shall be and we shall come back.

And if Israel is till struggling today and still does not know peace, Ani maamin [I still believe]. We believe, we are certain, we have faith. And if on the path to peace, here and there, we again are criticized because we do not bow, because we stand erect, because we cannot compromise on the question, to be or not to be, it is because we have decided that come what may, we are, and we will be.

And I say to Gideon: You are fortunate. You look upon a generation that is older than you are. You know them. You know their younger brothers; you know their parents. We know that not all those that go forth come back. But we know that they live with us.

From the very depth of my heart I wish that you, like my grandchildren, will not be required to go forth to fight. May you be preoccupied in producing and sowing. May you sow in joy and reap your harvest in joy. But whatever will be, let us remain strong and let us live. Amen.

# CONCLUSION

During the seventies, Washington gradually regained its composure. While government remains Washington's major industry and determines its economic health, the District of Columbia is more than a collection of marble monuments, massive staircases, and Corinthian pillars; it is home for a vast diversity of people. Although many Jewish families moved to the suburbs in the years following the riots, eventually a good number, weary of commuting, cautioned by gas shortages, and often no longer dependent on public education, returned to the city; former home-owners moved to high-rise condominiums in the District or close-by neighborhoods. In the city one could find world-class theaters, museums, symphonies, and libraries. An efficient and rapid Metro system transcended boundaries. Tourism returned.

Soon, Adas Israel regained its positive outlook. Newcomers added their strength to the congregation. Each year, hundreds of children continued to turn to the synagogue for instruction, fellowship, and confirmation of faith.* The congregation reached out to Jews by birth and Jews by choice. With its dignified affirmation of a contemporary Judaism and its respect for diversity in worship, the congregation attracted a membership from many areas of the community and from all walks of life.* It has remained a congregation for those who affirm a strong commitment to Judaism and want to transmit its beliefs and practices to their children.

New and old members continue to produce the leadership for Jewish and civic activities in the community. Members of Adas Israel have headed virtually every Jewish organization and many civic

*1992 school registration, 669 children; 344 live in the District, 310 in Maryland, and 15 in Virginia.

*1992 total membership, 1504 families; 688 live in the District, 683 in Maryland, and 133 in Virginia and elsewhere.

institutions in the area. They respond generously to the needs of the local community and to Israel's appeals for support; they are to be found among the sponsors and board members of Washington's theaters, symphony orchestra, ballet company, and art museums. Their names are incised on the facades of several university buildings in Washington and in Israel.

Among its members are many who have achieved distinction in higher education,* scholarship, the judiciary,* public service, and elected office.* Several have been named to important diplomatic posts.* One member, Miriam Ottenberg, was awarded a Pulitzer Prize for her reporting in the *Washington Star*.

The first three synagogue buildings were built under the leadership of foreign-born or first-generation Americans who achieved success in the New World and left their mark upon the community. Remembering their emergence from early poverty, they were motivated by the desire to express their gratitude for the opportunies afforded them; they also retained a respect for traditional Jewish values.

*Marver Bernstein, the president of Brandeis University; Stephen Trachtenberg, the president of George Washington University; Seymour Alpert, the vice-president of George Washington University; Walter Lacquer, political analyst.

*David Bazelon, chief judge of the U.S. Court of Appeals; Leonard Garment, adviser to Presidents, Samuel Dash, chief counsel for the Senate Watergate Investigation, Associate judges of the D.C. Superior Court, Samuel B. Block, Alfred Burka, and Bruce S. Mencher. Montgomery County judges Irma S. Raker and Paul Weinstein.

*In 1992, Representatives Sam Gejdenson of Connecticut and Meldon Levine and Henry Waxman, both of California.

*Arthur Goldberg, Supreme Court justice and U.N. ambassador; Joseph Gildenhorn, ambassador to Switzerland; Max Kampelman, ambassadorial head of the U.S. delegation to the Geneva talks on nuclear and space-arms reductions; Sol Linowitz, ambassador to the Organization of American States and Middle East peace negotiator; Richard Stone, ambassador to Denmark; Richard Schifter, Assistant Secretary of State for Human Rights and Humanitarian Affairs.

Motivation is difficult to transmit; nostalgia, ethnic loyalty, and philanthropy cannot be depended upon to motivate succeeding generations. Children in the congregation now include the fifth and sixth generations in the United States. It is for them and their parents to maintain the momentum of the past by discovering for themselves the meaning and dynamic of Jewish faith and identity.

The second century presents its challenge to the Assembly of Israel, the Adas Israel Hebrew Congregation.

# APPENDIX I

Officers and Clergy of Adas Israel Congregation

## Presidents

| | |
|---|---|
| 1869–1872 | Bendiza J. Behrend |
| 1872–1874 | Nathan Gotthelf |
| 1874– January–June | Jacob Rich |
| June–July | Nathan Gotthelf |
| 1874–1877 | John Jacob Boyer |
| 1877–1880 | Jacob Rich |
| 1880–April–June | Bernard Rich |
| July–October | Julius Baumgarten |
| 1880–1882 | Manassas Oppenheimer |
| 1882–April 1887 | Jacob Rich (died in office) |
| 1887–1888 | Felix Greenapple |
| 1888–1924 | Simon Oppenheimer |
| 1924–1928 | Louis Rosenberg |
| 1928–1929 | Fred Gichner |
| 1929–March 1953 | Joseph Wilner (died in office) |
| 1953–1955 | Isaac Jacobson |
| 1956 | Fred S. Kogod (died in office) |
| 1957–1960 | Julius Wolpe |
| 1960–1961 | Stanley Wiener |
| 1961–1964 | Joseph Blumenthal |
| 1964–1967 | Samuel Lebowitz |
| 1967–1969 | Milton Baldinger |
| 1969–1973 | Joseph Mendelson |
| 1973–1977 | Donald Wolpe |
| 1977–1979 | Leon Shinberg |

| | |
|---|---|
| 1979–1983 | Max Goldberg |
| 1983–1987 | Jack Lish |
| 1987–1991 | Stuart Fidler |
| 1992– | Bernard Segerman |

**Hazzanim**

| | |
|---|---|
| 1872 | Joseph A. Cohen |
| 1876 | Jacob Voorsanger |
| 1877 | Adolph Boerenstein |
| 1879 | Isadore W. Samuels |
| 1885 | Isaac Stempel |
| 1887 | Philip Bernstein |
| 1889 | Leopold Heiman |
| 1891 | Isadore W. Samuels |
| 1891–1894 | Emanuel Rosenzeig |
| 1894 | Isadore W. Samuels |

**Rabbis**

| | |
|---|---|
| 1898–1901 | Morris Mandel |
| 1901–1907 | Julius T. Loeb |
| 1907–1908 | Isadore W. Samuels (Hazzan) |
| 1908–1911 | Louis Egelson |
| 1914–1920 | Benjamin Grossman |
| 1920–1921 | Nathan Colish |
| 1921–1922 | Theodore Shabshelowitz |
| 1924–1929 | Louis Schwefel |
| 1930–1951 | Solomon Metz |
| 1951–1959 | David Panitz |
| 1960–1986 | Stanley Rabinowitz |
| 1986– | Jeffrey Wohlberg |

## Cantors

| | |
|---|---|
| 1908–1909 | L. J. Gargunsky |
| 1910–1914 | Samuel Glushak |
| 1914–1925 | Adler Shefferman |
| 1923–1946 | Louis Novick |
| 1946–1958 | Jacob Barkin |
| 1958–1960 | Burton Lowell Kaplan |
| 1961–1972 | Raphael Edgar |
| 1973–1976 | Donald Roberts |
| 1977–1979 | Robert Toren |
| 1979–1981 | Glenn Groper |
| 1981– | Arnold Saltzman |

## Executive Directors

| | |
|---|---|
| 1937–1961 | Abe Shefferman |
| 1961–1974 | Stanley Wiener |
| 1974–1985 | Sanford Cohen |
| 1985–1992 | Thelma Becker |
| 1992– | Glenn Easton |

## Assistants–Associates

| | |
|---|---|
| 1947–1969 | Samuel Weiss |
| 1968–1969 | Stanley Dreifuss |
| 1969–1971 | Jacob Garfinkle |
| 1971–1980 | Richard Yellin |
| 1980–1986 | Stephen Listfield |
| 1986– | Avis Miller |

## Sisterhood Presidents

| | |
|---|---|
| 1897 | Julia Oppenheimer (Mrs. Gustave) |
| | Carrie Oppenheimer (Mrs. Simon) |
| | Mrs. George W. Levy |
| | Yetta Pilzer (Mrs. George) |
| | Frances Gewirz (Mrs. Morris) |
| | Mary Veax (Mrs. Jacob) |
| | Mrs. Joseph Kaminsky |
| 1936–1939 | Fanny Tashoff (Mrs. Leon) |
| 1939–1942 | Helen Levinson (Mrs. I. Elliot) |
| 1942 | Mrs. Sylvan Steiner |
| 1942–1944 | Mildred Ostrow (Mrs. A. Harry) |
| 1944–1946 | Isabelle Gichner (Mrs. Henry) |
| 1946–1949 | Frances Goldberg (Mrs. Meyer) |
| 1949–1952 | Leonore Goldstein (Mrs. Philip) |
| 1952–1954 | Ethel Dubit (Mrs. Louis) |
| 1954–1956 | Fannye Berman (Mrs. Bernard) |
| 1956–1957 | Clara Smith (Mrs. William) |
| 1957–1959 | Mildred Fisher (Mrs. Jess) |
| 1959–1961 | Rhoda Smith (Mrs. Edward) |
| 1961–1963 | Anne Cohen (Mrs. Louis) |
| 1963–1965 | Ida Hellman (Mrs. Louis) |
| 1965–1967 | Frances Margolis (Mrs. Sidney) |
| 1967–1969 | Ida Rod (Mrs. Harry) |
| 1969–1970 | Ryna Cohen (Mrs. Melvin) |
| 1970–1971 | Bertha Bernstein (Mrs. Joseph) |
| 1973–1975 | Barbara Cooper (Mrs. Alan) |
| 1975–1977 | Muriel Grossman (Mrs. Harris) |
| 1977–1980 | Estelle Jacobs (Mrs. Irving) |
| 1980–1983 | Annette Morchower (Mrs. Adrian) |

| | |
|---|---|
| 1983–1985 | Marsha Boymel (Mrs. Paul) |
| 1985–1987 | Gilda Snyder (Mrs. Daniel) |
| 1987–1989 | Fern Ingber (Mrs. Kenneth) |
| 1989–1992 | Hope Powers (Mrs. David) |

## Brotherhood and Men's Club Presidents

### Brotherhood

| | |
|---|---|
| 1930 | Irving Stein |
| 1941 | Irvin Goldstein |
| 1942 | David Hornstein |
| 1945 | Matthew M. Epstein |

### Men's Club

| | |
|---|---|
| 1948–1950 | Samuel Lebowitz |
| 1950–1953 | Stanley A. Wiener |
| | Hobart Rowan, journalist, secretary |
| | Joseph Mendelson, secretary, National Federation |
| 1953–1955 | Philip Goldstein, president, National Federation 1961–1963 |
| 1955–1957 | Stanley Korman |
| 1957–1959 | Jacob Lish president, National Federation 1971–1973 |
| 1959–1961 | Max Goldberg, president, National Federation 1981–1983 |
| 1961–1963 | Sidney Margolis |
| 1963–1965 | Morton Levin |
| 1965–1967 | Joseph Laskin |
| 1967–1970 | Reuben Bender |

| | |
|---|---|
| 1970–1972 | Samuel Littman |
| 1972–1974 | Jack Herman |
| 1974–1976 | Joseph Cohen |
| 1976–1978 | Louis Hellman |
| 1978–1982 | Harry Bodansky |
| 1982–1984 | Paul Boymel |
| 1984–1986 | A. Hershel Muchnick |
| 1986–1988 | Irving Jacobs |
| 1988–1990 | Mark Berlin |
| 1990– | Leonard Schachter |

**Shem Tov Award Recipients**

| | |
|---|---|
| 1964 | Abraham S. Kay |
| 1966 | Isador S. Turover |
| 1967 | Joseph Andelman |
| 1968 | Leopold V. Freudberg |
| 1969 | Tina Gichner |
| 1970 | Charles E. Smith |
| 1971 | Hymen Goldman |
| 1972 | Samuel Lebowitz |
| 1972 | Yitzchak Rabin |
| 1973 | Sylvia and Alexander Hassan |
| 1974 | Nehemiah M. Cohen |
| 1975 | Robert J. Rothstein |
| 1976 | Seymour Alpert |
| 1977 | Louis C. Grossberg |
| 1978 | Simcha Dinitz |
| 1978 | Martha and Joseph Mendelson |
| 1979 | Hyman S. Bernstein |
| 1980 | Edward Rosenblum |

| | |
|---|---|
| 1981 | Nat Popick |
| 1982 | Arthur J. Goldberg |
| 1983 | Isabelle Gichner |
| 1984 | Mr. and Mrs. Melvin Cohen |
| 1985 | Sol Linowitz |
| 1986 | Stanley Rabinowitz |
| 1987 | Leon M. Shinberg |
| 1988 | Samuel Cohen |
| 1989 | Estelle Gelman |
| 1990 | Max M. Goldberg |
| 1991 | Norman Bernstein |
| 1992 | Max Kampelman |

## Membership List at Dedication of Synagogue, 1876

### Board of Managers

| | |
|---|---|
| John Boyer, President | Jacob Peyser, Vice-President |
| R. Sanger, Treasurer | Morris Cohen, Secretary |
| Manassas Oppenheimer | Philip Cohen |

### Membership

| | |
|---|---|
| Jacob Rich | M. Jollowitch |
| Manassas Oppenheimer | S. Goldstein |
| M. Baerman | John Boyer |
| Morris Cohen | Isaac Levy |
| Raphael Sanger | B. Schlossberg |
| A. Wallskey | Sam Hartong |
| Bernard Rich | L. Block |
| Felix Greenapple | H. Alexander |

A. Michaelis
Jacob Levy
J. Hirschfeld
Max Roginsky
F. M. Goldstein
Philip Peyser
Kaddish Oppner
Edward Hartogensis
Simon Coblenzer
Aron Herman
Sol Lewis
Herman Baumgarten
Morris Goldstein
Julius Baumgarten
H. Levenstein
F. Richards
Mark Abraham
Morris Coleman
Elias Rascher
Moses Salomon
Morris Richards
S. Roseman
Markus Goldsmith

# APPENDIX II

## The Architectural Restoration
Leon Brown, F. A. I. A.*

Preserving or restoring a building without proper architectural documents presents multifold problems. This is particularly the case when parts of a structure have been remodeled for uses other than those for which it was originally intended. From people who in their youth were familiar with the building, some recollections of how the building was used are useful.

In the restoration of the Adas Israel Synagogue, these were among the factors confronting the architect. In addition, there was fear the building would collapse in the three-block move. The specialized engineering knowledge of the firm moving the structure was some reassurance.

Measured drawings had been prepared by the Office of Archeology and Historic Preservation under the direction of the National Park Service, and a handsome scale model had been furnished through the generosity of Bernard S. Glassman. However, these were based on assumptions of the building without complete knowledge as to the first floor before it had been altered for commercial use.

Once the facade of the shops were removed and the first floor dismantled, many discrepancies were found. There were three openings on the front facade, two of which had been covered up by the shops. The entrance to the upper floor was a metal stair and railing, from the street level to the stair landing, an alteration made

*Editor's note: Leon brown's firm, Brown and Wright, received a merit award Oct. 30, 1975, from the Washington Metropolitan Chapter of the American Institute of Architects for planning the preservation.

years ago to provide usability of the second floor as storage facility. The original entrance, a large arched opening, had been covered by the shops. Once the lower level was dismantled, it was revealed the original building had two stairs, and the entrance was in this large arched opening at grade level. Fortunately, the arched opening was intact.

When the synagogue was constructed a century earlier, it was a very simple two-story brick building, with the sanctuary on the second floor. The ground floor, which originally contained two classrooms, and was used as the daily chapel, is the part which had been gutted and used for carry-out shops.

Window trim, wainscoting, stair railings, newel and doors were of inexpensive design and materials, with the main emphasis on the doors to the Ark and the pediment over the Ark. Even these were of plane late-colonial design. Fortunately, the window trim, wainscoting, Ark doors and pediments had not been materially damaged. Door trim, stair railings, baseboards, newel post and ballusters were of typical stock run-of-the-mill pine. There was no evidence of any hand carved woodwork. The hand rail on the stair was oak, typical of the material used in the 1870s.

Part of the balcony was in place. Upon examination of the original flooring, we could ascertain the location of the original posts or columns before the rest of the balcony was removed. Likewise with the size and location of Bemah. There were never any stained glass windows.

Whether the congregation which financed the original building was affluent is immaterial as the building with its architectural simplicity explains social implications of a group of people who preferred their religious services in a modicum of simplicity not unlike the early Quaker meeting houses of a century before this building was conceived.

Fortunately, the wood sun-burst design was over the main entrance and early photographs revealed only those windows on the street frontage also had a sun-burst design. The original cupola was in place but required repair. The interior wainscot of tongue and grooved wood was also in place and required some repair and replacing. The original two paneled doors to the Ark were in place. The paneling was not stock material and had to be specially made. The post or columns supporting the balcony were champhored with a plain cap and base and were easy to match.

When the disintegrated plaster was scraped from the walls, it was found to have been put directly on the masonry,which allowed penetration of moisture. In the restoration, the new plaster surface was furred from the masonry walls.

The history of the Jewish people for more than two thousand years had never developed an architecture which could be referred to as Jewish or Hebrew. In fact, it is not evident that, even before the dispersal, there was a Jewish architecture. Wherever these people migrated and formed a congregation, they adopted the current style of the time as their place of worship, without regard to the religious philosophical differences of their religion and that of the adopted country. This is evident in Florence, Italy; Curacao; Newport, R. I.; Temple Emanuel in New York, and the beautiful Hazel St. Greek Revival Synagogue in Charleston, S. C. The only "traditional architecture" of the ancient Jews was a tent.

The *Evening Star* of June 10, 1876, in describing the then new Adas Israel, wrote: "in the neat block edifice the lower part contains the vestry. The upper part or main room has a gallery on both sides and across the west end, the east end being occupied by the Ark, the reading desk, etc. Over the Ark in Hebrew characters were the words 'How Beautiful Are Thy Tents.'" Unfortunately, this inscription was painted over, but it has been restored with the same Hebrew characters.

The sanctuary's original brass chandelier was lost and has been replaced with a chandelier of the period. Likewise with the eternal light. From sketches of the original building, it was surrounded by a wrought-iron fence, long ago removed. Through the generosity of the Gichner family, a wrought-iron fence has been installed. The fence is unique with alternating Stars of David and Menorahs.

Saving this structure as an architectural expression of 1875 became a cause celebre and as a monument of our past culture. Too many people have had little concern for the preservation of architecturally-distinguished or historically-important buildings. This, coupled with the American zest for demolition—tear it down—progress for new construction—has left us with a landscape almost barren of cultural landmarks.

The original Adas Israel Synagogue is not illustrative of great historical architectural expression. However, in its simplicity it is an expression of a great heritage and is distinguished as an important landmark.

*Reprinted through the courtesy of the Jewish Historical Society of Greater Washington, publishers of* The Jews of Washington D. C., *1985, edited by David Altshuler.*

## Adas—"Restored but Forlorn"
Wolf Von Eckardt*

When the old Adas Israel Synagogue was dedicated for the first time a hundred years ago—with President Ulysses S. Grant leading the dignitaries in attendance—the unpretentious, two-story brick building proudly stood its own in the jumble of wood shacks, solid row houses, stores with big awnings, banks, churches, taverns, a few ornate six story office buildings and a horse-drawn streetcar that were downtown Washington.

The synagogue's second dedication finds it restored but forlorn shoved three blocks down the street to the brink of a freeway canyon—pathetic relic of a more civilized past.

It now stands on a little patch at Third and G Sts. N. W. which has been fenced in and densely planted with evergreens and reminds us that the city once had human dimensions and people who would walk to church or temple.

On the first floor, where the classrooms used to be, is now a touching little museum of mementos—someone's cradle, someone else's daguerrotyped grandmother in her wedding lace.

The sanctuary upstairs had been restored to the way it was when the last Jewish service was held there 68 years ago. But regular religious service will not be resumed in this marvelously simple space. Who would walk there now?

Instead, tourists are likely to come by the bus-load to get a glimpse of the Jewish presence in the history of the capital city.

*Reprinted from the *Washington Post,* June 14, 1975. Mr. Von Eckardt was the architecture analyst for the *Post* and wrote its Cityscape column which featured this article. This article is reprinted once again through the courtesy of the Jewish Historical Society of Greater Washington from its volume *The Jews of Washington D. C.*, 1985, edited by David Altshuler.

Adas Israel was the first synagogue building in Washington, erected in 1876 by 35 families who formed their own congregation when the Washington Hebrew Congregation began to reform.

By 1907, Adas Israel abandoned the building and moved to a larger temple at Sixth and I Sts., N. W. For a while it was used by the Greek Orthodox Church of St. Sophia and when that congregation also needed a larger building, the evangelical Church of God took over.

In the end, the old synagogue became a warehouse with a carry-out sandwich shop. In 1968 it was found to be in the way of the new Metro headquarters and about to be torn down.

But everyone rushed to its rescue. At the request of the Jewish Historical Society and its old congregation, Mayor Walter Washington, the City council, the Planning Commission, Congress, Metro, the Department of Housing and Urban Development, the Smithsonian, the National Trust for Historic Preservation and even the Federal Bureau of Public Roads all figuratively put their shoulders to the 28 wheels of a dolly and moved the old building down the road.

The restoration of what is now officially known as the Lillian and Albert Small Jewish Museum of Washington was financed with the help of a $100,000 HUD matching grant and under the architectural supervision of architect Leon Brown.

The effort was not lavished on a great work of architecture, but a dear and lovable little building which is actually a bit awkward in its proportions and design. It is Colonial in style more than a hundred years after it had any business being Colonial.

As Leon Brown has pointed out, the Adas Israel congregation could undoubtedly afford something more stylish and elaborate. But it preferred a building of utmost simplicity, an interior of run-of-the-mill pine, reminiscent of the early New England Quaker meeting houses.

This simplicity is all the more remarkable if you consider that the synagogue was built at a time when many Jewish congregations began to build elaborate temples adorned with Romanesque or Byzantine domes, concocted into a mishmash that has been aptly described as "meshugothic."

The simplicity is positively refreshing today as the "meshugothic" downtown temples have given way to lavish suburban religious plants where the kitchen is often as prominent as the Ark.

The simple Adas Israel synagogue is far more impressive.

# NOTES

## Chapter One Notes Pages 1-12

1. Maurice R. Davie, *World Immigration* (New York: Macmillan, 1949), p. 162.

2. Henry L. Feingold, *Zion in America* (New York: Twayne, 1974), pp. 70-71. Guido Kish, "The Revolution of 1848 and the Jewish 'On to America' Movement," *Publications of the American Jewish Historical Society* 27 (March 1949): 188.

3. Mark Wischnitzer, *To Dwell in Safety* (Philadelphia: Jewish Publication Society, 1949), pp. 18–19.

4. Moses Aberbach, "Early German Jews of Baltimore and Washington"; *Jewish Historical Society of Greater Washington Record* 6, no. 2 (May 1971): 11-23; Dieter Cunz, *The Maryland Germans* (Princeton, 1958), p. 202; Isidor Blum, *The Jews of Baltimore-Washington* (1910), p. 7.

5. Evelyn Levow Greenberg, *Isaac Polock: Early Settler in Washington, D.C.* (American Jewish Historical Society, 1958); *Encyclopaedia Judaica* (1971), 16:356; Saul Jacob Rubin, *Third to None: The Saga of Savannah Jewry, 1733–1983* (Savannah, 1983), pp. 5, 36, 49, 52.

6. Bob Arnebeck, *Through a Fiery Trial: Building Washington* (New York: Madison Books, 1991), pp. 288–289.

7. *Washington Sunday Star*, July 23, 1950.

8. Bob Arnebeck, "Tracking the Speculators," *Washington History* 3, no. 1 (Spring 1991): 119.

9. *Georgia Gazette*, Jan. 3, 1793, p. 1, col. 3, quoted in Rubin, *Third to None*.

10. Rubin, p. 49.

11. Bernard Postal and Lionel Kopman, *American Jewish Landmarks* (New York: Fleet Press, 1972), p. 62.

12. *Washington Sunday Star*, July 23, 1950.

13. Ibid.

14. Hillel Marans, *Jews in Greater Washington, 1795–1960* (Washington, 1961), pp. 10–11, citing *Washington Star*.

15. Bernard Postal and Lionel Kopman, *A Jewish Tourist's Guide to the United States* (Philadelphia: Jewish Publication Society, 1954), p. 93.

16. Gertrude S. Metz to Stanley Rabinowitz, Jan. 2, 1989.

17. H. G. Reissnerf, "The German-American Jews (1800–1850)," *Leo Baeck Institute Yearbook* 10 (London, 1969), pp. 68–70; Karl G. Wurst, "German Immigrants and Their Newspapers in the District of Columbia," *Society for the History of Germans in Maryland, 30th Report* (1959); idem, "Germans in the District of Columbia" (unpublished manuscript).

18. Arnebeck, Through a Fiery Trial, p. 29.

19. *Census 1940* (Washington, D.C.: Government Printing Office), vol. 1, table 1, p. 201.

**Chapter Two Notes Pages 13-36**

1. *Occident* 9, no. 6 (September 1852): 137.

2. Joseph L. Blau and Salo W. Baron, *The Jews of the United States, 1790–1840*, vol. 2 (New York and London, 1963), p. 576. Quoted by Abraham J. Karp in *The American Synagogue*, ed. Jack Wertheimer (Cambridge, Mass., 1987), p. 2.

3. *Occident* 12 (May 1854).

4. Ibid. 14 (July 1866). Quoted in Moshe Davis, *The Emergence of Conservative Judaism*, pp. 98–99.

5. Stern, *History of the Washington Hebrew Congregation*; Abraham Simon, *History of the Washington Hebrew Congregation*.

6. *Occident* 13, no. 1 (April 1856): 41.

7. Ibid.

8. *National Intelligencer*, May 23, 1859.

9. *Occident* 18, no. 32 (November 1860): 195.

10. Philps, *Washington Described: Complete View of the American Capital* (New York: Rudd & Carleston, 1861), p. 210. The inside front cover of the volume contains an advertisement for Philps and Solomons, 332 Pennsylvania Avenue. The publisher was Solomons's partner.

11. *Occident* 21, no. 6 (September 1863): 273.

12. I Kings 8:27.

13. Oscar Handlin, *The Uprooted* (Boston, 1951), p. 124. Also, A. Karp's chapter in *The American Synagogue*, ed. Jack Wertheimer (Cambridge, Mass., 1987), p. 15.

14. Minutes, September 8, 1867.

15. Nathan M. Kaganoff, "The Education of the Jewish Child in the District of Columbia," pt. 1, pp. 186–191; *Record* 2, No. 1 (January 1967): 43–51. Reprinted in *The Jews of Washington, D.C.*, David Altshuler, p. 140.

16. *Occident* 26, no. 2 (18XX): 94.

17. Kaganoff, "Education of the Jewish Child in the District of Columbia," p. 142.

18. Exchange of correspondence in the *Jewish Messenger*, January to April, 1872.

**Chapter Three Notes Pages 37-60**

1. Benjamin to Samuel L. M. Barlow, Dec. 9, 1860 (Barlow Papers, Henry E. Huntington Library). Quoted in James M. McPherson, *Battle Cry of Freedom*, p. 237.

2. Simon, *History of the Washington Hebrew Congregation*, p. 20.

3. McPherson, *Battle Cry of Freedom*, p. 254. Letters to Barlow, Dec. 3 and 9, 1860 (Barlow Papers).

4. Simon, *History of the Washington Hebrew Congregation*,. p. 19.

5. *Universal Jewish Encyclopedia* (1941), 2:181.

6. See Eli N. Evans, *Judah P. Benjamin: The Jewish Confederate* (New York: Free Press, 1988).

7. Rowland H. Landman, "Judah Benjamin," *Transactions of the Jewish Historical Society of England* 17 (1953).

8. Bertram Korn, *American Jewry and the Civil War* (Philadelphia: Jewish Publication Society, 1951), p. 44.

9. *Jewish Messenger* 9, no. 3 (January 24, 1862): 28.

10. Korn, *American Jewry and the Civil War*, p. 108.

11. *Jewish Messenger* 14, no. 25 (June 26, 1863): 211.

12. Ibid., no. 8 (February 26, 1864): 59.

13. Ibid., 14, no. 22 (December 11, 1863).

14. Robert Shosteck, "The Jewish Community of Washington, D.C., During the Civil War," in *The Jews of Washington, D.C.*, ed. David Altshuler, pp. 155–183.

15. *Encyclopaedia Judaica* (1971), 16:607.

16. *Jewish Messenger* 9, no. 21 (May 26, 1861): 165.

17. Louis Levy, ed., *Simon Wolf: The American Jew as Patriot, Soldier and Citizen* (Philadelphia: Brentano's, 1895), preface.

18. Korn, *American Jewry and the Civil War*, pp. 203–204.

19. Eric Foner, *Reconstruction: America's Unfinished Revolution* (New York: Harper & Row, 1988), p. 14.

20. For a full treatment of this subject, see Korn, *American Jewry and the Civil War*, chap. entitled "American Judaeophobia."

21. Ibid., p. 122.

22. *Richmond Examiner*, July 22, 1862; James M. McPherson, *Battle Cry of Freedom* (New York: Ballantine, 1988).

23. Korn., *American Jewry and the Civil War*, pp. 121 ff.

24. *Washington Star*, January 7, 1863; *Washington Chronicle*, Jan. 8, 1863. also Korn, *American Jewry and the Civil War*, p. 129.

25. *New York Times*, January 18, 1863.

26. Abraham Lincoln Papers, Manuscript Division, 441, Library of Congress, Archives, January 5, 1863.

27. Korn, *American Jewry and the Civil War*, loc. cit.

28. Adolphus Solomons Papers.

29. McPherson, *Battle Cry of Freedom*, p. 442.

30. Samuel H. Holland, "Charles H. Liebermann, M.D.," *Medical Annals of the District of Columbia* 38, no. 9 (September 1969).

31. Henry S. Morais, "Sabato Morais—A Memoir," *Proceedings* of the 6th Biennial Convention of the Jewish Theological Seminary Association (New York, 1898), p. 83.

32. *Occident* 23, no. 2, p. 84; Korn, *American Jewry and the Civil War*, p. 207.

33. *Occident* 23, no. 5 (May 1865): 95.

34. Ibid., no. 44 (July 1865): 162–163; Korn, *American Jewry and the Civil War*, p. 215.

35. *Washington Evening Star*, April 20, 1865.

36. *American Hebrew* 84 (1909).

37. Korn, *American Jewry and the Civil War*, p. 137.

38. I. Dolinsky, *National Jewish Ledger*, April 19, 1940. A letter from Rosa Mordecai to Rabbi Metz, 1936, written shortly before her death.

**Chapter Four Notes Pages 61-78**

1. *Washington Star*, November 21, 1859.

2. Nordlinger, *History of the Washington Hebrew Congregation*, p. 21.

3. *Israelite* 16, no. 20 (November 19, 1869).

4 Abram Simon, *A History of the Congregation: In Commemoration of Its Jubilee* (Washington, 1905), p. 24.

5. The two rabbis who wrote congregational histories were Louis Stern, who served from 1872 to 1902, and Simon, who served from 1904 to 1938. Bernard Nordlinger summarized their works in his *The Jews of Washington, D.C.*

6. Simon, *History of the Congregation*, p. 25.

7. Nordlinger, *Jews of Washington, D.C.*, p. 25.

8. See the symposium in *Publications of the American Jewish Historical Society* 78, no. 2 (December 1988).

9. Robert E. Fierstien, *A Different Spirit* (New York: Jewish Theological Seminary, 1990), p. 19. sourced in Stanley F. Chyet, "Isaac Mayer Wise: Portraits by David Philipson," in *A Bicentennial Festschrift for Jacob Rader Marcus*, ed. Bertram W. Korn (New York, 1976). David Philipson was a member of the first graduating class of Hebrew Union College and later its president.

10. Ibid, p. 18. sourced in Rebekah Kohut, *As I Know Them: Some Jews and a Few Gentiles* (Garden City, N.Y., 1939), p. 206.

11. Herbert Parzen, *Architects of Conservative Judaism* (New York: Jonathan David, 1964), p. 9.

12. *Occident* 2 (December 1844): 412.

13. *Occident* 7 (October 1849): 344.

14. (Publication of the American Jewish Historical Society) June, 1959: 223, n. 83.

15. *Israelite*, February 14, 1868.

16. *Israelite* 16, no. 20 (January 7, 1870).

17. Minutes, Washington Hebrew Congregation, January 17 and 29, 1870.

18. I. J. Benjamin, *Three Years in America*, trans. Charles Reznikoff (Philadelphia: Jewish Publication Society, 1956), pp. 76–77, quoted by Karp in *The American Synagogue*, p. 7.

19. *Israelite* 16, no. 20 (November 19, 1869).

**Chapter Five Notes Pages 79-97**

1. Itzig Behrend, "Unsere Familien Chronik," *Jahrbuch fuer juedische Geschichte und Literatur* 12 (1909): 114–130. Copy in Hebrew Union College Library. Translated from Yiddish into German by Dr. Magnus Cohen and into English by Prof. A. Berliner. Extracts reprinted in *Jewish Historical Society of Greater Washington Record* 3, no. 2 (November 1968): 36–64, by Samuel H. Holland.

2. Paul Johnson, *The History of the Jews* (New York: Harper & Row, 1987), p. 256.

3. *Universal Jewish Encyclopedia* (1943), 10:643.

4. *Washington Evening Star* and Washington Post, May 12, 1916.

5. For further details, see "The Behrends: Six Generations of a Washington Family," *Jewish Historical Society of Greater Washington Record* 2 (November 1968).

6. *Publications of the American Jewish Historical Society* 20 (1911): 166–170 and 33 (1934): 211–230.

7. In 1866, Solomons published Gardner's photographic sketchbook of the Civil War. See William Safire, *Freedom* (Garden City, N.Y.: Doubleday, 1987), p. 1352.

8. George Meany Memorial Archives, AFL-CIO.

9. Joseph Hirsh and Beka Doherty, *The First Hundred Years of Mount Sinai Hospital*, 1852–1952 (New York, 1952).

10. Moshe Davis, *The Emergence of Conservative Judaism* (Philadelphia: Jewish Publication Society, 1963), p. 325.

11. *Washington Post*, Mar. 13, 1932.

12. Barton Papers, Carton 29, 1892—Russian Famine.

13. *Jewish Messenger* 11, no. 3 (Jan. 24, 1862): 24.

14. Ibid. 23, no. 4 (Jan. 14, 1868): 5.

15. Minutes, Sept. 8, 1872.

16. March 11, 1906.

17. Simon Wolf, *The American Jew as Patriot, Soldier and Citizen* (New York: Brentano's, 1895), p. 429.

**Chapter Six Notes Pages 99-109**

1. I. Dolinsky, in *National Jewish Ledger*, April 19, 1940.
2. Naomi Rozenblit, "Choosing a Synagogue," in *The American Synagogue*, ed. Jack Wertheimer (Cambridge, Mass., 1987), p. 327.
3. Minutes, January 26, 1954.

**Chapter Seven Notes Pages 111-130**

1. *Washington Sunday Star*, July 23, 1950.
2. *Washington History*, Historical Society of Washington, (Spring Summer, 1992) 4:1 p.29.
3. Roberts, "History of Washington's Cemeteries" (master's thesis, District of Columbia Historical Society).
4. Minutes, May 2, 1886.
5. Ibid., March 1890.
6. Ibid., April 9, 1893.
7. Ibid., Nov. 14 and Dec. 7, 1890.
8. Ibid., July 4, 1875.
9. Ibid., June 6, 1880.
10. Ibid., Nov. 3, 1919.
11. Ibid., Jan. 12, 1913.
12. Ibid., Jan. 12, 1913, pp. 48–49.
13. Ibid., Jan. 3, 1886, vol. 3, p. 3.
14. Ibid., Nov. 16, 1873.
15. Ibid., Jan. 27, 1888.
16. Ibid., Jan. 6, 1901.
17. Ibid., April 20, 1908.
18. *Western States Jewish History* 23, no. 4 (July 1991): 321–323.
19. Norton B. Stern, editor of *Western States Jewish History*, to Stanley Rabinowitz.
20. Minutes, Apr. 6, 1873.
21. *Washington Star*, Dec. 27, 1972.
22. The letter *i* was confused with *e* and *r* with *n*, hence Rogersky instead of Roginsky.
23. *New Palestine*, December 1946, p. 16.

**Chapter Eight Notes Pages 131-153**

1. *Jewish Messenger* 31, no. 8 (Feb. 23, 1872).
2. Ibid. 31, no. 13 (Mar. 29, 1872).
3. Minutes, Aug. 11, 1872.
4. Ibid., Dec. 1, 1872.
5. Ibid., Feb. 2, 1873.
6. *Jewish Messenger*, April 5, 1872.
7. Minutes, May 4, 1873.
8. Ibid., Dec. 7, 1873.
9. Ibid., Sept. 16, 1874.
10. Ibid., April 4, 1875.
11. Dedication committee minutes, May 10, 1876. Despite his efforts to press the congregation, Kleinman's bill was not paid until after the dedication.
12. Minutes, July 11, 1875.
13. Ibid., Sept. 5, 1875.
14. Ibid., Feb. 20, 1876.
15. Ibid.
16. Ibid., Apr. 2, 1876.
17. He signed as Lewis Abraham. Evelyn Levow Greenberg, "An 1869 Petition on Behalf of Russian Jews," in *The Jews of Washington*, ed. David Altshuler (Washington, D.C.: Jewish Historical Society of the District of Columbia, 1985), p. 216.
18. Minute Book, vol. 2, p. 253.
19. *Jewish Encyclopedia* (1904), 7:45.
20. *Washington Evening Star*, June 10, 1876.
21. *Washington Chronicle*, June 10, 1876.
22. *Washington Evening Star*, June 8, 1876, p. 1.
23. *Jewish Messenger*, June 16, 1876.
24. *Washington Post*, June 14, 1975. Quoted by Evelyn Levow Greenberg, "Adas Israel Washington, D.C.: A Unique Synagogue Restoration Project," in *The Jerusalem Papers*, 1–2 (Jerusalem: Jerusalem Center for Planning Historic Cities, 1986), pp. 152–154, and in *Jewish Historical Society of Greater Washington Record* 16 (August 1989): 12.
25. Ibid., p. 154.

**Chapter Nine Notes Pages 155-176**

1. Minutes, August 4, 1872.
2. Ibid., October 13, 1872.
3. Ibid., October 27, 1872.
4. Ibid., August 27, 1873.
5. Ibid., November 14, 1873.
6. Ibid., December 21, 1873.
7. Ibid., March. 15, 1874.
8. Ibid., June 21, 1874.
9. Ibid., August 16, 1874.
10. Ibid., August 23, 1874.
11. Ibid., June 6, 1875.
12. Ibid., October 3 and 10, 1875.
13. Ibid., October 24, 1875.
14. Ibid., January 2, 1876.
15. Ibid., June 3, 1877.
16. Ibid., July 1, 1877.
17. *Washington Times,* July 26, 1903, p. 3.
18. Minutes, September 5, 1891.
19. Ibid., September 8, 1872.
20. Ibid., November 12, 1876.
21. Ibid., June 13, 1897.
22. *Washington Times,* Sunday, July 26, 1903.
23. The recollections of Rose Hornstein, a lifelong member, were delivered at the congregation's centennial meeting, November 1969.
24. Joseph Blumenthal, president of Adas Israel, 1961–64, addressing the congregation's centennial meeting, November 1969.
25. For further details, see *Encyclopaedia Judaica* (1972), 14:1337–38.
26. Minutes, April 13, 1873.
27. Ibid., March 7, 1875.
28. Nathan Kaganoff, "The Education of the Jewish Child in the District of Columbia," *Jewish Historical Society of Greater Washington Record,* March 1968, pp. 43–45.
29. *Washington Times,* July 26, 1903, p. 3.
30. From Rose Hornstein's address delivered at the centennial meeting, November 1969.

**Chapter Ten Notes Pages 177-187**

1. Bernard I. Nordlinger, History of the Washington Hebrew Congregation, and David Altshuler, ed., *The Jews of Washington, D.C.* (1985), pp. 30–31.

2. Abe Shefferman, *Adas Israel Dedication Pamphlet* (1951). The pamphlet erroneously names John Boyer as the first president.

3. Minutes, December 6, 1874.

4. Ibid., October 29, 1876.

5. Nordlinger, *History of the Washington Hebrew Congregation*, p. 42.

6. Minutes, October 21 and November 4, 1877.

7. Robert Shosteck's chapter in Altshuler, *History of the Jews in Washington, D.C.*, p. 164.

8. Mrs. John Safer, "Origins of Hadassah, in Altshuler, *History of the Jews in Washington, D.C.*, p. 111.

9. Minutes, May 6, 1877. "The recommendation of the Board of Managers that the Congregation shall join the Board of Delegates of American Israelites was not concurred in and the whole matter was ordered to lay on the table."

10. *Washington Evening Star*, July 3, 1881.

11. *Washington Evening Star*, October 6, 1881.

12. Busey, *Personal Reminiscences* (Washington, D.C., 1895), pp. 222–223.

13. Minutes, March 4, 1877.

14. Barton Papers, Carton 25, McClenney Nurses, quoted by Abram Vossen Goodman, in "Adolphus S. Solomons and Clara Barton," *Publications of the American Jewish Historical Society*, no. 3 (1970): 331–356.

15. Minutes, September 5, 1886.

**Chapter Eleven Notes Pages 189-208**

1. Minutes, September 1, 1872, p. 17.

2. Minutes, July 9, 1876.

3. Ibid., October 6, 1872, p. 25.

4. Ibid., January 5, 1873.

5. Ibid., August 23, 1874.

6. Ibid., November 10, 1872, p. 32.
7. Ibid., November 17, 1872.
8. Ibid., December 8, 1872.
9. Ibid., August 17, 1873.
10. Ibid., August 24, 1873.
11. Ibid., January 18, 1874.
12. Spelled incorrectly in the minutes as Neveveh Israel.
13. Minutes, May 17, 1874
14. Ibid., May 6, 1877.
15. Ibid., May 27, 1877.
16. Ibid., September 1, 1878.
17. Ibid., September 22, 1878.
18. Minutes, January 1, 1882.
19. Ibid., April 4, 1886, p. 12.
20. Ibid., August 7, 1887.
21. Ibid., December 16, 1888.
22. Ibid., June 11, 1905.
23. Ibid., February 2, 1896.
24. Lois Hechinger England, "The Lulley family," *Jewish Historical Society of Greater Washington Record* 18 (1991): 24–29.
25. Minutes, October 8, 1899.

**Chapter Twelve Notes Pages 209-231**

1. Leon A. Jick, "The Reform Synagogue," in *The American Synagogue*," ed. Leon Wertheimer (Cambridge, Mass., 1987).
2. Paul Wilkes, *The Atlantic Monthly*, Dec. 1990, 266:6.
3. Bernard I. Nordlinger, "The Washington Hebrew Congregation," in *The Jews of Washington, D.C.*, ed. David Altshuler (Washington: Jewish Historical Society of Greater Washington, 1985), pp. 21–22.
4. Ibid., p. 25.
5. Pamela S. Nadell, *Conservative Judaism in America*, (New York: Greenwood Press, 1988), p. 147.
6. Minutes, September 1, 1872, p. 17.
7. Ibid., March 1, 1875.
8. Ibid., August 27, 1876.

9. *Jewish Encyclopedia* (New York, 1905–16), 12:451; *Encyclopaedia Judaica* (1971), 16:223.

10. Kenneth C. Zweren and Norton B. Stern, "Jacob Voorsanger: From Cantor to Rabbi," *Western States Jewish Historical Quarterly* 15, no. 3 (April 1983): 195–202.

11. Minutes, September 10, 1876.

12. Simon Wolf, in Emanu-el, Sept. 25, 1908, p. 9.

13. Minutes, December 10, 1876.

14. Ibid., April 1, 1877.

15. Zweren and Stern, "Jacob Voorsanger," p. 198.

16. *Jewish Messenger*, June 27, 1879.

17. Martin A. Meyer, ed., *Jacob Voorsanger: Sermons and Addresses* (New York: Bloch Publishing Co., 1913), introduction.

18. Ibid., p. 199 and other citations.

19. *Jewish Encyclopedia*, 12:451.

20. Ibid.

21. *American Hebrew* 72, no. 20 (October 20, 1903).

22. Marc Lee Raphael, *Profiles in American Judaism: Reform, Conservative, Orthodox, and Reconstructionist Traditions in Historical Perspective* (New York: Harper & Row, 1984).

23. Ibid.

24. Raphael, *Profiles in American Judaism*, p. 15; William Popper, in *Emanu-El*, August 28, 1908, p. 3.

25. Zweren and Stern, Ibid., p. 195.

26. Ibid., p. 200. The Emil Hirsch account first appeared in the *Reform Advocate*, Chicago, May 2, 1908, p. 325.

27. Ibid., p.223.

28. Minutes, October 21, 1877.

29. Minutes, April 21, 1988.

30. Ibid., July 20, 1879.

31. Ibid., January 2, 1881.

32. Ibid., March 6, 1881.

33. Ibid., July 14, 1881.

34. Ibid., August 7, 1887.

35. Ibid., July 3, 1887.

36. Ibid., June 3, 1888.
37. Ibid., October 28, 1888.
38. Ibid., July 6, 1890.

**Chapter Thirteen Notes Pages 233-261**

1. Moshe Davis, *The Emergence of Conservative Judaism* (Philadelphia: Jewish Publication Society, 1963), p. 13.
2. *Israelite* 14, no. 7 (August 16, 1867).
3. *Occident* 26, no. 9 (December 1868): 25.
4. S. Morais, Report "To the Council of the Union of American Hebrew Congregations," 1877, Morais Papers; Robert E. Fierstien, *A Different Spirit* (New York: Jewish Theological Seminary, 1990), p. 13.
5. John J. Appel, "The Treyfa Banquet," *Commentary*, February 1966, p. 75.
6. *Israelite,* November 27 and December 18, 1885.
7. *Jewish Theological Seminary Semi-Centennial Volume* (New York: Jewish Theological Seminary, 19xx), p. 37.
8. *American Hebrew*, December 4, 1885.
9. Jewish Theological Seminary Association, Constitution and By-Laws. Certificate of Incorporation dated February 23, 1887.
10. Davis, *Emergence of Conservative Judaism*, p. 236, quoted from the *American Hebrew* 25 (February 5, 1886).
11. *Israelite,* March 12, 1886.
12. *American Hebrew*, January 7, 1887.
13. Minutes, March 7, 1886
14. Minutes of Chizuk Amunah, April 7, 1878.
15. Morais Correspondence at Dropsie College; Israel Goldman, "Henry W. Schneeberger: His Role in American Judaism," *Publications of the American Jewish Historical Society* 57, no. 2 (December 1967): 177.
16. Minutes, May 2, 1886.
17. *Western States Jewish History* 23, no. 3 (April 1991): 256.
18. Minutes, May 1, 1898.
19. Ibid., August 23, 1898.
20. Ibid., p. 237.

21. *American Hebrew*, September, 18, 1896, p. 508.

22. Ibid., October 9, 1896 and October 22, 1897.

23. Ibid., December 17, 1897.

24. Fierstien, *A Different Spirit*, p. 99.

25. Moshe Davis, *Emergence of Conservative Judaism*, opposite p. 243.

26. Minutes, November 6, 1898, p. 241.

27. Minutes, December, 4, 1898, p. 243.

28. Ibid., January 6, 1901, p. 280.

29. Cyrus Adler, *I Have Considered the Days* (Philadelphia: Jewish Publication Society. 1941), p.248.

30. *Cyrus Adler, Selected Letters*, ed. Ira Robinson, (Philadelphia: Jewish Publication Society, 1985) 1:112. Letter dated June 4, 1905.

31. Wilcomb E. Washburn, *The Cosmos Club of Washington* (Washington: Cosmos Club, 1978), p.31.

32. Cyrus Adler, *Jacob H. Schiff: His Life and Letters* (New York: Doubleday, 1929), 2:53.

33. *American Hebrew*, Apr. 4, 1902, p.598, quoted in Fierstien, *A Different Spirit*.

34. Cyrus Adler, *Selected Letters*, ed. Ira Robinson. (Philadelphia: Jewish Publication Society, 1985), 1:86–818.

35. Adler to Schechter, Aug.26, 1901 in *Selected Letters of Cyrus Adler*, ed. Ira Robinson. (Philadelphia, Jewish Publication Society) 1:90-91.

36. Adler to Solomons, May 15, 1901 in Ibid, 1:86-88.

37. Adler to Schechter, Aug.26, 1901 in Ibid.1:90–94.

38. Talmud Berachot 45a.

39. Minutes, September 6, 1908.

40. Adler, *I Have Considered the Days*, p. 243.

41. *American Hebrew*, June 14, 1901, pp. 95–96.

### Chapter Fourteen Notes Pages 263-282

1. Morris Alex, *Rabbis in Washington* (1938). In Yiddish.

2. *Washington Times*, July 26, 1903.

3. Cyrus Adler, ed., *The Voice of American on Kishineff* (Philadelphia: Jewish Publication Society, 1904), pp. 204–213, 459-462.

4. Minutes, January 6, 1901, p. 282.

5. *Washington Times*, July 26, 1903.

6. Evelyn Greenberg, "Adas Israel: A Unique Synagogue Restoration Project," *Jewish Historical Society of Greater Washington Record* 16 (August 1989).

7. Minutes, May 7, 1905, p. 337: "Authorization to sell building 617 and 619 6th St. syn and house, above description, $14,000. Purchaser to assume a trust of $10,000 and to pay in cash 4000. All furniture and benches not to be included."

8. Minutes, July 9, 1905. p. 343. "Lot 18, Square 453, Southwest corner of 6th and I, N.W., frontage of 85 feet on 6th and 75 feet on I Street. Price: $17,500. Terms, $7,000 in cash, balance payable in one year at 4 1/2%."

9. Minutes, January 5, 1905.

10. *Washington Times*, October 28, 1906.

11. Ibid.

12. *Washington Star*, November 22, 1906.

13. Ibid.

14. Genesis 28:10. The same text was used by Rabbi Jacobs in dedicating the first Adas Israel synagogue in 1876.

15. *Washington Post*, November 23, 1906.

16. Ibid.

17. Ibid., June 30, 1907.

18. Ibid.

19. *Washington Post*, December 15, 1942.

20. Minutes, November 13, 1907.

**Chapter Fifteen Notes Pages 283-298**

1. *Jewish Messenger*, December 3, 1869. For a fuller treatment of the Washington Jewish community's intercession with the Grant administration in behalf of Russian Jewry, see Evelyn Levow Greenberg, "An 1869 Petition on Behalf of Russian Jews," in *The Jews of Washington, D.C.*, ed. David Altshuler (Washington, 1985), pp. 213–243, reprinted from *Jewish Historical Society of Greater Washington Record* 4, no. 1 (May 1969): 33–50.

2. Moshe Davis, *The Emergence of Conservative Judaism*, (Philadelphia, Jewish Publication Society), p. 187.

3. Raphel, Marc Lee, *Profiles in American Judaism: Reform, Conservative, Orthodox and Reconstructionist Traditions in Historical Perspective* (New York: Harper and Row), 1984, p. 147.

4. Letter from Mrs. Aaron Friedenberg to her son. Typescript, Alexandra Lee Levin, "The Friedenwalds and Chizuk Amuna," quoted by Israel Goldman, Henry W. Schneeberger,(Publication of the American Jewish Historical Society) 57:2, p.171.

5. Proceedings, (Jewish Theological Seminary Annual, 1898, p.32. Fierstien, *A Different Spirit*, p.103.)

6. Ibid. p.103.

7. Minutes, July 3, 1887, p. 49.

8. Ibid., October 20, 1908, p. 396.

9. Ari L. Goldman, *The Search for God at Harvard* (New York: Times Books, 1991).

10. From her reflections at the centennial meeting, November 1969.

**Chapter Sixteen Notes Pages 299-314**

1. *American Hebrew*, Dec. 18, 1885, quoted in Fierstien, Ibid., p.62.

2. J.D. Eisenstein, *Ozar Zikhronothai*, p.208, quote in Fierstien, Ibid.,p. 72.

3. Pamela Nadell, *Conservative Judaism in America*, (New York: Greenwood Press, 1988) p.301.

4. Report to the United Synagogue of America, 1913, p.19. Herbert Parzen, *Architects of Conservative Judaism* (New York: Jonathan David, 1964), p. 64.

5. Ira Eisenstein and Eugene Kohn, *Mordecai M. Kaplan, An Evaluation*, (New York: Jewish Reconstructionist Foundation, 1952), p. 299.

6. Minutes, December 11, 1910, p. 467.

7. Citations and quotations pertaining to the career of Egelson at Adas Israel are based on two reports in the American Hebrew, January 13, 1911, p. 321, and January 20, 1911, p. 359.

8. Herbert Parzen, *Architects of Conservative Judaism* (New York: Jonathan David, 1964), p. 67.

9. From her reminiscences at the centennial meeting, November 1969.

## Chapter Seventeen Pages 315-331

1. Minutes, October 9, 1909, p. 414.
2. Ibid., February 5, 1911.
3. Ibid., January 12, 1913, pp. 48–56.
4. Ibid., March 19, 1913, p. 65.
5. Ibid., July 8, 1914.
6. Ibid., February 18, 1914, pp. 100–102.
7. Ibid., May 15, 1913, p. 68.
8. Ibid., May 20, 1914, p. 106.
9. Ibid., May 23, 1914, p. 108.
10. Ibid., August 9, 1914, p. 118.
11. Ibid., July 21, 1914. p. 112.
12. Annual message, January 10, 1915.
13. Ibid.
14. Letter from Grossman, December 3, 1919.
15. Letter from Grossman, November 28, 1919.
16. Letter from Grossman, January 9, 1920.
17. Minutes, December 12, 1915. Other defenders of Grossman were Max Kamerow, M. Pressler, and W. Hornstein.
18. For further details, see Hannah Sprecher, "'Let *Them* Drink and Forget *Our* Poverty': Orthodox Rabbis React to Prohibition," *American Jewish Archives* 43, no. 2 (Fall–Winter 1991): 135–179.
19. Minutes, November 27 and December 6, 1922.
20. Ibid., April 14, 1921, p. 193.
21. Minutes, June 8, 1922.
22. The eulogy was reprinted in *Proceedings of the Rabbinical Assembly Convention*, 1968, pp. 199–200.
23. Minutes, January 13, 1924.
24. Minutes, March 31, 1925.
25. From his recollections at the centennial meeting, November 1969.

## Chapter 18 Notes Pages 333-342

1. Minutes, March 5, 1925, p. 273.
2. David S. Wyman, *The Abandonment of the Jews* (New York: Pantheon Books, 1984), pp. 193 ff.

3. *Washington Star*, April 11, 1926.
4. Minutes, June 11, 1925.
5. Ibid., March 24, 1927.
6. Ibid., June 3, 1929.
7. Ibid., November 4, 1929.
8. Toba S. Herzenberg to Stanley Rabinowitz, April 17, 1988.

**Chapter Nineteen Notes Pages 343-361**

1. Charles and Mary Beard, *America in Midpassage* (New York: Macmillan, 1939), p. 115.
2. Louis Novick to Cantor Raphael Edgar, March 3, 1969.
3. Testimony of Charles Pilzer, son of the chairman of the ritual committee.
4. Minutes, October 1936.
5. Ibid., November 12, 1940.
6. Annual report, October 1, 1942, and others.
7. *Adas Israel Chronicle* 16, no. 2 (1953).
8. *Washington News*, March 23, 1950.
9. Barkin to Wolpe, June 26, 1959; Wolpe to Barkin, June 27, 1959. Files.
10. *Jewish Historical Society of Greater Washington Record* 11, no. 1 (July 1982): 13.
11. From his recollections at the centennial meeting, November 1969.

**Chapter Twenty Notes Pages 363-379**

1. Minutes, November 4, 1929.
2. "Spinoza and Amsterdam Jewry," delivered December 2, 1932.
3. Address on WRC, Washington, February 12, 1945.
4. Hasia R. Diner, *Fifty Years of Jewish Self-Governance* (Washington, D.C.: Jewish Community Council, 1989), p. 44.
5. Jack Wertheimer, ed., *The American Synagogue* (Cambridge, Mass., 1987), p. 119.
6. Aaron Blumenthal, "Presidential Address," quoted in Pamela S. Nadell, *Conservative Judaism in America* (New York: Greenwood Press, 1988), p. 317.

7. Minutes, April 17, 1939.

8. Letter addressed to Rabbi Metz. *National Jewish Ledger*, Washington, D.C., Mar. 2, 1934.

9. *Jewish Historical Society of Greater Washington Record* 11, no. 1 (July 1982): 10–24.

## Chapter Twenty-one Notes Pages 381-403

1. Salo Wittmayer Baron, *Steeled by Adversity* (Philadelphia: Jewish Publication Society, 1971), p. 251.

2. Minutes, January 7, 1886.

3. Arthur Hertzberg, *The Jews in America* (New York: Simon & Schuster, 1989), p. 234.

4. From the memoirs of Rebecca (Mrs. John) Safer, mimeographed.

5. *Adas Israel Chronicle* 12, no.1 (September 1948).

6. Minutes, December 9, 1940.

7. See Frederic William Wile, *Biography of Emil Berliner* (Indianapolis: Bobbs-Merrill, 1926), pp. 15–16, 40

## Chapter Twenty-two Notes Pages 405-425

1. Joseph L. Ruah, Jr., in *Jewish Historical Society of Greater Washington Record* 17 (1990): 15.

2. Minutes, January 6, 1941.

3. Ibid., September 27, 1945.

4. Kathryn Schneider Smith, *Washington at Home* (Washington, D.C.: Windsor Publications, 1988), p. 265.

5. Minutes, January 3, 1946.

6. Ibid., June 24, 1949.

7. Ben Zion Bokser to Abe Shefferman, March 31, 1949.

8. Blumenthal to Bureau of Highways, June 15, 1952.

9. Minutes, January 25, 1950.

10. Ibid., March 6, 1950.

11. Ibid., April 10, 1950.

12. Ibid., June 15, 1950.

13. Ibid., June 29, 1950.

14. *Rabbinical Assembly Proceedings*, 1960, p. 254.

15. Minutes, March 15, 1951.

16. Ibid., April 5, 1951.

17. Ibid., May 31, 1951.

18. Israel Goldstein, *My World as a Jew* (New York, Herzl Press, 1984), 1:263.

**Chapter Twenty-three Notes Pages 427-447**

1. *Washington Post*, December 10, 1955.

2. Bokser to Panitz, August 31, 1959.

3. Mortimer Cohen to Julius Wolpe, August 31, 1959.

4. Ibid., May 5, 1955.

5. Ibid., May 24, 1955.

6. Ibid., November 9, 1955.

7. Shefferman files, 1946; letters from Shefferman to the president and the chairman of the school board.

8. Ira Robinson, ed., *Cyrus Adler: Selected Letters* (Philadelphia: Jewish Publication Society, 1985), address at the second commencement of JTS, June 18, 1905, pp. 113–114.

**Chapter Twenty-four Notes Pages 449-462**

1. Minutes, August 2, 1891.

2. Ibid., April 21, 1878.

3. Ibid., Oppenheimer's report, January 1901.

4. Rose Hornstein's recollections at the centennial meeting, November 1969.

5. Minutes, September 8, 1930.

6. Mrs. Herbert S. Goldstein, president of the Women's Branch of the Union of Orthodox Congregations, to Rabbi Judah T. Loeb.

7. They included Mrs. M. Stein, Mrs. George W. Levy, Mrs. H. Jeffrey, and Mrs. B. Weiss, with the later addition of Mrs. I. Freund, Mrs. Henry Gichner, and Mrs. Charles Pilzer. Mrs. H. Oxenberg and Mrs. Morris Gewirz were added in 1930. In the early decades of the congregation's history, married women's given names were not mentioned in the minutes and other records.

8. Minutes, July 12, 1954.

9. Ibid., February 7, 1957.

10. Ibid., November 25, 1957.

11. Jonathan Sarna, "Debate Over Mixed Seating," in *The American Synagogue*, ed. Jack Wertheimer (Cambridge, Mass., 1987), p. 377.

12. Ibid., p. 380.

13. Minutes, May 9, 1921, p. 194.

14. Ibid., March 24, 1927, p. 35.

15. Annual Report, October 6, 1936.

16. Minutes, January 16, 1939.

17. Robert Gordis, "Seating in the Synagogue: Minhag America," *Judaism* 36 (1987): 53.

18. Minutes, May 5, 1958.

19. The Conservative Movement's Law Committee authorized including women in the count for a minyan in 1973, the ordination of women as rabbis in 1983, and the ordination of women as cantors in 1987.

20. From her recollections at the centennial meeting, November 1969.

21. Minutes, February 3, 1930, p. 95.

22. Minutes, October 26, 1947.

### Chapter Twenty-five Notes Pages 463-475

1. Shefferman to President Julius Wolpe, May 2, 1960.

2. Minutes, May 2, 1960.

3. Ibid., January 25, 1960.

4. Mandelbaum to Stanley Rabinowitz, May 10, 1990.

5. Minutes, January 26, 1960.

6. Mandelbaum to Rabinowitz, May 10, 1990.

7. Albert I. Gordon to Rabinowitz, March 8, 1960.

8. Max Arzt to Rabinowitz, Mar. 22, 1960.

9. Minutes, June 15, 1960.

### Chapter Twenty-six Notes Pages 477-523

1. Rabinowitz to Cantors Assembly, December 19, 1960.

2. Ritual committee minutes, January 25, 1961.

3. Ibid.

4. Minutes, October 18, 1961.

5. Ritual committee minutes, November 3, 1965.

6. Ibid.

7. Stanley Rabinowitz to Samuel Lebowitz, June 18, 1962.

8. Stanley Rabinowitz to Simon Hershman, September 25, 1962.

9. Ritual committee minutes, October 3, 1960.

10. Minutes, August 16, 1961.

11. Minutes, February 16, 1967.

12. Minutes, October 16, 1963.

13. Talmud, Berachot 48b.

14. Harlan Cleveland to Stanley Rabinowitz, December 30, 1963.

15. Marjorie Williams, "Cafritz v. Cafritz," *Washington Post Magazine*, February 25, 1990, p. 16.

16. Ibid.

17. *Adas Israel Chronicle* 2, no. 8 (April 1939).

18. John A. Sessions to Stanley Rabinowitz, May 3, 1968.

19. Minutes, January 18, 1967.

20. Isaac Franck to Rabbi Bernard Mandelbaum, November 27, 1968.

21. Stanley Rabinowitz to the Congregation, November 26, 1967.

22. *The Jewish Population of Greater Washington* (Washington: Jewish Community Council, 1956): *A Demographic Study* (Washington: United Jewish Appeal of Greater Washington, 1983).

23. Eugene B. Borowitz, "His Majesty's Opposition, As It Were," in *The Seminary at One Hundred*, ed. Nina Beth Cardin and David Wolf Silverman (New York: Rabbinical Assembly and Jewish Theological Seminary, 1987), p. 309.

24. "The Business of Washington" and "The *Regardies* 100: A Look at the Richest People in Washington—How They Made Their Money and What They Do with It," *Regardies* 6, no. 1 (September 1985). Since many of the 100 wealthiest people had families, the number of super-wealthy in the District actually amounted to more than 100 persons.

25. Charles E. Smith, *Building My Life* (Washington: Privately published, 1985).

26. A selfstyled Black Caucus was part of the National Conference in New Politics in 1947.